ABSENT PRESENCES IN THE COLONIAL ARCHIVE

Dealing with the Berlin Sound Archive's Acoustic Legacies

IRENE HILDEN

D1598817

LEUVEN UNIVERSITY PRESS

The publication of this work was supported by the Open Access Publication Fund of Humboldt-Universität zu Berlin, funded by the Deutsche Forschungsgemeinschaft (DFG, German Research Foundation) – 491192747, the Centre for Anthropological Research on Museums and Heritage (CARMAH), the Alexander von Humboldt Foundation, and the KU Leuven Fund for Fair Open Access.

The research was funded by the Deutsche Forschungsgemeinschaft (DFG, German Research Foundation) – 265331351/RTG 2130 minor cosmopolitanisms.

Published in 2022 by Leuven University Press / Presses Universitaires de Louvain / Universitaire Pers Leuven. Minderbroedersstraat 4, B-3000 Leuven (Belgium).

ISBN 978 94 6270 340 7 (Paperback)
ISBN 978 94 6166 469 3 (ePDF)
ISBN 978 94 6166 470 9 (ePUB)
https://doi.org/10.11116/9789461664693
D/2022/1869/36
NUR: 764

Layout: Crius Group
Cover design: Daniel Benneworth-Gray

Absent Presences in the Colonial Archive

Dealing with the Berlin Sound Archive's Acoustic Legacies

To my grandmother (1927–2019),
for and against whom I write.

Contents

List of Figures

Acknowledgments

The Voices of the Other—was the title of a seminar that sparked my scholarly interest in sound and initiated my exploration of the history of the Berlin *Lautarchiv*. Since then, my concern with the post/colonial legacies of sound archives has failed to diminish. I am deeply indebted to Britta Lange and Anette Hoffmann—the instructors of the seminar—for their thorough and extensive research, which has been a rich and motivating source for many—and certainly for me—over the past years. Britta Lange continues to be an important inspiration to me, and I cannot thank her enough for always encouraging me to proceed with my work in and on the *Lautarchiv*, for always taking the time to share her expertise with me, and for providing advice and support.

The research for this book, a revised version of my doctoral dissertation, would not have been possible without Regina Römhild and Anja Schwarz. Both as a fellow of the Deutsche Forschungsgemeinschaft's Research Training Group *minor cosmopolitanisms* at the University of Potsdam, which generously funded my research, and as a colleague at the Institute for European Ethnology at the Humboldt-Universität zu Berlin, they could not have made me feel more welcome and appreciated. I thank Regina for helping to make me the anthropologist I am today, for sharpening my ethnographic eye, and for trusting the analytical strength of historical imagination. Regina and Anja constantly challenged me to look at the bigger picture and to see my research against the backdrop of the colonial pasts and presents of the European project. Their critical readings of earlier versions of different chapters of this book have shaped my work, and their emphatic mentoring remains important to me.

Being surrounded by, exchanging thoughts with, and listening to such wonderful colleagues within the interdisciplinary Research Training Group enriched my thinking process tremendously. When I recall the many discussions during the numerous colloquia, events, lunch and coffee breaks, I feel a great sense of gratitude. My special thanks go to Sergio Costa, Lars Eckstein, Lucy Gasser, Yann Le Gall, Anouk Madörin, Sara Morais dos Santos Bruss, Oduor

Obura, Rajni Palriwala, Anna von Rath, Nicole Waller, and Dirk Wiemann for providing insightful comments at different stages of my research. I would also like to thank Anke Bartels, Judith Coffey, and Lina Fricke for their open ears and meticulousness in administrative matters. Rajni Palriwala, together with her amazing colleagues, Shaswati Mazumdar and Ira Raja, not to forget Sachita Kaushal and Neyha Tyagi, gave me a warm welcome at the University of Delhi, where I was fortunate enough to conduct some field research. I thank Rajni Palriwala for sharing her thoughts and knowledge with me.

The Humboldt-Universität zu Berlin and the Institute for European Ethnology do not only feel like academic homes to me, but have also become the sites of many memories: memories of the numerous hours spent reading and writing, but also memories of countless intriguing and precious encounters with colleagues and guests, all of whom I could never mention by name here. I would, however, especially like to thank Friedrich von Bose, Silvy Chakkalakal, Larissa Förster, Sharon Macdonald, Alik Mazukatov, Margareta von Oswald, Anna Szöke, and Daniela Weber. Sharon Macdonald's extensive body of work and writing have fundamentally influenced my academic thinking to this day. It is a very enriching experience to work with her and many other colleagues at the Centre for Anthropological Research on Museums and Heritage, where I was able to build on my previous research and work on this publication as part of the project *Making Differences. Transforming Museums and Heritage in the 21st Century*, funded by Sharon Macdonald's Alexander von Humboldt Professorship.

The Berlin *Lautarchiv* has seen many people come and go. Having worked there myself as a student assistant, I know firsthand how rewarding and some-times exhausting working with archival material, university administration, and visiting researchers, artists, and the interested public can be. I would like to thank the people who have made critical work on the sound archive's legacies possible and who have been mindful of the ethical responsibilities the institu-tion carries: Celine Couson, Paula Hanitzsch, Jochen Hennig, Christopher Li, Marie Lührs, Herdis Kley, and Michael Willenbücher.

In addition to the *Lautarchiv*, my thanks go to the following insti-tutions for providing access to archival materials and images: Archiv der Berlin-Brandenburgischen Akademie der Wissenschaften, Archiv des Zoologischen Gartens Berlin, Bildarchiv der Deutschen Kolonialgesellschaft / Universitätsbibliothek Frankfurt am Main, Bundesarchiv, Hausarchiv der Stiftung Deutsches Historisches Museum, Hausarchiv der Stiftung Stadtmuseum Berlin, Politisches Archiv des Auswärtigen Amts, Universitätsarchiv der Humboldt-Universität zu Berlin.

Many more people have contributed significantly to this book. I thank Jasmin Mahazi for collaborating with me on the collective listening workshop, for her help with translations, and for her critical comments on my writing. My thanks also go to G. Manoja, Madhumeeta Sinha, and Viswajith for their indispensable translation work. Among the group of collaborators, I would like to count my interlocuters in New Delhi who shared time and knowledge, meals and drinks with me. The many supporters and friends, more than I can possibly list here, are, partly anonymised, Rubaiyat Biswas, Rana Chhina, Rangan Da, Hammaad Danish, Wanphrang Diengdoh, Oeendrila, Armita, Manimughsha Sharma, and Anam Sheikh. My gratitude must also go to the workshop participants in Berlin, Rukia Bakari, Frank Daffa, Lutz Diegner, Vitale Kazimoto, Stephanie Lämmert, and Asmau Nitardy, who were willing to participate in an experimental listening session that would lay the cornerstone of one of my chapters.

I do not know what I would have done without the meticulous readings and comments of Rosa Barotsi and Julia Schulz. I owe a great debt of gratitude to their sharp eyes and infinite patience. I also want to thank my editor Mirjam Truwant and her team at Leuven University Press, Marc Lange from the Open-Access Team at Humboldt-Universität zu Berlin, and not least my two reviewers: Noel Lobley and another who wishes to stay anonymous. Any remaining errors or misjudgements are my responsibility.

There are plenty of other colleagues and friends whom I would like to thank and mention here, not forgetting my students, who have broadened my horizons in unique ways. Thank you, dear friends, Adela, Anaïs, Andrei, Anna, Brenda, Duane, Fabio, Katrin, Lea, Lucy, Manon, Mèhèza, Pato, and Sara, not only for reading and discussing my work, but also simply for being there and accompanying me along the way.

Finally, from the bottom of my heart, I thank those whom I am lucky to share all my ups and downs with, who always believe in me and build me up when I am in doubt, who care for me with their unwavering trust and support: my parents, my brother and sister, and last but not least, Julia, Malte, and Nora.

Abbreviations

AZGB	Archiv des Zoologischen Gartens Berlin
BJP	Bharatiya Janata Party
DOMiD	Dokumentationszentrum und Museum über die Migration in Deutschland
EASA	European Association of Social Anthropologists
GDR	German Democratic Republic
HUB-Archive	Universitätsarchiv der Humboldt-Universität zu Berlin
ICOM	International Council of Museums
IIC	India Independence Committee
IfL	Institut für Lautforschung
JNU	Jawaharlal Nehru University
LA	Lautabteilung
LAHUB	Lautarchiv der Humboldt-Universität zu Berlin
PK	Phonographische Kommission
POW	Prisoner of War
SSG	Subaltern Studies Group

Use of Names

Unless otherwise indicated, the names of historical figures are used as they appear in the archives. This may include the reproduction of spelling mistakes of the archival records. The names of interviewees are used as preferred by my interlocutors (by first/last name, institutional affiliation, or anonymised). When mentioning German institutions, I mostly used the English names. For the original German names, see the Appendix.

1
Introduction

Colonial Situations and Sonic Events

German Colonialism. Fragments Past and Present—this was the title of a temporary special exhibition at the German Historical Museum in Berlin, which opened in October 2016.[1] At the time, an exhibition dedicated to Germany's colonial past and its legacies was a project long overdue at a major German institution. At the same time, it was a project destined to disappoint the high expectations of many postcolonial scholars and activists who had been dealing with colonial pasts and presents for years and decades. In spite of all criticism— sometimes more, sometimes less justified—, the exhibition and the negotiations surrounding it have decidedly influenced a growing debate on colonial entanglements among the German public.

In my role as an external research assistant, I was involved in the archival research for the exhibition. Based on my previous work, I was asked to compile a list of topics and objects to be incorporated in a display on colonial sound recordings. I believed that the inclusion of historical sound recordings was an enriching addition to the exhibition for addressing discourses on colonial knowledge production. But I was also hesitant to contribute to an exhibition project that I knew had major flaws in terms of its conceptual and institutional framing. This structural and inner conflict remained a close companion throughout both the preparation and duration of the exhibition and my ensuing research project, which forms the basis for this book. Often, I have felt torn between my commitment to historical research, analysis, and critique within an institutional setting and the awareness that much more radical and insistent measures are needed to work through and transcend colonial thinking. At the exhibition opening, I was *inside* the museum and it was my perception that there were both inspiring talks but also rather reactionary welcome speeches. A close colleague of mine remained *outside* the building, joining a small protest in front of the museum entrance. As postulated for years, the protest demanded an official apology from the German government for the Herero and Nama genocide in present-day Namibia between 1904 and 1908. The protest also criticised the museum's failure to provide better conditions for the inclusion of more Black and activist voices in the exhibition's earliest curatorial concept. The slogan 'not about us without us' of the protesters gathered at the entrance served as a gateway, literally and figuratively—one that every invited guest had to walk through when entering the museum.

Although the exhibition did address current postcolonial struggles and included at least some decolonial initiatives, this was not its main focus, but rather appeared as an afterthought. At the core of the exhibition stood the curators' aim to display objects derived from the colonial archive as testimonies of colonial situations. In this way, they sought to negotiate German colonialism as a violent system of domination, legitimised by a racist ideology of European superiority, while at the same time producing intersecting experiences and relations of power. For the curators, the point of departure was the understanding of the colonial archive as determined by the Eurocentric and colonial gaze, but—as the exhibition wished to demonstrate—also full of ruptures and contradictions (Hartmann 2018: 49).

In this book, I follow the curators' approach of trying to productively link object histories to globally entangled colonial histories. Bringing together macro and micro levels in global history, as the historians Rebekka Habermas and Susanna Burghartz (2017: 306) argue, allows for questioning static spatial concepts and problematic epistemic orders. Looking at object histories as the physical traces of colonial situations offers the possibility to analyse the enduring coloniality of power inherent in colonial practices and hegemonic legacies. Moving beyond global and object histories, this book also deals with more intangible histories, that is, acoustic histories. Those histories derive from the sound archive of the Humboldt University—now known as the *Lautarchiv*. The core of the archive consists of an extensive collection of shellac records, compiled for scientific purposes by German scholars between 1909 and 1944. The content of the sound recordings ranges from short stories and songs, poems and personal testimonies to standard texts and phrases, lists of words and numbers.[2]

The focus of this study is on the archive's holdings whose production was underwritten by colonial arrangements in the metropolis of Berlin. This book therefore proposes to conceptualise the *Lautarchiv* as a colonial archive, consisting of sound objects generated 'at home,' in the heart of the metropolis, under colonial signs. In this sense, I wish to understand the *Lautarchiv* as a colonial

project involving the production, practice, and preservation of specific structures of power and knowledge which have, in part, survived to the present day.

The central concern of this book revolves around the question of how
to deal with the *Lautarchiv*'s sonic material that is at once project, product,
and testimony of a colonial regime of power and knowledge. How to deal
with archival material in which the ambivalence of colonial discourses and the
tensions between coloniser and colonised, metropolis and periphery manifest
themselves in a unique way. How to deal with the legitimising strategies that
constitute the colonial archive, its racist ideology of European superiority, but
also its imbalances and ambivalences, its silences and voids. How to deal with
the marginalised traces of colonial presences that have found little or no place
in established national narratives and collective memories. In other words, how
to deal with the *absent presences in the colonial archive*.

This book examines colonial situations through single sound events preserved as historical sound objects. The archival objects indicate institutional,
disciplinary, and personal histories; and they attest to colonial knowledge
production. They point to narratives embedded in larger histories of media,
science, and the project of Europe. As the visual anthropologist Elizabeth
Edwards pointed out in relation to colonial photography, photographic images
are "visual incisions through time and space" (2001: 3) that constitute 'little'
narratives. Yet, for Edwards, these 'little' narratives are simultaneously "constituted by and [...] constitutive of the 'grand', or at least 'larger', narratives" (3).
This study seeks to augment Edwards' position with colonial sound recordings. According to sound scholar Jonathan Sterne, historical sound recordings
"are the result of one particular moment in a much larger and unequal sphere
of cultural interchange" (2003: 331). "Recording is a form of exteriority," he
writes: "it does not preserve a preexisting sonic event as it happens so much
as it creates and organizes sonic events for the possibility of preservation and
repetition. Recording is, therefore, discontinuous with the 'live' events that it
is sometimes said to represent" (332). This discontinuity becomes manifest in
the changing social presence (or absence) ascribed to the *Lautarchiv*'s historical
sound recordings in the course of time. Initially recorded for linguistic, musicological, and anthropological purposes and archived for an anticipated future,
the sound recordings now bear witness to a colonial knowledge system and
colonial subjects often silenced in the grand narrative. Notions of exteriority
and discontinuity reveal the complex condition of colonial sound recordings.
Their contents cannot be separated from the situations in which they were produced—from the practices of recording and preserving underlying the creation

and organisation of sonic events. I therefore agree with Anette Hoffmann and Phindezwa Mnyaka (2015: 6), who argued that it is not possible to engage with and listen to the recordings outside the colonial situation.

Neither a Media History nor an Institutional History

This book is not a media history of the scientific use and implementation of early sound technology in Germany. Nor is it an encompassing institutional history of the *Lautarchiv*. Rather, it is a historical ethnography of constitutive moments of a metropolitan, colonial archive and its guiding concepts and aspirations. By considering sound objects, each dating from a different time and context, this study addresses the desideratum of a transversal investigation of the *Lautarchiv*'s diverse colonial collections. It sheds light on the entanglements, conflicts, and relationships that come to the fore in the little narratives emerging in and through the colonial archive. I argue that taking a closer look at sonic events allows us to recognise the fragility and ambiguity of seemingly fixed and naturalised dichotomies of coloniser and colonised, materiality and ephemerality, the dominant and the minor. Moreover, this book seeks to engage with Germany's colonial past as not taking place only on formal colonial territory; nor as ending after the First World War in 1918 and with the Treaty of Versailles, concluded in 1919. Colonial ambitions, desires, and imperatives found expression in different ways and in different contexts. They triggered a multitude of reactions, resistances, and affirmations and brought about other hegemonies beyond the opposition between coloniser and colonised (Herzfeld 2002: 922–923). The recordings of colonial subjects recorded in or near the metropolis of Berlin are just one form among many in which complex colonial entanglements materialise. In contrast to other sources, the sound recordings of the *Lautarchiv*, however, have survived astonishingly well in the shadows of the colonial archive.

The range of approaches to different historical sound recordings that underpin this book draw on and add to important past and ongoing research on colonial legacies. This study addresses both conceptual and methodological questions relevant to strands in cultural anthropology as well as cultural theory and history. My research follows and contributes to research agendas concerned with the relation between memory and media; with historical ethnographies of colonial knowledge production and the making of historical archives; and with questions of agency and institutional practices.[3]

Absent Presences

> *The absence [...], although [...] final in the physical sense, can be transformed into a 'meta-physical' or media-based presence.*

> (Balke 2009: 74)[4]

In a physical sense, the absence of the speakers and singers in the *Lautarchiv*'s sound recordings is final—they are dead, their bodies no longer exist. According to media scholar Friedrich Balke, however, in a meta-physical sense, their absence has been transformed into a sonic or medial presence. If not the presence of their voice, it is this medial presence that extends to find expression in my writing—on the pages of this book.

My ethnographic interest lies in presences hitherto marginalised in established historical narratives. What I am particularly concerned with is the constitutive character of these marginalised presences, which is precisely defined by their absence or omission in collective, or rather selective, memories. For Stoler, the "'present-absence' is not so much a contradiction as a marker of the phenomenon itself" (2002a: 158). It is a characteristic feature of the colonial archive and the production of history and cultural memory, determined by mechanisms of inclusion and exclusion. Rebekka Habermas (2017: 331) pleads for not thinking exclusively in terms of omissions or gaps, but for considering absence and silence as active production, an active production of ignorance. A main aim of my work is to address this imbalance; and to redress it by raising awareness of the archival presence and absence of colonial subjects, generated under colonial conditions and epistemic violence.

While physical gaps exist in the archive itself due to missing information, actual loss or damage of records, silences also appear in an epistemological sense. The scientific procedures underlying the archival project of the *Lautarchiv* intended to focus on a certain kind of knowledge and consequently deemed only certain information valuable and discursively knowable. Likewise, the archival process considered only certain contents as "qualified knowledge" (Foucault

1978: 60) and "archivable material" (Mbembe 2002: 20). Contemporary politics of history and memory similarly ensure that certain (often subaltern) histories remain silenced, hidden, and forgotten. These politics do not depict history
as intertwined and a reciprocal process of exchange and transfer. Rather, they
approach history from a Eurocentric standpoint, in order to maintain the idea
of a stable and monocausal European and national identity (Habermas 2017:
346; see also Römhild 2021: 691).

The sound recordings of colonial subjects are meaningful sources that
have thus far only had a minor or even absent status within contemporary
German colonial historiography—even though, or maybe rather because, the
Lautarchiv's acoustic stories, songs, and personal testimonies can offer new narratives and alternative histories. The sound files bear witness to transnational
mobilities between Europe and colonised territories up to the first half of the
twentieth century. Both established historical narratives as well as collective
memories in Germany show a lack of awareness of diasporic, migratory, and
cosmopolitan dynamics that have shaped German society, the academy, and the
economy for centuries. These dynamics are not considered an integral part of
Germany's or, on a smaller scale, Berlin's history. The matter of selective historical narratives and eclectic collective memories is, however, of great concern
given the *Lautarchiv*'s relocation to the contested Berlin Humboldt Forum, an
architectural copy of the City Palace (*Stadtschloss*).[5]

Both the decision to partly reconstruct a Prussian king's castle and to
realise the museum project of the Humboldt Forum have triggered intense
debates within political circles as well as within German and Berlin civil society.[6] The resulting discourse has ensured that Germany's colonial legacies are
now a distinct point of discussion not only at a political and academic level but
also in public discourse and the media. While the actual construction work
started in 2013, the discourse on what historical narratives the urban site does
or should stand for began much earlier (Bach 2017; Binder 2009; Ha 2014).[7]
Over the years, the Humboldt Forum has become a focal point of fierce con-
troversy about the politics of memory and history, about competing and/or
entangled historical narratives and cultures of remembrance in Germany and
beyond. For some, the Humboldt Forum is a Eurocentric and reactionary project that contradicts notions of global equality and postcolonial justice (e.g.
NoHumboldt21! 2017). Others hope that the project could point in the direction of a new cosmopolitan German culture of remembrance (e.g. Thiemeyer
2019). Following several delays and the setback of the COVID-19 pandemic,
the Humboldt Forum celebrated its digital and subsequently its physical open-

ing in December 2020 and July 2021. The institution exhibits collections of the Ethnological Museum of Berlin and the Museum of Asian Art.[8] In addition, the Stadtmuseum Berlin Foundation, along with Humboldt University, have their own exhibitions and project spaces. At the time I finished my research, the Humboldt Forum remained closed to visitors, but it was already known that a portrayal of the *Lautarchiv* featuring a number of acoustic and tangible objects would be included in the opening exhibition curated by the so-called Humboldt Lab. However, it was rather unclear how the archive's collections would continue to be accessible to international research communities and whether establishing collaborations with other stakeholders would be a major component of the new location.

Due to limited financial and personnel resources, the *Lautarchiv* has had a complicated status within the university over the past decades. Although large parts of the holdings were included in a digitisation project that started in 1999, the collections' accessibility always depended on temporary employment contracts and the courtesy of the respective staff. For many years, the management of the collection and research inquiries was largely left to student assistants, which, if one is looking for a silver lining, at least meant that the archive never had to close.[9] The increased attention prompted as a corollary of the Humboldt Forum project raised hopes that the call for lasting ethical care and a sustainable future for the archive's holdings would finally be met. So far, however, it seems that the authorities in charge have hardly been able to satisfy any of the desired commitments.

Un/linear Historical Moments

This book rejects linear narratives; it refuses to follow only one story. It is far from a mere examination of dates and facts, as one might expect from a more conventional account of an institution's history.[10] It is not a history inching teleologically along historical events, leading up to the present. Rather, this book reconsiders and cross-references the *Lautarchiv*'s collection history in a threefold manner: within the overarching history of science and the history of acoustics, within the wider context of the history of the university, and finally within the post/colonial history of Berlin. Seen from today's vantage point, this book brings together different archival collections from different times and situations, and correlates them with other sources and current discourses. In other words, it approaches the *Lautarchiv* as a space in which different histories—histories of the past and the present, of here and there, absence and presence—meet and converge.

The book is particularly concerned with the period in which the medium of the shellac record was formative for the *Lautarchiv*.[11] Roughly divided into three institutional phases, these stages ultimately also determined the selection of the three case studies in this book. My case analyses proceed from three colonial situations in or near the metropolis of Berlin, from three globally entangled histories that manifest themselves in sound, materialise in historical sound objects, and each stand for different colonial collections of the *Lautarchiv*. The case studies involve different social spheres—military, public, and academic—but also overlap at times. In all three analyses, I contrast and correlate acoustic and previously neglected sources with other media formats and supposedly dominant forms (i.e. written and visual, *white*[12] and male).

The first phase relevant to this book is characterised by recording activities of the so-called Royal Prussian Phonographic Commission (*Königlich Preußische Phonographische Kommission*). Founded in late 1915, the Phonographic Commission was set up to compile sound recordings of prisoners of war (POWs) in German internment camps during the First World War. In addition to recordings produced for language learning[13] and a voice collection of public figures[14], the set of recordings generated during the First World War is one of the oldest and most extensive archival collections of the *Lautarchiv* today. At the time, a range of well-established professors—in English, Romance, and Slavic linguistics, African and Oriental studies, musicology and anthropology—headed off to a considerable number of German POW camps throughout the German Empire. Their mission was to compile sound recordings for linguistic and phonetic, musicological and anthropological purposes. Among the soldiers and civilian internees were several people from the colonies, most of whom had either been fighting for the British and French Armies on the Western Front or had remained on German soil and waters at the beginning or during the war (e.g. Hoffmann 2014; Lange 2015a/b; Roy, Liebau, and Ahuja 2011). The Orientalists and Africanists among the Commission's members were especially interested in recording the voices of non-*white* people. For them, it meant that they did not have to travel to the 'non-European field' or colonial territories in order to explore 'their' research objects. For some of the scholars, this had been a common, but always costly and time-consuming practice. Instead, they could benefit from the state of war and the fact that numerous colonial soldiers and civilian internees had become prisoners of war in Germany, where they would remain for what was, for them, an indefinite period.

The book's first case study, discussed in Chapter 3, revolves around a couple of sound recordings of two Indian prisoners of war, Baldeo Singh (approx. 1888–?) and Keramat Ali (approx. 1897–?). The Orientalist Helmuth von Glasenapp (1891–1863) recorded the Hindi-speaking colonial soldier Singh in a POW camp located on the outskirts of Berlin in January 1917. His superior, Heinrich Lüders (1869–1943), was in charge of recording a group of Bengali seamen, among them Ali, one year later, in February 1918.

For Reinhart Meyer-Kalkus (2015: 47), the initial collection history of the *Lautarchiv* proves to be a revealing example of research practices in the humanities and social sciences during the rule of the German Empire, and more particularly in relation to imperialism and the conditions of repressive colonial politics. The collection compiled during the First World War thus joined the endeavours of ethnographic and natural history museums in Germany and Europe as implemented during the nineteenth and the first half of the twentieth century.[15]

After the war, the Phonographic Commission was dissolved and the collection of shellac records became part of the Prussian State Library's newly founded Sound Department (*Lautabteilung*). The vision of a Sound Department formed around different collection foci already existed as a notion since before the war. The ambitious intention had been to collect (1) languages of all nations of the world, (2) all German dialects, (3) music and songs of all nations of the world, (4) voices of leading public figures, and (5) miscellaneous (Doegen 1925: 9). While the 'war recordings' formed the basis of the department's stock, one of its new aims was to systematically compile a collection of German dialects recorded in different parts of Germany and Switzerland. The making of recordings of non-German languages and non-European people lost importance but still occurred from time to time. Recordings of non-Europeans spending time in post-imperial Berlin were made for a variety of reasons. For example, non-*white* diplomats and researchers, or non-*white* artists came to the department in order to be recorded.

The second case study, discussed in Chapter 5, deals with two sound recordings of the female performers Venkatamma (approx. 1905–?) and Rajamanikkam (approx. 1901–?) from India. The sound recordings in Telugu and Tamil did not originate at the Sound Department but at a so-called *India Show* at the Berlin Zoological Garden in September 1926. The zoo, as well as many other urban 'places of amusement,' represented sites where colonial phantasies were fuelled and where they resumed after the formal end of German colonialism.

At the beginning of the 1930s, the sound collections were again transferred, this time to the Friedrich Wilhelm University in Berlin (today's *Humboldt-Universität zu Berlin*). Here, the archival holdings were assigned to the Institute for Sound Research (*Institut für Lautforschung*), newly founded in 1934. The Africanist Diedrich Westermann (1875–1956) became head of the department and divided the institute into three research areas, focusing on linguistics, phonetics, and music. A specialist headed each section: Westermann was in charge of the linguistics department, Franz Wethlo (1878–1960) managed the phonetics lab, and Fritz Bose (1906–1975) led the (folk) music section.[16] In addition, Westermann assumed responsibility for the editorship of the so-called Sound Library (*Lautbibliothek*). The Sound Library (published since 1926) consisted of records and textbooks in the form of small brochures, intended for phonetic studies and language learning. In some cases, the issues were based on sound recordings of prisoners of war recorded during the First World War. In most of the publications, however, there is no mention of the circumstances under which the recordings were made. Apparently, the inclusion of these details was not considered meaningful or necessary—a point I will discuss in more detail in Chapter 6. During Westermann's incumbency, recordings were made of so-called African language assistants teaching Swahili and Ewe, among other languages, at the Berlin University. Amongst those who attended the classes were people who sought to qualify for future colonial service, meaning for the moment when Germany would reclaim colonial territories. A recording of the language assistant Bayume Mohamed Hussein or Husen (1904–1944) dates from this period. Lending his voice, Hussein was recorded for the purpose of teaching and learning Swahili in July 1934. The joint examination of Hussein's recording together with Swahili speakers from present-day Berlin forms the basis of the last case study, discussed in Chapter 6.

After the Second World War and during the time of German partition, research foci shifted to more experimental and phonetic research. Relegated to the background of research interests, the collection of shellac records was slowly sliding into obscurity. This was due to media change and the end of the era of the shellac record, which had started to unravel in the 1940s. But it was also due to institutional and political influences, and not least to the post-war changes in the academic landscape in Berlin and Germany. In the following years and decades, the collection of shellac records moved between different departments. It was only at the beginning of the 1990s that a renewed interest and a comprehensive indexing of the holdings began (Bayer and Mahrenholz 2000; Mehnert 1996). Digitised and made accessible online, the shellac records have ever since been subject to (historical) research on specific holdings of the *Lautarchiv*. With the growth of academic interest, so has public attention grown. In recent years, this was in large part due to the aforementioned decision that the *Lautarchiv* would be the only university collection to be moved to the Humboldt Forum.

Sensitive Collections and Contentious Heritage

In institutions such as museums and universities, processes of dealing with Germany's colonial past and present have been described as "slow and erratic" (Fründt 2019: 138) in comparison to other former imperial powers. According to interdisciplinary anthropologist Sarah Fründt, it is only in the last decade that three important shifts shaping debates on the colonial past within German museums, as well as within political and medial discourses, can be observed. A first shift began with the process of a slowly increasing consciousness about Germany's colonial legacies and the responsibilities towards formerly colonised regions. Building on this, a nuanced understanding of colonial contexts developed. Although there is still a considerable judicial and ethical need for the resolution of formal and violent colonial crimes committed under German rule (e.g. in the case of present-day Namibia), there are also contexts that are more subtle and epistemic in nature; contexts that are still very effective today. Related to this and to Fründt's own field of expertise, a new type of contested objects emerged. These were objects related to cultural heritage and colonial knowledge production in general, and to anthropological and racial research in particular. National and international debates have influenced these developments. For the German-speaking landscape, a volume of essays on *sensitive collections* by Margit Berner, Anette Hoffmann, and Britta Lange (2011) has provided a thought-provoking impulse for the discourse.

Berner, Hoffmann, and Lange introduced the concept of sensitive collections in their engagement with practices and objects of anthropological and ethnographic research of the late nineteenth to the middle of the twentieth century. Proceeding from the guidelines formulated by the International Council of Museums (ICOM) in 1986, which define human remains and artifacts with a religious or spiritual meaning as sensitive material, the authors made a case for a broadening of this definition. By directing their interest to the depots of museums and scientific institutions, they focused on visualisations of anthropometric data, sound recordings and plaster casts of body parts. They not only looked at collections that have largely been excluded from historical inquiries, but argued that research should not focus solely on the physical objects and artifacts themselves. Instead, research should also consider the coherent practices and power relations involved; the processes that turned the material into epistemic objects. In doing so, they advocated a *sensitive* approach to objects and to their history of provenance, transfer, and circulation.

Often not sufficiently listed in the institutions' catalogues and inventories, sensitive collections, such as those negotiated by Berner, Hoffmann, and Lange, are less visible and accessible to the wider scientific community and the public. This is not least because plaster casts and historical sound recordings have to be stored and preserved differently. They also seemed more difficult to translate into other media and digital formats than, for instance, research data and photographic images (Lange 2011a: 37–40). Yet, over the past decades, historical sound recordings on wax cylinders or shellac records have increasingly been included in cataloguing and digitisation projects.

With the increased opening of archives and their inventories through digitisation, many institutions have undergone enormous changes in recent years and are facing ever new challenges. While these processes enable a democratisation of access to knowledge, the shift to digital archiving practices continues to affect questions of hegemonic knowledge production in and of the archive. As already mentioned, large parts of the *Lautarchiv*'s sound recordings, as well as accompanying scripts, have been digitised. Searchable via a digital catalogue, the sound recordings are listed with information about the respective language, type, and date of the recording, as well as about format, length, and the name of the person recorded, among other things. Though intended to simplify the search pattern, the systematically designed categorisations of the catalogue yielded terms with pejorative and outdated connotations, as well as new exclusions and errors. Moreover, the decision over whether the sound recordings themselves ought to be published online has yet to be made. This decision touches upon ethical, cultural, and legal issues and may vary depending on the collection corpus (Hartmann, Hennig, and Lange 2015). At present, users can browse the metadata but cannot listen to nor download the sound. Only after personal or online contact with the archive's staff will users be given access to a selection of requested digital files.

In this book, I seek to discuss the *Lautarchiv*'s holdings against the backdrop of discourses on collections that have been described as sensitive, but also on heritage depicted as difficult and contentious (e.g. Hamm and Schönberger 2021a; Macdonald 2009, 2021). What do the *Lautarchiv*'s acoustic legacies signify today? In what way do colonial sounds from the past affect the current postcolonial situation? How does one assess sounds that may reveal more about colonial knowledge regimes and archival practices than the historical subjects recorded? How does one assess the ethical, legal, and social responsibilities of a researcher such as myself, as well as of the archive's custodians? While it may be the custodians' task to maintain and preserve the archival collections, it is also important to allow open and democratic access to the collections that prevents an exclusive power of interpretation as well as a restrictive sense of agency. What needs to happen to reconcile these two sides? What would an ethics of the *Lautarchiv* look like, as Lange (2019: 12) asks?

European Imaginations and Archival Projects

The *Lautarchiv* with its sonic collections both meets and disturbs the master narrative of European heritage. As pointed out in a companion on contentious cultural heritage, the "classic master narrative of European heritage was built from the centre: Technical and architectural achievements found in large cities; language, knowledge and customs as signifiers of a nation; art and science as expressions of the rise of the middle class" (Hamm and Schönberger 2021b: 33). With its innovative implementation of early sound technology in the academy, its location in the imperial capital of Berlin, and its aim to document and preserve language and music as markers of cultural difference, the archival project of the *Lautarchiv* fits the above listed parameters. However, as critical Europeanisation and heritage studies seek to prove, European imaginations and hence European heritage are not as stable and static as they may seem. Regina Römhild (e.g. 2009, 2021) therefore suggests a reflexive stance towards processes of Europeanisation, the construction and reconstruction of imaginations of Europe. What defines reflexivity in this context is a "social practice of re-assessing and challenging given normalities" (Hamm and Schönberger 2021b: 33). The approach of reflexive Europeanisation allows for the contestation of naturalised ideas and concepts of Europe and the development of new European imaginations that acknowledge the making of Europe as built on global transfer and unequal power relations. "Rather than seeing Europe – and its core identity labels of enlightenment, modernity, science, secularism etc. – as being autopoetic products of self-making," Römhild argues, reflexive Europeanisation "aims at understanding both Europe and its intellectual, cultural and political histories as products of global entanglements" (2021: 691). Understanding the *Lautarchiv* precisely and explicitly as an intellectual, cultural, and political project, I follow the aim of making the archive's "effective entanglements visible, approachable and reflectable" (689).

This book proceeds from an understanding of history as entanglement and histories of entanglements (Conrad and Randeria 2013 [2002]; Randeria 2019). In doing so, I seek to avoid the terminology of concepts of a shared history (and heritage), which tend to silence rather than stress the unequal relationships from which globally entangled histories result. In her account of a shared history and an entangled modernity (*Geteilte Geschichte und verwobene Moderne*), Shalini Randeria therefore highlights the connotations of shared *and* divided histories as expressed in the double entendre of the German verb *teilen* (1999a; see also Conrad and Randeria 2013 [2002] and Chapter 3). The sound recordings of colonial subjects made in or near Berlin are the products and physical evidence of a globalised world of (often unequal) interaction and mobility. At the same time, the making of the sound recordings relied on and reinforced the scientific and political understanding of cultural difference and European superiority. Linguistic and anthropological research of the time met the desire to provide legible and audible proof of racial categorisations.

Following the concept of entangled histories means to proceed from concrete situations and connections rather than to assume universal and transhistorical totalities. According to Conrad and Randeria (2013 [2002]: 40), it means to accept histories as fragmentary and porous rather than holistic and comprehensive. The analysis of entanglements allows for a change of perspective. It allows us to investigate moments of multidirectional exchange and relations of transfer that run transversely to dominant patterns (Bruns, Hampf, and Kämpf 2018). These dominant patterns may refer to the structures of European colonialism but also to the discursive production and order of knowledge in Western institutions. In addition, focusing on global and entangled histories offers the opportunity of a methodological change of perspective by taking into account non-Eurocentric and non-teleological analytical lenses. In this way, it becomes possible to turn away from the classic European master narrative and, instead, to get closer to the project of decentring and provincialising Europe (Adam et al. 2019a; Chakrabarty 2000; Conrad and Randeria 2013 [2002]).

Voicing and Listening

What distinguishes this study from other analyses of colonial archives is its focus on objects of sound and practices of listening. While students of colonialism have long been concerned with voice and speech, with the question of who has a voice and who can speak, who is heard and remembered, attention has rarely been drawn to practices of listening. Hence, shifting the focus to the politics of listening means to acknowledge that it is insufficient to concentrate on the speaker and the act of speaking alone. Following Hoffmann and Mnyaka (2015: 8), this book therefore intends to revisit the colonial archive and its acoustic traces by deploying different modes of listening.

According to Jenny R. Lawy, one needs to question the focus on voice and the claim that only the speaker or singer is responsible for what is said or sung. She warns, "using presence as evidence that voice is being heard is a rather superficial measure to use" (2017: 196). How do these arguments relate to the acts of speaking and singing—the sonic events—as performed in the recording situations I have chosen to place at centre stage in this book? As indicated at the outset of this introduction, no act of speaking and singing can be divorced from the situation and context in which it was performed *and* recorded. The situations of recording created a prescribed and scripted mode of speaking, an act of speaking often practiced in advance and then repeated in front of the technical device. But not only was the speech act prescribed; so too was the mode of listening. The mode of listening, as practiced by linguists and musicologists, objectified the act of speaking and the recorded voice. Content and content producers were usually not the focus of interest. What mattered to the recordists was the phonetic quality of the voice and its exemplary nature of a specific language type. Here, Hoffmann and Mnyaka speak of an excess of meaning and information that had no significance for the listeners at the time but has nevertheless been registered in sound. It is for this reason that they suggest applying a different way of listening—"one that seeks to retrieve what the collection of and files on statement-things omit" (2015: 8). In this book, I follow their attempt to explore modes of engaging with the excess of meaning; to ask whether the acts of both speaking and listening were always as restricted and limited as the colonial setting suggests. Are there moments or forms of subversion, irritation, and fragmentation? How does one approach these glimpses? Where does one fail to reach them? Applying different modes of listening seeks to contest the prescribed mode of listening as stipulated by disciplinary and normative logics.

But what kind of listening practices enable what kind of strategies in dealing with the *Lautarchiv*'s recordings today? These concerns form guiding questions for this book.

Once again, according to Lawy, "it is the ways that the audience or listener reacts to, accepts, or rejects what has been put out into the social milieu that reveals the (political/social) impact of that voice" (2017: 194). Therefore, when wishing to shed light on voicing and speaking, we must also address hearing and listening. In a similar vein, Tom Rice points out that "listening practices must be understood by reference to the broader cultural and historical context within which they are formed" (2015: 102). For Nina S. Eidsheim, a focus on perception reveals that listening is never neutral or passively practiced. Rather, listening "always actively produces meaning," which prompts Eidsheim to think of listening as "a political act" (2019: 24). Finally, this also points to one of the reasons why hearing and listening should not be equated. "Listening is a directed, learned activity: it is a definite cultural practice," Sterne reminds us. "Listening requires hearing but is not simply reducible to hearing" (2003: 19).

Irrespective of the prescribed setting, the desire remains to mis/interpret historical sound recordings as vehicles for the authentic and unmediated expression of a historical subject. Voice is, however, always mediated: it emerges from the body of a person, but is also detached from its source. Historical voice recordings are both disconnected from their corporeal source and separated in time. Corporeality, mediality, and temporality are significant notions that will resonate throughout this book. Again referring to Sterne, recapitulating the temporal contradiction, the practice of recording "created sound events designed to be reproduced later and elsewhere, even though the method was justified in terms of saving tradition in the 'here and now'" (324).

The Structure of this Book

The book consists of six main chapters comprising both theoretical and empirical elements. The triad—*the Ethnographic, the Archival*, and *the Acoustic*—forms the larger framework. I understand these parts as introducing overarching concepts, but I also see them as references to the deployment of reflexive practices. In this sense, I consider ethnography, the archive, as well as sound and listening as analytical tools, as methods and practices, and as sites of knowledge production. However, these three stages are not to be understood as separate, isolated modules. Rather, the sections stand for the transdisciplinary discussions within which I wish to situate this study; for debates on historical anthropology (Chapter 2), archival theory (Chapter 4), and sound studies (Chapter 7). Yet aspects of postcolonial and cultural studies, as well as media and memory studies, also influence this broader framing.

Apart from this larger structure, the core of the study consists of three case studies (Chapter 3, 5, and 6), informed by and positioned against the backdrop of notions of the ethnographic, the archival, and the acoustic. Three modes of listening—*failed listening*, *close listening*, and *collective listening*—form a second framing of this book. The listening modes that I develop in the three case analyses or apply to the material provide an additional frame. As with the theoretical accounts, I do not assume that the case studies stand in complete isolation. Rather, I propose three different modes in which to approach different colonial collections of the *Lautarchiv*. By deploying these modes, I show how different listening practices allow us to illuminate the complex and interdependent positionalities and practices connected to the project of the *Lautarchiv*.

* * *

Under the heading of *the Ethnographic*, Chapter 2 revolves around the question of what it means to approach the *Lautarchiv* reflexively and under the premises of the project of historical anthropology. Hence, this part explores conceptual considerations and methodological instruments that appear useful for a historical ethnography of the *Lautarchiv*. From the perspective of the present, historical ethnography offers the possibility of analysing subjects, practices, and events of the past, which in their interplay constitute social realities and collective memories. The chapter endorses the conceptual idea of a historical ethnography as aiming at correlating past and present beyond clearly separated temporal modes. It thus suggests a multitemporal and multidirectional practice that allows an investigation of the relationships between past and present. On the one hand, this means to examine how the past is experienced, understood, and produced in the present, a practice that Sharon Macdonald (e.g. 2003, 2012, 2013) conceptualised as that of 'past presencing.' On the other hand, the suggested approach goes beyond a presentist perspective, by also interrogating immanent logics in the past.

How does the past materialise? How is history documented, encoded, archived, and thus continuously selected? What are the mechanisms ensuring that certain material and stories survive over time and are regarded as evidence of the past, while others do not count as such or get lost? What characterises the approach I adopt here is a methodology of mobility and juxtaposition. By this, I mean both the productive comparison of different perspectives and temporalities as well as their relational juxtaposition. This involves, for instance, the approach of reading the *Lautarchiv* both along and against its grain or of examining different modes of listening—listening then and listening now.

The first case study on *failed listening* follows my reflections on the heterogeneous field of historical anthropology and takes ethnographic episodes as starting points. Those episodes do not stem from my research in the *Lautarchiv* in Berlin, but occurred during a research stay at the University of Delhi in India. Short extracts from my interview transcripts and field notes set the ground for my approach to sound recordings of Indian prisoners of war housed at the *Lautarchiv*. The ethnographic material includes conversations I had and observations I made in Delhi. The extracts presented in the chapter concern sound recordings of the Indian prisoners of war Baldeo Singh and Keramat Ali and the failed wish to get closer to these historical figures.

Consequently, Chapter 3 explores whether and how the notion of failure can be productive in ethnographic work. It suggests the mode of a *failed listening* as one way of dealing with the *Lautarchiv*'s colonial sound recordings. It acknowledges the difficulties of coming to terms with the past, which will always leave a sense of dissatisfaction behind. In this chapter, I ponder over different listening positions: the positions of the recordists and internees in the past, my own position today, and the positions of my Indian interlocutors. I depict the positions as both separated from each other in temporal, spatial, or epistemological terms; but also interconnected in unique ways. Since my positionality as a *white* and female anthropologist belonging to the very same university as the researchers that first recorded the voices of prisoners of war indicates a certain continuity, I ask how to both reveal this fact and break with it. Proceeding from Kamala Visweswaran's proposition of a *feminist ethnography as failure* (1994), the chapter introduces an intersectional position towards the *Lautarchiv*. It argues that the *politics of listening* are closely connected to the *politics of location* (Rich 1987; Braidotti 1994). It matters from where you think, speak, write, and listen. It matters who is recording and who is being recorded, who is speaking, who or what is heard at what moment in time, who is listening or who is listening in.

Problematising these formations is crucial to the outline of the chapter and the discussions that follow this first case study. Although the chapter also deals with the colonial dimensions of the First World War and the marginalisation of non-European perspectives within its history and memory, the conceptual core of the discussion seeks to negotiate the limitations and constraints of my research endeavour and positionality. Pointing to the existing, but sometimes rather complex, imbalance of the availability of ostensibly subaltern and dominant sources, the chapter develops a critical stance towards the colonial archive. Dealing with the colonial archive entails acknowledging the inability to know everything, accounting for the archive's limited and incomplete condition. Dealing with the colonial archive is not merely about stories of the past, but also about the history of the present and how it is interrupted by the past (Hartman 2008). Lastly, and inspired by perspectives in queer studies, the chapter introduces the notion of failure as a form of critique (Halberstam 2011): a critique of normative standards of historical narratives and source analysis that not only tend to ignore silences and their active production, but also the diversity of archival traces.

Chapter 4 is dedicated to the archive and *the Archival* and is preceded by a discussion of genealogies of archival theories. My reflections on the archive begin with classic accounts by Michel Foucault (1972 [1969]) and Arlette Farge (2013 [1989]), Jacques Derrida (1996 [1995]) and Carolyn Steedman (2001a/b), and end with contributions by Ann L. Stoler (2002, 2009), Saidiya Hartman (2008), and Anjali Arondekar (2009), among others. While Derrida famously went back to the Greek *archons*, the guardians of parchment and law, I conclude with a recourse to the archival technology of sound reproduction (Hoffmann 2004; Lange 2017a). On the basis of theoretical reflections on the archive—on knowledge and power—, the chapter seeks to discuss how the *Lautarchiv* can be grasped in its discursive order and hegemonic logic. Here, considerations of the imperial, the colonial, and the European archive help to conceptualise the *Lautarchiv* as a colonial archive 'at home.' Furthermore, the chapter deals with the power dynamics between the making of archives and the production of history (Trouillot 1995).

Drawing on the *archival turn*, I plead for an understanding of the archive as simultaneously a "subject of inquiry, site of research and critical practice" (Eichhorn 2013: 4). Hence, I advocate for a conception of the archive not as a place where the past can be reconstructed, but rather as a methodological approach to an investigation of the legacies and the epistemic forms and formations of the past that influence present and future. This book is thus based on a twofold notion of the archive—the archive as institution and workplace, but also the archive as concept and metaphor.

In my second case study, in Chapter 5, I examine the gendered and racialised orders of the *Lautarchiv*. The focus of this case analysis is on two sound recordings by the female performers Venkatamma and Rajamanikkam from India, recorded at the site of a so-called *Völkerschau* in the Berlin Zoological Garden in 1926. As the majority of the *Lautarchiv*'s recordings are of men, the 'femininity' of these sources represents a unique feature. By concentrating on female colonial subjects, I argue that it is possible to defy much of the scholarship on historical migrations and transnational mobilities. For a long time, a large part of the literature focused on male and physical labour. Although the *Lautarchiv* is another good example of the paucity of sources attesting to female presence and historicity, the chapter allows me to highlight Indian temporary workers and their artistic background.

The chapter suggests another mode of listening, that of a *close listening*. Assuming that the recordings housed at the *Lautarchiv* contain more than verbally communicated content, namely non-verbal information, Hoffmann (2015) and Lange (2014) first introduced the method of close listening. For this approach, it is important to recognise that, in addition to the noise of the technical apparatus, the recordings contain pauses and silences, unplanned speaking and misspeaking, coughing and laughing. As part of my analysis, I argue that a close listening offers the possibility of perceiving interruptions, if not disruptions, of the otherwise very strict and rigid recording process. I put forward the argument that a close listening allows for paying attention to aspects that appear imperceptible or inaudible within the archival or media order that underlies the production of the recordings. I demonstrate that these aspects are nevertheless part of the archive and can become visible and audible by means of a close reading *and* listening.

In my investigation of the archival traces of the two performers (on the level of technology and materiality, of the recording device and discourse networks, as well as of the subject), I show that the logic of the scientific recording procedure of the time followed a patriarchal norm and a gendered order of knowledge. I discuss whether Venkatamma's laughter and Rajamanikkam's free narration can be understood as disruptions of the procedure and thus, to a certain extent, as subversions of the archival and hegemonic order. I contemplate to what extent this touches upon moments of agency of the recorded subjects, who had otherwise been degraded to objects. Are they marginalised by and within the patriarchal system, exploited by the colonial labour regime? Are they early cosmopolitan workers 'from below,' subversive in their artistic practice and speaking position? Or is neither the case? Instead, do the archival traces of the two women point to the ambiguities of colonial dialectics?

In my third and final case study, in Chapter 6, I develop the mode of a *collective listening* in order to investigate the historical and current meanings of a sound recording by Bayume Mohamed Hussein. Hussein is a prominent figure in the historical reappraisal of colonial migration to Berlin. Compared to the other colonial protagonists in this book, there is quite a lot of knowledge about Hussein's life. Hardly any other biography seems so closely entangled with German (colonial) history. Hussein was born in Dar es Salaam in 1904 and fought as a child soldier in the First World War in the then colony of German East Africa. At the end of the 1920s, he came to Berlin, where he worked as a waiter and actor, but also as a Swahili language assistant at the Berlin University. Denounced for 'racial defilement' by the Nazis in 1941, he died in the *Sachsenhausen* concentration camp in 1944.

Hussein's voice recording was produced at the Institute for Sound Research in July 1934. The sound recording features a text read by Hussein in Swahili, dealing with Swahili wedding traditions. The recording was primarily intended for language teaching purposes and was published as a companion to a language-learning booklet. In order to approach this specific sonic source, I organised a listening workshop together with the anthropologist Jasmin Mahazi. We invited Swahili speakers to share views on the conditions under which the recording was produced, about the content and its meaning. By bringing together different expertise, perspectives, and positionalities, we intended to produce a collective, collaborative, and open-ended investigation of the historical material. The chapter explores whether collective listening presents a way to overcome traditional forms of academic knowledge production by recognising a variety of knowledges and experiences.

The workshop revealed that the research and recording practice at the time was accompanied by several—culturally- and gender-specific—border crossings. Today's listening experiences showed how fundamentally necessary it is to classify historical voice recordings as the results of unequal power relations and the product of research and teaching methods of a colonial knowledge system. Any present or future engagement with Hussein's recording must take into account the doubly sensitive character of the recording. The recording is sensitive because of its conditions of origin in an apparatus of colonial knowledge production. But not only the recording situation, also the content of the recording itself is sensitive. The recorded and published text stands for an *othering* and for the gendered, colonial gaze.

With the perspective of collective listening, the chapter moves between three, at times contradictory, premises. Does the approach taken here simply complement the colonial archive and thus update it? Does it allow for the establishment of an alternative or 'second life' for the colonial archive? Or does it create an entirely new archive consisting of contemporary and intersubjective projections and speculations?

By taking into account perspectives from the field of sound studies, the final chapter, before the coda, tackles the notion of *the Acoustic*. It further interrogates the relationship between sound preservation and the paradigm of 'salvage anthropology,' and hence relations between race and sound. I show that the 'salvage paradigm' was emblematic of the archival project of the *Lautarchiv*. It was the attempt to preserve not only the voices of the deceased, but the sound of (native) culture. As the chapter points out, this notion runs like a red thread throughout the book.

Introducing a variety of approaches to the object of sound, I take up the proclamation to break with static and naturalised conceptions of sound (e.g. Novak and Sakakeeny 2015). Such critical voices wish to understand sound events as highly dynamic and multisensory phenomena. Eidsheim, for instance, postulates the necessity to reject a static and essentialist "figure of sound" (2015: 2). Instead, she seeks to conceptualise sound as a composite of visual, structural, and discursive information. As indicated above, Eidsheim advocates for a shift away from the source of sound, as well as ostensibly given qualities of mediated sound. Instead, one should concentrate on the processes of hearing and listening, including not only acoustic but also tactile, spatial, and physical sensations. Accordingly, the focus is no longer on the sound subject or object alone, but on reflecting and historicising listening practices. This, then, reflects the purpose of developing three diverging listening modes in the preceding case studies. In summary, the chapter suggests that, in dealing with sound objects of the *Lautarchiv*, one ought to detach oneself from both the archival objects themselves as well as from the recorded historical subjects and instead focus more on listening, then and now.

* * *

In negotiating my position in relation to the contested project of the Berlin Humboldt Forum, I understand my case studies and the three different modes of listening as a way to develop a stance towards the Forum's present and future. In my opinion, it is essential to reflect upon and problematise the limits of the

Western institution and decentre its position. It is crucial to pay close attention to archival forms, to contextualise the sources, to historicise practices of
listening, and to consider ambivalence and ambiguity. Lastly, it is important to
approach colonial material from different perspectives and, if feasible, collaboratively. For only then—if at all—does a post- and decolonial approach to the
acoustic legacies of the *Lautarchiv* become possible.

All in all, my research has largely remained outside the institution of the
Humboldt Forum, keeping a critical distance from the planning process and
personnel decisions regarding the *Lautarchiv*'s relocation to the Forum. But
just as the activists in front of the German Historical Museum expect to be
heard at some point, I humbly hope that this book will encourage more critical
and reflexive engagements with the *Lautarchiv*'s colonial holdings at its new
location.

2

THE ETHNOGRAPHIC ...

On Entangled Histories

What does it mean to conduct a historical ethnography *in* and *of* the *Lautarchiv*? What exactly does an entangled approach to the sound archive's history imply? And what kind of analytical concepts and methodological tools are useful and necessary to deal with the sound objects and histories selected for this study? This chapter sets out to discuss the strengths and possible pitfalls of carrying out historical research from a cultural anthropology perspective. How does one reflect upon diverging notions of historical anthropology within the multi-faceted discipline of anthropology, or better, anthropologies (Restrepo and Escobar 2005)? How does one assess other disciplinary strands, such as those of cultural, social, or micro-history? And how do notions of time and temporality translate into epistemic concepts when trying to grasp the past in relation to the present and future? Arguing that it does not seem worth thinking either in static intra-disciplinary and disciplinary divisions or in temporal constraints, this chapter advocates for an understanding of the project of historical anthropology as a genuine transdisciplinary field and a multidirectional practice. This understanding values different epistemological and methodological perspectives in order to challenge homogenous and constraining notions of temporality, spatiality, and materiality.

While this chapter does devote special attention to one field of study, namely European ethnology, it is equally certain that my academic home in the German-speaking scientific landscape cannot be described as a discipline in the singular. Rather, the field must be conceived as a project that is constantly in the making, self-reflexively seeking to reinvent itself time and again and trying to cope with its difficult legacies (Kaschuba 2006 [1999]: 96). Two characteristics are important when it comes to defining and historicising the discipline of European ethnology. First, one needs to consider Germany's particular genealogies of nation-building, imperialism, colonialism, and, of course, National Socialism. Second, one must take into account the nineteenth-century division between two anthropologies, which technically still exists in German-speaking institutions. In the nineteenth century, two scholarly fields became institutionalised: one placed attention on studying the non-European and the 'foreign' (*Völkerkunde*), while the other concentrated on European and folkloristic traditions (*Volkskunde*). As cultural anthropologists and European ethnologists Regina Römhild and Michi Knecht (2019: 68) point out, both disciplinary legacies continue to hover over the current project of European ethnology.

Set against the background of the discipline's history, this chapter shows that it is crucial to spend some time dwelling on institutional genealogies, as well as on the categories of 'European' and 'Europe.' Perceived as allegedly spatially and culturally distinctive, these categories often appear as unquestioned markers. I share the opinion that postcolonial and entangled approaches in particular benefit from incorporating a critical account of these dominant categories into their analyses (e.g Adam et al. 2019b; see also Randeria and Römhild 2013). While some students of postcolonial or area studies deliberately turn their attention away from the dominant centre of Europe, in order to bring the hitherto marginalised and peripheral into focus, they in fact often sustain the naturalised binary between 'the West and the Rest' (Hall 1992). This study, by contrast, offers relational perspectives that concentrate on the centre and the periphery in one analytical field, carving out relationships, inequalities, and conflicts in and of a globalised world. In this way, I argue, it is possible to challenge and decentre not only the often unquestioned and unmarked notion of the European centre, but also other allegedly fixed, normative, and dichotomous categorisations (see also Chapter 3 and 5). As Römhild (e.g. 2009, 2021) and others propose, this is exactly what characterises core questions of an approach of reflexive Europeanisation. I follow the editors of a volume on decentring Europe in their suggested program of combining postcolonial approaches with the intellectual capital of anthropological reflexivity (Adam et al. 2019b: 16). I share their wish to examine the making and re-making of European hegemony, both in political and epistemic terms. This hegemony remains incomprehensible if one does not account for centuries of social, cultural, and political mobility, migration, and inequality on a global scale. I believe that the historical depth of historical ethnography is key to understanding and challenging this hegemony under the auspices of the current European project.

My thinking in this chapter is oriented towards a range of different accounts of historical anthropology stemming from German-speaking positions in European ethnology, but also from Anglophone traditions in cultural and social anthropology. In doing so, I wish to react to and situate this study within broader disciplinary discussions on the project of historical anthropology and the concept of historical ethnography. The debate on what it means to conduct cultural analysis in historical terms is an abiding one—obviously not exclusively reserved for the German-speaking landscape. Rather, it seems that such discussions are continuously revived, from theoretical as well as methodological standpoints in multiple contexts. The chapter seeks to show how my study contributes to and at the same time complicates these academic discourses.

Notes on a Reflexive and Situated Access (to History and the Archive)

By drawing on my own archival work, and by reflecting on the experiences I have had in the archives within the scope of this book, I am constructing my very own archive of reflexive selections and situated interpretations, projections, and affects. This personal archive, however, is not disconnected from the archives I am referring to. Different notions of what it means to construct a new, or one's own, archive through ethnography, as suggested by anthropologists Jean and John Comaroff (1992: 34), accompany this chapter and the book overall.

While some may argue that, by lingering on a reflexive approach, the research process is more transparent and intelligible; others might say that shifting the attention to situated interpretations of historical sources runs the risk of losing a critical distance to the material. Some hold the opinion that a reflexive form of de-familiarisation, as a classic anthropological tool, rather than an emphatic proximity, allows for a productive analysis of historical issues (Kienitz 2012: 119–121). Still others warn against overstepping the mark when applying anthropological terminologies of fieldwork, participant observation, and auto-ethnography in an excessively literal way to archival work. It is assumed that reference to a co-presence of, or even a dialogue between, historical subjects and researchers would be detrimental to the research process. This understanding would favour a mistaken notion of a symmetrical relationship between observers and subjects, when in fact the interaction is anything but equal and synchronous. Further, it would foster a difficult sense of subjectivism, which runs the risk of losing sight of the (f)actual matter of historical material (Wietschorke 2010: 206).

Aware of these rather critical or at least cautious positions, I nonetheless attend to a reflexive and situated historical methodology. Throughout this book, I reveal when, how, and why I refer to my subject position in relation to my object of study. In this way, I aim to unfold and reflect upon my situated perspective and possible blind spots. Joining Donna Haraway (1988), who famously brought attention to the situatedness of knowledge production, I depict knowledge as always contextual and limited. On that note, I also wish to emphasise the importance of past and ongoing debates on questions of representation and positionality in shaping my academic training. My engagement with various disciplinary discourses on writing culture, politics of representation and knowledge (e.g. Clifford and Marcus 1986; Hall 1997; Visweswaran 1994), postcolonial thinking (e.g. Spivak 1988; Stoler 2009; Trouillot 1995), as well as queer/feminist and Black critique (e.g. Arondekar 2009; Haraway 1988; Hartman 2008) has had and continues to have a decisive impact on me personally, but more importantly on my academic practice and my writing. Not least in light of this broader framing of scholarship influencing my approach to the *Lautarchiv*, I understand this study to be a crucial intervention in the project of historical anthropology.

Historical Ethnography and the Epistemological Bracketing of Past and Present

The dialogical relation between the disciplines of history and anthropology, which results in a reciprocal exchange of methods and theories, is perhaps one of the most frequent arguments put forward when debating the project of historical anthropology. Advocates of the project commonly suggest that conventional historical and archival research would profit from an ethnographic lens, just as ethnographic approaches focusing merely on contemporary discourses would benefit from historical perspectives. In this sense, my study seeks to show what historical research on the *Lautarchiv* gains from applying ethnographic methods to the investigation of the archive; and vice versa, why, within the scope of anthropology, researchers benefit from paying more attention to the interplay of pasts and presents. To illustrate my point, I draw on the conception of historical ethnography, as discussed by European ethnologist Jens Wietschorke, before augmenting his approach by considering further anthropological accounts, by aforementioned Jean and John Comaroff, Regina Römhild, and Sharon Macdonald, among others.

Committed to an ethnographically-inspired historiography, Wietschorke (2012: 35) introduces the figure of thought of an epistemological bracketing (*Verklammerung*) of past and present. He explains that this means, on the one hand, historicising the present and, on the other, examining the past by treating it as a quasi-ethnographic present. In a Foucauldian sense of a genealogy of the present, he believes that one cannot understand the present without looking into the past, just as one cannot grasp the past without thinking about how certain issues are addressed in the present (see also Hall 2001). Wietschorke (2010: 209) therefore argues that history ought to be understood as nothing other than a past present, since the present appears as nothing other than a history that has not yet passed. This understanding is fundamental to his further elaboration of what he understands to be the concept of historical ethnography.

Discussing the usefulness and limitations of historical ethnography, Wietschorke (2010: 207) points to three crucial conditions, emphasising that the concept is more than just a set of methods. For him, historical ethnography entails a heuristic and epistemological moment in its approach to cultural and micro history. First of all, Wietschorke (2013: 210) understands historical ethnography to be an epistemological approach to source analysis and interpretation. The concept offers the possibility to carve out and contextualise ostensible minor details and aspects of the mundane. For him, historical ethnography is an epistemological access point to historic source material allowing for a thick description—in a Geertzian sense—of agents, practices, and events. Second, Wietschorke depicts ethnography as epistemological *brackets* encompassing an analysis of both past and present. This moment of bracketing has the ability to unsettle supposedly fixed boundaries between the two temporal modalities. Lastly, the concept demands a reflection of the researcher's positionality. This also entails the aforementioned mediation of situated knowledges, which has been a subject of discussion, particularly in feminist schools of thought.

As opposed to social and cultural history, a particular strength of (historical) ethnography is its focus on practices and the (historical) agents applying them (Wietschorke 2010: 209, referencing Maase 2001: 259). Here, however, a methodological problem arises: how does one grasp practices if not by being there, by participant observation, or by entering into dialogue with one's counterparts? How does one examine practices based on written and visual—and in my case acoustic—material? Accordingly, the simple, yet challenging, question is how to proceed from text to practice. One possible way to address this obstacle is to assume that all historical material—be they texts, images, or sounds—contain traces indicating practices, social relations, and specific logics of agency. Hence, what I take from Wietschorke's account is an analytical lens to examine traces of past and changing practices. His exhortation to pay special attention to moments of difference and relationality materialising in historical sources are of particular importance for the case studies presented in this book. It is in a similar vein that John and Jean Comaroff define all social fields, including historical ones, as "swept by contrary waves of unity and diversity: by forces that diffuse power and meaning and by counterforces that concentrate and fix them" (1992: 31). The following pages draw on the Comaroffian conceptualisations of ethnography and historical imagination, as developed by them almost three decades ago.

The Poetics of History

Right at the beginning of their eminent book *Ethnography and Historical Imagination* (1992), Jean and John Comaroff promote a "historical anthropology that is dedicated to exploring the processes that make and transform particular worlds—processes that reciprocally shape subject and context, that allow certain things to be said and done" (31). From this, I understand the Comaroffs' pondering over historical anthropology and ethnography—then still in its early formation stage—as both conceptual and methodological. At the same time, their thinking connects two of the three major conceptual frameworks scaffolding this book—namely *the Ethnographic* and *the Archival*. As highlighted in my introduction, I understand the theoretical vantage points taken from ethnography and the archive as practices and sites of knowledge production in their own right. Following anthropologists Elizabeth Edwards and Christopher Morton (2009: 9–11), ethnography and the archive can imply both a powerful institution and a reflexive practice epitomising dynamic, fluid historical processes and opening up new interpretative space.

A quintessential contribution of the Comaroffs is the assertion that conducting historical ethnography "must begin by constructing its own archive" (1992: 34). In order to be able to deconstruct colonial archives allegedly consisting of social facts and historical evidence, the Comaroffs recommend that anthropologists "must work both in and outside the official record, both with and beyond the guardians of memory in the societies we study" (34). As I will point to in more detail in Chapter 4, anthropologist Ann L. Stoler (2002c/d, 2009) convincingly took up this proposition in her account of reading the colonial archive along the grain. According to Stoler, three different types of responses followed the Comaroffs' proposal. Some students of colonialism adopted the idea of creating a new colonial archive by interrogating new kinds of sources. Others understood the assertion as an invitation to access familiar archives under the premise of posing new research questions and establishing new reading strategies. Finally, Stoler's own approach took up the Comaroffs' suggestion to dwell on the "unexplored fault lines, ragged edges, and unre-marked disruptions to the seamless and smooth surface of colonialism's archival genres" (2009: 52). By examining official archival records, Stoler aimed at unravelling governmental formations that evolved in and came from archival categorisations and classifications.[1]

As far as my own research on the *Lautarchiv* is concerned, I see some influence on my work from each approach described by Stoler. I am dealing with new kinds of sources—sources which, for the most part, have been nei-ther examined nor considered as meaningful additions, completions, or coun-terweights to already evaluated archives on which established historiographies rest. Concurrently, I approach the *Lautarchiv* through a postcolonial lens, rais-ing new analytical questions relating to colonial situations in the metropolis. This also entails developing new reading strategies of familiar material, consid-ered dominant or hegemonic and usually produced by *white*, male, or otherwise privileged subjects.[2] In this way, as I demonstrate, it is possible to contrast and contest a variety of sources, challenge their ostensibly stable and static status, and point to moments of difference and conflict, ambiguity and contradiction. Lastly, I follow Stoler in her attempt to read the archive both along and against its grain. Ultimately, all of this may lead to the construction of a new archive, based on the work of an already existing archive (see also Chapter 4 and my reference to Arlette Farge). As a new archive, this study is not detached from or located outside of the colonial archive. For me, responding to the *Lautarchiv* speaks to a discursive practice. It is the attempt to react to an acoustic matter in textual form, which hopefully entails more than another layer of appropriation (see also Edwards and Morton 2009). In Chapter 3 and 6, I will come back to the question of whether a refigured archive or archival practice appears as an addition to or extension of archival power and the existing colonial archive, rather than a counter-archive and/or counter-history.

Similar to Wietschorke's understanding of the concept of historical ethnography as a systematic analysis of social relations and cultural differences in their praxeological dimensions, the Comaroffs likewise lay their focus on practices. Their interest concentrates on possible ways to study the tensions and reciprocities of the individual and the personal on the one hand, and social facts and cultural imaginations on the other: "For only then," they argue, "can we situate individual expressions and signifying practices within a wider field of representation. After all," the Comaroffs continue, "locating fragments requires a sense of the way in which they ride the crosscurrents of division and unity in any moment" (1992: 34).

In line with the above, the Comaroffs make it very clear that their "methodological concern is less with events than with meaningful *practices*—which, perhaps, remains one of the principle distinctions between historical anthropology and social history" (37, my emphasis). My key takeaway from the Comaroffs, then, is the invitation to be "more preoccupied with ambiguous processes than with contained acts or isolable incidents" (37). To me, this means to look for the 'poetics of history' revealing themselves in ambiguous processes and practices, rather than in recorded facts constituting the notion of a singular 'truth' or allegedly stable figurations:

> We would insist [...] that a historical ethnography must always go beyond literary traces, beyond explicit narrative, exegesis, even argument. For the *poetics of history* lie also in *mute meanings* transacted through goods and practices, through icons and images dispersed in the landscape of the everyday. (35, my emphasis)

As the notions of silence and absence, blank spaces and (forced or voluntary) muteness take on a significant role throughout this book, I understand the assertion of 'mute meanings' both in a literal and figurative sense. I seek to take the Comaroffs' insistence of 'going beyond' to a different level: my focus on absences and gaps is not only a change in perspective and emphasis but a possible form of critique. As suggested in the aforementioned anthology on decentring Europe, the contributions in that volume are predominantly concerned with different positions of the omitted, the *Other*, or the marginalised, amounting to a *critique of and through gaps* (Adam et al. 2019b: 17). Just as they seek to broaden and complicate the prospects of what constitutes the European project, I, for my part, explore the possibility of widening the perspectives on what constitutes the colonial archive.

For a Postcolonial Anthropology of Europe

Insisting on the notion of gaps, this section draws on Regina Römhild and Michi Knecht's account of a twofold gap in anthropological research, which prompted them to suggest a newly inspired anthropology of Europe. Römhild and Knecht (2019: 67–68) begin their argument with two assumptions: first, they point out that despite the fact that anthropological research in and of Europe has become an established field of study, postcolonial perspectives on Europe remain marginal. Second, they argue that cultural and social anthropology informed by postcolonial theory generally does not address Europe—understood as a globally and historically entangled unit—as a potential empirical field site. In other words, research in and of Europe neglects postcolonial perspectives, while postcolonial discourses disregard Europe. In response to this dual gap, the scholars advocate for a critical and reflexive investigation of Europe and processes of Europeanisation from a postcolonial standpoint. For them, Europeanisation processes include both past and present practices as well as politics, projects and conflicts constitutive to the production of Europe. Here, Europe is understood as a relational space, a space that is defined by a constant transfer and migration of people, objects, and knowledge. As Römhild (2019: 2) points out elsewhere, Europe is seen as a heterogeneous political, cultural, and discursive project, which means depicting it as both co-producer and by-product of global injustices, mobilities and movements, conflicts and tensions (see also Randeria and Römhild 2013: 11). By shifting the focus to global entanglements, Römhild and Knecht aim at moving beyond explicit, but also more subtle and unquestioned, Eurocentric research traditions. Given the contentious history of anthropology, they wonder why it is still not commonplace to formulate a postcolonial critique of the epistemic origins of their discipline *and* of Europe, even though both are genuine colonial and imperial projects (2019: 67).

As indicated in the introduction to this chapter, Römhild and Knecht emphasise the special case of anthropological research in the German-speaking academic landscape. In the nineteenth century, the discipline of anthropology split into two fields of study: the discipline of ethnology, or *Völkerkunde*, with a focus on the non-European world, and the discipline of *Volkskunde*, with an initial interest in folkloristic traditions.[3] While the first was concerned with constructing a 'foreign' and 'othered' (often derogatory or antithetical) reflection of the European and 'rational' Self, the latter served not least to legitimise the historical origins of the ideology of the German nation or *Volk* (*ethnos*) (Kaschuba 2006 [1999]: 26).[4] What both disciplines shared, however, was the fact that scholars usually approached their object of study—the *Other*—from the position of the urban bourgeoisie. For *Völkerkunde*, it was indigenous groups and practices that were of interest, for *Volkskunde*, rural peasants and traditions.[5]

Although epistemological interests and practices have certainly changed, not least by convergences and interactions between the two disciplines, anthropologies in German-speaking contexts remain divided in this post/colonial way.[6] This disciplinary distinction faces the challenge of sustaining the 'imperial division' of a knowledge production in which Europe is constituted as the subject and the colonised world is considered to be the object (Römhild and Knecht 2019: 69, referencing Conrad and Randeria 2013 [2002]: 43).[7] To Römhild and Knecht, it seems particularly peculiar that the entanglements between academic traditions and Germany's colonial and fascist pasts are not taken as a starting point to decentre Europe. Instead, they observe how an implicit Eurocentrism further excludes Europe as an object of research, thus perpetuating its hegemonic position (2019: 70).

All in all, and in the vein of the important attempt to provincialise Europe, famously brought to the fore by postcolonial scholar Dipesh Chakrabarty (2000), Römhild and Knecht argue against an omission and instead for a decentring of Europe. That is to say, in order to overcome the stated gaps, they advocate for a stronger inclusion of postcolonial perspectives in the discipline of European ethnology—demanding that they ought to be invested in the diachronic study of Europeanisation processes. At the same time, they plea for tackling questions of Europe in postcolonial-oriented studies in order to challenge Europe's dominant status, which is still all too often regarded as normative. In their opinion, there is a plethora of cases where Europe remains unmarked, thereby appearing as the unquestioned and naturalised centre of former (but today also neo-)colonial hegemony. What they wish for is a reflexive Europeanisation and cosmopolitanisation of the anthropological project prepared to study entangled spaces and mobilities, both of the past and in the present (2019: 76).

What I take from this line of reasoning for my own research is the move to re-focus on the former centre—the metropolitan archive and colonial knowledge production—in order to decentre it in a next step by carving out its globally entangled conditions. If one understands the *Lautarchiv* as a site where alleged European promises of modernity, progress, and superiority materialised, it seems therefore particularly worthwhile to apply approaches from a globally-oriented and postcolonial anthropology of Europe. In this way, previously *absent presences*, unquestioned relations and dynamics, untracked past and future ideas of and for the *Lautarchiv* come to the fore. Following from this epistemic shift, the next section argues *that*, and *why*, this change of perspective also requires a methodological consideration.

'Past Presencing' and Multiplying 'Past Presences'

Whereas discussions of methodology may not be the most pressing issue in other fields of the humanities, for anthropology and ethnographic research, methodological reflection is crucial. In simplified terms, I could say that the methodology I deploy in order to approach the *Lautarchiv* is (historical) ethnography. Yet, I believe it is important to elaborate on how I explore the historical object of study located in a postcolonial European metropolis and in an imperial space. I argue that my object of inquiry can neither be isolated in time (as I am interested in studying the intersections and connections between past, present, and future) nor in space (since the material I am looking at *and* listening to refers to different intersecting topologies and imagined topographies). In what follows, I therefore draw on Sharon Macdonald's account of processes of 'past presencing' and employ her assertion of a multidirectional temporal practice on the *Lautarchiv*.

In order to investigate connections between past(s) and present(s), Macdonald suggests concentrating more on historical dimensions. As part of her book, *Memorylands: Heritage and Identity in Europe Today* (2013), the social anthropologist calls for broadening the scope of anthropological research.[8] One of the central arguments of her work is to look at memory processes and projects of memorialisation constitutive of the production of Europe *today*. Similar to Römhild, Macdonald understands present-day Europe as shaped by and itself shaping specific imaginations of what ought to be Europe and European. With respect to my study, I consider her reasoning for expanding the scope of historical research within European contexts and against the background of European memory banks, social practices, and (museum) collections as particularly productive (see also Macdonald 2021).

Important in Macdonald's work is the observation that anthropological research on the past in general, and on (collective) memory practices in particular, is usually concerned with the question of how and by whom the past is constructed and used in the present. According to Macdonald, the following questions matter in anthropological approaches to the past:

> What is recalled, when and why? Whose pasts are told in the public sphere? What is forgotten, not mentioned or perhaps only told in whispers? And what notions of continuity, change, repetition or rupture shape or are expressed in recounted memories? (2013: 27)

In order to deal with this set of questions, Macdonald suggests conceptualising practices of 'past presencing.' In her opinion, the discipline of anthropology is particularly suited to digging into and juggling the different (temporal) notions addressed by these questions. "If past presencing is the empirical phenomenon of how people variously experience, understand and produce the past in the present," she writes, "the challenge for anthropologists is how to approach it. This can be seen as a multitemporal challenge" (52).

While Macdonald conducted a lot of her (field) research on the politics and practices of memory in Germany, she has always concentrated her work on broader contexts, understanding her studies as part of an anthropology of Europe. For the past decades, as Macdonald explicates, the anthropology of Europe was largely concerned with studying conceptions of identity, difference, and belonging in changing localities, spaces, and temporalities. When looking at Europe today, the question of so-called identity politics matters every step of the way and from either end of the political spectrum. In this vein, and particularly addressed to the profession of social anthropology, Macdonald emphasises the need to shed light on the practices of how identities and rights are produced, claimed, or appropriated with recourse to historical formations and the past. This interest is directed towards both (trans)nationally-bounded levels as well as smaller communal or urban spaces.

In her investigation of how the past is recalled and recounted, Macdonald draws on the development of different concepts of history and historical consciousness in anthropology. She begins her elaboration by introducing anthropological approaches to historical research that remain rather unidirectional. She problematises tendencies of a certain kind of 'synchronism' when, for instance, scholars use the ethnographic present, thereby implying false notions of stability and an "enduring reality" (53).[9] While Macdonald acknowledges that historical ethnography allows both to conduct microanalysis of past moments *and* to study instances of transformation and rupture on a larger scale, she argues that these approaches need to be thought of as rather one-sided too. To her, there is always the risk of laying too much emphasis on a fixed sequence of time that linearly leads to the present. In opposition to this, Macdonald mentions accounts that mainly concentrate on "present uses of the past" (54). While she understands this focus as an important contribution from the side of anthropology, and not least as a type of corrective to teleological models, Macdonald also warns against a certain kind of 'presentism.' When solely considering the past as capable of conferring meaning in and for the present moment, other temporalities are excluded. Consequently, one can ascribe to this perspective yet another sense of unidirectionality. Previously, attention was more focused on normative ideas in which the past led to the present. Then the perspective changed, and attention turned to practices that aimed at viewing the past only to the extent that people perceive, use, and stage the past in the present.

Given these different yet seemingly one-sided approaches, Macdonald proposes a *multidirectional temporal practice* in ethnographic research. In her view, a multidirectional temporal practice is able to grasp the multiple meanings and different temporal layers associated with the past. In this way, it becomes possible to go beyond not only conventional historical accounts but also rather normative approaches in historical anthropology when restricted to a specific time span. On yet another level, and in keeping with Wietschorke, Macdonald speaks out in favour of a multitemporal practice in order to overcome binary divisions within cultural analysis of either the past or the present. In a striking way, similar modalities are at play when attempting to bring entanglements—of past and present, here and there—into focus, as proposed in my introduction and again at the outset of this chapter.

For a Multidirectional Temporal Practice

In a schematic manner, Macdonald (2003: 100) elaborates on the different temporal modes one has to take into consideration when dealing with historical material and the interplay of pasts and presents. For her, there is, first of all, *the present in the past*; second, the past that is referred to, *the documented and encoded past*; third, the *past presents* the material survived since its original production; and, lastly, *the past in the present*, the current moment. In what follows, I apply the suggestions provided by Macdonald to historical material from the *Lautarchiv*. It is a conscious decision to do this before diving into my more detailed investigations of specific archival collections and single sound files. In the coming chapters, I account for distinct colonial situations as they material-ised in sound and under metropolitan conditions (see Chapter 3, 5, and 6). At this point, however, I conceive the archival institution and material as rather coherent bodies in order to carve out their relation to notions of time and tem-porality. What kind of temporal modes and dimensions is one confronted with in the present when dealing with historical sounds compiled for the future?

When translating the different levels to my object of research, I first need to ask how the historical events (the act of recording and archiving sound) and the historical material (the sound recordings and written scripts) were per-ceived at the time of their original production, meaning the *present in the past*. Following the logic of the time, and thus going along the archival grain, one way to define these moments is to consider them under at least three premises, that is to say, erstwhile understandings of science, technology, and time.

For one thing, the act of recording ties in with the encyclopaedic doctrine of producing a range of speech and music samples (Balke 2009: 70; Lange 2012: 68–71). The possibility of capturing a whole set of examples was emblematic of the then epistemic paradigm of practices of systematised collecting and cat-aloguing, classifying and comparing. Jonathan Sterne subsumes this paradigm under the motif of a Western "ethos of preservation" (2003: 324; see also Chapter 7). Another primary purpose for compiling voice samples was the mere technical possibility of recording, reproducing, and preserving sound. At the time, sound technology had been rather newly introduced to and adopted in academic contexts (e.g. Hoffmann 2004; see also Chapter 4 and 7). In temporal terms, and given the technological and institutional possibilities of producing and archiving sound, the now was imagined as the future past—a past which, in fact, had never been the present. Understood as a highly modern device repre-senting innovation and progress, the phonograph's technical means to preserve the present for future generations was a decisive factor in terms of the tempo-rality of modernity. In this respect, it becomes clear how special and unique the nature of the sound archive is in relation to time and temporality, in terms of the configuration and reconfiguration, imagination and representation of pasts, presents, and futures. For the present, the recordists envisioned the opportunity to conduct research on 'live objects' by means of new recording media and for-mats. It was assumed that such unique opportunities might not reoccur in the near future. In addition, the act of recording was regarded as a distinct cut into the present, a present that—by the flow of history—would soon become the past and was therefore deemed valuable for future scientific research.

On yet another note, it is important to mention that due to the labora-tory-like setup, the individual person behind the sample did not seem to mat-ter. The objectifying, archival, and encyclopaedic practices of the time made the subject disappear. This is a crucial point I will keep coming back to in my detailed analyses of single sound documents and my attempt to get closer to the vocalisers and recordists. Both historical subjects tend to disappear behind the scientific procedure and technology, behind colonial positions and practices. In Chapter 3, I further outline how introducing postcolonial perspectives in earlier contexts of engagement with the *Lautarchiv* contributed to shifting the focus to questions of (inter)subjectivity.

Secondly, as suggested by Macdonald, one needs to examine in what ways historical events were documented and encoded. In other words, this means considering the ways past moments and practices materialised. Such materialisations are characterised by an interplay of the technical prerequisites and archival dispositive. As much as the medium dictated the recording act, the recordists still had to instruct the singers and speakers in order to achieve the documenting of a 'specific performance.' In other words, the "recording diaphragm and wax medium captured a specific performance, a performance designed and modified specifically for the purposes of reproducibility" (Sterne 2003: 314). In this, the power of both the medium and the archive, and the power of specific processes of exclusion and inclusion, become manifest. At the same time, archival practices are embedded in larger historical formations and knowledge constellations. In view of documenting and encoding, as well as with regard to the first reflection on *presents in the past*, this temporal layer also touches upon the question of how historians perceive and represent events in and as part of historiographical accounts. Answering the question of how estab-lished historiographies understood the historical situations I am dealing with in this book seems rather easy. The events scarcely appear in standard histories or the grand narrative. Only in the more recent past are the sound recordings of colonial subjects acknowledged as historical sources relevant for historiograph-ical accounts, collective memories, as well as cultural and media analysis.

On a tangible level, the events the sound recordings initially refer to are materialised in wax. The act of capturing a human voice with the technical apparatus of the gramophone meant inscribing the voice in horizontal cir-cles on a wax plate. This template constituted the negative for the shellac disc and ultimately the digital file. Matrixed, copied, and played back, the sound files' contents were in many, but not all, cases transcribed and translated into German; the files were entered on lists and stored in filing cabinets. Later, they were 'rediscovered,' digitised, indexed, and browsed through. Just as every literal translation is accompanied by a slight change in meaning, every medial transmission entails a shift in how users may perceive or use the respective medium (see also Chapter 7). What, then, can one take from and read into these processes? How does one assess shifting meanings and materialisations?

Pertaining to the third level, Macdonald asks about the ways in which *past presents*, or more precisely past fragments, survive over time. Why do certain traces subsist? Why do others disappear, get lost, or are destroyed? When and why are sources regarded as historical evidence? Examining the volatile history of the institution of the *Lautarchiv*, one can only wonder why the archival material—shellac records, other recording media and devices, visuals, written files, and specialised literature—survived over time. The status of the collections was often anything but secure, as was the conservational situation of the objects they contain. There was little or no interest either in assessing the scholarly (particularly the phonetic or linguistic) relevance or in coming to terms with the collections' multi-layered histories. For a long time, the collections gained little attention regarding both their historical and scholarly impact. In recent years, however, one can observe that many different (politically charged) agendas have been associated with the acoustic legacies of the sound archive (e.g. Hennig 2016; Hilden 2018a; Lange 2017a).[10] This new attention was and is linked to the controversial debates surrounding the project of the Humboldt Forum, as addressed in my introduction.

This contemporary momentum also leads to the fourth and last aspect laid out by Macdonald. The fourth layer concerns the question of how and by whom events and historical material are perceived and used today, in *the present of the now*. As far as the Humboldt Forum is concerned, the question for me is how the sound archive could be used and reconfigured *in* and *by* a German post-migrant society and an international (academic) community.[11] What role does a public and national institution have to play in this as stakeholder? According to its former speakers, the aim of the Forum is to present a cosmopolitan Berlin, bringing together diverse perspectives on Germany's (colonial) past and present (Parzinger 2011). However, having followed the planning of the Humboldt Forum and its final opening, I continue to have serious doubts about the institution's ability to offer alternative ideas of belonging. I remain sceptical that it can provide narratives that are not bound to essentialised positions and instead contribute to multidirectional, non-Eurocentric forms of historical consciousness and collective memory (I will return to this notion at the end of this book).[12]

Going through Macdonald's schema, which she adopted from social anthropologist Edwin Ardener (1989), one can explore the different conjunctions and often fluid and entangled boundaries between pasts and presents. As anthropology seems to be particularly apt to attend to the phenomenon of processes and practices of 'past presencing,' it seems useful to focus on these different temporal moments with respect to the *Lautarchiv*. In accordance with the suggested temporal trajectories, one can examine in what ways the past shapes the present and how the past is construed and enacted in present as well as past moments. What is missing, however, both in this and in the previous accounts on historical anthropology, is an anthropological approach to the future and its imaginations.[13]

It was Arjun Appadurai who famously suggested focusing more on notions of futurity and less on ideas of the past in anthropological research. For many years, Appadurai has been invested in studying global inequalities and ways to overcome them. In his call for the *capacity to aspire*, the anthropologist places the notion of futurity at the core of thinking about culture. For him, "it is in culture that ideas of future, as much as of those about the past, are embedded and nurtured" (2013: 179). As opposed to the past, however, Appadurai suggests that an orientation towards the future serves not only abstract academic interests, but also those of the disadvantaged. By acknowledging this cultural capacity for aspiration, the possibilities for the underprivileged to participate and be heard in debates on (global) development might increase. While Rebecca Bryant and Michael D. Knight (2019: 13) appreciate Appadurai's influential and much-quoted orientation towards the future, they point to the lack of adequate methodologies in order to move beyond anthropology's tendency (they call it burden) to study societies of the past. In their book *The Anthropology of the Future* (2019), it is their aim to offer analytical and methodological tools for assessing the future's role in the anthropological investigation of society, culture, and everyday life. Like Appadurai, Bryant and Knight ask why the discipline of anthropology has so far not put a similar emphasis on the study of the future as it has on the past. In their view, it is odd that there is a plethora of anthropological scholarship "that claims to address time and temporality while focusing almost entirely on the past-present relationship" (7). As far as the attempt to include future into anthropological research is concerned, I consider these current interventions to be crucial for my own thinking in terms of a multitemporal practice. Below, I will come back to Bryant and Knight's revived understanding of teleology.

With the different layers of time and temporality in mind, it follows that major contradictions are in place between what the *Lautarchiv* material was supposed to document and how and by whom it is read in the course of time. An extract of time, a present moment, was imagined as the past to be captured for an anticipated future. At the same time, the knowledge institution of the archive was and continues to be crucial to imaginations of the nation and European supremacy. Capturing markers of difference in sound and speech helped imagine a national Self.[14] "Because of national political and ideological priorities," Andre Gingrich argues, "the methodological focus in these [linguistic] studies was usually not comparative, but particularist" (2010: 364). Compiled under the pretext of science and research, practices of ordering and archiving, the sound recordings were produced with a strong belief in the achievements of modernity and objectivity. One of these achievements was the possibility of reproducing and preserving the ephemeral entity of the human voice. Today, early sound recordings appear as materialisations of modernity's imperatives. When emphasising conceptions of scientific paradigms and modes of knowledge production that change(d) over time, I do not wish to circumvent either the relationships between them or their continuities. To the contrary, I believe that Macdonald's multitemporal approach allows me to point to the interferences and entanglements of history—of pasts, presents, *and* futures.

All in all, Macdonald's account makes a case for a "methodology of juxtaposition and mobility, for moving between different perspectives and trying to see them in relation to one another" (2003: 101). In this way, she "attempts to develop a multidirectional relationship between past and present, and to move beyond a purely documentary approach to find ways of dealing with and theorising other kinds of 'past presences'" (102). As the title of this book suggests, I pursue the goal of dealing with, not only 'other kinds of 'past presences'' in a temporal sense, but also with the *absent presences* in (meta)physical terms. My ethnographic interest lies with marginalised presences that are, however, constitutive in their absence or omission. The aim is to show that the marginalisation of sounds as historical source material, the absence of colonial subjects in grand narratives and collective memories, and the omission of the constitutive condition of social, economic, cultural, and political entanglements are integral components to the legitimisation of the epistemic power of disciplinary and national figurations.

Through an ethnographic lens, it is not only possible to address *absent presences* but also to identify the contingency of history. While there are strands in critical historical theory concerned with the contingency of history, there remains a strong branch in social history that discards contingency and coincidence (e.g. Hoffmann 2005). I, for my part, understand contingency as constitutive of history. To me, this also relates to the question of perspectivity, of who looks back, when and how.[15] For a long time, also in the discipline of anthropology, notions of modernity and progress were the driving force for recounting the past. This coincided with a teleological understanding of history, of following history linearly in one direction. As indicated above, Bryant and Knight (2019: 2) do not wish to discard teleology altogether but instead advocate for a different kind of teleology. In their proposal for a new anthropology that directs attention to the future, they suggest an open-ended and indeterminate teleology of everyday life. In their line of reasoning, teleology does not necessarily have to be linear and progress-orientated, referring solely to the temporality of modernity. Instead, Bryant and Knight propose an indeterminate teleology as a future-oriented activity leading to a multiplicity of possible trajectories and ends. As for the *Lautarchiv*, I argue that not only the archivists and recordists envisioned a certain future but so did the people recorded. They might have had a future audience in mind when lending their voice to the academic project. In part, their aspirations simply served the needs of the scholarly enterprise. Yet some of the people recorded also managed to interrupt or undermine the archival and colonial order. In this way, the past offers trajectories that do not fit into the mould of modernity's temporality, but rather break with it by indicating different future pasts.

Conclusion

> Historical anthropology is innovative both theoretically and thematically, not least because it learned to ask questions allowing us to assume a wider understanding of human traces and, conversely, because it combined this sensitivity for *tracing* the past with new epistemological and methodological reflections on the question of how 'historical facts' are constructed. (Tanner 2009: 153, emphasis in the original)[16]

In closing the chapter with this quote, I would like to note that the project of historical anthropology can be seen as an innovative mode of knowledge production. Coinciding with Tanner's dense depiction of historical anthropology, I find his emphasis on a 'wider understanding of human traces' and the 'sensitivity for tracing the past' particularly convincing. From my point of view, the accounts of historical anthropology I have presented in this chapter stand for a certain widening of human traces, which can be linked to my focus on practices and my interest in the sense of hearing. Also, the call for 'new epistemological and methodological reflections' appears as a common thread running through the suggested ethnographic approaches. As emphasised at the beginning of this chapter, this common thread also connects to the question of accounting for positionality and situatedness regarding one's own research practice and knowledge production. Finally, and as I have been able to show in more detail in the previous pages, an access to the past must consider differing temporalities and multidirectional processes of temporalisation—including the notion of futurity.

I assembled these analytical and methodological considerations, stemming from both German-speaking discourses in European ethnology and Anglophone strands in the fields of social and cultural anthropology, in order to outline a set of tools and concepts for approaching the *Lautarchiv*. While I do not claim that this selection is in any way exhaustive, I am convinced that it offers the right instruments to reflexively study the reciprocal relationships between historical subjects and technical, as well as medial, systems on the one hand, and cultural practices and social structures on the other (Tanner 2009: 148). This reciprocity also ties in with the conception of the project of historical anthropology as outlined by European ethnologist Silvy Chakkalakal (2018). For Chakkalakal, historical anthropology is not only about decentring European history by means of 'de-familiarising' the view on one's own history. It should also be about making the interconnection (*Verschränkung*) between history and culture visible. Chakkalakal understands history and culture both as practices and epistemic concepts (174). In response, my own analytical aspiration is to historicise audio cultures and practices of listening by means of examining the epistemic and material status of archived sounds. Following the call to decentre Europe, hitherto marginalised entanglements become visible in and through the archive, emerging in practices and conflicts, ruptures and continuities, transfers and movements.

At the beginning of this chapter, I posed the question of what it means to carry out a historical ethnography *in* and *of* the *Lautarchiv*. One possible answer comes from Stoler who simply stated, "no single answer will do" (2009: 32). According to her, "ethnography in and of the colonial archives attends to processes of production, relations of power in which archives are created, sequestered, and rearranged" (32). For Stoler, the most explicit and noteworthy example in this regard is Michel-Rolph Trouillot's *Silencing the Past* (1995), which I will draw on in more detail in Chapter 4. It is the aim of the following chapters then to show how I deal with the notion of an ethnography in and of the colonial archive; how I attend to the production of the archival sounds and the relations of power between recorded people and recordists; how I navigate the different (temporal) modes in which the *Lautarchiv* was and is discursively constituted, forgotten, and reconfigured.

3
Failed Listening

From my Interview Transcripts

There was this one person who was singing a song and that song is actually, it's still in work. [...] That song is something, I have heard it in my lifetime, it is still common. And I was like: 'Oh my god, I know this song. And this person back then is singing the same song.' And that was really, it was fun. [...] It's about women. [...] It's a very popular song in the sense, OK, it has just been there through the test of time. (Armita [name changed], 20 January 2018, New Delhi)

This snippet of my conversation with a doctoral student in New Delhi resonated with me profoundly. I had asked my interlocutor to describe the experience she had when listening to a set of Bengali sound files from the *Lautarchiv*. The files had been recorded in a German POW camp during the First World War in February 1918. Today, they belong to a collection of sound recordings of prisoners of war from South Asia housed at Humboldt University's sound archive. This chapter outlines my efforts to trace the story behind the sound document mentioned in the epigraph, to get closer to the story of its content and creation.

I had met Armita at a public lecture at Jawaharlal Nehru University's School for Arts and Aesthetics, which I attended during a research stay at Delhi University's Department of Sociology. She was one of several people I met with, informally talked to, or conducted semi-structured interviews with during my research stay in late 2017 and early 2018. Most of the people I interacted with were, in one way or the other, professionally concerned with the histories and memories of the First World War in South Asian contexts. My interlocutor had heard about the Berlin sound collections in her undergraduate studies. She was familiar with the literature available in English on Indian prisoners of war held captive in German POW camps during the First World War. But it was only after our first encounter, when I sent her a selection of recordings, that she would listen to the Bengali files of three so-called *lascars*.[1] The comparatively small set of ten records belongs to the otherwise ample collection consisting of almost three hundred sound documents of colonial soldiers from South Asia—so-called *sepoys*.[2]

On the one hand, I was intrigued by the fact that my interview partner recognised one of the recorded songs, which is still in use—withstanding the 'test of time.' On the other hand, I was fascinated by the (commonly made) observation that many of the archived songs and stories are about women—irrespective of whether they were recounted by interned soldiers or seamen. Disclosing her thoughts on the situation of prisoners of war, Armita said:

> *They were talking about, they were singing songs, the very typical folk songs back home. And then, it kind of got me into this feeling that being a soldier does not always mean soldiery. It's not all about the Army. So when you are in the front, when you are fighting, or in this case you are prisoner of war, you still think about, the prominent thought in your head is your home. You think about the songs that you would have sung back home, or people you miss, or lots of people are talking about women. [...] It kind of feels like singing about women was their way of dealing with it. And, I mean, they were missing the women that they had left back home.* (20 January 2018, New Delhi)

My interlocutor's observation and the listening experience she shared were the reasons to embark on a mission to learn more about this particular sound file. Impelled by the acousmatic questions—*Who is this? Who is singing?*—I wished to overcome the division between the mediated sound and its source (Eidsheim 2019: 1–2). I wanted to know more about the recorded person, named Keramat Ali. From the archived files, I learned that Ali was born in Mymensingh, a city in what is now northeastern Bangladesh. On February 7, 1918, he had sung the folk song in one of the barracks of the so-called Half Moon Camp in Wünsdorf, a special POW camp situated on the outskirts of Berlin. I sought to find out more about the song—its use and circulation, find someone to translate it, and try to situate the acoustic trace against the backdrop of the present. I meant to tell the story of this particular song and its singer, of how the digital file travelled to present-day India—and thus, in a way, also withstood *the test of time*.

As it turned out, my intended goal to gain insights about the specific historical subject and the traditional folk song was not meant to be the crux of this chapter. I did not find an answer to the acousmatic question. I did not find out much about who was singing—about the historical figure of Keramat Ali. According to musicologist Nina S. Eidsheim, the acousmatic question tells you, the listener, "only who is listening: who you are" (24; see also Chapter 7). Consequently, my research led me to discover more about my own subject position and my role in this endeavour: about what it means to conduct historical research concerning a temporal, geographical, and cultural frame I am neither particularly adept in nor familiar with. This is one of the reasons this chapter turned out to be *a chapter of failure(s)*. I do, however, refuse to understand the notion of failure in a purely negative sense. Rather, this chapter aims at fleshing out its illuminating and productive aspects. Moments of failure in ethnographic research sometimes turn out to be serendipitous, allowing for prolific juxtapositions and new research questions (e.g. Martínez 2018; Rivoal and Salazar 2013). Moreover, this chapter introduces approaches in and of feminist ethnography, discussing the question of the *politics of location* (Rich 1987; Braidotti 1994). In particular, I go back to the notion of *feminist ethnography as failure* (1994), as developed by anthropologist Kamala Visweswaran.

In this first of my three case studies, I wish to carve out the importance of acknowledging one's situated, limited, and contextual points of reference when engaging with colonial archives (see Chapter 2). Here, I ask what might emerge from my research experiences and feelings of failure. Rejecting the expectation to understand failure as a dead end, I argue that failure can function as a lens of productive reflection and a form of critique in order to engage with the politics of location and my subject position as a *white*, female, Western-trained, and institutionally privileged researcher.[3] I proceed to show how pondering over failure and failing helped me to establish a nuanced theoretical and methodological framework, which turned out to be valuable also for the approaches exercised in other sections of this study (see Chapter 5 and 6).[4]

After a second glimpse into my ethnographic archive, this chapter recounts an ethnographic anecdote by Kamala Visweswaran. I draw on her theory of ethnographic failure in order to discuss what my own failures might provide for a postcolonial engagement with the *Lautarchiv*'s colonial histories. This chapter is thus to be understood as a first appeal to the future handling of the *Lautarchiv* at its new location, the Humboldt Forum. In addition, the chapter offers detailed (re)contextualisations of four historical figures I encountered in the archive, before bringing my failed—albeit productively failed—journey of tracing the subjects behind the *Lautarchiv*'s historical sound recordings full circle.

From my Field Journal

Soon after I arrived in New Delhi and made myself familiar with the university grounds, I had the opportunity to meet a group of young undergraduate students at Delhi University's Department of Germanic and Romance Studies. One of the department's lecturers invited me to visit a course she taught during that semester, focused on German translation. My attendance provided me with the opportunity to introduce the history of the *Lautarchiv*'s collection of sound recordings of South Asian prisoners of war to an Indian audience. When I visited the class for the first time, I concentrated on giving an overview of the archive, my project, and my research questions. The second time, I presented a selection of Hindi sound recordings and their accompanying scripts. My aim was to listen to and discuss the recordings in a collective and possibly multidirectional setting.

After one of the students helped me to set up the provisional technical sound equipment, two groups of four clustered around the two small loudspeakers. The sound quality was poor. All heads gathered closely around the small sound capsules in order to grasp the sound. I started the play back of a religious song in Hindi chanted by the prisoner of war Baldeo Singh in January 1917. The students listened mesmerised.

The singer's voice sounded strong and ardent, hitting even the high-pitched tones. For I knew the melody from another recording, it sounded somehow familiar to me. However, as ever so often, and in contrast to the Indian students lending their ears, my listening experience was limited to the melody, the quality of the recording, and the texture of the singing voice. I thought that this is the experience to which Wilhelm Doegen was bound. As the recording commissioner, Doegen managed the technical set up on the campsites and supervised the sound technician Mr. Goile. Doegen made notes on the attached personal information form concerning the phonetic quality of the respective speaker or singer's voice. Yet he never referred to the music or content.

Listening to the repeating lines, the students, in turn, understood the song and the narration; they could relate to the names of the gods mentioned. Had they heard the song before? Did they know the tale? Listening closely, and in due consideration of the written transcripts, they were able to apprehend the recited lines on the recording. Yet deciphering parts of the written texts in Devnagari script turned out to be a bit more difficult. One of the students explained that the person who wrote the text did not leave clear spaces between the words. It was another student who showed the most interest for the recording's content. When I asked about the meaning(s) of the song and possible connections to the war or camp situation in Europe, she was always the first to respond. Her fellow students did not seem to disagree with her, but also did not add to her interpretations. (Field note, 23 October 2017, New Delhi)

This episode from my field journal conveys a comprehensive picture of the situation I found myself in as a researcher in India. While I was welcomed as a guest and interlocutor, appreciating the opportunity to exchange ideas with local researchers, experts, and students, my field note also indicates a sense of unease. Never before had the discrepancy between 'my' material and myself been so obvious. Never before had I compared myself to Wilhelm Doegen (1877–1967) in such drastic terms. This was a discomforting experience since Doegen is one of the most controversial figures associated with the *Lautarchiv*'s history. Contemporaries accused him of having always been more concerned with the commercial innovation and success of 'his' archive project than with scientific achievements in linguistics (Lange 2017c: 338–340). Initially trained as an English teacher, he became interested in technical sound innovations at an early stage. Prior to the First World War, he produced Anglophone gramophone recordings for Alois Brandl (1855–1940), a professor of English at the Friedrich Wilhelm University in Berlin. Doegen played a decisive part in compiling the archive's initial and largest collection during the First World War. I will come back to Doegen's role during the emergence of the Royal Prussian Phonographic Commission and its aftermath leading to the establishment of the Sound Department at the Prussian State Library (see also Chapter 5).

What I would like to further pursue in this section are notions of continuity and discontinuity, connection and disconnection. I do so by drawing on two distinct listening acts, which differ in temporal, spatial, and epistemological terms. On the one hand, there is the moment of recording and listening in the past, which happened almost exactly one hundred years ago in a POW camp located close to Berlin, Germany. On the other hand, there is the listening experience today, taking place in a university classroom in New Delhi, India. In equal measure, connected and disconnected across time and space, each of these two moments indicate selective hearing and a plurality of listening positions. Hence, not only are the politics of location at stake here, but also the politics of

listening: who is recording and recorded, who is hearing and heard, who is listening and listening in? When thinking in terms of continuity and discontinuity, it is important to understand listening as a *sense formation* (Lacey 2013) and
to grasp the nuanced *sonic skills* (Bijsterveld 2019) that include different practices of hearing and listening, interpreting and assessing sound.[5] The emphasis
on different, yet interrelated, temporal levels also leads back to the notion of a
multitemporal challenge, which I discussed in the previous chapter. I argued for
shifting one's attention to the interplay between pasts and presents, introducing
Macdonald's conceptualisation of a *multidirectional temporal practice*.

But what characterises the notion of a failed listening? What unfolds
when depicting a failed listening from a conceptual and epistemological standpoint? When it comes to the failed listening I alluded to in my field journal, it is
neither that I did not hear anything nor that I did not listen. Naturally, I tried to
interpret and make sense of the things I heard. However, and as stressed above,
my listening remains limited and the same holds true for Doegen. What Doegen
heard phonetically was a "very silvery falsetto voice," as one can read on the
personal information form (*Personal-Bogen*) referring to Baldeo Singh's recordings.[6] Concerning the sound files of Keramat Ali introduced at the beginning
of this chapter, Doegen's judgment reads as follows: "silvery inner voice with
sufficiently clear consonance and nasalized sounds."[7] As it becomes obvious in
these 'commissioner's judgments' (*Urteile des Fachmanns*) one can find on each
of the forms filed at the *Lautarchiv*, the phonetician Doegen was not interested
in the recordings' contents. Equally, there is no evidence that he interpreted the
spoken or sung pieces against the backdrop of either their cultural meaning or
in connection to war, captivity, or homesickness. It is precisely this blank space
that leads me to the imperative necessity to revisit the recordings through the
lens of a postcolonial and cultural history that aims at shedding light on these
hitherto largely unacknowledged matters. On that note, Britta Lange (2012:
73) made a strong case for understanding the sound recordings of prisoners of
war as testimonies of a subaltern historiography of the First World War that has
not been considered yet.[8]

What other notions of failure am I pointing to by drawing on the episode
from my field journal and recalling my interactions with the group of undergraduate students? Initially, I was positive about the idea of engaging with a
group of people and not just with one single expert counterpart. In this way,
different people could share, exchange, and discuss their possibly divergent
knowledges, perceptions, and interpretations (see also Chapter 6). Sound in
general and sonic practices of listening and hearing in particular spawn a wide

array of associations. In addition, I thought that a course focusing on German translation would be a particularly convenient space in which to engage with the *Lautarchiv*'s recordings. The question of translation applies to the historical transcriptions, but also to the way in which one would (re)translate and (re)interpret the recordings today. However, when presenting my research project to the students, I faced two methodological constraints. For one thing, I felt it was counterproductive to be the only person who was able to properly contextualise and historicise the material. I clearly influenced the students and the discussion due to the selected background information I deemed relevant. In retrospect, I believe it would have been helpful to let the students read up on the topic first and give them time to think about their own views on it. Most of the students did not know much about the involvement of Indian soldiers in the First World War, not to mention their time in captivity in Germany and repatriation back to India.[9] In addition, the students understandably perceived me as an authority, since it was their professor who had invited me to visit the class. Consequently, I had to acknowledge that the uneven distribution of contextual knowledge and status interfered with the creation of a collaborative space in which to exchange ideas and discuss personal impressions.

Feminist Ethnography as Failure

Kamala Visweswaran (2003 [1994]) begins her essay with an anecdote she experienced while 'being there'—on a research trip in southern India. She narrates how she, as a young US-trained anthropologist, embarked on a trip to carry out ethnographic research on women and Indian nationalism.[10] She recounts her plan to conduct an interview with an elderly woman from Madras (present-day Chennai) in the southeastern state of Tamil Nadu, who was jailed during India's freedom movement. Showing up at the family's doorstep accompanied by a colleague from New Delhi, Visweswaran felt insecure starting the interview right away. When they visited the home a second time, there was some confusion between the family and the two researchers. Visweswaran got the impression of having fallen short of the hosts' expectations. One son showed visible irritation upon realising that the two women were particularly interested in female participation and, especially, in his mother's involvement in the liberation movement. Instead, the son wished to focus on his father and his right to a freedom fighter pension. When the anthropologists finally started talking to their aimed interviewee, the woman insisted that she went to jail because her husband wanted her to follow him. Yet another misunderstanding occurred because the daughters expected the two visitors to be working for a TV station and not for a research institution. They did not seem to understand why the scholars would be technically equipped when not employed by a news service. Visweswaran ends her short anecdote by saying: "Leaving the house, we concluded that the whole thing had been a disaster, a complete failure" (97).

Following this episode, Visweswaran explains how this field experience sparked her interest in failure, and more precisely, in failed feminist intentions. Opening up a discussion about the epistemological position of ethnographic fieldwork from a feminist perspective, she contends that it is feminist research in particular that is characterised by historically embedded and intrinsic difficulties and negotiations. Visweswaran argues that it might be a specifically feminist stand "that we [feminist ethnographers] use our 'fields' of failure as a means of pointing up the difficulties in our own epistemological assumptions and representational strategies" (98).

On an ethnographic level, Visweswaran's desire to capture the voice of a female person in order to shed a different light on the histories and memories of India's freedom movement was predestined to fail. Compared to the husband and father, neither the chosen female interlocutor nor her children seemed to see much relevance in her story. Too divergent expectations and incomprehensible intentions—or simply too many people in the room—kept the researchers from gathering the ethnographic data they had hoped for. Hence, in Visweswaran's view, the recounted anecdote implicated a failure of (feminist) ethnography in methodological but also epistemological terms. The approach had to fail, Visweswaran recapitulates, because the researchers neglected, or at least underestimated, the divergent effects of geography, history, and epistemology. In other words, they underestimated intersecting axes of nation, colonialism, class, age, and gender. In this way, Visweswaran points to the failures of Western feminism(s) and feminist theory. Notably originating in the 1980s, critique of Western feminism was put forward vociferously by transnational and postcolonial feminist ethnographers, such as Lila Abu-Lughod, Gloria Anzaldúa, and Chandra T. Mohanty, to name but a few. In broader terms, and beyond the scope of anthropology, Visweswaran's assessment also alludes to, now widespread, conceptions of the *simultaneity of oppressions* (Lorde 1984), the *politics of location* (Rich 1987; Braidotti 1994), as well as *intersectional feminism* (Crenshaw 1989, 1991).

In her concluding remarks, Visweswaran states that her opening account and the further framing and discussion of her ethnographic practice revealed at least two important lessons. First, she showed that, from an intersectional standpoint, gender alone—not to mention the alleged universal category of woman—is not meant to form the core of feminist theory and research. Second, Visweswaran suggests that 'being there' in the field is not the only and pivotal point in anthropology. Ultimately, Visweswaran argues that these two "epistemological shifts" (2003 [1994]: 113), as she terms them, imply two moments of failure, both of which point to the project of decolonisation. To put it in Visweswaran's words, they "mark decolonization as an active, ongoing process—incomplete, and certainly not one to be memorialized as past historical moment" (113).

In my opinion, Visweswaran's observations appear as timely as ever, even decades after the publication of her volume of essays. More than anything, my engagement with the *Lautarchiv* epitomises the significance of the ongoing and incomplete process of decolonising the archive. Without wanting to neglect crucial battles already fought and won, I follow Visweswaran in her view that the decolonial project remains in a provisional and unfinished state. In this sense, the demand to decolonise anthropology (and/or the archive) is a perpetual necessity and apparently always in some state of flux. The same can be said about the attempt to decentre rigid conceptions of gender and the ethnographic field as constitutive categories in anthropology and gender studies (Binder and Hess 2011: 17). Thus, processes of decolonising often imply an impossible notion. And yet recognising impossibility invites us—as feminist and queer anthropologists—to persevere. To Visweswaran, acknowledging the impossible, or the fact that one might fail, is important for a feminist practice invested in decolonising anthropology. Her views on decolonial thinking are one of the key points in her writing. Another crucial aspect is Visweswaran's reference to Gayatri C. Spivak, who influentially demanded to "question the authority of the investigating subject without paralyzing her, persistently transforming conditions of impossibility into possibility" (2003 [1994]: 100, referencing Spivak 2006 [1987]: 201). Accordingly, recognising modes of failure and limitation as constitutive parts of knowledge-making processes engenders new possibilities. Depicting failure as both "a sign of epistemological crisis [...], but also [...] an epistemological construct" (Visweswaran 2003 [1994]: 99–100) helps to understand failure not as a negative outcome or a paralysing condition, but rather as allowing for an accountable positioning.

An accountable positioning demands manoeuvring vectors of similarity, continuity, and difference. My schooling in colonial history, postcolonial studies, and intersectional feminism taught me to locate myself in discourses of race, class, gender, religion, and sexuality, among other variables. It taught me to recognise and scrutinise my privileges. The privilege of my institutional position, to give but one example, has different layers to it. Understood in a rather practical sense, my position allows me easy access to the *Lautarchiv*'s historical material.[11] It offers the possibility to disclose the material for critical contestation and sensitive examination, which is, however, as I was forced to realise early on, hardly possible if not in a collaborative manner. As emphasised previously, I soon came across certain obstacles as a consequence of my lack of language expertise and contextual historical/cultural knowledge. This evolved to be a frustrating, albeit eye-opening, experience, pointing me towards my distinct limitations and possibilities of unlearning. It exposed the experience of not knowing it all: of not being able to understand or translate the recordings at once, of not being able to follow the life stories of the colonial subjects beyond the limited sources available, of not being able to detach the sources from their hegemonic ballast. "Respect the limits of what cannot be known" (2008: 4) is a statement by Saidiya Hartman I was reminded of in this regard. To me, this form of disclosure also includes acknowledging the fact that the past is always only partially accessible. Each engagement with and assessment of the archive will be incomplete in different ways, depending on the location one is looking from— in my case, the location from which one is listening (in). In her *Notes Towards a Politics of Location* (1987), Adrienne Rich urges her readers to discuss and take responsibility for the point of location one inhabits while speaking, "the geography closest in" (212)—the body one is thinking, writing, and listening in from.

It is not just a fragmented past I am dealing with, but an entangled one too. It is a past deeply intertwined with global and local histories, with the (colonial) knowledge regime of the metropolis, with transnational complexities and conundrums. According to Shalini Randeria, the (modern) world we live in is constituted by histories that are both shared and divided. As mentioned in my introduction, Randeria coined the German term *geteilte Geschichten* (entangled histories), which captures the ambiguity of the German verb *teilen*, referring to both division and/or reciprocity, to something that encapsulates the act of both dividing and/or sharing (1999a; see also Conrad and Randeria 2013 [2002]: 39–44).[12]

Both notions of the entangled—the shared and the divided—become manifest when we address the histories related to the *Lautarchiv*'s sound recordings of non-European people. The recordings refer to shared histories insofar as one must acknowledge the *global* dimensions of the First World War. For a long time, established national narratives restricted these dimensions in favour of telling a single story of the Great War, as though it was an exclusively European war fought exclusively by European powers on European battlefields. The sound recordings provide physical evidence of the involvement of non-European subjects in the war, as well as the (unequal) interactions between recordists and people recorded. At the same time, one has to consider the notion of divided histories. Here, the sound files compiled by the Royal Prussian Phonographic Commission tell a story of an imperial and racial project. Seen in this light, the recordings mark the alleged supremacy of imperial Germany as a modern and progressive Empire. They illustrate the overarching project of modernity—a project based on maintaining cultural difference and division (see also Chapter 7).

Returning to the question of the politics of location, I am thinking of at least two significant effects. Drastically speaking, being born and brought up in a *white* West-German middle-class family, I am the product of a mainstream society of former colonisers and fascists.[13] Schooled and trained in cultural anthropology at a German university, my academic background is the product of a colonial discipline, of a classist and racist institution. By engaging with the archival material up to the point at which I seem to fail, I aim to acknowledge, but simultaneously also contest, the essentialising notions of these subject positions. I argue that, in this way, it becomes possible to negotiate the difficult enmeshment of these social, institutional, and personal trajectories. It is my hope that my engagement sets a cornerstone for further accountable research, for telling entangled histories. At the same time, my account both complements and complicates already existing research, unveiling both the shared *and* the divided. In this vein, I also call into question fixed binaries between perpetrator and victim, coloniser and colonised, privileges and precariousness (Binder and Hess 2011: 39). I argue that considering nuanced notions of failures and failing refuses a thinking in these normative binaries. Showing that it is possible to tell alternative stories with the available sources, my account oscillates between thick descriptions of the material and a contextualisation against the background of global and structural entanglements. This chapter moves between the concrete and the abstract, between ethnographic and archival situations and more conceptual and epistemological ideas. Before diving into my readings of the archival material, I will recall a selection of already completed accounts of histories associated with sound recordings of prisoners of war from South Asia.

Shifting Paradigms

Without any doubt, there already exists a variety of ('successful') approaches to and engagements with a number of (subaltern) sonic testimonies from the First World War POW camps housed at the *Lautarchiv*. This is another and rather simple reason why I decided to shift the chapter's focus. During the last decade especially, a range of studies have dealt with the involvement of non-*white* participants in the First World War in general, and the wealth of sound recordings of prisoners of war from South Asia recorded at the Half Moon Camp in particular. I am greatly indebted to the groundbreaking work carried out from different disciplinary angles and positionalities, and in different formats. It is not my aim to provide a comprehensive account but, rather, to highlight some of the approaches to sound recordings of South Asian prisoners that have been and continue to be important for my own work.

In his outline of the most recent history of the *Lautarchiv*, Jochen Hennig (2016: 359–360) proclaims the format of an experimental documentary film as the catalyst for a paradigm shift. To him, the film, *The Halfmoon Files* (2007) by filmmaker Philip Scheffner, set in motion a crucial shift towards a critical awareness and postcolonial appropriation of the *Lautarchiv*'s material. On the one hand, the film considered the recorded speakers and singers as historical subjects and not as mere representatives of a certain language or dialect. On the other hand, the film prompted a growing awareness of the fact that the sound collection should be located within current postcolonial discourses in Germany and beyond. In Scheffner's film, the director does not appear on screen. His voice remains off-camera as he tries to trace a soldier from the Punjab named Mall Singh (approx. 1892–?). Filed at the *Lautarchiv*, it was the recording's content in particular that struck the director. Under the title *Thoughts about himself* (*Gedanken über sich selbst*), Mall Singh's voice was recorded at the Half Moon Camp in Wünsdorf in December 1916.[14] Referring to himself in the third person, Singh relates to the war situation. In Punjabi, he narrates that a "man came to the European war," that "Germany captured this man," that the man "wishes to go back to India" (Das 2011: 1). This man became the protagonist of Scheffner's film and was thus recognised as a historical subject. Representing only one piece of a larger puzzle, Mall Singh's sonic imprint was the starting point for Scheffner's cinematic journey. Scheffner introduces the black screen as well as evocative, fuzzy visuals to convey an understanding for the fragmented condition of Singh's acoustic trace, and that of other South

Asian soldiers featured in the film. By means of an experimental documentary film, *The Halfmoon Files* not only blurs boundaries between different film genres but more importantly between allegedly authentic historical sources.[15]

Inspired by the film, Santanu Das followed the story of Mall Singh from a literary studies perspective. His academic interest, broadly concerned with the presence of non-*white* soldiers and labourers in the First World War, is driven by the wish to carve out the war's social and emotional implications for non-*white* agents (Das 2005, 2011a/b, 2018). Among the letters, songs, oral testimonies, and literature that Das takes into consideration, Mall Singh's sonic trace appears as a particularly striking testament. "As I listened to it," Das writes, "the body and emotion of the speaker seemed palpable, filling in, flowing out, lending physicality to an encounter with a disembodied voice from a hundred years ago. In some indefinable way, Mall Singh was present in it" (2018: 6). In his earlier article "The Singing Subaltern" (2011a), Das conceptualises the recording as a sign of the failure of communication and subaltern speech. With reference to Spivak's eminent essay, "Can the Subaltern Speak?" (1988), he concludes that there is no actual transaction between singer and listeners (Das 2011a: 5). Therefore, the attempted speech act was destined to fail. Considered as subalterns, the recorded prisoners of war spoke but were—for structural reasons—not heard. Thus, they were "muted in the very act of speaking" (4).

Britta Lange was involved in the intensive research process that preceded Scheffner's work, the final version of the film, as well as a joint exhibition project.[16] As part of her own extensive academic research on the linguistic and anthropological studies on prisoners of war in both German and Austro-Hungarian POW camps, Lange examined the various anthropological and ethnographic methods, data, and media in an impressive number of publications (Lange 2011a/b/c, 2012, 2013a/b, 2014, 2015a/b, 2017b, 2019). Her focus laid on both phonographic recordings as well as practices of visualisation (see also Chapter 7). On the one hand, Lange directed her interest towards a (cultural) history of science perspective and located this emphasis within a history of knowledge and the historicity of academic paradigms. On the other hand, she dealt with the question of how to frame methodical approaches to sonic and visual material. Together with Anette Hoffmann, she developed the concept of a close reading of, or rather close listening to, sonic testimonies. What motivated both scholars was the search for a methodology that would make it possible to handle the complex layers of textual and visual material, but above all one that would respond to acoustic data (Lange 2013a; Hoffmann 2015; see also Chapter 5). Lange (2013a: 40–42) has always been concerned with the potentiality of moments of resistance and subversion in sonic material. Consistently, she touches on questions of identity, subjectivity, and the political status of the recorded people.

In an essay from 2015, Lange introduces two motifs in order to explore two separate sound recordings of soldiers from the British Indian Army imprisoned in the Wünsdorf camp. She conceptualises the sonic traces as *poste restante*[17], and messages in bottles reaching their recipients almost one hundred years after their creation. By alluding to messages in bottles, the image of a sealed sound box (*Schalldose*) comes to mind; a box capturing someone's voice, to be opened some time in the future. In her essay, Lange closely studies a self-authored song recorded by the Gurkha soldier Jasbahadur Rai (approx. 1893–?) in June 1916.[18] In the music piece, the singer poetically refers to his body, which "has become like a string" (2015a: 95). He laments that he does not want "to stay in a European country," pleading "please reach me to India" (86). The recurring refrain—"listen, listen"—prompts Lange to imagine an audience to which the singer addresses his heart-rending verses. In her concluding thoughts, she asks, "are we, am I the recipient, when I listen to these messages, of which I—without knowledge and competence regarding country, literature or language—only understand a fraction" (95). The second recording examined by Lange contains a text recited by the Sikh soldier Sundar Singh (approx. 1885–?) in January 1917.[19] In his text, the speaker refers to the *Guru Granth Sahib*, the principal scripture of Sikhism. He complains, though very implicitly, about the fact that the Sikh soldiers' book is lacking a special blanket to wrap it in in the camp. Lange understands the text as a kind of petition, as a request directed towards the Germans to respect and enable the religious habits of the Sikh. It is not known whether the camp authorities complied with the speaker's request, or whether the petition was deposited in the archive to be received much later—*poste restante*.

In the form of a more conventional historiographical account, Heike Liebau (2018) traces the life story of yet another colonial soldier by means of exploring visual, auditory, and textual evidence. Liebau follows the Gurkha soldier Gangaram Gurung (approx. 1881–?). In the archives, the historian came across not only an acoustic testimony but also three drawings and a portrait photograph.[20] Liebau understands her investigation as being in line with the growing interest for the social lives of members of the colonial troops, shifting scholarly attention to the global and entangled dimensions of war.[21] Gangaram Gurung's sound file was recorded in English and not in his first language or a local dialect. He read out the biblical story of the prodigal son, which was considered a standard text in comparative linguistics at the time.[22] Because of his English skills, Liebau assumes that Gangaram Gurung acted as a translator and mediator between different languages and camp hierarchies (11). In her essay, she argues that tracing the individual life story of the Gurkha soldier allows us to draw conclusions about the social and cultural ramifications of military interactions, which have implications far beyond combat operations.

Following Das, Lange, and Scheffner, what motivated my own initial engagement with the POW recordings was the ambivalent condition of the sonic sources. I was interested in the tensions between the recordings' objectifying status and moments of articulating political subjectivity (Hilden 2015, 2018a). In previous research, I too investigated sound testimonies of Gurkha soldiers imprisoned in the Half Moon Camp in Wünsdorf. Together with the ethnomusicologist and visual anthropologist Ranav Adhikari, we closely examined songs of the *sepoys* Motilal (approx. 1885–?) and Him Bahadur (approx. 1885–?).[23] In June 1916, the soldiers sang about the war, their longing for home and loved ones, the wish to end the fighting. By concentrating on the songs' contents, we proved that the singers adapted their music pieces to the war situation they found themselves in on European soil. The songs' titles, *Tidings from Germany* (*Kunde aus Deutschland*), *Lament of a Prisoner* (*Gefangenenklage*), and *Sepoy's Life* (*Sepoy Leben*) are revealing of the unsettling, yet deeply poetic contents the song lines revolve around. In my work, I grappled with the discrepancy between the recordists' intentions and the poetic qualities of the recordings. On the one hand, the recordists reduced the contents to a representation of language samples. On the other hand, the recordings contained political statements addressed to an undefined audience. The songs reveal a political subject position muted for structural reasons. The voices, questioning the benefits of war and lamenting over the tragic conditions, percolated in the archive's shallows. However, almost one hundred years later, the soldiers' voices bear witness and help to convey new perspectives from within and on the First World War.

The following pages return to the historical protagonists introduced at the outset of this chapter. I take up the thread from the beginning in order to convey why I decided against tagging along with (my) previous work, and decided to shift the analytical attention. It is not that I do not trust the historiographical importance and value of the accounts invoked above. Yet I strongly believe in the recognition of failure as a form of critique, as advocated by Jack Halberstam (2011: 88). Nonetheless, the above-mentioned scholars and I might share similar post- and/or decolonial agendas. In this way, it becomes clear that the attempt at decolonising the *Lautarchiv* has to emerge from different directions.

I base the following portrayals on my points of access to the acoustic and written material from the archive. By bringing together my archival research with secondary literature, only a vague impression of the historical subjects emerges. But even if the portrayals remain incomplete, they outline one possible reading of the archive—my own—and the personal histories it entails. I deal with the historical figures of Keramat Ali and Baldeo Singh—as the ones being recorded—as well as the recordists Heinrich Lüders and Helmuth von Glasenapp. It is my aim to correlate historical contexts with archival traces and information about these four individuals, thereby also drawing on the notion of alleged 'subaltern' and 'dominant' traces. I move between the individuals' tangible traces and broader contexts and concepts. Although the sources and my access are limited, I believe that a nuanced recontextualisation of 'dominant' and hitherto marginalised histories matters, not least in order to identify moments of limitation and failure.

Ali and Singh

Keramat Ali was not a soldier. He was an Indian civilian. His trajectory leading to the Half Moon Camp is different from the one of the *sepoys* recruited and shipped to the theatres of war, first in Europe and later Mesopotamia and other places.[24] In 1914 and 1915, a large number of soldiers of the British Indian Army fought on the Western Front in France and Belgium, before being deployed on other battlefields. Yet, for many members of the colonial troops, the combat operations on the Western Front were followed by German captivity. By early 1915, many of the *sepoys* ended up in different internment camps on German soil—including the Half Moon Camp in Wünsdorf. However, Keramat Ali did not belong to the group of colonial soldiers. He was one of five Indian *lascars* that the Orientalist Heinrich Lüders recorded in February 1918.[25] The Germans detained Ali and other *lascars* at the so-called India Camp (*Inderlager*), which was part of the Half Moon Camp. Between the recordings Lüders had been in charge of since early 1916 and the recordings of the seamen that he compiled two years later, one can thus notice a clear temporal gap. Today, Lüders' intentions and the question of what it was that he expected from this new set of sound samples remain rather unclear (a point to which I will return below).

Seen from a present point of view, one of the sound documents in the collection of recordings of *lascars* sticks out. Divided into three separate recordings, the *lascar* Mohammed Hossin (approx. 1868–?) recalls the story of his capture. It is the story of the *Möwe* (seagull), as one can read in the archive's neatly kept recording journal (*Aufnahmejournal*).[26] The story of the *Möwe* refers to the *SMS Möwe*—a German raider, also known as the 'Kaiser's pirate.' Between 1915 and 1918, the German ship captured a number of 'enemy ships' belonging to the British Empire. In the archived sound recordings, Hossin recounts the day of the capture. At the time, he was a steward of the *SS Clan MacTavish*, a ship requisitioned by the British government and belonging to the British cargo shipping company *Clan Line*. Built in 1912, the vessel operated between ports in Britain and Australia.[27] In January 1916, the *SMS Möwe* shelled and sank the *Clan MacTavish* off the Portuguese island of Madeira in the Atlantic Ocean. The hostile take-over cost the lives of eighteen people. Hossin narrates how he boarded the *SMS Möwe*. As it says in the translation, both groups of crew members—"the English and Muslims"—entered the ship raider.[28] Bringing them to the mainland, the Germans allocated the crew to different internment facilities—among them the Half Moon Camp at Wünsdorf.

Almost one hundred years later, literary scholar Santanu Das transcribed and translated Hossin's story. Britta Lange published it in a volume about South Asian prisoners of war in World War One Germany (2011c; see also Lange 2015b, 2019: 277–302). It is thanks to Das and Lange that this story, told from a steward's—and, if you will, subaltern—point of view, became known to an international public. "His story," Lange writes, "which he [Mohammed Hossin] describes in such detail and which bears testimony hitherto unknown in Europe to an event in the First World War, has not been printed prior to the publication of this book" (2011c: 182).

The *lascar* Hossin was fifty years old at the time of the recording. He went to sea at the young age of ten, as one learns from his personal file. I imagine that he must have stood out among the *sepoys* and other *lascars* who were mostly in their early twenties and thirties when taken as prisoners of war. It is not known whether Hossin and Ali shared employment on the *Clan MacTavish*. Less than half Hossin's age, Ali was only twenty-one years old when Lüders captured his voice on altogether five different records (see figure 3-1). According to the personal files, Hossin and the other three *lascars* recorded were all born in Kolkata and were sailors or "captain's boys." Only Ali was born in Mymengsingh and his occupation was noted as "Signeller [sic] of Railway Line." His personal file says that he went to a "Minor School" in Bajitpur, a city, like Mymengsingh, in what is today East Bangladesh. At the age of sixteen, he moved to Rangoon (today's Yangon) in then British Burma (today's Myanmar). Besides Bengali, he also knew a bit of Hindustani.[29]

Lfd. Nr.

PERSONAL=BOGEN

Lautliche Aufnahme Nr.: P.K.1158 Ort: W ü r s d o r f

Datum: 7. 2. 1918.

Zeitangabe: 6 Uhr

Dauer der Aufnahme: 3 Min.   Durchmesser der Platte: 27 cm.

Raum der Aufnahme: Baracke 7.

Art der Aufnahme (Sprechaufnahme, Gesangsaufnahme,
    Choraufnahme, Instrumentenaufnahme, Orchesteraufnahme):   2 Volkslieder.

_____   B e n g a l i   (Osten).

Name (in der Muttersprache geschrieben):

Name (lateinisch geschrieben):   K e r a m a t   A l i

Vorname:

Wann geboren (oder ungefähres Alter)?   21 Jahre alt

Wo geboren (Heimat)?   Maymeng Sing, Post Bijidpur
                                                  Provence Bengal.

Welche größere Stadt liegt in der Nähe des Geburtsortes?

Kanton — Kreis (Ujedz):

Departement — Gouvernement (Gubernija) — Grafschaft (County):

Wo gelebt in den ersten 6 Jahren?   Maymeng Sing

Wo gelebt vom 7. bis 20. Lebensjahr?   mit 16 Jahren nach Rangoon

Was für Schulbildung?   Pathiala and Minor School

Wo die Schule besucht?   Bajidpur

Wo gelebt vom 20. Lebensjahr?

Aus welchem Ort (Ort und Kreis angeben) stammt der Vater? Bajidpur

Aus welchem Ort (Ort und Kreis angeben) stammt die Mutter?

Welchem Volksstamm angehörig?   Sekh

Welche Sprache als Muttersprache?   Bengali

Welche Sprachen spricht er außerdem?   etwas Hindustani

Kann er lesen?   Ja   Welche Sprachen?   Bengali Alphabet

Kann er schreiben?   "   Welche Sprachen?   "   "

Spielt er ein im Lager vorhandenes Instrument aus der Heimat?

Singt oder spielt er moderne europäische Musikweisen?

Religion: Islam   Beruf: SigMeller of Railway Line

Vorgeschlagen von: 1. gez.: Dr. Lüders.
                   2. gez.Wilh.Doegen.

                                    | 1. Urteil des Fachmannes
                                    | (des Assistenten):
        Beschaffenheit der Stimme: <
                                    |
                                    | 2. Urteil des Kommissars: Helle Mittelstimm
                                                                 mit hinreichend
                                                                 lautlicher Konsonanz und
                                                                 resonierter Lauten.
                                                                 gez.: Wilh.Doegen.

Figure 3-1: Personal information form (*Personal-Bogen*), PK 1158.
February 7, 1918. LAHUB.

It seems remarkable, yet not surprising, that the histories of *lascars* in general, but particularly the life stories that fragmentarily derive from the *Lautarchiv*'s documents are characterised by this high degree of mobility. Especially from the late eighteenth to the middle of the twentieth century, European ships increasingly employed *lascars*. The sailors originated from many places, namely from Southeast Asia, but also the Arab world. Particularly during the eighteenth and nineteenth centuries, the British East India Company recruited many Bengali Muslims. Accordingly, migration and movement between South Asia and Europe had been ongoing for centuries. However, the First World War marks a new quality of mobility and labour migration, not only between South Asia and Europe, but also in other translocations, such as between European and French colonies on the African continent, as well as other British dominions (Roy and Liebau 2011).

But the recordings of the group of Indian *lascars* also point to the discontinuities of the archive for other reasons. Although the histories of non-*white* combatant soldiers have long been neglected in historiographical accounts of the First World War in general, the presence of *lascars*, not to mention of thousands of non-combatant soldiers and labourers, is an even more unrecognised chapter in global history (e.g. Diengdoh 2017; Roy 2011).[30] Under the condition of labour regimes, a vast number of workers, labour and porter corps, were transferred to the theatres of war in Europe and elsewhere from many parts of the world (e.g. Singha 2010). It was Das who pointed out that the recruitment of Indian combatant and non-combatant labour during the First World War has not only long been absent from historical research, but also from elitist (nationalist-inclined) memories in India and the West (2011a; see also Roy and Liebau 2011).[31] With regard to India, Das (2005, 2011b, 2018) has been concerned with the overlooked aspects of the military conflict of the First World War for many years. His academic inquiries focus on the war's global, social, cultural, and emotional ramifications. In regards to the paucity of sources, he emphasises:

> In a context when the sepoys did not leave behind the thousands of diaries, poems and memoirs that form the corner-stone of European war memory and when the colonial archives are remarkably silent, a dialogue between different kinds of sources—archival, oral and the literary—become all the more important. (2011a: 8)

Set against the backdrop of the methodological aspiration of 'creating a dialogue between different kinds of sources,' what I offer in this study is a dialogue

Lfd. Nr

PERSONAL=BOGEN

Lautliche Aufnahme Nr: *P.H.647*   Kriegsgefangenenlager: *Wünsdorf*

Datum: *3. 1. 1917*

Zeitangabe: *12 Uhr*

Dauer der Aufnahme: Durchmesser der Platte: *27 cm*

Raum der Aufnahme:

Art der Aufnahme (Sprechaufnahme, Gesangsaufnahme, Choraufnahme, Instrumentenaufnahme, Orchesteraufnahme): *I. Gesang von 3 Sängern gesungen. (1. Baldeo Singh 2. Mahatap Singh 3. Teodulari Singh Hauptsänger I.) II. Moralbegespr. v. Baldeo Singh). Hindi (Thakur)*

Name (in der Muttersprache geschrieben):

Name (lateinisch geschrieben): *1. Baldeo Singh 2. Mahataj Singh 3. Teodulari*

Vorname: *Pers. einliegend?*

Wann geboren (oder ungefähres Alter)? *30 Jahre*

Wo geboren (Heimat)? *Kera*

Welche größere Stadt liegt in der Nähe des Geburtsortes?

Kanton — Kreis (Ujedz): *Itava*

Departement — Gouvernement (Gubernija) — Grafschaft (County): *Upper India*

Wo gelebt in den ersten 6 Jahren? *Kera*

Wo gelebt vom 7. bis 20. Lebensjahr? *Mit 18 Jahren ins Regt 9. Bhop. Inf. Faizabad*

Was für Schulbildung? *Dorfschule*

Wo die Schule besucht? *u. in Udi*

Wo gelebt vom 20. Lebensjahr? *Faizabad u Sihore*

Aus welchem Ort (Ort und Kreis angeben) stammt der Vater? *Kera*

Aus welchem Ort (Ort und Kreis angeben) stammt die Mutter? *im Distr. Banda*

Welchem Volksstamm angehörig? *Thakur*

Welche Sprache als Muttersprache? *Hindi*

Welche Sprachen spricht er außerdem? *nei*

Kann er lesen? *ja*   Welche Sprachen? *Nagari*

Kann er schreiben? *ja*   Welche Sprachen? *Nagari*

Spielt er ein im Lager vorhandenes Instrument aus der Heimat? *nei*

Singt oder spielt er modern europäische Musikweisen? *nei*

Religion: *Hindu*   Beruf: *Zamindar*

Beschaffenheit der Stimme:

1. Urteil des Fachmannes (des Assistenten):

2. Urteil des Kommissars: *1. Stelle kräftig ...*

3. Urteil des Technikers:

Figure 3-2: Personal information form (*Personal-Bogen*), PK 647. January 3, 1917. LAHUB.

between different material, sensory, and temporal dimensions attached to the acoustic documents (see also Chapter 5 and 6). Following Das, the recordings of the *sepoy* Baldeo Singh are significant, not least in the sense that they seem to cut across all three notions of the archival, the oral, and the literary.

Baldeo Singh's recordings belong to the comparatively large collection of songs and narratives from northern India stored in the *Lautarchiv*. From the archival scripts, one learns that Singh was born in Kera (Etawah District) in the Indian state of Uttar Pradesh (see figure 3-2). He received his basic education at a rural school in Faizabad, where he would also join the British Indian Army. At the age of eighteen, he became a member of the Regiment of the Ninth Bhopal Infantry. In September 1914, the Regiment arrived at the Mediterranean Coast in Marseille in order to support the British battalions that had suffered heavy losses during the first months of the war. It is likely that Baldeo Singh was among the Indian soldiers who fought in the battles of Neuve Chappelle or Ypres—attacks which cost the lives of many soldiers on both sides of the front lines. Contrary to many of his fallen comrades, Singh survived the trench warfare. Together with hundreds of other soldiers, he was held captive as a prisoner of war. Ultimately, he ended up in a POW camp in Germany and was not able to follow his regiment to the battles of the Mesopotamian campaign. Archived at the *Lautarchiv*, his recordings bear witness to his survival, though it is not known whether and when he was repatriated to India. It is not known what happened to him during and after his time of captivity, as is the case for so many of the (colonial) internees.[32]

Compared to the *lascar* recordings, Baldeo Singh's acoustic testimony stands out from the archive in different ways—in part also alluding to notions of failure. For one thing, it seems striking that Singh was recorded on three different days: on January 2, 3, and 5 in 1917.[33] When looking through the recording journals, one usually reads the same name only in conjunction with one single date. Might Singh have been of particular scholarly interest for the recordists, Helmuth von Glasenapp and Wilhelm Doegen? Or did he distinguish himself from the other soldiers for different reasons? On day three, Doegen noted on the back side of the personal file, regarding the sound recording with the serial number PK 673: "At the end, Baldeo Singh shouts 'Guten Abend' ['good evening'] without being asked."[34] I understand this as one striking example of the discontinuities and failures of the archive (see figure 3-3). "The unforeseen is not desired," says the off-screen voice of Philip Scheffner (2007) in his documentary film. "It endangers the scientific comparability and creates additional work," the narrator continues. The sound document PK 673 did not conform

Figure 3-3: Personal information form (*Personal-Bogen*), PK 673. Back side.
January 3, 1917. LAHUB.

to what the recordists intended to record, as the accordance between the written and the sonic file was one of the main objectives of the archival enterprise. Ideally, the targeted procedure allowed for the production of a sound piece with a corresponding transliteration, transcription, and German translation. From my point of view, the notion of failure has a practical as much as an epistemological layer to it. "Without being asked," Baldeo Singh neglected the rigid recording procedure by the simplest act, for the briefest moment. Since the recordist felt the urge to list the 'misbehaviour,' I read it as a rupture of the scientific practice (see also Chapter 5)—performed by the 'unruly' object of study that was Singh. It was a minor and modest gesture. At the same time, it appears humane and almost a bit humorous. Lange (2019: 331) even sees the appropriation of the German language as a way of taking control of the situation.

It is the presence of migrant labour and moments of subaltern agency that is manifest in the recordings of Keramat Ali and Baledo Singh. It is here that the colonial archives are not silent (to recall Santanu Das), but literally sounding and resounding. The recordings referred to, resonate with the attempt to shift dominant historical narratives and memories of the First World War.

Lüders and Glasenapp

If one reads the colonial archive along its grain, it appears natural to follow the official records of dominant figures in history—usually *white* and male (see also Chapter 5 and 6). Considering the points of reference in this chapter—sound recordings of Keramat Ali and Baldeo Singh—, one needs to take a closer look at Heinrich Lüders and Helmuth von Glasenapp. The two Orientalists differ from each other significantly, despite sharing certain characteristics. They differ with regard to their age, educational training, and career prospects, but also their research focus and findings in the POW camps. The ominous, yet influential, academic discipline of Oriental studies was launched as an academic field of research concerned with societies, languages, and histories of the 'Eastern world' and the 'Orient.' In his groundbreaking book, *Orientalism* (1978), Edward W. Said famously deconstructed the political and academic discourse pervaded by the Eurocentric gaze that legitimised and perpetuated the racist ideology of European superiority.[35]

As a renowned philologist at Berlin University, Heinrich Lüders was one of the leading members of the Royal Prussian Phonographic Commission. In December 1915, the Prussian Ministry of Science, Art, and National Culture approved and (largely) funded the activities of the Phonographic Commission. Doegen acted as the Commission's technical and logistic director, whereas the influential musicologist, professor of psychology, and founder of the Berlin Phonogram Archive, Carl Stumpf (1846–1936), was appointed first chair of the board. The Phonographic Commission consisted of altogether thirty members divided into seven teams, composed of (mostly) well-established linguists with expertise in different Western and non-Western languages. In addition, there were two groups focusing on anthropological and musicological research. For the first, Felix von Luschan (1854–1924)—then director of the Berlin Ethnological Museum—was in control.[36] For the latter, Stumpf and his student Erich Moritz von Hornbostel (1877–1935) were initially in charge.[37] However, as things developed, Georg Schünemann (1884–1945) would conduct most of the music recordings.

The musicologists used an Edison phonograph for their practice, which meant saving songs and instrumental music exclusively on wax cylinders.[38] In 1877, Thomas Alva Edison (1847–1931) had invented the phonograph. It did not take long for anthropologists to introduce the technical device to ethnographic research, commissioning missionaries, travellers, and colonial administrative staff to record voices with the portable apparatus (e.g. Stangl 2000). To contemporary ears, the sound quality of recordings made on wax cylinders is substantially lower than that of shellac records. The cylinders were fragile, quickly wore out, and thus not well-suited to long-term preservation. However, back then, the well-tested and easily transportable phonograph still seemed most convincing to the group of musicologists. Unlike the gramophone, the phonograph operated with a mechanical crank and did not require electricity in the form of heavy batteries. Moreover, one could play back the recorded sound immediately after the moment of recording. Nevertheless, the linguistically- and phonetically-oriented researchers used the far more elaborate device of the gramophone, which promised the production and (commercial) distribution of easily duplicable recordings. Ten years after Edison had introduced the phonograph in the US, German-born Emile Berliner (1851–1929) developed the gramophone. The technical requirements of the gramophone meant setting up a provisional sound studio each time a group of linguists set out on a trip to one of the camps. Depending on their field of expertise, the language experts belonged to different subgroups, traveling to different internment camps installed throughout Germany. Among the exclusively male members were pro-fessors of English and Romance languages, Orientalists and Africanists, and a number of Indo-Germanic philologists.

Lüders was head of the group for Indian and Mongolian languages, work-ing in close collaboration with his colleague, Wilhelm Schulze (1863–1935). The young Helmuth von Glasenapp also became a member of his team. In 1908, Lüders became professor of ancient Indian languages and literature at the Friedrich Wilhelm University in Berlin. His research focused on the analysis of ancient Indian and Nepali handwritings and inscriptions, as well as ancient Buddhist narratives. For his studies in the POW camps, he slightly shifted his interest to historical linguistics, wishing to trace the genealogies and divisions of Indo-Aryan and Tibeto-Burman languages. As part of his camp studies, Lüders mainly concentrated on soldiers of so-called Gurkha regiments. He was particularly interested in studying Nepali speakers who, in some cases, also knew non-Indo-Aryan languages (Lüders 1925: 137). After several trips to the Wünsdorf camp, Lüders and Schulze followed some of the soldiers they had worked with to camps in southern Romania.[39]

As I have shown elsewhere, Lüders did not seem entirely convinced of the sonic scientific enterprise—despite his efforts (Hilden 2015). For him and many other Commission members, the sound recordings represented a by-product of the transliteration, which scholars continued to build their analyses on (Hennig 2016; Kaplan 2013; Meyer-Kalkus 2015). Moreover, Lüders' attitude and actions suggest that he had ethical concerns regarding the anthropometric studies of Felix von Luschan and his student Egon von Eickstedt (1892–1965). Lüders believed that the two anthropologists were disrespectful towards the religious beliefs of, for instance, Sikh soldiers. Lüders was in support of a protest letter by members of the India Independence Committee (IIC) to the Ministry of Foreign Affairs.[40] While Lüders' research had a linguistic (rather than a racist, albeit racialising) focus, the work of Eickstedt provides strong evidence of his scientific stance towards racial theories gaining ground at the time. Eickstedt became one of the leading advocates of racial theory under National Socialism, occupying a professorship in anthropology at the University of Breslau (today's University of Wrocław) since 1933.[41] At this point, I would not be able to do justice to a nuanced description of the development of racial science in Germany and the complicity between linguistic and anthropological research. Andrew D. Evans (among others) notably analysed the wartime and camp studies as turning points for the discipline of (physical) anthropology in Germany. Evans (2002, 2003, 2010) claims that a new generation of anthropologists moved away from its allegedly 'liberal' roots, paving the way for further racial studies under eugenic auspices (see also Penny and Bunzl 2003; Zimmerman 2001). Andre Gingrich and Britta Lange disagree with Evans, insofar as they argue that the proclaimed liberal roots in German-speaking anthropology were not necessarily innocent, but had already manifested chauvinist, orientalist, racist, and anti-Semitic tendencies long before the First World War (Lange 2013a: 27, referencing Gingrich 2010: 372).

Between a New Ethnology and an Archival Project

Edited by Wilhelm Doegen in 1925, the volume *Among Foreign Peoples* (*Unter Fremden Völkern*) assembles a range of linguistic and ethnological contributions by members of the Phonographic Commission, but also by other scholars. Most of the contributors do not directly address the studies in the camps, but concentrate on general anthropological remarks concerning their respective area of expertise. Heinrich Lüders is one of the few people who refer to the insights derived from the camp studies in detail. His contribution concerns "the Gurkhas," whereas he does not mention his studies on Bengali speakers at all. In the following quote, Lüders addresses "the Gurkhas" as a homogenous group, while, in fact, they were very heterogeneous in terms of identity and belonging, as the Orientalist himself points out (1925: 129 and 136).[42] Characterising the soldiers he interacted with, Lüders writes:

> When Professor Wilhelm Schulze and I allocated our attention to the study of Khas [Nepali] in the prison camps, we could of course not make *our loyal* Gurkhas understand the actual purpose of our quest for knowledge. But that did not stop them from *willingly* helping us. They seemed to feel a certain pride that we were paying so much attention to their language. Many, perhaps most, were literate in reading and writing; however, they had not learnt the script used for their language as children, but only during their service. Some were also able to write down longer stories from their memory. [...] Most of them, however, did not dare to tell a coherent tale. They preferred to recite a song, either alone or in a group. Among the songs, there are certainly some sounding at festivals since ancient times [...]. (135–136, my emphasis)[43]

Analysing this paragraph in light of the context of the time, the discrepancy between researcher and 'research object' and the vilification of the soldiers' subject positions seem manifest. By describing the soldiers as 'loyal' and 'willing,' Lüders infantilises the singers and speakers. Consequently, he denies them their own volition as well as their own understanding of the sound recordings' potential purpose and meaning. Instead, this passage suggests difference and alterity between the *white* and modern academics, on the one hand, and traditional, unmodern non-academics on the other. It also implies a sense of nostalgia for 'indigenous culture' embodying elements of the past in the modern present (a point I will come back to in Chapter 7).

Driven by a positivistic and unilineal understanding of history and 'cultural progress,' Lüders intended to trace the genealogies and changes in the use of different languages and vocabulary. In line with the paradigm of 'salvage ethnography,' he pointed out that non-Indo-Aryan languages among the Gurkha regiments were on the brink of extinction because of labour migration and global transformations (see also Chapter 7). I argue that Lüders' attitude is a striking example of what prompted anthropologist Johannes Fabian to explore Western techniques of time-related dissociation and racialised forms of *othering*. In *Time and the Other* (1983), Fabian observes that anthropology's distancing practices produce and reproduce the constructed dichotomy between the Self and the *Other* by constituting different temporal zones. In this way, Lüders located 'his' research objects in a separate and preceding temporal stage in order to deny a possible synchronicity and coeval existence. In fact, Lüders points out that Tibeto-Burman languages are on a 'lower cultural stage' compared to the Indo-Aryan language of Nepali, which he refers to as the language of a "herrenvolk" (1925: 135).

As mentioned earlier, it is not known what motivated Lüders to compile the set of Bengali speech samples. What prompted him to study the linguistic repertoires of the highly mobile seamen? Was it for practical reasons and the relocation of the Gurkha soldiers who initially mattered most to him? Or did Lüders actually show an interest in the diverse linguistic influences on and skills of the Indian sailors? Even if the archival files do not indicate the initial scientific interest that led to the compilation of the Bengali recordings, they do, as emphasised before, bear witness to the situation of Indian *lascars* detained as civilian internees in German POW camps.

In view of his overall published work, the output based on Lüders' extensive camp studies seems rather limited. Yet his colleague Glasenapp appears to have extracted even fewer findings from his studies in the camps. Glasenapp was only at the early stages of his academic career when the war broke out. Back then, he wished to become a military volunteer. Because of an injured knee, however, he had to withdraw from service. By December 1914, his regiment in Berlin had discharged him from his duties. Later, Glasenapp (1964: 70–71) would write in his memoirs that he sought employment that was essential to the war effort. Consequently, he not only became a member of the Phonographic Commission, but he also started working for the Intelligence Bureau for the East (*Nachrichtenstelle für den Orient*). Founded by the law graduate and Orientalist Max von Oppenheim (1860–1946) on the eve of the First World War, the Intelligence Bureau was attached to the German Foreign Office.[44] Through the recommendation of a state secretary at the Imperial Colonial Office (*Reichskolonialamt*), Oppenheim had hired Glasenapp for his academic expertise in 'Indology.'

In his autobiography, published one year after his death in 1963, Glasenapp (1964: 90–91) addresses his camp studies only in one single paragraph. In his further published work, there is no mention of his linguistic research and experiences in the POW camp (see also Lange 2011b: 126). It is, however, noteworthy that Glasenapp contributed three essays to Doegen's 1925 volume. Unlike Lüders, he did not once mention whether his strongly ethnicised characterisations of "Hinduism," "the Rajputs," and "the Sikhs" stem from, or were complemented by, his encounters with Hindu, Rajput, or Sikh soldiers in the POW camp (Glasenapp 1925a/b/c). Concerning his studies during the war, he explains in his memoirs:

> The main task was to have the Indians first write down the text of a story or a song, which I then discussed with them and Professor Doegen recorded. Performing this task was often difficult because the prisoners of course could not speak English, so I could only communicate with them in Hindi; there were also those who were illiterate, whose texts I could only listen to and transcribe. Although the results of these studies had, by their very nature, to involve some potential errors, a large collection was assembled, which unfortunately was not published in a book as planned. (1964: 90–91)[45]

Even though one can sense a certain reservation towards the camp studies in these lines, Glasenapp still admires the size of the collected data. He considers it a pity that Doegen did not manage to publish the findings as planned. However, one has to keep in mind that Glasenapp wrote these words decades after working for the Phonographic Commission. At this point, he was looking back on an eminent academic career in comparative theology. While Lüders' working papers and files full of notes and transcriptions are stored at the Archives of the Berlin Brandenburg Academy of Science, the scripts of Glasenapp's recordings are filed at the *Lautarchiv*. This suggests that, ultimately, neither Glasenapp nor, presumably, any other researcher had used the transliterations, transcriptions, and translations for further scholarly research and editing. It depends on the historical moment and epistemological position whether this circumstance is considered a failure of the Commission's linguistic enterprise. With regard to the recordings' scientific relevance, Britta Lange writes:

> These recordings had no scientific 'afterlife'—until their rediscovery as historical holdings of the archive *through the archive itself*. Thus in the case of recordings of prisoners of war, it also seems justified to speak of an 'archival' project, a collection project (Scheer 2010), which owed much of its existence to the interests of the archive itself and was accordingly not fully compatible with any of the scientific disciplines involved—anthropology, ethnography, oriental studies, linguistics, comparative musicology. (2013a: 139, emphasis in the original)[46]

The outcomes of the linguistic research may have been minor; Doegen's 'collection project' and his encyclopaedic vision, however, succeeded. Doegen's vision of collecting, studying, and archiving languages of *all* nations of the world, appears as the very basis for legitimising the Commission's project and its 'archival afterlife.'

Doegen gives plenty of reasons why the opportunity to carry out phonetic recordings 'among foreign peoples' in German POW camps was so unique. No less than *A New Ethnology* (*Eine neue Völkerkunde*) is what Doegen promises in the rather presumptuous subheading to the aforementioned anthology.[47] In the preface, he emphasises that the book offers more than mere travelogues. Doegen highlights the fact that the volume turned out to be an anthropological companion grown out of 'lively' linguistic research. To him, the archival documents form 'a historical museum of sounds.' In his often overstated manner, Doegen furthermore describes the archival venture as "the creation of living cultural testimonies that will last for thousands of years" (1925: 6, emphasis in the original).[48] Contemplating the question of how these claims relate to other strands in German anthropology of the time, I argue that Doegen's publication stands for Germany's status quo after the First World War; after the former Empire had lost control over its colonies and German academic as well as political landscapes were rendered weak. For me, Doegen's tendency to exaggerate reads as an attempt to compensate for Germany's diminished position after the Treaty of Versailles.[49]

In this section, I focused on the people on the other side of the recording device, the recordists Lüders and Glasenapp. It was my intention to consider their role in and for the Phonographic Commission, not least in order to account for the scientific and archival logics behind the camp studies. It became evident that the scientific outcome was limited, if not a failure. However, for the archival project, the POW recordings laid the foundation of what is today considered the *Lautarchiv*. In the next section, I return to my attempt to follow the acousmatic voices behind the sound documents.

From my Mailbox

On 21 January 2018 at 10:37 AM, Irene wrote:

> *Thanks again for your time and sharing your thoughts and observations. [...] May I ask you again for the serial number of the song you were mentioning?*

On 21 January 2018 at 11:58 AM, Armita wrote:

> *I haven't had the chance to go through the audio records yet, once I do, I will send you the serial number of the song that I was talking about.*

As is sometimes the case in our busy and fleeting digital times, Armita never replied to the inquiry I had sent her shortly after the interview. For my part, I was probably not persistent enough and missed the opportunity to get in touch with her again. Instead, I decided to reach out to other Bengali speakers I met during and after my research trip to India. What this kind of ethnographic detour reveals is that my initial interlocutor may simply not have had the time or interest to learn more about the recorded song and to invest in a joint study of the acoustic file. Rather, it was my assumption and ascription that an Indian researcher, like her, who was working on the effects of the (military) history of the First and Second World Wars on the Indian subcontinent, would be keen to collaboratively investigate Keramat Ali's sonic testament. Looking back, I understand that thinking in terms of an entangled history does not necessarily mean a shared interest and commitment. Although this may seem obvious, my ethnographic approach in a way unveiled my naively assumed and rightly disappointed prejudices.

On my further path to track down the recorded song, I received a couple of responses similar to the first reaction. I would ask people whether they knew the song and where from. I would ask for their thoughts on the woman addressed in the lyrics. One of the answers I received came from yet another person who had graduated from Jawaharlal Nehru University (JNU).

On 13 April 2018 at 2:58 AM, Oeendrila wrote:

> *I have heard this song before when I was a child—the refrain is familiar. I don't remember from whom but I suppose a lot of people from the older generation know this song—as well as a lot of Bangladeshis would know this song. [...] The man in the song is inquisitive about the identity of this woman who he sees fetching water from the Yamuna—'Kader kul-er bou'—which family is she married into? He is intrigued by the fact that she is unaccompanied at the riverbank. This is the crux of the song. Clearly, this is an aberration on part of the woman, and I am not sure if he is excited by it or disapproves it. There are a couple of lines I do not understand. I'll have to ask my mother or someone [else] to listen to it.*

At the time of my research, Oeendrila was a Melbourne-based researcher, with a PhD from JNU's English Department. I was introduced to her and her husband (a German anthropologist) through Wanphrang K. Diengdoh—a musician and filmmaker from Shillong in Northeast India. I had met Diengdoh after one of his screenings at a cultural centre in New Delhi in 2017, where he showed his documentary film *Because We Did Not Choose* (2017). In the experimental film, Diengdoh draws on historical traces of indigenous Khasi labourers from northeastern India who were recruited by Welsh missionaries during the First World War. The film is an important contribution to the engagement with the histories of the war's direct and indirect effect on different (indigenous) communities in India.

Oeendrila did indeed send the sound file to her mother and aunt in order to add to or correct her first assumptions regarding Ali's song. As she had suspected, both relatives were familiar with the song. They identified it as belonging to the popular traditions of the Bengali folk theatrical forms of *jatra* and/or *tappa*.[50] However, neither Oeendrila nor her mother and aunt commented on the role of the female character, which had initially sparked my interest. Attached to an e-mail, the recorded file continued its digital journey to Melbourne, Australia, and back to Oeendrila's family in West Bengal, India. However, its interpretation remained incomplete and situational, depending on the connections people would establish to the historic sound object.

Some of my readers may find it disappointing or inconsistent that I leave them with these fragments from my ethnographic work, and that I am content not to include the recordings' transcriptions. Others may agree that this abrupt ending marks the logical consequence of my line of reasoning throughout this chapter. The unaccomplished wish to follow the two individual speakers, Keramat Ali and Baldeo Singh, to somehow grasp their personalities and the meaning of their sonic testaments, taught me to acknowledge my limitations and the boundaries of the archive rather than perpetuating problematic representational regimes. Instead, I learned to respect archival gaps and, in a way, unlearn the consistent and urgent desire to fill them. For me, this perspective marks both a form of critique and a possible counter-history, as suggested by Halberstam and Hartman. In a compelling way, I was yet again reminded of Hartman, who recalls how she failed to narrate the "romance of resistance" (2008: 9) when drawing on the archives of slavery and the topos of the captive and enslaved Black woman. As for me, I failed to do justice to the acoustic traces of Ali and Singh, to recover their status as historical subjects, to retrieve them from the archival project. In the next part of this book, I will come back to the notion of why an archival recovery seems neither particularly advisable nor actually possible (see Chapter 4).

Conclusion

In the final remarks of her essay, Kamala Visweswaran understands that her "opening account of 'being there' has been displaced by an emerging narrative of 'getting there'" (2003 [1994]: 112). Something similar happened to the narrative that unfolded in this chapter. I set out to describe two experiences of 'being there'—at sites where I imagined I would gather important insights for my research. As it turned out, neither my speaking/listening position nor that of my ethnographic acquaintances seemed capable of grasping the many layers of the sonic material. As a result, I portrayed my personal journey of 'getting there,' arriving at a point where the recognition and implementation of an accountable positioning seemed more important than the attempt at a detailed reconstruction of the historical data. In her essay, Visweswaran describes how she turned away from her field site in order to return home to do her homework. For her, a crucial aspect of doing one's homework means destabilising the "epistemological weight" (102) fieldwork carries for the discipline of anthropology. In a similar vein, I see an epistemological burden associated with not only the notion of fieldwork but also with the situated colonial legacies of my disciplinary position. As indicated earlier, I saw and continue to see myself as confronted with a certain notion of continuity, raising the question of what exactly it is that distinguishes my listening position from the one of the researchers back then. In this first of my three attempts at dealing with specific sound recordings from the *Lautarchiv*, I intended to carve out and draw on this unsettling and destabilising moment of discomfort, irritation, and not least, failure—the failure to answer certain questions that initially seemed most important. It was my wish to show that the sense of failure can be an opportunity to re-think and re-position. Failure is a constitutive part of not only feminist ethnography, but really any form of knowledge production. It is constitutive to the making of situated knowledges.

Thinking in terms of 'getting there,' of my evolving research process, also meant acknowledging the recordings' existence against the backdrop of entangled histories marking both the shared and the divided. In this way, the failures I described at the outset of this chapter turned out to be serendipitous moments of my ethnographic work, directing me to reflexively reconceive the heterogeneity of modes of listening. These modes of listening seem both connected and disconnected through time and space. Going back to Hartman once again, I understand this chapter as "written with and against the archive" (2008: 12). I addressed the archive, I responded to the desire to engage with the past, I wished to tell counter-histories, yet I refused to fill the gaps.

Investigating and simultaneously correlating two single sound recordings from the *Lautarchiv*—one of a Bengali *lascar* and one of a Hindu *sepoy*—was the chapter's initial aim. In the end, I primarily analysed my situated, and thus limited, subject and knowledge position. I contextualised the sonic testimonies by studying primary written documents and secondary literature. By drawing on the recordists, I followed and went along with the archive. Yet the acoustic data—the actual sound—only emerged more thoroughly through my ethnographic encounters. In the rest of this book, the notion of the acoustic will occupy a more detailed role (in Chapter 5, 6, and 7). Yet I do not quite see the following approaches of a *close listening* (Chapter 5) and a *collective listening* (Chapter 6) as counterpoints to the approach of a *failed listening*. Similarly, I do not see them as opposed to it, and thus as successful approaches. Rather, these different attempts mirror the complexity and ambiguity of the material I study. In Chapter 4 and 5, I draw in more detail on the ethnographic experiences of 'being here'—in Berlin, in the colonial archive 'at home.'

At the beginning of this chapter, I raised the question of what qualifies as the notion of a *failed listening* and how this notion shapes my analytical and methodological standpoint. In what followed, I described my way of dealing with the material and the open questions, unavailable, or fragmentary information I was confronted with. With these tools, I negotiated the relationship between subject positions and structural formations. One additional answer to the question of failure stems from Halberstam's *The Queer Art of Failure* (2011), which I have been alluding to at different points in this chapter. In the book, Halberstam claims to explore "what happens when failure is productively linked to racial awareness, anticolonial struggle, gender variance, and different formulations of the temporality of success" (92). It was my intention to build this chapter on these linkages, and it remains my aspiration to return to them in the course of this book.

4
... THE ARCHIVAL ...

The Politics of the Archive

> *One could argue that 'the archive' for historians and 'the Archive' for cultural theorists have been wholly different analytic objects: for the former, a body of documents and the institutions that house them, for the latter, a metaphoric invocation for any corpus of selective collections and the longings that the acquisitive quests for the primary, originary, and untouched entail.*

(Stoler 2009: 45)

My theorising of the archive addresses the analytic distinction between 'the archive' and 'the Archive.' Engaging with the tension between two archives adds to my conceptual framework for approaching the *Lautarchiv* and its politics. My readings of the extensive scholarship on archives and archival theory stem from a variety of disciplinary bodies of knowledge and locations. Historians and archivists as well as philosophers, cultural theorists, and anthropologists shaped this literature. By bringing together a whole range of prominent positions on the archive, this chapter discusses a particular set of theoretical and analytical instruments. Opening with ideas from poststructuralist philosophy, the chapter also explores more recent approaches, arising out of postcolonial theory, queer and Black critique, and media history. However, it is not my aim to present a comprehensive overview of everyone who has been addressing and writing about the archive. Rather, this chapter places particular notions of archival thinking in relation to one another in order to see what kind of theoretical responses they elicited and how they influenced each other. At the same time, I wish to rethink archival theory by means of looking at and incorporating notions of archival practice in my analysis, so as not to run the risk of getting lost in the archive's abstractions (Ebeling and Günzel 2009: 20). Ultimately, I wish to elucidate my own position in the 'struggle over archives.'

> Contesting the hegemony of cultural meaning has always been linked to the politics of the archive in academic research. Struggle over archives has been central to Black, feminist, postcolonial, decolonial, and queer challenges to the literary canon, to the writing of history books as well as the material preservation of artefacts and the concomitant pedagogy in museum spaces and ethnographic collections. (Haschemi Yekani and Michaelis 2014: 280)

Sharing this commitment, expressed here by postcolonial and queer literary scholars Elahe Haschemi Yekani and Beatrice Michaelis, I aim to contribute to the establishment of an intersectional perspective and a transdisciplinary methodology in archival studies. Such a methodology illuminates the sound archive's epistemic status as well as its physical, and by now also digital, shape. In Chapter 2, I addressed a number of crucial vectors important to historical and archival research, focusing in particular on the project of historical anthropology. I stressed a multitemporal and entangled perspective of a postcolonial and reflexive anthropology of Europe, which found an echo in the following chapter on failed listening.

Michel Foucault is widely considered to have defined the archive as a conceptual space where mechanisms of inclusion and exclusion of knowledge operate. Many, following him, carried forward his thinking by drawing on the motif of revealing or returning to some sort of origin, 'truth,' or the 'real.' The *archival turn*, which emerged in part because of such assertions in the late 1980s and early 1990s, can be understood as the attempt to think of the archive in a variety of ways. While the more abstract understanding of the archive brought new possibilities for addressing larger issues of knowledge and power, memory and history, I also share the ambivalent feeling of historian Regina Kunzel, who says:

> Sometimes I worry (along with others) that *the archive* referenced by the 'archival turn,' understood as a universal metaphor for memory structures, information storage, and knowledge production, might become so expansive as to include nearly everything and that, as a result, it will lose any relationship to what I'm tempted, with some embarrassment, to call 'real' archives. (Kunzel in Arondekar et al. 2015: 229, emphasis in the original)

In response to this sentiment, brought to the fore at a round table on queering archives, I am hopeful that the contradiction inherent in the *archival turn* pushes scholars to work with this ambiguity between ephemeral/metaphorical and tangible/material archives. Approaching the analytic object of the *Lautarchiv* in this way inspires both a theoretical and empirical engagement with *the Archive* and archival objects—be they texts, visuals, or sounds.

The Archive and Knowledge (From Foucault to Farge)

> *[The archive] is the border of time that surrounds our presence, which overhangs it, and which indicates it in its otherness [...].*

(Foucault 1972 [1969]: 147)

Like many accounts of the archive, this one begins with Michel Foucault. Still today, his influence on theories of the archive resonates in a variety of fields and academic discourses. In 1969, Foucault re-introduced the singular form of the archive, which for a long time was almost non-existent in the French language and French writing. With this move, Foucault wished to establish a distinction between archives, understood as institutions and archival material, on the one hand, and the archive as a more conceptual and metaphorical idea on the other.

In *The Archaeology of Knowledge* (1972 [1969]), Foucault intends nothing less than to rethink history, historiography, and the history of ideas. As is so often the case in his writing, Foucault defines this singular form of the archive not in positive but in negative terms first:

> By this term [archive] I do not mean *the sum of all the texts* that a culture has kept upon its person as documents attesting to its own past, or as evidence of a continuing identity; nor do I mean *the institutions*, which, in a given society, make it possible to record and preserve those discourses that one wishes to remember and keep in circulation. (145, my emphasis)

Rather, Foucault continues, the archive appears as "a whole *set of relations* that are peculiar to the discursive level"—it is constituted of "things said" or "systems of statements," which "are born in accordance with specific regularities; [...] in *the system of discursivity*, in the enunciative possibilities and impossibilities that it lays down" (145, my emphasis). The archive, in a Foucauldian sense, can hence be understood as an epistemic figure dealing with the regularities and conditions of the distribution and transformation of knowledge and of things known and knowable: "The archive is *the law of what can be said*, the system that governs the appearance of statements as unique events" (145, my emphasis). On a more empirical level, Aleida Assmann translates this much-quoted suggestive trope into: "The archive is the basis of what can be said in the future about the present when it will have become the past" (2008: 102). In this way, Assmann situates the archive, conceived as cultural memory, between remembering and forgetting. Memory and its practices constitute one of the many meanings ascribed to the archive. As opposed to positivist methods with a linear understanding of historiography, the archive, in Foucault's interpretation, does not simply record and then mirror the past but it produces history and memory and constitutes their orders. This is what Foucault calls the *historical a priori*: the archive precedes historiography which therefore can be considered one of the effects of the archive. In line with this, the archive can be read as a medium of history encoding certain statements, knowledges, and memories.

With his take on archaeology, Foucault brought to the fore concrete methodological and (new) historiographical suggestions, which he also applied to his earlier case studies of the clinic, the prison, or the object of 'madness.' However, in *The Archaeology of Knowledge*, he avoids referring to formal archival institutions, repositories, as well as recording media (a point I will come back to in Chapter 7). Rather, Foucault concentrates on the notion of a transcendental dispositive deploying the possibilities and impossibilities of particular statements. As a result, the medial status of the archived knowledge remains uncertain. By contrast, schools of thought like media archaeology and mediology, which nevertheless are very much influenced by and build on Foucault's thinking, lay their focus specifically on the relation between the material data storage device and the recording/inscription device. Philosopher Régis Debray states that, through "a perpetual re-inscribing of the archives," stored layers of knowledge can be accessed: "The most recent layer of signs reaches us through the older ones [...] such that the new takes effect in, by, and on the old" (1996 [1994]: 17). Accordingly, the archive is to be conceptualised not only as the medium of history and memory, as set out above, but as the medium or *device of transmission* of knowledge. In turn, Foucault's notions of "*possibilities of re-inscription and transcription*" (1972 [1969]: 117, emphasis in original) or *"the general system of the formation and transformation of statements"* (146, emphasis in original), as he defines the archive at a later point in his text, derive from "the rule of *repeatable materiality* that characterizes the statement" (114, emphasis in original). This speaks to a dynamic reading of the archive as a discursive formation shaped by constant modifications. At the same time, it seems to completely undermine the crucial archival process of a tangible fixation, or at least the attempt to achieve it. On yet another level, and as media scholar Wolfgang Ernst claims, approaches in media archaeology expand Foucault's 'law of what can be said' by a *medial law* which regulates the *order of things* in its very production. Ultimately, according to Ernst, this way of thinking allows us to include the conceptual question of the technical device in the theoretical analysis of the archive (2002: 19).

In his introduction, Foucault states that history is used to memorise or even memorialise monuments of the past by transforming them into documents ostensibly embodying, and in unmediated manners speaking of, the past. As a response to this view, he proposes a transformation of documents into monuments, into elements "that have to be grouped, made relevant, placed in relation to one another" (1972 [1969]: 8) in order to turn traces and fragments into history. Foucault, thus, pleads for an archaeological practice that foresees an "intrinsic description" (8) of the object of study and its materiality and mediality. One could argue that this early differentiation, set by Foucault, led other cultural, and particularly postcolonial, theorists to specifically engage with the nexus between "documents of exclusion and monuments to particular configurations of power" (Hamilton et al. 2002: 9, referencing Stoler in the same volume). Achille Mbembe famously drew attention to the entanglement of buildings and documents (fulfilling certain criteria of *archivability*) which, according to him, defines the status of the power of the archive or, as he also terms it, the "status of proof" (2002: 21). This material, as well as imaginary, status is what urges Mbembe to speak of an *"inescapable materiality* of the archive" (19, my emphasis).

As indicated above, Foucault did not consider the archive primarily as a workplace, but rather concentrated on other facets of *the archival*. Together with the historian Arlette Farge, he was, nonetheless, involved in archival work, as in the case of the joint publication *Disorderly Families* (2016 [1982]). The book comprises an early attempt to trace and write about marginal(ised) lives hidden in hegemonic archives. Farge, in turn, engaged with archival labour from the very beginning of her academic career. Still today, her essay *Le Goût de l'archive* (1989) represents an indefeasible account of the archive. For some, it still seems remarkable that it was Farge—a historian—who wrote this compelling essay with the sensitivity of an ethnographic participant observer. Well before the general 'archive fever' arose in the mid-1990s, Farge describes the experiences and feelings she underwent when combing through scripts from the eighteenth century, hour after hour, in Parisian archives.[1] In her essay, Farge elaborates on the materiality of archives; and how this materiality appeals to different senses: feeling the cold in the archives' reading rooms, tasting the different layers of dust on stacks of paper, or trying to decipher notes on a document's margins by reading them aloud.[2] She also speaks about various emergent emotions: *The Allure of the Archives*, as the English title of her essay hints at. The archival allure oscillates between the researcher's fear of damaging centuries-old scripts and the desire for the 'undiscovered,' of being the first to reveal hitherto hidden stories.

As demonstrated previously, concepts of media and communication studies as well as cultural theory are highly influenced by Foucault's archival thinking and his archaeology. For this book and my approach to the *Lautarchiv*, Farge's phenomenology of the archive has a similar impact. Her account moves between descriptions of archives as a workplace for researchers and as the site where hegemonic power structures evolve. Being a historian but also ethnographer and philosopher of the archive, Farge walks a tightrope when writing about the insights she draws from the archive. In her words, the archive plays with notions of 'reality' and 'truth,' with moments or effects of the 'real' emerging in the archive as "an infinite number of relations to reality" (2013 [1989]: 30). Later, she continues:

> Archival research starts off slowly and steadily through banal manual tasks to which one rarely gives much thought. Nonetheless, in doing these tasks, a *new object* is created, a *new form of knowledge* takes shape, and a *new 'archive'* emerges. As you work, you are taking the preexisting forms and readjusting them in different ways to make possible a different narration of reality. [...] Each process corresponds to a choice, which can sometimes be predictable and sometimes appear surreptitiously, as if it were imposed by the contents of the documents themselves. (62–63, my emphasis)

Drawing a line back to her own academic discipline of history, Farge argues that this newly created object, the interpretation or meaning one finds in the archives, is framed by and "within systems of symbols—systems for which history attempts to be the grammar" (12). With reference to Michel de Certeau's *The Writing of History* (1988 [1975]), she explains that archives have to be understood as 'forever incomplete' in the same way as knowledge has been defined as ever-changing through its incompleteness. Consequently, Farge advocates: "Today, to use the archives is to translate this incompleteness into a question, and this begins by combing through them" (2013 [1989]: 55). I therefore agree that using and translating archives is tied to a subjective selection of material and research questions and the exclusion of others; archival work and practice are bound to the production of *new forms of knowledges, histories, archives*, and the silencing of others (see also Chapter 6).

The 'Foucault effect,' as coined by Kate Eichhorn (2013: 4), led to the constant reassessment of his accounts by various fields and disciplines, thus providing a theoretical basis for wide-ranging reflections on the archive. Based on Foucault's notion of the power and control of the archive, what follows turns to Jacques Derrida's account of what he termed *mal d'archive* (1995), which has been, in its English translation, turned into the above-mentioned 'archive fever' (1996). For Derrida, not only *law* but *place* forms the starting point of his elaboration on the archive (singular) as a concept. Similar to Foucault's thought, his writing is less about literal archives or history, and more about notions of time, memory, and technology. It was Derrida who introduced the idea of a 'general archivology' which became, and still is, an important point of reference for many working in and on archives—be it in empirical, conceptual, or aesthetic terms. I therefore welcome his invitation to "imagine [...] a project of general archivology, a word that does not exist but that could designate a general and interdisciplinary science of the archive" (1996 [1995]: 34).

The Archive and Power (From Derrida to Steedman)

The archive: if we want to know what that will have meant, we will only know in times to come. Perhaps. Not tomorrow but in times to come, later on or perhaps never.

(Derrida 1996 [1995]: 36)

Derrida's account of the archive as concept or metaphor concerns interferences between archival techniques and technologies and their power-political implications: "In Derrida's description," Carolyn Steedman summarises her reading of Derrida, "the *arkhe*—the archive—appears to represent the *now* of whatever kind of power is being exercised, anywhere, in any place or time" (2001a: 1, emphasis in original). In her view, the essay may also represent "an intermittent dialogue between Foucault and Derrida on [...] topics [such as]: the archive as a way of seeing, or a way of knowing; the archive as a symbol or form of power" (2).

Derrida introduces the idea of 'archontic power' by tracing the archive back to the Greek *archeîon*, the house and residence of the *archons* (the magistrates) who were initially responsible for retaining and preserving official documents and files. Only the *archons* had the right and authority to interpret the archives (1996 [1995]: 2–3). From this vantage point, a place where power originates, and where someone exercises the power to choose, Derrida draws his attention to the relations between place and law. "At the intersection of the topological and the nomological, of the place and the law, of the substrate and the authority," he writes, "a scene of domiciliation becomes at once visible and invisible" (3). The archontic power is thus tied to the power of consignation, meaning the gathering of signs and techniques of preservation. "*There is no archive without a place of consignation, without a technology of repetition, without a certain exteriority. No archive without outside*" (11, emphasis in original). Subsequently, by speaking of an 'archontic principle,' Derrida declares: "The archivization produces as much as it records the event" (17). Applying his observations to Sigmund Freud and psychoanalysis, Derrida states that the project of psychoanalysis is not only a theory of memory but a theory of the archive.[3] He gives the example of repression, understood as a form of archiving, a form of storing things out of consciousness or public circulation. This notion also alludes to Assmann's (2008: 98) conceptualisation of archival institutions and practices of active and passive memory and forgetting. At the same time, Derrida highlights that the possibility of memorisation underlies the logic of repetition; "to want to make an archive in the first place is to want to *repeat*" (Steedman 2001b: 1161, emphasis in original). Ultimately, this quest constitutes one of the important aspects of what Derrida calls *le mal d'archive*, the 'archive fever' (or *das Archivübel* in its German translation).

This ambiguous meaning of 'archive fever' is what anthropologist David Zeitlyn focuses on. According to him, Derrida plays with the notion of fever, which can be read both as a disease (as in being sick *of* the archive) and as a desire (as in being sick *for* the archive), seeking to find beginnings and origins and to even possess these inceptions (2012: 463). Anthropologist Rebecka Lennartsson, on the other hand, relates 'archive fever' to the "ethnographic ballast" (2012: 84) one has to carry and deal with when conducting fieldwork in historical archives. In a similar vein as Zeitlyn, Lennartsson describes 'archive fever' as the ethnographer's—inevitably unaccomplished—"desire to find the origin, the point at which experience and its impression remain intact and where the question of representation is unproblematic" (85). Modern forms of power are, in Lennartsson's view, immanent in the practice of ethnography and manifest in the desire to portray lived realities as studied by anthropologists. Ethnography, whether it is a historical ethnography in and of the archive, or of present phenomena, remains always an extract, an interpretation. Consequently, Lennartsson sees her role as an "ethnologist of the past" as "questioning and dest-abilizing truths that have been established in archive material" (86). In line with her, I am inclined to see myself as an 'ethnologist of historical sounds,' attempt-ing to challenge the notion of fixing a moment of a present 'truth' on record.

Historian Carolyn Steedman, in turn, lays her focus on literal forms of 'archive fever.' On the one hand, she elaborates on the historian's anxiety, triggered by archival research. Coming on "at night, long after the archive has shut for the day" (2001a: 17), it describes the feeling of uneasiness about the fact that "you *will not finish*, that there will be something left unread, unnoted, untranscribed" (18, emphasis in original). On the other hand, Steedman traces the history of *anthrax meningitis*, a disease emerging, for instance, in the leather and papermak-ing industries in Great Britain during the eighteenth and nineteenth centuries, or caused by leather bindings and parchment stored in archives. Considering dust as the central motif of her book, Steedman develops the notion of "Real Archive Fever, or Archive Fever Proper" (27). First, Steedman gives an overview of schol-ars—including herself—who wish to draw history out from the archive, though their search "for origins and original referents cannot be performed, because there is actually nothing there: only absence, what once was: dust" (2001b: 1179). She then introduces the French historian Jules Michelet (1798–1874) who had famously described his experiences in the *Archives Nationales* in Paris as meeting the dead and bringing the past back to life. Steedman points out that Michelet "breathed in: the dust of the workers who made the papers and parch-ments; the dust of the animals who provided the skins for their leather bindings. He inhaled the by-product of all the filthy trades that have, by circuitous routes, deposited their end-products in the archives" (1179).

Archive Story I

Without wanting to overestimate Michelet's romantic depiction of the archive, I still think, to some extent, that I can relate my own experi-ences in the sound archive to the ones described by Steedman. In the

Lautarchiv, *I am confronted, not with multiple-century-old parchment and leather bindings, but with the century-old natural material of shellac. Shellac is the resin secreted by female lac bugs, which is still today mostly collected from trees in South India and Thailand. Since the end of the nineteenth century, shellac was used for gramophone records first introduced and developed by Emil Berliner in the United States. The era of shellac records, lasting until the middle of the twentieth century, is only one of the peaks of the colonial trade system of the shellac industry—an industry which can be traced as far back as the East India Company of the sixteenth and seventeenth centuries.*

Each playback of a shellac record leaves behind its traces on the record, but also sets free the smallest shellac particles, when the gramophone needle moves over the inscribed rills. Because the traditional gramophone was equipped with a steel needle attached to a heavy arm, this was even more true in the past. Nowadays, record players come with special needles. But even if one frequently replaces the needles, one still cannot completely prevent the record's abrasion. Paradoxically, the physical collection of archived shellac records is not actually the focal point of my research. In my archival practice, I am usually not listening to the shellac records themselves. I am not combing through the archive's metal filing cabinets but rather browsing through the digital catalogue. Saved on my private computer in an online cloud, I can access the digitised sound files wherever there is an Internet connection. What role does knowledge of the different (in)tangible materialities of the sound objects play in the quest to learn more about the technical and epistemic processes of reproducing and preserving sound? How do practices of listening to actual shellac records (with the negligent or naïve expectation of experiencing some form of the archive's or object's aura) or to digital files (a series of zeros and ones) shape my approach to and perception— my breathing in—of the sonic objects?

For some, Steedman reacted in a rather unexpected manner to the deconstructionist Derrida. She emphasises the puzzlement among historians about what the archive was doing in Derrida's essay in the first place. In his *strangely* structured text, Derrida elaborates largely on someone else's writing, namely on Yosef Hayim Yerushalmi's *Freud's Moses* (1991). In response to Derrida's assertions, Steedman claims that her "book repeats a *strange* move, which is to concentrate on what Derrida did not say, on that which was not the focus of his attention" (2001a: 5, my emphasis). In doing so, Steedman uses Derrida's account to reflect on her own discipline of (cultural and social) history. According to her, history is made of the "smallest fragment of its representation [...] [which] ends up in various kinds of archives" (2001b: 1176). History, thus, is composed of fragments, loss, and absence. It is in this respect that Steedman's idea of dust represents an archival metonym. Referencing Jacques Rancière's *The Names of History* (1992 [1994]), she points out that history is based upon a dialectic of absence, a dichotomy between a passion for the past, something that is "*no longer there*," (2001b: 1177, emphasis in original) and something that was never "*such as it was told*" (1177, emphasis in original). On top of that, rather bluntly and dryly, Steedman concludes that the 'stuff' in the archive

> is indexed, and catalogued, and some of it is not indexed and cat-alogued, and some of it is lost. But as stuff, it just sits there until it is read, and used, and narrativised. In the Archive, you cannot be shocked at its exclusions, its emptiness, at what is *not* catalogued [...]. (2001a: 68, emphasis in original)

It is therefore that the power to choose and the power to exclude holds true not only for the control of the archive, which Foucault and Derrida draw upon, but for the more empirical status of history and its making. This fact was famously presented by anthropologist Michel-Rolph Trouillot in his previously mentioned book *Silencing the Past* (1995). The following pages relate Trouillot's conceptual ideas to the object of study of this book—the *Lautarchiv*—and the dominant historical narratives connected to it.

The Archive and Silence (From Haiti to Berlin)

Proceeding from rather theoretical understandings of the archive and the dialectics between formation and transformation, mediality and materiality, as well as inclusion and exclusion, Trouillot's thoughts provide further conceptual insights for analysing the making of archives. With the analytical instruments offered by Trouillot, it is possible to investigate different moments of historical production and processes of silencing. In what follows, I aim to transfer Trouillot's thinking onto moments associated with the *Lautarchiv*. In his much-quoted theorising of the conditions of the making of history, Trouillot highlights the notion of silences at four different points:

> [1.] the moment of fact creation (the making of sources); [2.] the moment of fact assembly (the making of archives); [3.] the moment of fact retrieval (the making of narratives); and [4.] the moment of retrospective significance (the making of history in the final instance). (1995: 26)

With regard to the *Lautarchiv*, I am, first of all, interested in the production of the sound archive's *sources* and sound material, i.e. the first moment described by Trouillot. Here, it seems equally important to focus on the *practice*, the *process*, and the final *product*. How did the selection of recorded people and texts come about? Is it possible to reconstruct the decision-making process and the historical contingency connected to it? How can I assess the role of the technical apparatus and procedure, and its links to a strong belief in alleged 'objective' scientific practices, as the result of a rigid and systemised protocol? What did the actual moments of recording look like? Who was supervising and running the technical process in the different recording situations? Who else was present? Who could understand and relate to the recordings' contents? All these questions point to the crucial account of the interrelation between *form*, *context*, and *content*, as laid out by Ann L. Stoler (2002c/d, 2009), and as I will discuss in more detail below.

If we consider sound archives as specific types of formal archival institutions, the second moment—that of fact assembly and the making of archives— stands out. Conventional archives contain (mostly) written documents that were not actually produced for archival reasons as such, but entered the archive later as a result of specific collection strategies. By contrast, the sound archive's objects are created for archival purposes. This fact is reflected in the numerical order of the sound recordings, something that can also be observed at the *Lautarchiv* in Berlin. Each sound document was numbered in the moment of its production (what is referred to as *numerus currens*) rather than afterwards, when it entered the archive's classification system. In this context, the power to choose and the question of who has the right to choose appear once again.

The third moment, which Trouillot identifies as fact retrieval and the process of producing specific narratives in and of the sound archive, is multi-layered, given the many different aims and agendas connected to the *Lautarchiv*'s history. Here, two of the recordists' initial and salient desires arising from the archival material and its configuration are particularly striking. On the one hand, there is the aforementioned narrative of collecting and preserving languages of *all* nations of the world by, for instance, taking advantage of the global dimensions of the First World War. On the other hand, the narrative, or rather the imperative, of 'objectivity' plays an important role, which must be analysed from a perspective of (media) anthropology as well as the history and philosophy of science. One correlation between the desire for 'objectivity' and the attempt to collect languages of *all* nations seems to reside in the illusion of an encyclopaedic totality, which was not only pursued in academia but also in museums and comparable contexts during the nineteenth and beginning of the twentieth century (see also Chapter 7).

Grasping the actual moment of the making of history, defined by Trouillot as the final instance, is one of the greater, and most compelling, challenges. Considering the grand narrative, one must recognise the dominance of the *white*, male, and bourgeois elite: of men trying to understand the world (if nothing else, by means of collections and categorisations), believing in the progress of civilisation, gaining more and more power and authority and in so doing stabilising their interpretational sovereignty. Against this backdrop, I ask for the history-making moments of the *Lautarchiv* and suggest that these moments should be again under contestation when it comes to the project of the Humboldt Forum. At the same time, I seek to understand the (actively) muted and silenced moments, which are nonetheless constitutive and telling of the grand narrative. Throughout his book, Trouillot comments from different perspectives on the under-represented, or rather missing, anti-slavery and anti-colonial history of the Haitian Revolution (1791–1804) and its forgotten protagonists in Western historiography:

> The presences and absences embodied in sources (artifacts and bodies that turn an event into fact) or archives (facts collected, thematized, and processed as documents and monuments) are neither neutral nor natural. They are created. As such, they are not mere presences and absences, but mentions or silences of various kinds and degrees. By silence, I mean an active and transitive process: one 'silences' a fact or an individual as a silencer silences a gun. One engages in the practice of silencing. Mentions and silences are thus active, dialectical counterparts of which history is the synthesis. (1995: 48)

Once more, this citation highlights the tension between active and passive, presence and absence, mentions and silence. While Trouillot emphasises the engagement in practices of silencing in the making of history, archival silences also imply other notions. "Speech and silence are dependent and defined through the other," archivist Rodney G.S. Carter (2006: 223) writes. "There is no speech without silence, otherwise there would be unmodulated cacophony; likewise there would be no silence without speech, just a universal meaningless, emptiness" (223). It is in this respect that the meaning of silence ought not to be understood only in negative terms or simply equated with muteness. Silence can be a conscious choice, or even imply moments of resistance.

Engaging with archives after the *archival turn*, it seems hardly possible to disregard the conceptions of the archive as theorised by Foucault and Derrida. Nor does it seem possible to investigate the archives solely in empirical terms. Trouillot, I argue, manages to do both, by, on the one hand, focusing on practices of silencing and, on the other, emphasising the absence (and its meaningful ramifications) of the Haitian Revolution and specific subaltern agents in Western history books.[4] Proceeding from this crucial moment of the Haitian Revolution in the account of histories of colonialism, the following concentrates on notions of colonial and imperial archives.

The Archival and the Colonial (From Richards to Stoler)

The archive, the sum total of the known and knowable that once seemed an attainable goal hovering on the horizon of possibility, became and has remained utopia.

(Richards 1993: 44)

At the end of the first chapter of *The Imperial Archive* (1993), Thomas Richards arrives at the conclusion that the imperial archive has always remained utopia. Throughout his book, Richards tries "to understand what it means to think the fictive thought of imperial control" (2). He does this by claiming that "the alliance between knowledge and power [had never] been more clearly presented than in turn-of-the-century fiction" (5). Tracing literary, cultural, and scientific, alongside imperial, trajectories of colonialism, Richards establishes modes of thinking about the utopian archive and utopian spaces, as well as about imperial imaginations and imagined epistemologies. Thereby, he pursues the objective of grasping, as he calls it, the "positivist project of comprehensive knowledge" (46) in and of the late Victorian era. According to him, the project of comprehensive knowledge was characterised by "the sense that knowledge was singular and not plural, complete and not partial, global and not local, that all knowledges would ultimately turn out to be concordant in one great system of knowledge" (7). This archival quest for a total set of knowledge attained through technologies and practices of surveillance and information gathering is what Richards uses to put forward the argument that the (imperial) archive can only be read as a utopian institution understood as an epistemological complex. "In imperial mythology," he argues, "the archive was less a specific institution than an entire epistemological complex for representing a comprehensive knowledge within the domain of Empire" (14). This *archival complex* encompasses a number of definitions, ranging from collective imaginations to fantastic epistemologies:

> This operational field of projected knowledge was the archive. The archive was not a building, nor even a collection of texts, but the collectively imagined junction of all that was known and knowable, a fantastic representation of an epistemological master pattern, a virtual focal point for the heterogeneous local knowledge of metropolis and empire. (11)[5]

As opposed to Richards, visual and historical anthropologist Elizabeth Edwards neither deals with the utopian archive nor focuses on Victorian times. On the contrary, Edwards discusses the present situation of archival institutions, namely visual archives in postcolonial Britain. Her aim is to shed light on the question of the possibility of a dystopian archive. Yet with reference to Richards, she asks: "what happens when the utopian archive of an inclusive, instrumental and even fantasy of knowledge that constitutes colonial power [...] becomes a potentially dystopian force?" (2016: 53) Edwards proposes an understanding of the dystopian archive as a "site of 'misrule,' destabilisation and disruption, the inverse of the inclusive and unproblematized utopian hope" (53). Consequently, she argues for a consideration of the *dystopic potential* of colonial archives that is "not only metaphorical but literal, in that they have the power to disturb dominant, and utopian, political desires and narratives" (54).

Edward's article was published in the special issue, entitled "Utopian Archives, Decolonial Affordances" (2016), which represents one prominent outcome of the attempt to connect imperial and colonial archives to notions of utopia and/or dystopia. This endeavour appears as a common strategy for dealing with both literal and metaphorical archival spaces. One point of reference for the special issue's editors, Paul Basu and Ferdinand De Jong, is that "all utopias are [...] structured by present conditions and are necessarily constructed, bricolage-like, from resources available in the present sociocultural milieu" (2016: 9). Hence, the utopian archive cannot only be traced back to actual imperial conditions and desires but is, in fact, constitutive of these circumstances. In a similar vein, Kirsty Reid and Fiona Paisley explain: "More than capturing some external actuality, they [imperial and colonial archives] created the very subjects on which they claimed to report" (2017: 2). According to Reid and Paisley, one has to understand that the act of founding archives for reasons of collecting information and knowledge served the exercise and consolidation of colonial rule. Secondly, they state that archives are not passive but active sites of power, and have, thirdly, consequences in and for the present.

Turning from notions of the imperial and utopian/dystopian archive to notions of *the colonial*, the following shifts attention to the question of knowledge, its politics and connections to the colonial project. With respect to this ostensibly more encompassing terminology, the notion of *the archival* represents only one conceptual perspective. It is in this regard that Ricardo Roque and Kim A. Wagner share the observation:

> During the last three decades 'knowledge' – under distinct conceptual terminologies such as 'discourse', 'culture', 'text', 'information', or 'archive' to name but a few – has come to the forefront of inquiries of the colonial; it has been posited as the central feature of colonialism. (2012: 6)

The aim of their work is to rethink common strategies and hence develop new readings of colonialism. This goal includes bringing European archives as repositories of epistemic legacies of European hegemony and imperialism into focus. In doing so, one point of departure is to access new avenues leading "beyond both conventional positivist historiography and postcolonial literary approaches" (26). Emphasising that 'colonial' cannot simply be reduced to 'European,' Roque and Wagner plead for a broader (and entangled) understanding of colonial knowledge. They stress that colonial knowledge must include an account of "indigenous involvement, exchanges, and interferences" (23) and caution against a negligent or too simplistic equation of colonial knowledge and Western agency, since this would neglect conditional dynamics of colonialism.[6] Roque and Wagner argue in support of a more complex perspective on colonial knowledge that shifts the focus to its heterogeneity, historicity, and entanglements (see also Chapter 2). Hence, colonial knowledge should be seen neither as simply fictitious, nor as a factual or 'pure' reflection of Western hegemony.

Another crucial aspect of the suggested alternative reading strategies of colonial discourses and archives is to read them "as epistemic traces mediated by bodily actions and enmeshed in the materiality of colonial situations" (5). Speaking to the notion of materiality, but even more importantly to the location from which the archive is read today, Antoinette Burton argues for a re-materialisation of not only processes of archival production, but especially of history writing and its contingencies. In her introduction to the volume *Archive Stories* (2005), Burton states that archival logics must be strictly historicised and variably situated. She pleads for:

> interrogating how archive logics work; what subjects they produce; and which they silence in specific historical and cultural contexts; enumerating the ways in which archival work is an embodied experience, one shaped as much by national identity, gender, race and class as by professional training and credentials; pressing the limits of disciplinary boundaries to consider what kind of archive work different genres, material artifacts, and aesthetic forms do, for what audiences and for what ends; recognizing, and accounting for, the relative evidentiary weight given to sources of various types [...]; imagining counter-histories of the archive and its regimes of truth in a variety of times and places. (9)

Another facet that touches upon the *politics of location* is the question of whether the focus on the colonial archive 'at home' does not also run the risk of reproducing the metropolis as the core of the colonial project and imperial power (Burton 2011: 15; see also Falola 2017). Why focus on colonial knowledge in and of Western archives, when, at the same time, the objective is to challenge and overcome the normative dichotomy between centre and periphery? In terms of my own study, and as mentioned many times before, this issue is of particular importance due to the fact the *Lautarchiv*'s holdings were all compiled in Berlin and remain located there. Understood as always already hegemonic and determined by complex entanglements, I believe that it is crucial to consider Western archival and historical narratives. As pointed out in the previous chapters, and as Burton suggests, it is therefore not only necessary to re-materialise archival activities and logics but also to decentre notions of the European metropolis and its epistemic legacies.

In her approach to, and empirical work on, visual archives in postcolonial Britain, Edwards discusses the notion of "the colonial archival imaginaire at home," as well as the concept of "the historical elsewhere" (2016: 52). In her argumentation, Edwards elaborates on three forms of the 'elsewhere:' the temporal, the spatial, and the disciplinary. Against the backdrop of the former, Edwards argues, the colonial would commonly be constituted "as something that happened long ago" (56). In this perception, the colonial has hardly any impact on local histories, nor on contemporary British society. As an example of the temporal 'elsewhere,' Edwards describes how museums in Britain represent narratives of the trans-Atlantic slave trade and its abolition. She contends that museums often tell these stories as narratives with a beginning and an alleged end, without reference to any kind of continuities with or within the present. In a similar way, the spatial 'elsewhere' imagines the colonial archive and its relevance not as issues with which one must engage locally and in the present. According to Edwards, an example of this attitude is the assumption that colonial histories mostly belong overseas. In the case of the *Lautarchiv* in Berlin, a spatial 'elsewhere' is clearly at stake. As pointed out in my introduction, the sound archive must be interpreted as a colonial archive enabled and established in the heart of the metropolis. As a colonial archive 'at home,' this study conceives of the *Lautarchiv* as a site to locally engage with narratives of the colonial, with epistemic violence, and more generally with different modalities of imperial knowledge production. Edwards characterises the final form of the 'elsewhere' in a disciplinary sense: the 'elsewhere' of anthropology. In her argument, Edwards points out that anthropology "as a discipline or category of museum collecting, [...] has also become an 'elsewhere' into which problematic categories of action and objects can be safely sequestrated" (59). In this way, the colonial past can be separated from local, social, and political (and, in the specific case of the *Lautarchiv*, also academic) histories. Instead, the colonial past is constructed as 'not here.'

Coming back to Roque and Wagner and their claim for an engagement with colonial knowledge, it seems worth mentioning their postulate of "the commitment towards an understanding of colonialism, and its manifold dynamics, through critical attention paid to the political and epistemic productivity of its archival traces" (2012: 4). This plea for and commitment to an "alternative methodological attitude" (26) ultimately leads me to Stoler and her theorisation of archives as part of her broader effort to come to terms with imperial tensions and formations of knowledge. There is no doubt that Stoler's work offers an important framework for thinking about the archive, knowledge systems, and regimes of truth.

The Archive Against and Along Its Grain

> *How can students of colonialisms so quickly and confidently turn to*
> *readings 'against the grain' without a prior sense of their texture and*
> *granularity? How can we compare colonialisms without knowing the*
> *circuits of knowledge production in which they operated and the racial*
> *commensurabilities on which they relied?*

(Stoler 2002c: 92)

Stoler initially formulated this set of questions at a conference on *Ethnography in the Archives,* which took place at the University of Rochester in 1996. Her essay, "Colonial Archives and the Arts of Governance" (2002c/d), published both in the eminent South-African volume *Refiguring the Archive* and in what was then a newly founded journal on *Archival Science*, followed the initial conference. At that time, Stoler articulated her concerns regarding a reading of the archives *against the grain* as prominently postulated by postcolonial and feminist scholars. Stoler, by contrast, stood up for a different reading practice to set in before attempting modes of approaching the archive from below and beyond, across and against. As a response to her questions, she writes:

> If a notion of colonial ethnography starts from the premise that archi-
> val production is itself both a process and a powerful technology of
> rule, then we need not only to brush against the archive's received
> categories. We need to read for its regularities, for its logic of recall,
> for its densities and distributions, for its consistencies of misinfor-
> mation, omission and mistake, along the archival grain. (92)

In her later, much more detailed, book, *Along the Archival Grain* (2009), Stoler advocates a "commitment to a less assured and perhaps more humble stance— to explore the grain with care and read along it first" (50). Against this back- drop, Stoler pleads for treating

> archival events more as moments that disrupt (if only provisionally)
> a field of force, that challenge (if only slightly) what can be said and
> done, that question (if only quietly) 'epistemic warrant,' that realign

the certainties of the probable more than they mark wholesale rever-
sals of direction. (51)

While Stoler appreciates the work of other scholars who, like her, aim to offer
a postcolonial critique of the archive and the making of the grand narrative,
she claims to enter a different path concerning her critical accounts of colonial history. For one thing, and as already pointed out at the end of Chapter 2,
Stoler refers to Trouillot's *Silencing the Past* (1995) as still the most significant
example of an ethnography in and of colonial archives, their relations of power
and their manifestation in established historical narratives. Published in the
same year, Stoler argues that Shahid Amin's *Event, Metaphor, Memory* (1995)
represents another instance of the importance of the author's ethnographic sensibility "when writing histories of the unlettered" (Amin 1995: 1) from a perspective of alternative histories. Stoler also honours the work of Ranajit Guha as
an influential actor and pioneer of the Subaltern Studies Group (SSG). Aimed
at assessing histories from below, members of the SSG sought to make subalternity the point of departure for any narration. In particular, Stoler points to the
book *Dominance without Hegemony* (1997), in which Guha elaborates on the
"effort to resituate those who appeared as objects of colonial discipline as subaltern subjects and agents of practice who made – albeit constrained – choices
of their own" (Stoler 2002c: 91). Stoler emphasises that this form of objectification, which needs to be contested and reconsidered, is all the more valid when
it comes to female subjects and the attempt of locating them in the colonial
archives not simply as objects or as the absent.

Although Stoler references the work of a number of historians, her analytic
strength, as an anthropologist engaged in postcolonial studies and history, seems
to reside in her turn to epistemology (rather than history) and to what she terms
"grids of intelligibility" (2009: 1). "Focus on the politics of knowledge," Stoler
argues, "is a methodological commitment to how history's exclusions are secured
and made" (45). While she shows interest in the archive's gaps and exclusions,
Stoler nevertheless tries to avoid the danger of merely seeking out ostensible lost
voices. As long as attention lays only on marginalised traces, as it was the agenda
of, for instance, members of the aforementioned Subaltern Studies Group, the
archive's power and its formation would remain unsolicited.[7] Recovered stories
of subalternity may be added to historical narratives, but they would not actually
change or contest dominant epistemic frameworks. Stoler, therefore, intends
to decode the colonial logics and hegemonic texture, supporting silences and
absences in the first place. Her aim is to explore the epistemic formations and

practices that are responsible for uncontested conventions in hegemonic contexts. At the same time, accepting the ambivalent status of archival documents,
which appear both as the result of colonial processes and the source of historical
production, Stoler argues for a twofold approach to colonial archives. "In turning from an extractive to a more ethnographic project," she writes, "our readings
need to move in new ways through archives, along their fault lines as much as
against their grain" (2002c: 99–100). This shift also implies that the archive,
archival material, and practices of archiving are to be treated with an ethnographic sensibility. As emphasised above, it is precisely this sensibility that allows
for illuminating the powerful relationship between *form*, *context*, and *content*.

    As one point of criticism concerning Stoler's account of the archive, queer
scholar Anjali Arondekar (2009: 9) wonders why Stoler does not sufficiently
cover notions of sexuality, affect, and intimacy in relation to archival imperatives. This is particularly salient as Stoler otherwise engages precisely with issues
of the interrelation between the colonial, the intimate, and sex in her scholarship (see also Chapter 5). In my view, Arondekar's critique, and her study of sexuality and the colonial archive in India, also touch upon more general questions
of how and why one turns to the past and seeks access to the colonial archive.
In the following section, I therefore concentrate on notions of a queer critique
and the call for using the past to question the present. This is of relevance not
least regarding the conditions of an ethical queer archival academic practice, as
it was and continues to be claimed, for instance, in the eminent work of Ann
Cvetkovich (Arondekar et al. 2015: 222 and 225).

The Archive and the Promise of a Future

> *One must grasp, precisely to not fix. To read without a trace [...] is*
> *not a mandate against archival work, but rather a call to interrogate,*
> *without paralysis, to challenge, without ending the promise of a future.*

(Arondekar 2009: 4)

Situating herself in queer, sexuality, and postcolonial studies, Anjali Arondekar
commits to an engagement with minoritised historiographies. The logic of her
(archival) work and her book, *For the Record* (2009), is based upon two crucial

points of critique regarding scholarship on colonial archives. For one thing, Arondekar argues that, against the backdrop of the *archival turn*, the emphasis on and interest in marginalised and lost knowledges runs into danger of lacking historical specificity. In her study, she therefore follows specific archival figurations and refuses to accept that the history of sexuality in the colonial archive appears merely as a lost one or as located at the archive's margins. On the other hand, Arondekar strives against the recovery model of archival research or, as she puts it, the "recovery imperative" (99). In this respect, Arondekar distances herself, firstly, from "the additive model of subalternity" (6)—famously brought to the fore and then criticised by members of the Subaltern Studies Group. Secondly, she renounces the desire to make marginalised historical subjects visible. Last, but not least, the historian abdicates the idea of (sometimes nearly fetishised) archival 'discoveries.' "The critical challenge," Arondekar points out, "is to imagine a practice of archival reading that incites relationships between the seductions of recovery and the occlusions such retrieval mandates" (1). Following this, her aim is to navigate "figurations of archival evidence that move the act of archival recovery into narratives of profound undoing" (17).

In a similar vein, Elahe Haschemi Yekani and Beatrice Michaelis (2014) argue against the tendency towards possibilities of recovery and a consolidation of past and present. In their work, they lay focus on "unhappy archives" (Ahmed 2010) of race and slavery as well as the notion of queer temporalities. For them, the process of queering the archive brings with it the potential to reconsider archival material and to read it in a different way. "Rather than attempting to consolidate hegemonic archives of race in the past with a version of 'positive diversity' in the present," they state, "we would like to enquire into contemporary efforts to make 'race' speak differently to us today" (Haschemi Yekani and Michaelis 2014: 270). The two scholars draw attention to the ambivalence of the attempt to trace moments of agency and/or resistance in hegemonic archives and avoid valorising the diversity of subaltern subjects.

> A queer critique of the temporal politics of [...] archival practices shows that in specific contexts it might make sense to criticize the lack of engagement with an early version of 'multiculture' and racialized difference while in others the mere celebration of the spectacular early Black presence can also procure problematically happy archives of race and slavery. (281)

In a more drastic sense, this also speaks to Saidiya Hartman's argument against using the archive to recover or repair historical violence and traumas. Instead, and as pointed out in Chapter 3, Hartman (re)claims to "respect the limits of what cannot be known" (2008: 4) as a form of Black critique. She advocates writing a history of the present which "strives [...] to write our now as it is interrupted by this past" (4). For Hartman, it is more about "a history of an unrecoverable past; it is a narrative of what might have been or could have been; it is a history written with and against the archive" (12). As summarised by Eichhorn, the archive, understood in an intersectional sense, should therefore not be regarded "as a place to recover the past but rather as a way to engage with some of the legacies, epistemes, and traumas pressing down on the present" (2013: 5).

Aspects of queer and Black critique offer the potential to not only reflect on one's own position and desires, as well as the location from where I approach and investigate the *Lautarchiv*. It also allows me to ask to what extent looking at the past illuminates the now and the future, and how one may contribute to writing a history of the present. Problematising and historicising past practices of producing and archiving sound by means of generating scientific knowledge must include a reflection on my very own and present practice of academic knowledge production.

Archive Story II

In approaching the Lautarchiv, *I am impelled by the attempt to engage with the archive's gaps and silences. Archival voids appear in the material itself but also need to be traced in terms that are more abstract. There are various ways of defining and dealing with the archive's gaps—gaps in historical records and cultural memory. Do we understand archival voids as characterised by the interruptions and traumas that disturb and disrupt the now, as described by Hartman and Eichhorn? Or, do we regard the archival gap as the essence of the archive, as George Didi-Huberman (2007: 7) proclaimed? According to him, the archive is defined by its gap—its perforated being. The philosopher and art historian poses the question whether one should not always contemplate* how *a text came to us; what prevented an image from vanishing or being destroyed. So many texts have been burned, images obliterated, voices silenced. This is what prompts Didi-Huberman, following Arlette Farge, to claim that the essence of the archive is its gap—a consistent absence. The archive's essence are not the preserved vestiges of texts,*

images, and sounds. It is not about what is there but how a particu-
lar assessment, classification, or highlighting of a past event is enabled
(Ebeling and Günzel 2009: 15). Any attempt to shed light on inclusion
and exclusion, destruction and recovery, remembrance and forgetting
must take into account archival voids. Even though my research seeks
to investigate the how, the mechanisms of selection and formations of
archival processes, I feel it is important to recall that the intention of this
work is not to simply fill the existing gaps. It is important to reflect on
what motivates oneself to visit and re-visit the archive, to look for and
mark the gaps in historical records, memories, and archives.

The Archive, the Apparatus, and the Acoustic

After examining a variety of multi-faceted and rather theoretical approaches
to the archive and the different possibilities of addressing its politics, I come
back to this work's analytical object—the sound archive. What kind of considerations does one have to take into account in order to grasp the specificities
of the project of (re)producing and archiving sound, voices, and music? How
can one assess the relation between the archive and notions of the acoustic, the
apparatus, and the act of speaking, recording, and listening? To what extent
does the previously described tension between theoretical and literal notions of
the archive apply to sound archives?

First, establishing modes of thinking about acoustic archives requires a
consideration of the differences between text archives and sound archives.
While the former consists of written documents and textual sources, the latter
contains silent sound objects and acoustic files that "do not sound until they
are activated by the user" (Lange 2017b: 49). Second, it is of importance to lay
focus on the recording and playback equipment. In the case of the *Lautarchiv*,
one has to concentrate on the apparatus of the gramophone, as much as on
the infrastructural and socio-cultural conditions enabling the advent and development of sound archives. At the end of the nineteenth and the beginning of
the twentieth century, the emergence of such archival institutions occurred in
different urban locations throughout Central Europe and North America. It is
important to pay particular attention to the interrelationships between technological innovations, scientific aims, and socio-political processes, as well as

cultural practices of collecting and archiving, and their institutionalisations (see also Chapter 7).

Reflecting on the formation of the Phonogram Archive in Vienna, founded in 1899 as the first of its kind, scholar of science Christoph Hoffmann puts particular emphasis on technological components. He regards the emergent technical requirements as being most constitutive for the establishment of sound archives.[8] The very idea of an acoustic archive is thus based on the potentiality and possibility of recording. It is precisely this capability that prompts Hoffmann (2004: 281) to speak of a doubly effective imperative, which is, on the one hand, characterised by the technical ability of the apparatus to form an archive and, on the other hand, by the archival demands on the apparatus.

Concerning the distinction between historical archives of textual material as opposed to sound objects, Hoffmann points out that, for the former, the relation between transmission and its inherent gaps requires particular modes of reflection. The sound archive's configuration is, in turn, always already present and immediate in the archival medium and its materiality (285). The order and control of the archive (and the past) is always already part of the act of recording and the decision of what and whom to record. Similar to Derrida's above-quoted statement that "archivization produces as much as it records the event," (1996 [1995]: 17) Hoffmann (2004: 290) states that all events captured by the phonograph only served the purpose of a transmission into the future. Similarly, it is nothing but the will to record that precedes the archival object, nothing but the agenda of the particular recordist or archivist (291). Hoffmann also discusses aspects specific to the archiving of sounds and voices that are not under total control of the historical subjects in charge. Aside from the material and technical dimensions inscribed in the record, one needs to take operational conditions as well as spatial circumstances into account. For a long period of time in the history of the reproduction of sounds, it was simply not possible to capture, and for that matter archive, someone's voice without their willingness to speak or sing in front of the recording device. Hence, acoustic testimonies in historical sound archives can only be found of those who were willing to be recorded, and not of those who decided to remain silent. In terms of sound recordings compiled in colonial contexts and shaped by asymmetrical and complex power relations, this willingness, however, has to be examined in a nuanced manner and in its discursive quality.

With respect to logistical constraints, it must be noted that the phonograph as well as the gramophone could not be set up that easily in any place, although there were soon attempts to design a phonograph that was portable and could be taken on field trips (e.g. Stangl 2000; see also Chapter 3). On top of that, the recorded person had to be accurately positioned in front of the apparatus. They had to have a powerful voice and be able to express and practice something—a story or a song, a series of words or numbers—without pause or interruption. As opposed to material circumstances, these operational conditions are only indirectly perceptible (Hoffmann 2004: 286–287). By listening to historical sound recordings, one learns next to nothing either about the surrounding and the recording situation, or about how the willingness to speak or sing came about—unless the recorded person addresses these issues on the actual recording and the listening person is able to understand the content. Additional information and textual material are therefore inevitable in order to be able to (re)contextualise historically recorded sound.

Elaborating on the specificity of the history of the *Lautarchiv*, Britta Lange, too, refers to the implementation of both the Vienna and the Berlin Phonogram Archive at the turn of the twentieth century. Similar to Hoffmann, Lange discusses the difference between textual and acoustic archives. First, she highlights the "archive's *own* production of the archival material" (2017a, emphasis in original) and the fact that sound documents were not simply studied and stored but actively generated. Second, Lange points to the materiality of sound recordings, taking into account that one can access recorded sound only with the help of a technical device. Lange sees a third distinction in the perception and reception of sound recordings. According to her, sound recordings "preserve sounds as sounds, language as spoken or sung language and, in this way, reproduce a dimension of corporeality—voice, performance—that textual sources lack" (2017a). The resulting question of immediacy appears as an important but also difficult one, since the perception of the quality of immediacy is culturally coded and varies in different times and contexts. In the following chapter on *close listening*, I will come back to the excess of meaning and information that voice recordings potentially entail.

Conclusion

As a final point of my theorising of the archival, I wish to contemplate where forging a bridge from Foucault's understanding of the archive as the 'law of what can be said' to the archival imperative of the recording apparatus of the gramophone has led me. In closing this chapter, I wish to highlight some of the arguments and concepts discussed above, which informs my approach and analysis in the following chapters.

By examining the *Lautarchiv* through a Foucauldian lens, it is possible to analyse the complex alliances between knowledge and power. How do positions of power generate knowledge, and how does generating knowledge enable power? In examining the extent to which these dimensions tie in with the *Lautarchiv*, the question arises as to how one can situate them in relation to both the literal and metaphorical archival space, the transcending archive, as well as to historical subjects. Farge's considerations, in turn, offer the possibility to grasp not only the archive's materiality but also its alleged 'truth effects.' What kinds of *truth claims* are attached to the *materiality of sound* and to the *Lautarchiv*'s overarching endeavour of archiving languages of *all* nations of the world? How can one critically assess and historicise these paradigms from a present point of view? And how might this relate to Derrida's attempt to deconstruct the conceptual space of the archive by drawing on larger issues, such as the power to choose (and exclude), the desire to repeat, and the quest for origins and beginnings? On the one hand, and as Steedman hints at, these notions only lead to dust, alluding to the idea of the archive as consisting of hazy fragments, loss, and absence. Following Trouillot, on the other hand, the aim must be to trace archival absences by looking at different moments in the making of narratives, so as to shed light on the processes of silencing the histories and historicity of colonial subjects in the metropolis of Berlin (see Chapter 5 and 6). As emphasised before, these processes apply similarly to the production of archives, historiographies, and collective memories.

Another crucial aspect of outlining the above theoretical framings was the attempt to carve out a conceptual understanding of 'the colonial' and 'the colonial archive.' For one thing, I pointed to the "positivist project of comprehensive knowledge" (Richards 1993: 46) associated with imperialism and European hegemony, a project which can only be characterised as a utopian model of the archive. Whereas Richards claims that the project of the imperial archive had to remain utopian, the potential of the dystopian archive to contest, disturb, and disrupt established narratives and epistemologies is particularly relevant against the backdrop of present moments of coloniality. It is in this respect that not only Edwards, but also Roque and Wagner, plead for a shift towards an engagement with colonial knowledges in Western archives in order to dismantle the concurrent political and epistemic impact of archival traces on and for the present and future. This shift might help to better understand the dimensions and dynamics of colonial legacies, which cannot be assessed without looking at their inherent heterogeneity, historicity, and entanglement. Applicable strategies to grasp these moments—marginalised and/or neglected for too long—can be found in remarks on global history, but also in Burton's writing, advocating the decentring of archival repositories.

The compelling work of Stoler (which goes way beyond her contribution to archival theory) is important to this work on various levels. Stoler's archival thinking, characterised by a turn to epistemology and philosophy as much as to historical anthropology and ethnography, complicates my approach to the *Lautarchiv* and its difficult epistemic status. For me, it is crucial to think both along and against (that is, both in terms of and counter to) the logics and formations of archival power and knowledge. Moreover, by turning to notions of a queer critique of the (colonial) archive, I show how notions of queer historiography can be productively used and applied to the *Lautarchiv*. While Arondekar's remarks urge me to consistently interrogate my own archival practice, Haschemi Yekani and Michaelis emphasise a queer critique of the archive's temporalities that speaks to an engagement with the past, not with the aim to recover it, but to position the past in critical tension to the present and future(s).

The most important insight gained from reading Hoffmann and Lange, is that—contrary to textual archives—acoustic archives do not simply preserve archival documents, but they also produce their own objects (see Chapter 7). Archival sounds can thus never be disconnected from the formal and technical setting they were generated in and through. This notion not only explains my broadly defined conceptualisation of the archive—understood both as institution and concept, workplace and metaphor (Ebeling and Günzel 2009: 10)—but also acts as a point of departure for my engagement with further sound objects and archival orders. In the next two chapters, I concentrate on additional sound recordings from the *Lautarchiv*, compiled in very different contexts and historical moments, trusting that a *close* (Chapter 5) and *collective* (Chapter 6) listening to the archive's voices offers intriguing ways to approach colonial discourses and their materialisation.

5
Close Listening

Reading Gender into Historical Sources

By speaking of female and male, subaltern and dominant, *white* and non-*white* sources, I am aware that I am not superseding the gendered and racialised categories used in historical records, but that I am reproducing them. In a postcolonial approach—informed by and intersectionally entangled with gender theory—, the dichotomising oppositions of coloniser-colonised, metropolis-periphery, dominance-resistance (and the list could go on) are inadequate when analysing colonial relationships and their trajectories, since these binaries are themselves products of hegemonic orders. How, then, can I deal with this difficulty of binary systems? How can I deal with the fact that self-imposed terms and positionalities cannot at all, or rarely, be found in historical archives?

Feminist scholar and writer Anne McClintock (among many others) pointed to gender as an important analytical category in postcolonial theory in order to analyse Western imperialism and its ramifications. In her book *Imperial Leather* (1995), McClintock set out to criticise "Western historicism and its entourage of binaries" (10). In her view, Eurocentric historiographical theories are not suited to apprehend the complex layers of power dynamics. "Drawn historically from the metaphysical Manicheanism of the imperial enlightenment itself," McClintock stated, "binaries run the risk of simply inverting, rather than overturning, dominant notions of power" (15). In a similar vein, Ann L. Stoler reflected upon the discipline of anthropology and its relationship to binary thinking. In the introduction to her book *Carnal Knowledge and Imperial Power* (2002b), Stoler contended: "students of colonialism, anthropologists in particular, have taken the politically constructed dichotomy colonizer/colonized as a given rather than as a historically shifting pair of social categories that needs to be explained" (13). Yet McClintock's critique took the debate another step further when she argued that postcolonial theory shifted from the binary axis of *power* (colonizer-colonized—itself inadequately nuanced, as in the case of women) to the binary axis of *time*, an axis even less productive of political nuance because it does not distinguish between the beneficiaries of colonialism (the ex-colonizers) and the casualties of colonialism (the ex-colonized). The postcolonial scene occurs in an entranced suspension of history, as if the definitive historical events have preceded our time and are not now in the making. If theory promises a decentering of history in hybridity, syncretism, multidimensional time and so forth, the singularity of the term effects a recentering of global history around a single rubric of European time. Colonialism returns at the moment of its disappearance. (1995: 10–11, emphasis in the original)

For the purpose of this chapter—that is, reading gender into my historical analysis and approaching the racialised dimensions in and of the *Lautarchiv*—McClintock's elaborate critique is important in at least two aspects. For one thing, it urges me to problematise and contest the binaries that I continue to use when focusing on so-called female traces, as opposed to the dominance of male sources in the *Lautarchiv*. Wishing to shed light on the gendered notions ingrained in the applied scientific procedures and their implications for the archival order, I follow McClintock's remark that "gender is not synonymous with women" (7). However, one might gather the impression that I am precisely keeping up with this ominous equivalence, if and when I divide archival material into, and in doing so denote it as, female and male, dominant and subaltern, *white* and non-*white*. My objective, therefore, is to carve out the complex dynamics and complicities between coloniser and colonised, thus acknowledging the fluidity and hybridity of heterogeneous identities. Secondly, an important analytical lens derived from McClintock's account touches upon the notion of time. According to the feminist scholar, the question of time is fundamental for a perspective and theory that holds the temporal prefix 'post' in its name. McClintock brings forward the argument that singular and predominantly Eurocentric notions of time and history, past and present, are not suitable to describe the multiple historieS and post/colonial situationS and effectS, that are isolatable neither in time nor in their alleged singularity. Again, I ask how I can grasp the complex temporalities and notions of power and resistance indicated in the material I am looking at (see Chapter 2 and 3). How can I grapple with the difficulty of trying to avoid ascribing colonial, Eurocentric, and hetero-normative categories to historical subjects? As one possible answer to these obstacles, I believe that it is of utmost importance to frequently return to and problematise my perspective and position, reflect on my conceptual prospects and epistemic framework.

In what follows, I link my analytical approach to a detailed description of the location and the historical moment the sonic events, which I have chosen for this chapter, occurred. As in Chapter 3 and 6, this chapter takes single sound recordings and a particular mode of listening—that is the mode of a *close listening*—as the focal point of its analysis. As a rare exception in the *Lautarchiv*'s holdings, the sound documents stem from two female subjects: the performers Venkatamma and Rajamanikam. It was the linguist Friedrich Otto Schrader (1876–1961) who recorded the two women at the site of a so-called *India Show* at the Berlin Zoological Garden in 1926. My close listening to the acoustic testimonies of female colonial subjects is punctuated by a close reading of the personal memoirs of a male colonial impresario: John George Hagenbeck (1900–1959). But before I turn to the recordings themselves, I discuss the history of what Andrew Zimmerman (2001) has called 'exotic spectacles,' and how the history of sound reproduction is connected to this particular metropolitan phenomenon.

Völkerschauen and the Berlin Zoological Garden

The history of *Völkerschauen* in Berlin traces back not exclusively to the Zoological Garden but to different urban places of entertainment.[1] The history goes far back into the nineteenth century and witnesses *Völkerschauen*'s expansion, starting in the 1870s, not only in Berlin and Germany but throughout Central Europe and North America (e.g. Blanchard et al. 2008 [2002]; Bruckner 2003; Demski and Czarnecka 2021). While there is a need to account for the specific past of the colonial amusement industry of many Berlin (and German) institutions, the following section will nevertheless focus on aspects of the colonial legacies of the Berlin Zoo.[2]

In September 2014, a representative of the Pirate Party Germany[3] and then member of the Berlin House of Parliament put out an official request to the ruling parties of the Berlin Senate. In his letter, he asked whether the Berlin government feels responsible for the process of coming to terms with the colonial history of the Berlin Zoological Garden.[4] The answers provided by the ruling representatives of the Berlin Senate less than a month later were neither particularly well-researched nor satisfactory to the inquirer. While the responses did provide an overview of the different *Völkerschauen* taking place at the zoo, of the number of participating performers (varying from less than ten to more than one hundred people), and of the hired organisers, the official paper did not imply that further action would be taken to reappraise the findings. It was rather the lack of information and the near absent negotiation of this chapter of Berlin history in public and political spheres at the time that resonated in the short and mostly poor answers.[5]

The formal reply states that after the Zoological Garden was founded in 1844, a total of twenty-five *Völkerschauen* took place, over a period of almost seventy-five years, between 1878 and 1952. Most of the exhibitions were organised by employees of the Carl Hagenbeck Company, and by members of the Hagenbeck family in particular. However, a clear sense of who exactly was involved in the organisation of the numerous exhibitions (which had different themes and focused on different regions) is still hard to depict, as Hilke Thode-Arora (1996: 110–111) explains in her work on the history of *Völkerschauen* in Berlin and other parts of Germany. Thode-Arora is one of the few scholars and museum experts working extensively on this part of Germany's colonial past. She has not only been examining plenty of archival material and media reports, but has also been looking at personal letters and journals, as well as further primary literature (e.g. 1996, 2001, 2008, 2014, 2021).

For the first two exhibitions in 1878, six people from Greenland and seventeen people from Sudan and southern Egypt, together with a number of animals, were brought to Germany in order to be put on display. The troupes performed for what was a growing *white*, urban Berlin middle-class audience at the time. In the following years, people from northern Scandinavia, Libya, Somalia, Sri Lanka (former Ceylon) and India, among other places, came to Berlin to take part in these commercial exhibitions. The performers were temporarily living in Germany and touring throughout Central Europe. To what extent they were engaging in public life and the urban space and interacting with Berlin citizens is difficult to trace due to the paucity of sources.[6] Obviously, the interactions also varied over time, among the different communities, and from person to person.[7] Oftentimes, the artists were additionally hired for circus shows and film productions, by cabarets and other places of entertainment. As a result, they extended their stay in, or frequently returned to, Europe.

From a conceptual point of view, Roslyn Poignant introduces the notion of a 'show-space' to describe the setting in which so-called ethnic shows and colonial spectacles took place in North America and Europe. For the anthropologist, the term 'show space'

> is more than a collective name for the actual show places; rather it defines a cultural space that is both a zone of displacement for the performers and a place of spectacle for the onlookers. It is a chronotopic space, that is to say, a conjunction of time and space, where certain stories can 'take place': where historically specific relations of power between colonisers and colonised were made visible. (2004: 7)

Poignant's depiction of time and space also alludes to the notion of the 'ethnographic present' (Fabian 1983), which describes techniques of distancing the *Other* not only in spatial but particularly in temporal terms (see also Chapter 7). This form of denying *Others* access to and participation in Western historicity and modernity, and thus depriving them of the right to their own history, seems to be reflected in show spaces—and even more so in museum spaces—of that time. As Poignant highlights, in these spaces, (colonial) relations of power were in fact made visible and simultaneously construed as the normative order of the world. In this way, a colonial matrix of *Others* vis-à-vis 'the West' was naturalised, a phenomenon Gayatri C. Spivak called "the epistemic violence of the *worlding* of worlds" (1985: 267, my emphasis; see also Römhild 2019: 3).

The Berlin Senate's reply furthermore states that, according to present knowledge, no relics of *Völkerschauen* can be found, neither in the possession of the city of Berlin nor in other institutional repositories. Even if one disregards the sound recordings I will be focusing on in this chapter, the substance of this statement by the political representatives seems rather evasive and imprecise, ignoring the political and ethical implication the existence of colonial remnants carries. It appears as a striking reminder of the fact that a more systematic investigation of the provenance of hundreds and thousands of relics and objects (or rather subjects) situated at Berlin museums and other German institutions has only just begun. It is thanks to the persistent efforts and extensive pressure by many activists and scholars that provenance research is now part of national political agendas. Not only is it important to grant access to what archives and depots hold. Provenance research should above all provide information on whether objects were acquired in unethical situations, or whether they indicate histories of problematic or violent circumstances regarding their production, appropriation, or circulation (e.g. Förster et al. 2018).

A similarly evasive answer was given with regard to the organising committees of the *Völkerschauen*. In the representative's (official) opinion, it was not the public venue of the events—in this case the Zoological Garden—but the operating partners in charge who were responsible for recruiting, hiring, and terminating contracts with the performers, taking care of their travels and everyday needs. Given other ongoing struggles in dealing with problematic institutional legacies, this answer points tellingly to the grey areas of political and historical responsibility. It points to the issue of who can and who has to be made accountable for negotiating difficult histories. Who demands an accounting of the past, symbolic or material reparation, restitution and repatriation? Who acts on and reacts to these demands? Who does not take responsibility and for what reasons?[8]

The Beginnings of the Berlin Phonogram Archive

The first sound artifacts compiled against the background of a colonial spectacle in Germany are six wax cylinders recorded by the psychologist, philosopher, and musicologist Carl Stumpf (1846–1936) and his colleague Otto Abraham (1872–1926). Recorded in September 1900, these wax cylinders contain music played by performers of a Siamese court theatre visiting Berlin. Today, the wax cylinders are considered to be the oldest set of sound objects of the Berlin Phonogram Archive (*Berliner Phonogramm-Archiv*). As the first of its kind in Germany, Stumpf officially founded the archive in 1904 following the Vienna model, established in 1899, together with his student and colleague Erich Moritz von Hornbostel (1877–1935). The archive was initially located at the Institute for Psychology of the Friedrich Wilhelm University in Berlin. It might not come as a surprise that quite a number of sound files stored in the Phonogram Archive today were produced in commercial entertainment settings.[9] Nevertheless, I was rather stunned to find out that the archive contains tapes of Sami performers from northern Scandinavia compiled during a *Völkerschau* at the Zoological Garden as late as 1952. Becoming director of the archive in 1906, Hornbostel was responsible for the continuous development and expansion of the sound project. In the course of the fascist takeover in 1933, Hornbostel, whose mother was Jewish, was dismissed from all his posts at the university and was forced to leave Germany.[10] After Hornbostel's emigration, the Phonogram Archive became part of the Ethnological Museum of Berlin. Together with the ethnographic museum collections, the acoustic holdings are now part of the Humboldt Forum.

Stumpf and Hornbostel are considered important figures in the making and shaping of ethnomusicology and comparative musicology, known as the Berlin School. Both disciplinary strands evolved during the nineteenth century and are deeply connected to colonial history. Although neither Stumpf nor Hornbostel have ever had formal chairs in comparative musicology, they are nevertheless known for developing new, highly technical-oriented methodologies and comparative practices of collecting, transcribing, and listening to music. Nowadays, their effort to institutionalise their 'achievements' in the city of Berlin is regarded as a particularly impactful avenue not only for the history of (ethno)musicology but also for the history of sound archives (e.g. Meyer-Kalkus 2015; Simon 2000; Sterne 2003).

In his article "The Sound of Evolution" (2003), literary and media scholar Eric Ames shows how nineteenth-century evolutionist theories have strongly influenced German comparative musicology. The discipline was closely linked to the obsession with collecting, cataloguing, and categorising; the obsession with describing ostensibly linear developments and finding the alleged missing links in these lineages. For my approach to the colonial archive 'at home,' an even more crucial insight of Ames' remarks is that Stumpf, Hornbostel, and Abraham would conduct most of their early research activities in Berlin and not 'on location' or 'in the field.' "Only from the viewpoint of the urban center," Ames argues, "could one construct a comparative taxonomy of cultures or an evolutionary history of origins" (301). Accordingly, the urban centre played an important role: urban sites where music could be found, recorded, and compared; sites where mass-cultural, economic, and scientific interests met and circulated. Sound recordings made in these contexts thus not only illustrate an intersection between commercialised colonial spectacles and academic research agendas, but also between the so-called periphery and the metropolis.[11]

> Between 1900 and 1912, they [Stumpf and Hornbostel] made their earliest and most important recordings not in the colonies—but in the metropolis. The music came to them. Live performances of non-Western music could be heard throughout Berlin, where they played a key role in the burgeoning industry of leisure and entertainment as stock features of cabaret programs, circus shows, and ethnographic exhibitions. Though the literature on nineteenth-cen-

tury visual culture maintains an awkward silence on issues of sound, music did not merely supplement these entertainments. On the contrary, live performances of foreign music were in at least one respect more sensational than the visual displays that they accompanied: Europeans were already familiar with images of cultural difference, brought to them through paintings and illustrations, but ethnographic entertainments made the sounds of non-European life available to mass audiences for the very first time. (301)

Here, Ames draws attention not only to developments in urban popular culture at the end of the nineteenth and the beginning of the twentieth century, but also to the asymmetrical division between visual and sound culture and the often merely one-sided exploration of it. Ames furthermore emphasises the tension between the showmen's attempt to present the 'authentic' and 'representative,' and at the same time excite the audience with something 'spectacular' and 'sensational.' Especially after the turn of the century, shows increasingly consisted not only of magic and animal acts, but also of professional dance and music performances. By contrast, the (stereo)typical continued to be put on display through orchestrated insights into the everyday life of the performers. For instance, people involved in the shows prepared their food in public; and organisers shipped entire residential buildings to Germany or recreated them 'authentically' at the show place. From this, a significant tension resulted in the contradictory understanding of labour. In one of the few archived contracts, between a representative of the Carl Hagenbeck Company and Samson Dido[12] from Cameroon from 1886, one of the agreements says: "Carl Hagenbeck does not demand any *labour* from the troupe but only the display of customs and practices" (cited in Thode-Arora 1996: 119, my emphasis).[13] The idea that the contracting party did not work but simply attended to their daily practices contradicts both the deployment of Prince Dido and his family as well as of other professional cultural labourers. According to the historian Susann Lewerenz (2017: 40–48), with the growing commercialisation of the shows, theatrical elements became increasingly popular with the audiences. It is my opinion that most critical research on migration and social history has so far been unable to comprehensively address and fully understand the histories of this different sort of labour migration of the nineteenth and twentieth century.[14]

In addition to these socio-economic factors, the close relationship between *Völkerschauen* and the academy is important to look at. Not only Stumpf but also anthropologists and physicians like Adolf Bastian (1826–1905) or Rudolf

Virchow (1821–1902) relied on the 'authentic' and thus scientific value of eth-nographic displays. It almost seems like both sides, the entertainment and the academic enterprise, required confirmation and legitimation from one another. For his argument, Ames reconstructs in detail how Stumpf would proceed in his scientific endeavour, how he would orchestrate the performance for the recording in order to capture and then 'objectively' dissect sound and music. He concludes that a strict division between showman and scholar no longer seemed very clear: "acoustic objectivity was therefore a function not of the dis-tance between science and entertainment, but of the power to choreograph. As 'participant observer,' the scientist became a kind of impresario in his own right" (2003: 308).

Yet another rather paradoxical discrepancy can be observed between colo-nialism as a general force of transformation, and the discipline of comparative musicology, which was mainly focused on the study of 'original' musical tradi-tions not yet influenced by imperialist expansion (see also Chapter 7). With regard to the early years of the discipline of ethnomusicology, this tension seems contradictory in the sense that "comparative musicologists assailed the infrastructure that made possible not only the ethnographic exhibition—their initial source of data—but also their own still nascent discipline" (309). The musicologists' aim was to collect, analyse, and preserve music traditions before further circulation of other musical styles would increase, and before mass cul-ture and sound technologies would gain influence.

> Whereas mass reproduction threatened to 'homogenize' non-Euro-pean music, recording promised to 'fix' or 'capture' that music in all its particularity. Thus phonography offered a unique means of pre-serving the alterity of 'exotic melodies,' which is to say, a means of constructing it technologically and discursively. (311)

As has already been shown, both *Völkerschauen* and scientific endeavours contributed a great deal to the discursive construction of alterity. In contrast to the Berlin Phonogram Archive, however, the holdings of the *Lautarchiv* include only one collection that was unmistakably compiled at the site of a *Völkerschau*.[15] In late September of 1926, the linguist Friedrich Otto Schrader from the University of Kiel recorded a total of nine individuals at the loca-tion of a so-called *India Show*.[16] From the beginning of July until the end of September 1926, the Berlin Zoological Garden was the venue for this 'show'—the largest up to that point and including more than one hundred people. In the archival records housed at the zoo, I came across a legal document providing a detailed list of the people involved in the *India Show*.[17] Apart from around seventy men, whose professions ranged from lathe workers and chefs, to acrobats, musicians, and dancers, the list reveals that the troupe also consisted of ten children (between the age of four and eight) and eleven women. Among the women were a weaver's wife, one basket maker, two lace makers, two juggler's wives, four dancers, and one "good-looking Tamil woman." While most of the other people involved are listed with their or their husband's profession, the designation "good-looking Tamil woman with two or three young children" stands out. It is likely that this woman's part in the show was the performance of the exoticising and sexualised representation of a woman, wife, and mother of Colour.[18]

Wilhelm Doegen, then head of the Prussian State Library's Sound Department, invited the linguist Schrader to Berlin to take advantage of the presence of people from South India and today's Sri Lanka who resided in Berlin during the summer.[19] As the Sound Department was predominantly using the gramophone for its acoustic operations, the recordists would not use the phonograph like Stumpf and his colleagues (see Chapter 3). Instead, they installed technical apparatus of the gramophone in a storeroom at the zoo. At times, the merchant and co-organiser of the exhibition John George Hagenbeck[20] was also present during the recording process. In his autobiographical writing about his journeys to South Asia as well as back to and through Europe, Hagenbeck highlights, if not boasts, that academics showed great interest in his work. Apart from Schrader and Doegen, Hagenbeck also mentions the anatomist Hans Virchow[21] (1852–1940) who was particularly interested in the anatomy of acrobats and even X-rayed the body of one of them (1932: 150–152). Generally, it should be mentioned that Hagenbeck and his mercantile relatives had always sought to be in close contact with influential members of German academia and the growing museum landscape.[22]

Among the *Lautarchiv*'s sound recordings—containing stories, songs, religious texts, and lists of words and numbers in Telugu, Tamil, Sinhalese, and Pali—one can find three recordings of two individuals designated as female in the historical scripts. As indicated at the outset of this chapter, this appears as a rare exception in an archive otherwise dominated by male presences—both among the recordists as well as the persons recorded.[23] Until today, none of these sound objects—neither those which include women nor those of others—have been considered either as testimonies by individual historical subjects or as relics of *Völkerschauen*.

Venkatamma

Leaving aside the larger historical context, the following turns to the *Lautarchiv* and one of the sonic traces recorded at the zoo. What kind of materialities and voids, noises and voices, sounds and scripts can be found at the archive today? Visiting the *Lautarchiv*, I have a close look at the material entity itself, at one of the shellac discs. The record I examine comes in a light brown record envelope. In the upper right corner, the serial number LA (for *Lautabteilung*) 824 is stamped on the cover. Inspecting the inscribed rills of the black surface of the record, I detect four different sections interrupted by blank parts with no rills. This indicates that the record contains four pieces of sound. In the middle of the record, a label inscribed with three different pencils states the language (Telugu), the content of the recording (love song, numbers), as well as the serial number (LA 824). Underneath the label, engraved on the shellac, I can feel, once again, the serial number as well as Doegen's signature. This signature can be found on several of the *Lautarchiv*'s records. Whereas well-known public figures recorded for the Darmstaedter collection were asked to leave their autographs on the record, other people recorded did not leave an engraved mark—at least not on bare wax. The personal information form (*Personal-Bogen*) attached to each record did include a designated rubric for the speaker or singer's name as written in their first language. However, on most of the files compiled at the zoo, this section remains blank.

The archive holds three duplicate copies of the shellac disc LA 824. Often regarded as 'the originals,' the duplicate copies actually constitute the third carrier medium. As part of the disc manufacturing procedure, the initially recorded wax disc is destroyed. A copper master resulting from the matrixing process forms the positive for the shellac disc, which can then be duplicated as often as required. In the course of the digitisation process starting in 1999, the four pieces of sound were divided into four digital MP3 and WAV files, which I can listen to and play back and forth on my personal laptop. Even during my visits to the *Lautarchiv*, I did not listen to records on the record player but on the archive's computer.

The personal information forms attached to the records are stored in acid-free cardboard boxes. Each box holds twenty-five files, containing the written documentation for each record. The forms comprise details about each person recorded, their biographical background, the recording location, and the recording's content, among many other details. The amount of information in these forms varies, but

Lautabteilung an der Preussischen Staatsbibliothek, Berlin

PERSONAL-BOGEN

Nr. ....

Ort: *Berlin for*

Datum: *29. 9. 1926*

Laut-Aufnahme Nr.: *M 824*　Zeitangabe: *4 Uhr*

Dauer der Aufnahme: ....　Duchmesser der Platte: *50*

Raum der Aufnahme: ....

Art der Aufnahme und Titel (Sprechaufnahme, Gesangsaufnahme,
　Choraufnahme, Instrumentenaufnahme, Orchesteraufnahme):

1) Liebeslied　2) dasselbe, Anfang, unterbrochen v. Lachen
3) wie 1)　4) Zahlwörter 1-20　1-3 m. Trommelbegl.
(s. P.A. 33)

Name (in der Muttersprache geschrieben): *(Kann nicht schreiben)*

Name (lateinisch geschrieben): *Venkatamma*

Vorname: ....

Wann geboren (oder ungefähres Alter)? *ca 28 J.*

Wo geboren (Heimatprovinz)? *Tutur, Carnul N.*

Welche grössere Stadt liegt in der Nähe des Geburtsortes? ....

Wo gelebt in den ersten 6 Jahren? ....

Wo gelebt vom 7. bis 20. Lebensjahr? ....

Was für Schulbildung? ....

Wo die Schule besucht? ....

Wo gelebt vom 20. Lebensjahr? ....

Aus welchem Ort (bzw. Sprachbezirk) stammt der Vater? ....

Aus welchem Ort (bzw. Sprachbezirk) stammt die Mutter? ....

Welchem Volksstamm angehörig? ....

Welche Sprache als Muttersprache? *Telugu*

Welche Sprachen spricht er ausserdem? *Tamil (etwas)*

Kann er lesen? *nein*　Welche Sprachen? ....

Kann er schreiben?　Welche Sprachen? ....

Spielt er ein Instrument (ev. aus der Heimat)? ....

Singt oder spielt er modern europäische Musikweisen? ....

Religion: *Rama madam*　Beruf: *Frau eines Jongleurs dessen Vorfüh-*
rungen sie auf der Trommel beglei-
tet

Vorgeschlagen von: 1. *F.O. Schrader*

　　　　　　　　　2. *H. Jergen*

Beschaffenheit der Stimme:　1. Urteil des Fachmannes
　　　　　　　　　　　　　　　(des Assistenten):

　　　　　　　　　　　　　　2. Urteil des Direktors der Lautabteilung
　　　　　　　　　　　　　　　(seines Stellvertreters):

Die Lauturkunde wird beglaubigt:

Figure 5-1: Personal information form (*Personal-Bogen*), LA 824.
September 9, 1926. LAHUB.

the people in charge of the recording mostly completed the questionnaires meticulously and supplemented them with additional notes, transcripts, and translations. In the case of the recording at hand, however, there are only a few pieces of information about the person named Venkatamma and her biography (see figure 5-1).[24] Did the recordists have no time to take down further details? Did they consider it unimportant? Or did the categories simply not fit the recording context?

On the form LA 824, it is mentioned that Venkatamma was approximately twenty years old at the time of the recording; she was born in the south of India, in a province called Tutur, her first language was Telugu, and she also knew a bit of Tamil. At the bottom of the form, it was noted that she—the printed "he" was crossed out and replaced by "she"—could not read or write. The category asking for the name as written in the person's first language was not left blank, but it was noted in brackets: "Cannot write." From the documents, one learns that it was another, literate Indian person, named Kovvali Viracaryalu (approx. 1896–?), who wrote down the accompanying transcription. Kovvali Viracaryalu, a goldsmith, had been recorded the day before.[25]

The act of crossing out the predefined "he" can be read as one of the indicators of the gendered scientific practice and archival order. On the one hand, it shows that the personal information form and the whole scientific procedure had been envisaged only for men; they had been designed for male subjects, who generally counted, and in this way were again construed, as the scientific norm (e.g. Hanke 2007).[26] From the outset, women had been excluded from the scientific endeavour; they had been made invisible. In this case, they had neither been considered a deviation from the norm—which usually happened by denoting women as the *Other*. Nor were they regarded as valuable complementary subjects. On the other hand, the overwriting of the pronoun indicates that the recordists felt the need to assign a certain gender to the recorded person. In general, the recording process did not include the production of visual footage, which could have been an additional marker of the gender role, based on the external gender performance through gender-conforming hairstyles, clothes, or jewellery.[27] Stating and codifying the visibility or audibility of gender and race in photographs or sound recordings always refers to a normative gender and racial dichotomy. A dichotomy in which people can be labelled as either male or female, *white* or non-*white* because of their appearance or voice quality and vocal timbre. Nina S. Eidsheim (2019: 49) makes a case for understanding voice and vocal categories as culturally-conditioned and performed material entities. For her, it is important to deconstruct how and why one associates a recorded voice with a certain gender, race, ethnicity, or age.[28]

The comment in the questionnaire's "occupation category" reveals the importance of the forms' restrictive and gendered nature as an element of the systematised recording procedure. Venkatamma's profession is described as "wife of a juggler whom she accompanies on drums during his performances."[29] Reading the archive today, this short note can be taken to imply an overlap between the gendered and archival logic of the time. Here, Venkatamma is understood as the companion of her husband. She is not considered a performer, singer, or artist in her own right. Hence, both the details given and the omission of several categories on the personal information form appear as an active production of gaps. The answer to the form's last question, regarding Venkatamma's occupation, symbolises the Eurocentric, patriarchal, and hetero-normative order of the underlying scientific practice. The questionnaire's gaps thus indicate archival voids in two different ways: on the one hand, information was simply omitted and apparently not considered meaningful; on the other hand, the given details are indications of the gendered order of knowledge.

Venkatamma's recording is one of five records made on September 29, 1926. At four in the afternoon, as it was noted on the form, Venkatamma started singing a song in Telugu in front of the gramophone horn. The musical piece, accompanied by a drum, forms the first of the four pieces on the record. The song's historical translation into German, which can be found in the archive's files, and a recent translation into English by G. Manoja, read as follows:

My translation into English of the historical German translation of the written file:

Translation in accordance with the voice record:

Oh beloved! If you leave me,
how shall I bear it?
Wicked Amor, in his cruelty,
has made me mad!
Is it right to torture me
as you listen to Evil's whispering?
How often did he say
'Stand up and come!'
and put patira[30] *on my neck.*
Even after a month it still smelled.
Oh beloved! If you leave me,
how shall I bear it?

Oh beau, your bereavement
how could I forbear
Sinful cupid cruelly
made me afflicted
made fervent
made me afflicted
Eared wicked inculcations
made me tormented
is it just to torment me
'bal' – torment me to extent
Elegant beau jocosed with me
where did that Charmer go

Oh girl, the words he said.
My thoughts vanished.
My own kind would not exist in this
world:
so I thought.
Oh beloved! If you leave me,
how shall I bear it?

oh! Dame, what to do
his words mote my heart
bal[31] – *mote my heart*
When in endearment
picking a peck
pitiless God separated us
bal – *separated us*
Assumed myself
unparalleled in this world
oh! Damsel, his words
mote my heart
affront every word
wanted me to go close to
put sandal paste on neck
make demoiselle smell aromatic

LAHUB, Personal information
form LA 824.[32]

Translation by G. Manoja (2018).[33]

Listening to the recording, one can hear a well-trained voice singing a love song in a quick tempo. The genre of the song is a simplified *javali*—a South Indian musical form usually associated with the practice of so-called *devadāsīs*.[34] Instead of focusing on the content and a musicological analysis, the following draws attention to the sound object's material and auditory qualities. In doing so, I concentrate on how I approach different kinds of source material, and whether and how I can establish a productive dialogue between different archival formats and auditory features.

Hearing and Seeing: 'the Gaze' and 'the Listen'

What we hear is not necessarily an addition or completion of what we see. We do not necessarily want to extend what we see by something audible. But we—Central Europeans—want to connect what we hear to something visual, to the source of the sound, the knowledge of its origin. (Lange 2012: 61)[35]

The quotation in the epigraph describes a telling contradiction for the sound recording at hand. Literature on colonial spectacles has often addressed visual archives that document the exoticising presentation of People of Colour (e.g. by focusing on commercial posters, postcards, photographs, and newspaper articles). Terms like *Völkerschau* or human zoo are likely to evoke immediate images of either violent and racist representations or no less drastic exoticising and romanticising images in many people's heads. How does one relate these mental images to Venkatamma's sound recording, which was most probably produced in a similar context? Might it be possible to approach the sound file detached from one's own presuppositions and stereotypical thinking? Or does sound, indeed, always demand a form of visibility and embodiment, a connection to its source? Listening to the recording, I wondered whether the *Lautarchiv*'s acoustic testimonials might offer an alternative access to the past and such racist practice.

The hegemonic gaze always shapes the display of visual testimonies, which document the exoticising practice of 'representing' People of Colour. Accordingly, the hegemonic gaze always reproduces the racist practice to some extent. Again, I wondered how this critique relates to acoustic material. Does sound material not bear witness to hegemonic power imbalances in a similar way? To imbalances between the recorded persons and the Western entrepreneurs who would mainly be interested in the economic benefits of putting human beings on display; or the *white* academics who would pursue the scholarly goal of exploring what for them were foreign languages and unfamiliar musical traditions in order to collect, catalogue, and preserve them for posterity? Does the current approach to the sound recordings and the current practice of playing back the sound simply reproduce the asymmetrical structures of power, which enabled the production of the collections in the first place? Considering the fact that the archival material is still situated in a German institution and that it is still predominantly *white* scholars who investigate the sources, I believe this question has to be answered in the affirmative. But is there nevertheless a way to bypass this dilemma? How can I, and can I at all, as a *white*, female, and Western-trained scholar, approach this *sensitive* material (see also Chapter 3)?

During my search for additional sources in other archival institutions, I came across a press photo by an international photographic agency.[36] Apparently, this photo was taken during the opening of the *India Show* at the Berlin Zoological Garden in July 1926. On the left side of the photograph, one can see a Woman of Colour sitting on the ground playing a drum. The woman is wearing a figured robe or a sari, which partially covers her long hair. Her gaze is

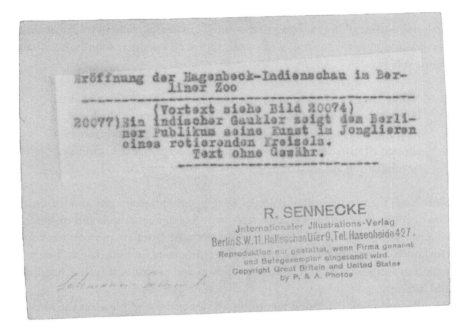

Figure 5-2: Back side of a photograph taken at a *Völkerschau* at the Berlin Zoological Garden in 1926. Stadtmuseum Berlin Foundation, Lehmann Collection.

directed straight ahead to the camera lens, to my gaze. On a blanket next to her, covered with different tools and instruments, sits a male juggler, as one can read in the captions on the back of the photograph (see figure 5-2). The performer "is presenting his art of juggling a rotating spin top to the Berlin audience." At the rear of the two performers, the picture shows the audience, seemingly *white* Berlin middle-class citizens of the Weimar era. They mostly seem to be paying attention to the juggler's show and not to the photographer's presence.

Might it be possible that the pictured woman sitting next to the juggler is the same woman who was recorded by Schrader in September 1926? Might it be the same woman who was described as "the wife of a juggler whom she accompanies on drums during his performances"? How does one relate this visual source to the archived sound? How do I deal with this colonial photograph; with the doubly effective colonial gaze—that of the historical Berlin audience on the one hand, and my own current gaze on the other? Do questions of the gaze, visuality, and the act of seeing equally apply to the practice of hearing and listening—to the listeners back then and my practice of listening, of analysing and ascribing meaning to the sound document today? Problematising the distinction between studies of visual culture and popular sounds, Jonathan Sterne states:

> While 'the gaze', as an act of seeing, is a central trope in studies of visual culture, there is no central auditory trope equivalent to 'the listen'. In its place, there are dozens of figures and figurations of audition, even though all structures of listening, whether interpersonal, institutional or mediatized are also configurations of power. (2012c: 19)

Since both the production of colonial imagery and photography and the creation of colonial sounds and records refer to problematic methods and epistemic violence, the question of whether the former or the latter are more or less contentious is, in my opinion, not the most pressing issue. In my analysis, I rather intend to focus on the configurations of power and practices of seeing, hearing, and listening.

Returning to the sound recording, the second sound piece on the record I have been discussing comprises a particularly important aspect of my account of the sound object's form, its material and auditory dimensions.[37] This second, fragmentary sound piece epitomises a significant difference between acoustic and visual or textual material. After twenty seconds, the recording ends; it is interrupted. Initially, and as was common practice, the recorded person was supposed to repeat the song. In this case, however, Venkatamma did not do so. In the written scripts, concerning the recording's second part, it is noted: "same, beginning, interrupted through laughing" and "cancelled through laughing."[38]

In her research on sound recordings of prisoners of war recorded during the First World War in German and Austro-Hungarian internment camps, Britta Lange (2011a: 36) argues that moments of subversion or resistance can be found in instances of simple pauses, verbal errors, coughing—or laughing. Together with Anette Hoffmann, Lange developed the methodological approach of a *close listening*. The two scholars claim that a close listening to historical sound recordings allows for addressing the multi-faceted layers of the phonetic material (see also Hoffmann 2015: 75–77 and 2020: 28–39). According to Lange,

> the recordings provide more non-verbal information than can be reproduced in a written form. As the recordings are not cut or dubbed, they contain the sound of the technical apparatus itself, pauses, laughing, coughing and murmuring. A careful analysis could

help to develop questions about the specific meaning of the pauses and errors, about what we do *not* hear, but which is still there and significant. (2014: 376, emphasis in the original)

Elsewhere, she writes:

> Sounds—not understood as humans' 'authentic' articulations, but as acoustic productions—give the recorded or rather interrogated person, more than measured data, photography, and plaster casts, the chance to, briefly and only within narrow bounds, act as a subject and to shake off the scientifically attributed object status. While they provide a language sample that pleases the researchers, on the technical level they also have the opportunity to irritate by pausing, laughing, modifying the agreed text or omitting parts of it. (2011a: 36)[39]

Following this view, the question for me is whether Venkatamma's laughing can be understood as a moment of resistance, or even as a moment of empowerment. Can the disruption of the scientific procedure be read as a self-empowering act? Or does this interpretation represent a mere speculation and falsely attributes (subaltern) agency and subjectivity to the act?

In his take on the recording procedures in POW camps, media scholar Friedrich Balke (2009) argues that the recording act in front of the gramophone cannot be considered an (inter)active speech act. He holds the opinion that the internees did not speak but merely verbalised a script (70). Yet Balke considers laughing as an act of speaking. With reference to another instance of laughter that occurred among the recordings of Indian prisoners of war, Balke contends that the speaker rises to speak in and through laughter. According to him, laughing allows the speaker to create a distance to the object or meaning of the anticipated statement (71; see also Lange 2019: 315–334).[40] Similarly, I could argue that Venkatamma only starts to express herself at the moment she interrupts her singing and rises to speak in and through her laughter. Whether or not Venkatamma planned or intended her interruption, whether it was supposed to be humourous or disruptive, whether it was a form of distancing or self-expression, it certainly had the effect of an interference. Venkatamma's laughing disrupted, and maybe even subverted, the rigid scientific process of recording. Hence, I read this rupture—and the notion of error or, if you will, failure—on several levels: on a structural and on a material, technical level, but also on the level of the subject.

Taking this fragile interpretation to different levels also means reflecting on the ambiguous role of the subject recorded. Venkatamma can neither be seen as the exploited and marginalised object and victim. Nor can she be viewed as a subversive and cosmopolitan worker 'from below.' Rather, I argue that the acoustic trace tells us something about the ambivalence of subjective practices. It tells us something about the dialectics of processes of transnational mobility and migratory movements, about the dialectic between politics of control and practices of appropriation. On the one hand, the practice of recording Venkatamma as part of her employment in the *India Show* is clearly a reflection of an unequal and exploitative labour regime. On the other hand, it was the same system that offered Venkatamma the opportunity to be mobile, to escape (other) exploitative conditions, and to earn a living. For Manuela Bojadžijev (2011: 142), migration is always characterised by the ambivalence of exploitation and escape from exploitation. Although I doubt that the people recorded received any sort of expense allowance, not to mention signing a consent form, it is nevertheless possible that they perceived the recording project as yet another context for presenting their artistic practice. The recording system was supposed to avoid the unexpected, but it was in fact prone to error and sensitive to appropriation. Research on contemporary politics of migration attempts to account for and grasp these dialectics by drawing on the concept of the *autonomy of migration* (see also De Genova 2017; Mezzadra 2011; Papadopoulos and Tsianos 2013).[41] This approach seeks to change the perspective *on* migration by adapting the perspective *of* migration, meaning to recognise migration as an essential component of any society both past and present (Bojadžijev 2011: 139). It seeks to shift the focus to the practices of subjects of migration, towards the heterogeneity of these practices, which always include (albeit limited) scopes of action, even under conditions of disenfranchisement. Sceptical voices criticise the concept as romanticising the figure of the migrant as a subversive and resistant subject, thereby losing sight of the dispositive of domination and exploitation. Proponents of the concept, in turn, say that by placing particular emphasis on subjective practices, the autonomy of migration approach does not merely focus on subjects, but rather establishes a complex understanding of subjects and societies in their global and entangled conditions. According to Bojadžijev, these dimensions characterise a substantial plurality of possible forms of agency (141).

What implications, then, derive from the sonic presence of a Woman of Colour in Germany? What does her presence reveal about transnational mobility and about Western systems of producing knowledge, collecting, and archiving based upon (time-)specific and hierarchically-constructed ideas and ideologies? By examining the sound recording today as the trace of a subjective moment, I argue that it is possible to gain insight into the imaginations and configurations of Western hegemony. Venkatamma's sound recording points to the possibility of investigating materialised forms of hegemonic knowledge production. Here, I showed that tensions between the material and epistemic formations that manifest in the archive's gaps and silences, in its ruptures and in differently marginalised or hybrid figures, are particularly crucial for the approach of close reading and listening.

John George Hagenbeck as a Hybrid Figure

Throughout my research, I was confronted with the ostensibly certain fact that sources of and information about male and bourgeois figures dominate the holdings of official (not exclusively colonial) archives. I was confronted with the certainty that traces of female and subaltern subjects can only be detected by reading the archive against its grain or by focusing on the archive's absences and silences. As plausible as they may sound, I nevertheless feel the urge to problematise, differentiate, and perhaps even revise these assumptions. Although this book intends to concentrate on the *absent presences* existent in and produced by the colonial archive, I am also inclined to account for seemingly dominant sources. It is not least the attempt to read the archive *along* its grain, to understand the texture of the archive, that drives this intention.

As I emphasised at the beginning of this chapter, students of colonialism today seem to agree on the notion that oppressors or colonisers, previously thought as fixed entities, can no longer be described in a homogenised manner. Stoler notes that a unifying view has been particularly applied to the colonisers, explaining that "colonizers and their communities are frequently treated as diverse but unproblematically viewed as unified in a fashion that would disturb ethnographic sensibilities if applied to ruling elites of the colonized" (2002b: 23). Further, she states:

> The populations that fell within these contradictory colonial locations were subject to a frequently shifting set of criteria that allowed them privilege at certain moments and pointedly excluded them at

others. This is not to deny that sharp distinctions divided those who were ruled and those who did the ruling but to highlight the fact that these divisions were not as easily (or permanently) drawn as the official discourse might lead one to imagine. (40)

With regard to the *India Show*'s organisers and performers, making sharp distinctions is rather difficult. It is especially difficult when taking into consideration different colonial locations—meaning "disparate origins and circumstances" (39)—and relations of power. In this way, neither the dynamics among the many performers traveling to Europe nor the dynamics back home in South Asia can be unambiguously described. The performers often considered the opportunity to go to Europe as an appealing possibility to earn comparatively good money in a relatively short amount of time and to transfer the earnings back home. However, the accessible sources do not reveal a lot about the performers' life histories and about their wants and needs. Little is known about their paths through life, whether they wished to stay in Germany, or what happened to them after returning to their homes.

At the end of his book *With India's Traveling People* (*Mit Indiens fahrendem Volk*), published in 1932, John George Hagenbeck recounts an anecdote about a group of performers he had toured with for one season. The impresario Hagenbeck recalls a scene at the train station, when the performers were about to leave the city of Munich by train. Mentioning a German woman, who worked in a pub at the station, Hagenbeck says that she would pity the troupe of artists because she assumed they could never afford to buy themselves a drink. She was surprised when, seemingly as a gesture of farewell, she saw them waving and throwing small coins out of the windows of the leaving train. Although Hagenbeck might have portrayed this story in a way that was slightly too glorifying, it still shows the misrepresentation or at least the abridged depiction of non-European people in Germany at that time. The description of the incident comes from a dominant, male, and written source. For my argument, I have to read between the lines. As the following will shows, analysing Hagenbeck's writing in more detail means to examine the impresario and his relationships as ambivalent and contradictory. Hagenbeck himself was born to a Sinhalese mother and a German father. Despite being married to the mother, his father only accepted his son as adopted, and not as his birth child.

Throughout her compelling work on the colonial, Stoler follows her interests in 'carnal knowledge,' 'genealogies of the intimate,' and entanglements between the construction of race and colonial rule. Stoler explores notions of the domestic, of sexual relationships, modes of reproductive and care work, and the status of *white* women as well as Women of Colour. Primarily, she is concerned with communities of the Dutch, but also French and British, empire ruling on the Asian continent. Her aim is "to identify the regimes of truth that underwrote [...] political discourse and a politics that made a racially coded notion of who could be intimate with whom—and in what way—a primary concern in colonial policy" (2002b: 2). By examining different Euro-Asian unions in the Dutch colonies, Stoler outlines the varying handling of these unions depending on the different social groups and locations among the Dutch colonial communities:

> There were some Euro-Asian marriages among the colonial elite, but government regulations made concubinage a more attractive option by prohibiting European men from returning to the Netherlands with native wives and children. For the middling colonial staff, the East Indies Company firmly discouraged Euro-Asian marriages. Households based in Euro-Asian unions, by contrast, were seen to bear distinct advantages. Individual employees would bear the costs of dependents, mixed unions would produce healthier children, and Asian women would make fewer financial and affective demands. (47)

With regard to the Dutch government regulations, developed and adjusted in a shifting mode between theory and practice, my interest here is to explore the impact of John George Hagenbeck's family history on his personal and professional life. The senior John Hagenbeck (1866–1940) had started his career as an animal dealer and recruiter of performers, working for his father's half-brother, Carl Hagenbeck. In 1891, he settled in Sri Lanka for the first time, where he became a planter for globally-traded goods such as tea, coconuts, and gum. During the First World War, he had to flee from the British back to Germany, where he founded a production company for (exoticising) colonial films before, again, returning to Sri Lanka in the early 1920s. During this time, his son, John George Hagenbeck, became an important part of his business activities, as he was now also recruiting performers, escorting them on their sea voyages to the European continent, and accompanying them on their touring enterprises throughout Central Europe.[42] As indicated above, and in comparison to his father and other showmen, John George Hagenbeck's biographical background provides the entry point for locating inner ambivalences and their influence on his life and actions. Hagenbeck's role thus points to unstable colonial relationships. Underlining his distinctive character, Thode-Arora describes Hagenbeck in the following way:

> Despite his European sense of superiority and the paternalistic atti-
> tude of a showman, no other impresario shows as much respect for
> people's artistic abilities, and as much sympathy and compassion for
> the performers. At each show place, he would, most of the time, per-
> sonally take care of the food for the performers bearing in mind all
> their different religious beliefs and dietary habits. Together with his
> wife, he would fulfil the children's wishes for toys, special clothing,
> entertainment outings, or endearing cuddling. (1996: 114)[43]

Similar notions can be found in Hagenbeck's travelogue, which, however, has to be read with caution because of the glorifying picture he seems to have wanted to draw of himself. With regard to Stoler's work on gender and moral-ity, Hagenbeck's remarks on (sexual) morality, in particular, are worth a closer look. In one of the chapters, Hagenbeck talks about the Sinhalese performer named Bodiya who became famous for his spectacular stunt, which entailed putting his head in an elephant's mouth without getting hurt. Hagenbeck had known and worked with Bodiya for some time. He tells that Bodiya's shows had been so impressive that a North American circus hired him, which he ended up touring with for more than two years. During this time, Bodiya got married to a "young, blonde woman" (Hagenbeck 1932: 67) and would, at some point, contact Hagenbeck to ask him for a pending salary in order to pay for his and his wife's journey back to Sri Lanka. Hagenbeck refused to give the money to him—not least, as he explains, out of moral concerns.

> I would like to point out that, as a European, I would never pay for
> the passage of a white woman who got married to an Indian, since
> this woman cannot anticipate what she would have to expect over
> there. The Europeans would not keep her company, and the man
> would only receive insults by his compatriots because they would
> not accept him being married to a white woman. An educated
> Indian would never ask a European woman to follow him to his
> home country and conform to the local rules and customs. (67–68,
> my emphasis)[44]

Hagenbeck continues his moral reflection by elaborating more generally on the differences between Asia and Europe and their people:

> The boundaries dividing Asia and Europe are still too strong, and it will probably take thousands of years to bring about the kind of fraternisation that many people imagine. To understand Asians, you have to be Asian yourself, to understand us Europeans, you have to be European. (68)[45]

It is striking and, at the same time, not surprising that Hagenbeck feels the urge to judge Bodiya's 'immoral' behaviour, while he might not have condemned a marriage between a *white* man and a Woman of Colour, like the one between his father and his mother. Hagenbeck's confidence in claiming to know how and when boundaries between Asia and Europe would decrease derive from the fact that he, despite referring to himself as European, considered himself to be a 'natural' expert of the cultural differences between the two continents and their people. This notion resonates throughout his writing. The book consists of thirty-five illustrative photographs and sixteen chapters, in which Hagenbeck elaborates on his experiences as a merchant of animals and recruiter of performers, portraying the life of an impresario and showman. Essentially, the book comprises a compilation of different anecdotes Hagenbeck had witnessed while traveling with performers and animals from South Asia. Particularly when reading the first chapters of the book, I, as a contemporary reader, get the impression that Hagenbeck does not necessarily distinguish between the humans, goods, and animals he was doing business with. In objectifying terms, Hagenbeck refers to the colonial subjects he was recruiting overseas as 'material' and 'attractions.' He reduces them to their 'suitability' and 'effort of performing.'

> It is not always easy to find the right thing among the available *material*. Often, one has to be there in person in order to prove the candidate's *suitability*. In most of the cases, one is disappointed when one sees a highly recommended *attraction*. Then, the candidate is stunned when he gets a negative answer because he cannot understand that his *effort of performing* was not enough although his compatriots were applauding him. Here, the obvious opposite taste between Europe and India is evident. (8, my emphasis)[46]

Consequently, most of his narrating is not immune to generalising and pejorative, racialising and racist remarks on people from the Indian subcontinent. In some parts of the book, the author loses himself in details about how many snakes of a specific kind he shipped to which harbour on what day. Stereotypical comments about the performers' alleged superstitious beliefs or their apparent penchant for alcohol and narcotics shape other parts of his writing. Against the backdrop of the historical moment in which he was writing down his memories, it does not come as a surprise that his descriptions and remarks are traversed by, at the same time, paternalistic and belittling, as well as stereotypical and rather romanticising statements.

Retelling these fragments of the life stories of male members of the Hagenbeck family, it is once again striking that the archives contain so much information about their biographies, either from their own published writing, or from other primary and secondary literature. Would the fact that there is so much existing information about the male Hagenbecks be reason enough for me to avoid recounting their stories altogether? Or would such an attempt to redress the colonial imbalance merely create new gaps and absences? In this book, I am allowing these dominant, male sources to take up space (see also Chapter 3 and 6). At the same time, I am careful not to silence and gloss over the marginalised or missing sources, but to seize them in contrasting, punctuating terms. In this way, I hope to fit into Stoler's observation that "students of colonial histories now direct their archival energies to the instabilities and vulnerabilities of colonial regimes, to the internal conflicts among those who ruled, and to the divergent and diverse practices among them" (2002b: 10).

Rajamanikkam

Returning to the *Lautarchiv*'s files, LA 823 is one of two recordings of yet another person designated as female in the historical scripts. The personal information form belonging to her recording includes even less information than in Venkatamma's case (see figure 5-3). It was noted that her name was Rajamanikkam, that she was approximately twenty-five years old at the time of the recording, that she was born in a province named Koviljalayan, and that her first language was Tamil.[47] According to the form, Rajamanikkam's sound recording was made only ten minutes before Venkatamma positioned herself in front of the gramophone. Were the two women present during each other's recordings? Who else was there? Who would listen to and actually understand or relate to what they heard? The first part of the record contains a story narrated by Rajamanikkam. The second, much longer part consists of Tamil sayings read out by the speaker Sanmuga Soragar (approx. 1894–?), a peasant and school-teacher, who had transcribed the texts intended for the recordings. Sanmuga Soragar had already been recorded the day before, on September 28, 1926.[48]

Rajamanikkam, who, like Venkatamma, was illiterate, had told the alle-gorical story of the *Judgment of Solomon*—"without notes" (*frei erzählt*), as it is pointed out on the form. This remark indicates that all the other recorded peo-ple delivered their stories and texts with notes. However, many of the recorded people recited them by heart—ideally in the exact way they had practiced the texts beforehand, because a lot of them (especially among the many soldiers and civilian internees recorded in POW camps during the First World War) could barely read or write. This is one of the reasons why so many songs and poems were collected, since traditional folksongs and poetry could usually be sung or recited without notes. Many of the recorded people would be more willing and less shy singing a song, reciting a poem, or simply counting from one to twenty, than narrating a story or delivering something of one's own composition.[49]

In the further remarks concerning Rajamanikkam's recording it was noted that she felt timid during the recording process and that, as a consequence, she would not recite the story without alterations or interruptions. The typed annotation says:

Sound recording no. 823, part 1, transcription

of the document in Tamil writing = of the dictation of the speaker that was initially meant for the recording, not used. The dictation, recited without any interruptions or alterations, shows to what extent the speaker was feeling timid *during the recording.* (LAHUB, LA 823, my emphasis)[50]

What made Rajamanikkam timid? What or who caused her discomfort? Was it the studio situation or being in front of the technical apparatus? Was it being exposed to the scholars, becoming the focus of attention? One might think that the recorded people—as artists and performers—might have been used to being put on the spot, to performing songs, dances, and stunts in front of a predominantly *white* audience.

Lautabteilung an der Preussischen Staatsbibliothek, Berlin

PERSONAL-BOGEN

Nr. _____ *823* Ort: _____ *Alin*

Datum: _____ *29. 9. 1926*

Laut-Aufnahme Nr.: _____ Zeitangabe: *3 Uhr 50 Min.*

Dauer der Aufnahme: _____ Durchmesser der Platte: _____

Raum der Aufnahme: _____

Art der Aufnahme und Titel (Sprechaufnahme, Gesangsaufnahme,
Choraufnahme, Instrumentenaufnahme, Orchesteraufnahme): _____

1) Salomonisches Urteil, frei erzählt

2) Sprichwörter

Name (in der Muttersprache geschrieben): *1)* ... *Rājamānikkam*

Name (lateinisch geschrieben): *2)* ... *Sanmuga Sonagar*

(4736)

Vorname: _____

Wann geboren (oder ungefähres Alter)? _____

Wo geboren (Heimatprovinz)? _____

Welche grössere Stadt liegt in der Nähe des Geburtsortes? _____

_____

Wo gelebt in den ersten 6 Jahren? _____

Wo gelebt vom 7. bis 20. Lebensjahr? _____

_____

Was für Schulbildung? _____

Wo die Schule besucht? _____

Wo gelebt vom 20. Lebensjahr? _____

Aus welchem Ort (bzw. Sprachbezirk) stammt der Vater? _____

Aus welchem Ort (bzw. Sprachbezirk) stammt die Mutter? _____

Welchem Volksstamm angehörig? _____

Welche Sprache als Muttersprache? *Tamil.*

Welche Sprachen spricht er ausserdem? _____

Kann er lesen? _____ Welche Sprachen? _____

Kann er schreiben? _____ Welche Sprachen? _____

Spielt er ein Instrument (ev. aus der Heimat)? _____

Singt oder spielt er modern europäische Musikweisen? _____

Religion: _____ Beruf: _____

Vorgeschlagen von: 1. *F. Otto Schrader.*

2. *Kittogegen*

Beschaffenheit der Stimme: 1. Urteil des Fachmannes
                              (des Assistenten):

                            2. Urteil des Direktors der Lautabteilung
                              (seines Stellvertreters):

Die Lauturkunde wird beglaubigt:

Figure 5-3: Personal information form (*Personal-Bogen*), LA 823.
September 9, 1926. LAHUB.

Taking into account my interpretation of Venkatamma's interruption through her laughing, how can one read Rajamanikkam's behaviour? Did her behaviour not also—though in a completely different way—disturb the scientific procedure? A comment on one of the documents says that the phonogram—as the scholars called the records—would "strongly differ" from the text Rajamanikkam had dictated before. It was noted that the sound recording was "in many ways inarticulate" so that the scholars could not transcribe the sound properly, and had to leave blank spaces, which they intended to fill with the help of an "informed native" at some later point.[51] My focus on different types of interruptions and discontinuities shows, on the one hand, how limited the applied scientific practices actually were; how easily deviations from the rule could occur. On the other hand, it demonstrates how possibilities of subverting these practices (whether conscious and intended or unwitting and unintended) could emerge.

We can neither completely know what the recording situation actually looked like, nor can we answer the question whether—or rather to what extent—personal, cultural, or even bodily boundaries were disregarded. What seems certain, however, is that the situation was influenced by or even made possible due to the use—or rather abuse—of a colonial and social position of power on the part of the academics as well as showmen. While it seems unlikely that the people recorded were actually (physically) forced to stand in front of the technical device in order to sing or speak into the gramophone's horn, the recording situation has to be described in the light of Gayatri C. Spivak's notion of epistemic violence. With reference to Michel Foucault, Spivak defines an instance of epistemic violence as "the remotely orchestrated, far-flung, and heterogeneous project to constitute the colonial subject as Other" (1988: 280–281). Hence, epistemic violence describes forms of knowledge production of and about the *Other* that, at the same time, embody techniques of hegemony.

Looking at the acoustic project of the *Lautarchiv*, at the sound recordings' production, the technical and practical circumstances, and not least the relationship between power and knowledge, the aim here is to approach the discursive order in which the recordings were made. How did they become epistemic objects—objects symbolising the gendered and racialised modes of knowledge production which, resting on the *Other*, guaranteed the self-assurance of the scholars and the scientific credibility of their academic disciplines? What kind of possibilities of agency remained for the person recorded, the subaltern woman? Once more with reference to Spivak, one has to be careful not to come up with speculative assumptions about the recording situation and the actions and reactions by the recorded, not to mention the unreflective attempt to speak for or give voice to subaltern women today (Morris 2010). Again, I am wondering whether a certain intentionality can be observed and reconstructed from the sound recording itself, the accompanying scripts, or further archival material. What can be read into the recorded person being uncomfortable during the recording procedure? Or the academics trying to meticulously document everything that happened during the recording? The scholars' aim was to create a sound object identical to the written words. This is also the reason why the texts were read out or recited, although, from a present point of view, this practice undermined the 'natural' flow or an alleged 'authenticity' of the speech act and language sample.

With respect to the content of the recording, another hardly answerable question for me is why the recordists or Rajamanikkam herself chose the *Judgment of Solomon*.[52] Why did they pick this story, which, in most parts of the Western world today, is known as a parable of the Bible? While many consider the origin of the folktale uncertain, some argue that it has Indian roots and that, for a long time, it had just not been documented in writing (e.g. Gunkel 1987 [1917]). The historical translation in Tamil was written down by Sanmuga Soragar and was supposedly based on the dictation of the speaker, Rajamanikkam. The current translation, by Viswajith, is not based on the write up but on the recorded sound.

My translation into English of the historical German translation of the written file:

Someone had married two women: Both women had a child each. He died. Later, one of the children died too. Both women would breastfeed the other child and raise it. After getting into a fight with each other, both said: 'The child is mine, it is mine!' They went to the judge and said (the same). Because He (plur. maj.) did not know who was right, He said: 'Cut the child into two pieces and give each person one piece!' The one

Translation in accordance with the voice record:

A man had married two women. He died after the marriage. The two women had, in all, two babies. One baby passed away. The other baby was taken care of by being breastfed by both women. Then a fight arose between them. 'My baby, your baby' fight ensued between them. They went to the judge. The judge was confused and so offered to slice the baby into two and give one half to each woman. One of them agreed. But the other said 'Fine!' The other one said: 'The child must not be cut! Give it to her!' Upon hearing that, He knew that the child was hers, He gave it to her and punished the other.

said, 'I don't want that baby, give it to her.' So the judge said, 'The baby belongs to this (latter) woman' and gave the baby to the actual mother. The judge punished the other woman for creating the problem.

LAHUB, Personal information form LA 824.[53]

Translation by Viswajith (2019).[54]

This narration is the only acoustic trace of Rajamanikkam preserved in the archives today. A second acoustic source is registered as lost in the *Lautarchiv*'s digital catalogue. Until now, it has not been rediscovered either at the archive or at another institution or private collection. This very first recording made at the zoo on September 28, 1926, at two in the afternoon, contained a performance of a so-called "temple dance," including choral singing and instrumental accompaniment. On the front page of the personal information form concerning the recording LA 733, only one name, the name of Rajamanikkam, is mentioned (see figure 5-4). Who else might have been part of the ensemble? Who played the instruments? On the back of the form, under the rubric "special remarks," six different names and three instruments were noted in looped cursive as well as in Tamil writing (see figure 5-5). From the remarks, it can be assumed that, apart from three people playing different musical instruments, four—including Rajamanikkam—"bayaderes" were part of the performance.[55]

Even though there is documentation to suggest that more musicians and dancers were present, it cannot be known what the performance looked like. What did the limited radius of the gramophone's horn capture? Usually, the technical apparatus could not catch background sounds or any kind of soundscape except for the sounds of musical instruments played directly in front of the device. However, not only the technological conditions determined what the medium would record. Sterne argues that the reproducibility of a live performance always remained an illusion and a fantasy:

> The recording diaphragm and wax medium captured a specific performance, a performance designed and modified specifically for the purpose of reproducibility. The promise of mediation was made but not fulfilled: the mediation of the life music and the dissolution of that mediation into transparency are at best imagined. The

Lautabteilung an der Preussischen Staatsbibliothek, Berlin

PERSONAL-BOGEN

Nr. ....   Ort: ~~Lagerraum des Zoo~~ *Berlin*

                                                   Datum: *28. September*

Laut-Aufnahme Nr.: *LA 733*   Zeitangabe: *2 Uhr Nachmittags*

Dauer der Aufnahme: .... Durchmesser der Platte: ....

Raum der Aufnahme: *Lagerraum des Zoo*

Art der Aufnahme und Titel (Sprechaufnahme, Gesangsaufnahme, *Tempeltanz*
   Choraufnahme, Instrumentenaufnahme, Orchesteraufnahme): ....

Name (in der Muttersprache geschrieben): [Tamil script]

Name (lateinisch geschrieben): *Rajamānikkham*

Vornahme: ....

Wann geboren (oder ungefähres Alter)? *ca. 35 Jahre alt*

Wo geboren (Heimatprovinz)? *Koṟil pālayam (Trichinopoly)*

Welche grössere Stadt liegt in der Nähe des Geburtsortes? *"*

Wo gelebt in den ersten 6 Jahren? ....

Wo gelebt vom 7. bis 20. Lebensjahr? ....

Was für Schulbildung? ....

Wo die Schule besucht? ....

Wo gelebt vom 20. Lebensjahr? ....

Aus welchem Ort (bzw. Sprachbezirk) stammt der Vater? ....

Aus welchem Ort (bzw. Sprachbezirk) stammt die Mutter? ....

Welchem Volksstamm angehörig? ....

Welche Sprache als Muttersprache? *Tamil*

Welche Sprachen spricht er ausserdem? ....

Kann er lesen? .... Welche Sprachen? ....

Kann er schreiben? .... Welche Sprachen? ....

Spielt er ein Instrument (ev. aus der Heimat)? ....

Singt oder spielt er modern europäische Musikweisen? ....

Religion: .... Beruf: ....

Vorgeschlagen von: 1. *F. Otto Schrader, Prof. John Hagenbeck jr.*
                          2.

Beschaffenheit der Stimme: 1. Urteil des Fachmannes
                             (des Assistenten):

                             2. Urteil des Direktors der Lautabteilung
                             (seines Stellvertreters):

Die Lauturkunde wird beglaubigt:

Figure 5-4: Personal information form (*Personal-Bogen*), LA 733. Front side.
September 28, 1926. LAHUB.

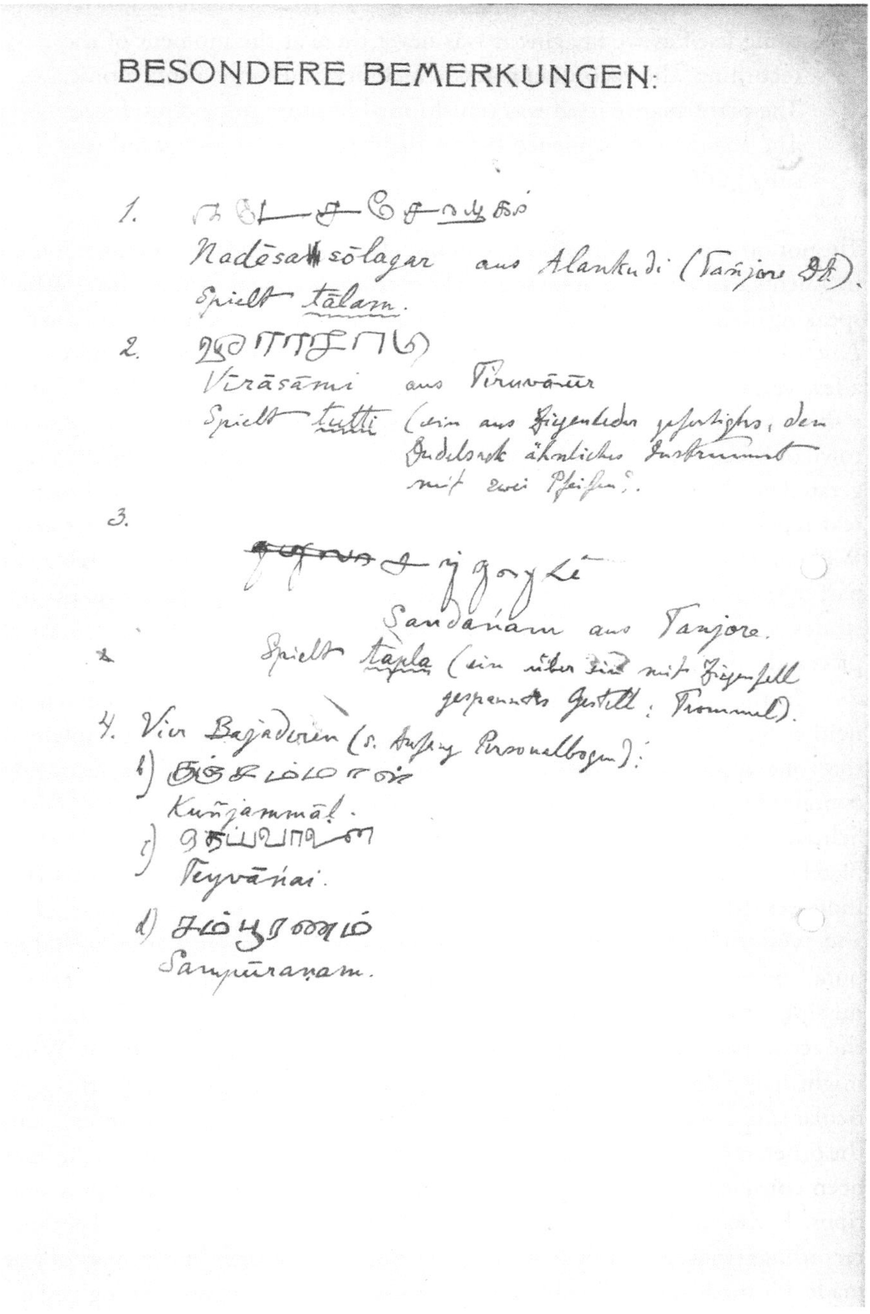

BESONDERE BEMERKUNGEN:

1. [handwritten Tamil script]
   Nadêsa sôlagar   aus Alankudi (Tanjore Dt).
   Spielt tālam.

2. [handwritten Tamil script]
   Vīrāsāmi   aus Tiruvārūr
   Spielt tutti (ein aus Ziegenleder gefertigtes, den
   Dudelsack ähnliches Instrument
   mit zwei Pfeifen).

3.

   [handwritten Tamil script]
   Sandanam aus Tanjore.
   Spielt tapla (ein über ein mit Ziegenfell
   gespanntes Gestell: Trommel).

4. Vier Bajaderen (s. Anhang Personalbogen):
   b) [handwritten Tamil script]
   Kuñjammāḷ.
   c) [handwritten Tamil script]
   Teyvānai.
   d) [handwritten Tamil script]
   Sampūraṇam.

Figure 5-5: Personal information form (*Personal-Bogen*), LA 733. Back side.
September 28, 1926. LAHUB.

thing itself as we imagine it was never there at the moment of the recording; the recording is less a memory and more a mnemonic. The performance itself was transformed in order to be reproduced. The abstraction happened before the cylinder spun or a word was sung. (2003: 320)

The notion of the recording as a mnemonic also refers to the other kinds of source fragments that give one hope to get closer to the moment of recording. When speaking of different kinds of sources, the collection of press reports housed at the *Lautarchiv* is a valuable additional source, even though the collection only covers a few years of the archive's institutional history. In one of the folders, I found a short newspaper clipping of a daily newspaper located in the small German town of Braunschweig. Published on October 11, 1926, under the slightly exaggerated heading "Sound Recordings of Indian Language Monuments," the short text reports that the head of the Prussian State Library's Sound Department, Wilhelm Doegen, had been conducting sound recordings in Tamil and Telugu as part of the zoo's *India Show*. Furthermore, it was written that apart from poetry, stories, and sayings, the recordists Doegen and Schrader would record musical pieces: the dance of the 'bayaderes' and the dance of the devil.[56]

In the accompanying scripts, the language expert Schrader commented neither on the dancing nor on the music. It was probably him who explained that one could only translate the monophonic beginning of the recording containing a performance of the 'temple dance' presented by Rajamanikkam. Schrader also claimed that the polyphonic rest—"even though maybe not completely justified"—could be described as "sheer onomatopoeia."[57] This remark indicates that the performance itself—on the textual level—defies the scholars and Western listeners, appearing as unapproachable. On another level, and in purely material terms, the sound recording remains inaccessible because it went missing. This circumstance symbolises yet a different kind of gap in the archive: the accompanying scripts still exist but the actual sound object is absent. What might have caused its loss? Who abstracted it from the archive? As this particular sound recording was also mentioned in the news report and differs from the other, mostly linguistically-motivated recordings, the sound file might have been considered as rather prominent and therefore used for public presentations. Earlier in the same year, Doegen would play some of the collection's recordings (most probably from the collection of recordings of prisoners of war made during the First World War) at an event called an 'Indian Evening' organised by the German Foreign Association of Academics (*Deutsch-ausländischer*

Akademiker-Club), founded in 1923.[58] Might Doegen have used this particular recording for similar occasions or lectures? Or did he trade the copies of the recording with other institutions? Since the exchange of records was a common practice, one can never be sure that the sound recording LA 733 will not reappear someday at some unexpected place.[59]

Conclusion

I began this chapter by problematising the tendency of reproducing dichotomies and modes of binary thinking both in historical accounts and in gender and postcolonial theory. By still being, to some extent, tied to thinking in terms of hetero-normative and dichotomising categories, but at the same time also questioning those categories, my aim was to shed light on the gendered and racialised notions in and of the *Lautarchiv*'s collection. I showed that the applied scientific techniques were first and foremost construed to record, document, and categorise the gendered (male) norm. Why, then, did Schrader record the voices of two female individuals? How did the decision to include the two women come about, while still disproportionate to the seven men who were included in the same context? Whereas Thode-Arora (1996: 115), in her work on *Völkerschauen*, emphasises the attempt to include women and children in order to show a comprehensive and 'authentic' picture of the communities' family lives, this was not a primary concern of the scientific aims pursued at the *Lautarchiv*.[60] In their writing, neither Doegen nor other scholars involved expressed the opinion that the lack of female speech samples could be considered an incomplete part of their general research. Concerning his anthropometrical work in Austro-Hungarian POW camps during the First World War, the anthropologist Rudolf Pöch (1870–1921) argued that racial characteristics could be 'diagnosed' regardless of gender and that his research at the camps could not be regarded as imbalanced. Similarly to Pöch (1916: 989), who had called the war situation a one-of-a-kind opportunity for his scientific research, Doegen and his colleagues would consider *Völkerschauen* (among other occasions) an appealing possibility to explore and record foreign languages in Berlin—'on location.' In this chapter, I thus highlighted the interrelationship between *Völkerschauen* and academic research and its entanglements with commercial interests and the reproduction of racial and racist stereotypes, reciprocally constructed both in public/popular spheres as well as in the scientific literature of that time. In 1973, Talal Asad observed that it was, and still is, the "colonial power structure [which] made the object of anthropological study accessible and safe" (1995 [1973]: 17)—not only in the colonies but in the metropolis, too. I regarded it as important to expand on the history of *Völkerschauen* at the Berlin Zoological Garden and discuss the history of sound artifacts compiled as part of, and actually made possible due to, the ethnographic event culture of the time. Further, my elaboration on the history of the Berlin Phonogram Archive and on the role of the musicologists Stumpf and Hornbostel, led me to my own approach to the two—or rather three—sound recordings of the *Lautarchiv* I focused on in this chapter.

Thinking in terms of dominant and subaltern sources, I tried to concentrate on marginalised and aberrant traces, which are nonetheless present in and constitutive of the colonial archive. The traces of the recorded subjects Venkatamma and Rajamanikkam seem in many ways marginalised: on a structural level, the two women are impeded from being able to speak. As women, they form an exception both in the archive and in the scientific data compiled. As illiterates, they were unable to read everything the scholars would want them to recite. However, as I was able to show, the variations between what had been recorded and transcribed entailed a certain form of productivity and maybe even agency. Finally, as performers, they may not have been hired for their artistic abilities, but as companions of their husbands or as care providers for their children.[61]

At first glance, the historical subjects only emerge in mediated, and mere objectified, manners: mentioned in the scripts, pictured on a photograph, or recorded on wax. At a second glance, and with the help of a close listening, I demonstrated that the recorded subjects do not only appear as objects. On the contrary, I revealed that they play an important part in shaping—in terms of both enabling and unsettling—the scientific practice and the production of epistemic objects. In this regard, the notion and the division of the dominant and the subaltern no longer seemed to be attributed that easily. Thus, both the method of a close listening and the investigation of different kinds of sources helped me to negotiate the gendered and racialised modes of the archive and colonial knowledge production. By including a critical examination of the controversial figure of John George Hagenbeck, I negotiated the meaning of allegedly dominant, male, and written documents, as opposed to silenced, female, and acoustic sources. My focus on Hagenbeck's writing and his role as a marginal and hybrid figure acted, on the one hand, as a counterbalance to the *Lautarchiv*'s archival material, its own order and logic. On the other hand, it was an attempt to show unstable aspects of those assumed to be powerful. Referring to Stoler's work on intimacy and sexuality in colonial rule, I showed that the Euro-Asian union of Hagenbeck's mother and father and his relationships with the people he hired influenced his views on (sexual) morality and, more generally, his personal and professional life.

Throughout this book, it is crucial for me to bring into focus different notions of the archive's gaps and silences. As mentioned before, one major gap addressed in this chapter stems from the fact that men and male sources dominate the *Lautarchiv*, like many other historical archives. Consequently, the material produced, collected, and archived for scientific purposes was based upon the notion of the male as the scientific norm. This notion also relates to epistemic violence as—to put it in Spivak's words—"an account of how an explanation and narrative of reality was established as the normative one" (1988: 281). In addition, as Spivak makes clear: "the narrow epistemic violence of imperialism gives us an imperfect allegory of the general violence that is the possibility of an episteme" (287). In the context of the *Lautarchiv* and with regard to modes of knowledge production, this 'general violence' refers to the power of excluding and at the same time being in need of and constituting the *Other*.

On the level of materiality, I discussed further gaps emerging in the personal information forms and scripts. In most cases, it is the written rather than the sound material that provides the point of departure for my archival research. I make more sense of the collected data concerning the recorded person, as well as of the historical transcripts and translations than of the archived sound. Due to my lack of language expertise, which is a recurring issue in this book, I do not understand the sound recording's content (see also Chapter 3 and 6). In the case of the missing recording LA 733 of the 'temple dance,' however, I was struck by the absence of the sound, combined with the fact that this recording probably contained the singing voices of more than one woman. Hence, the archival order is not just shaped by the decisions and selections of what is going to be archived, and by the categories chosen for documentation. It is also shaped by the omission and lack of consideration of certain categories and, ultimately, by what has and has not been preserved, and what can and cannot be accessed today.

6
Collective Listening

Early Black Presence and Historicity

zitendawili zishile,	*The riddles are already done,*
na hadisi zimalize	*and the stories are finished,*
ngano zihitimile,	*and the fables are completed.*
msisaili zote pia.	*Don't ask for more.*

(Unknown author: ca. 1895)[1]

In recent years, public awareness of and scholarship on histories of colonial migration(s) to Germany have increased. Likewise, the number of works accounting for early Black presence and historicity in Germany before the second half of the twentieth century has grown (e.g. Aitken and Rosenhaft 2013a/b; Ayim, Oguntoye, and Schultz 1986; Bechhaus-Gerst 2018b; Diallo and Zeller 2013; Grosse 2003). One figure prominently associated with these histories is Bayume Mohamed Hussein or Husen (1904–1944).[2] His biography is deeply entangled with Germany's colonial past. The different chapters of his life define turning points in terms of both Hussein's own chequered biography and Germany's military (see Chapter 3), public (see Chapter 5), and academic (the focus of this chapter) legacies.

Born as Mahjub bin Adam Mohamed in Dar es Salam in 1904, Hussein became a child soldier during the First World War.[3] As so-called Askari soldiers, Hussein and his father, like many other colonised men and boys, joined the German colonial army in the colony of German East Africa, which includes parts of present-day Tanzania, Burundi, and Rwanda. In 1929, Hussein came to Germany to claim an outstanding payment for himself and his deceased father. After the Foreign Office rejected Hussein's claim, he began working as an actor and waiter in the Berlin entertainment sector. With the world economic crisis and the rise of the National Socialists, Hussein witnessed how the exoticising amusement industry became an increasingly precarious employment, especially for Black people and People of Colour (Lewerenz 2017: 153–157). Finally, yet importantly for this chapter, Hussein held the position of a so-called African language assistant at Berlin University. Mainly serving to train future colonial officials, military personnel, and merchants, Hussein co-taught Swahili courses at the Seminar for Oriental Languages (*Seminar für Orientalische Sprachen*) from 1931.[4] When he started a family with a *white* woman, it was not least for this reason that he was exposed to racial discrimination, leading to his arrest by the *Gestapo* in 1941. After three years of imprisonment, Hussein died in the concentration camp *Sachsenhausen* in 1944.

Set against the background of these historical dates, it is obvious that one cannot recount Hussein's biography without considering Germany's colonial and fascist past and its global repercussions. Subsequently, drawing on the figure of Hussein appears in some sense as a culmination of the main arguments of this book. By exploring minoritised histories, sources, practices, and subject positions, it aims to not simply add missing aspects to established narratives, but rather to draw attention to always already entangled conditions. As emphasised before, the book is concerned with tracing these conditions as they materialise in parts of the acoustic holdings of the *Lautarchiv*. In this way, I wish to contest and transform hegemonic readings and, at the same time, avoid the danger of merely re-narrating history under the premise of an additive model (Bhambra and Santos 2017: 4; Randeria 1999a: 273) or even a recovery imperative (Arondekar 2009: 99).

This chapter revolves around yet another shellac record housed at the *Lautarchiv*. The sound recording contains the voice of Bayume Mohamed Hussein. It consists of an ethnographic text[5] about Swahili wedding traditions recited by the speaker in Swahili in July 1934. This archival source constitutes a compelling but nevertheless ambiguous expression of a colonial subject in the metropolis of Berlin. On the one hand, the acoustic file appears as a material expression of a Black person living and working in Berlin, produced and archived at the hegemonic knowledge institution of the university. On the other hand, listening to the voice of Hussein evokes a poignant experience of sensing a long-gone presence. An investigation of this particular sound object allows me to concentrate not only on historical figures; it also offers the possibility to focus on the practices connected to the production of the sonic document (see Chapter 2).

This chapter draws in more detail on the concept of *sensitive collections* as set out in my introduction. Developed by Margit Berner, Anette Hoffmann, and Britta Lange (2011), the concept indicates that, when dealing with anthropological collections, it is not only the collectibles themselves that are to be examined. The histories of their production, transmission, and circulation are also relevant. Only this broader framing, Lange (2011a: 19) argues, allows for shedding light on the practices, power relations, and contexts of epistemic or literal violence connected to anthropological collections and the institutions storing them. For a long time, in museum and academic contexts, only human remains and material of sacred or ritual significance were considered sensitive material. While there is no doubt that this material appears as the most drastic result of (colonial) contexts of injustice, it seems, nonetheless, important to broaden perspectives on anthropological knowledge production and its archives. Ultimately, this also entails reconsidering the understanding of what constitutes anthropological and ethnographic collections in the first place. Anthropological depots (be they in museums, universities, research institutions, or private homes) not only hold the knowledge attached to ethnographic artifacts. They also contain knowledges in the form of measuring data, mouldings, visuals, or sounds of bodily and thus personal features.[6]

For thinking through sensitive collections, the issue of how to deal with anthropological data in the present and future is a crucial point of consideration. Likewise, the question of who should be included in this discourse is of particular importance since, in most cases, sensitive collections are invisible and inaccessible to wider circles and the public. While I have frequently touched upon this discourse in previous parts of this book (see Chapter 3 and 5), this chapter adds further relevant aspects to the ongoing debate. In what follows, I continue the discussion on how the *Lautarchiv*'s colonial holdings could or should be treated today. Drawing on the concept of sensitive collections represents one dimension of this purpose; reflecting on how I approached and dealt with Hussein's recording is yet another. Apart from compiling and examining a variety of archival and primary sources, and following the attempt to take into account what cannot be found in the archives (either because information went missing or because it was never intended to be documented), my approach in this chapter can be described as joint endeavour. Proceeding from the conceptual framing, this chapter discusses methodological decisions I deemed necessary in order to engage with Hussein's recording in a *sensitive* and *collaborative* manner.

In order to approach Hussein's testimony today, and in order to make sense of the sonic source from a postcolonial point of view, I sought out collaborators. Once again, I not only lacked language skills and cultural knowledge, I also did not want to repeat an act of epistemic violence by perpetuating an exclusive power over interpretation. Together with the anthropologist and Swahili speaker Jasmin Mahazi, I therefore began working collaboratively on the acoustic trace of Hussein. A colleague had introduced me to Jasmin, and I first met her in person at the *Lautarchiv* in 2017. At that time, Jasmin was conducting research on Swahili sound recordings stored at both the *Lautarchiv* and the Berlin Phonogram Archive as part of a research assignment at the Ethnological Museum of Berlin. When I contacted Jasmin again in the summer of 2018 and asked her whether she was interested in working with me on the acoustic testimony of Hussein, she was about to complete her dissertation at the Berlin Graduate School for Muslim Cultures and Societies. Together, we set out to study the complexities associated with the sound file and its (social) content by following Ann L. Stoler, who urges us to attend both to "colonialism's archival content, but also to its particular and sometimes peculiar form" (2002a: 157; see also Chapter 4). Assuming that there are multiple layers of meaning to Hussein's sound recording, both in terms of content and form, Jasmin and I thought that not just the two of us, but several people and ears, should explore these layers. For this reason, we decided to organise a *collective listening* workshop in Berlin. Aiming to bring together different expertise, perspectives, and positionalities, Jasmin and I invited Swahili speakers from and to Berlin to take part in this workshop. The practice of collective listening aims at turning away from traditional academic knowledge production and towards a multiplicity of positionalities and bodies of knowledge. The workshop invited Swahili speakers to listen to the sound recording collectively and to share their listening experiences. In this way, it was our wish to enable a critical and sensitive engagement with Hussein's hitherto little-known recording.

In the course of the chapter, I touch upon a number of issues by understanding the sound recording as a point of reference for, on the one hand, the involved protagonists and applied research practices, and on the other hand, placing both against the background of broader discourses about colonial knowledge regimes and the colonial metropolis. Similar to Chapter 3 and 5, the following switches between microanalysis of moments and people in and of the past, and the study of larger structures and contexts. Wishing to focus on the making of the sound recording, but being aware of the difficulties that occur when aiming to reconstruct historical events, the chapter shows that even fragmentary (or in fact missing) information can say a lot about the historical figures present and active in the realm of the *Lautarchiv*, illuminating the discursive relations and hierarchies among them. Most central to this chapter, however, is the account of the collective listening, which offers another way to reflect on how to deal with colonial sounds in postcolonial Berlin—on how to remember Bayume Mohamed Hussein.

'How, then, can his story be told?'

mkusanyize hadisi,
mandishile na warisi,
ilimu zenye kiasi
pia mwalizipapia.

You've collected stories,
written by the descendants,
valuable knowledge,
also you consumed it.

The circle of experts invested in the histories of Black presence and historicity in Germany includes Paulette Reed-Anderson, Katharina Oguntoye, and Marianne Bechhaus-Gerst, to name but a few. Reconstructing Hussein's life story by consulting an impressive number of archives and sources, scholars and activists alike have done a pioneering job (e.g. Bechhaus-Gerst 1997, 2007; Oguntoye 1997a; Reed-Anderson 1997, 2000 [1995]). From an academic point of view, tracking down the existence of people of African descent living and working in Germany, and thus attempting to incorporate their stories into German historiographies, represent important milestones. Yet the effort has been even more important for challenging, and slowly shifting, dominant narratives and collective memories. For too long, stories of Black subjects in Germany were not told and remembered, but silenced and excluded. However, even after decades of considering the Black diaspora before the second half of the twentieth century, many open questions remain. Obviously, this is not only the case with regard to Hussein's path through life, but also with respect to many other people and their biographies.

A major gap in the already recounted stories on Hussein's life is the omission of a detailed examination of the voice recording, which can be found at the *Lautarchiv* under the serial numbers LA 1373 and 1374 (referring to the front and back side of the record).[7] According to the archival scripts, this sound file was recorded on July 25, 1934, at the Institute for Sound Research (*Institut für Lautforschung*), newly established at the then Friedrich Wilhelm University in that same year.[8] Arnulf Schroeder (1911–1945) supervised and edited the recording. At the time, Schroeder was a doctoral candidate supervised by Max Vasmer (1886–1962) and Diedrich Westermann (who had both been members of the Sound Commission[9] since 1928).[10] Schroeder had majored in Slavic literature and languages, while studying African languages and cultural studies (*Afrikanistik*) only as a minor subject in the German cities of Münster and, later, Berlin. Though mainly invested in phonetics and linguistics, he recorded the speech sample of Hussein for language learning purposes. Below, I come back to the short textbook edited by Schroeder containing a transcription, transliteration, and translation of the recording.

More than eighty-five years later, the then common practice of recording Hussein appears as an act of objectification, of turning a person into an object of research meant to represent both a language and an anthropological sample. Accordingly, one of my first questions was whether the archived file merely stands for modes of objectification and racialisation. These modes emerge not only against the backdrop of the recording activities and practices at the Institute for Sound Research, but also when exploring more broadly the role of the language departments' non-*white* teaching staff. Whereas Hussein started working as a so-called language and teaching assistant at the university only in 1931, many others began their appointment long before him, starting in 1887 (Pugach 2007). How, I had to ask, is my current account of Hussein any different from practices back then, when I also consider his sound recording as my point of departure and object of research?

Film director and scholar Eva Knopf raises a similar question. In her documentary film *Majub's Journey* (2013), as well as in her academic writing, Knopf is especially concerned with Hussein's role as a (background) actor in German colonial and propagandistic film productions.[11] Knopf's point of access for her cinematic work is the visual footage of Hussein, stored and made accessible in (national) archives. Explaining the dilemma she feels caught up in, Knopf writes:

> Showing these images also means updating the racist stereotypes shaping Hussein's film roles and carrying them into the future. Not showing them means forgetting Mohamed Hussein in the archives, or at least refraining from the attempt to write Hussein back into (film) history. *How, then, can his story be told?* (2018: 84, my emphasis)[12]

Similarly, I ask what postcolonial futures for the *Lautarchiv*'s records may look like. This concern is particularly important in light of the fact that the

Lautarchiv's material is the result of, and served as evidence for producing and shaping, colonial knowledge. Pointing to their "inexorable historical embeddedness in the logics of colonial power," Brian K. Axel states, "archival documents may be understood as simultaneously the outcome of colonial processes, integral to the continuing formation of such processes, and the condition for the production of historical knowledge" (2002: 14). I therefore plead for revisiting the archival documents in order to understand and challenge the logics of colonial power and alter the conditions under which historical knowledge and cultural memory are produced. In a different vein, Paul Basu and Ferdinand de Jong waver between two possible decolonial moments in their thinking about the colonial archive. On the one hand, they ask whether accepting archival decay ought not to be taken as a sign of decolonisation. On the other hand, they see possibilities of "second lives" (2016: 2) of colonial archives by means of a re-appropriation by postcolonial subjects. Through my engagement with Hussein's recording and the practice of collective listening, I wish to add further aspects to the debate of decolonising the *Lautarchiv*.

Created under Sensitive Circumstances

kwa hila zenu mpete,	*You got the things through your tricks.*
hamkuona utete,	*You never met any objection,*
killa neno mtetete	*every word was discussed,*
na daula yote pia.	*and all the powers as well.*

> The sound recordings of prisoners of war are undoubtedly a sensitive collection – a collection created under sensitive circumstances, taking advantage of a military and colonial position of power, violating cultural, religious, social, and possibly also physical boundaries of the speakers. (Lange 2012: 65)[13]

Voice recordings compiled in POW camps (see Chapter 3) or at sites of *Völkerschauen* (see Chapter 5) are *sensitive collections*. Yet applying the term to an audio object, made in an academic setting at a university, of a person who considered himself a consultant and teacher of Swahili, may not appear so straightforward—at least at first glance.[14] This ostensible ambiguity is one of the reasons why I return to the concept of sensitive collections, which was touched upon in the book's introduction, only now, against the backdrop of the last of my three case studies. As Britta Lange suggests in the epigraph to this section, a sensitive collection should be defined as such if and when its production and circulation can be traced back to the abuse of a (colonial) position of power and the violation of cultural and/or other boundaries. This chapter shows that once we look more closely at the recording of Hussein, it becomes clear why the sound object and its content must be considered sensitive; it shows why the document needs to be treated, researched, and presented (if at all) with caution and sensitivity.

The concept of sensitive collections has been important for dealing and coming to terms with heritage described as contested or difficult. It has been crucial particularly in light of anthropological and ethnographic collection practices refined and applied during the second half of the nineteenth and until the middle of the twentieth century. The authors of the book *Sensible Sammlungen* (2011), Berner, Hoffmann, and Lange, developed the concept with respect to German-speaking contexts and anthropological collections housed at German and Austrian institutions of knowledge. Since its first release, the concept has been applied in various contexts and to other types of collections (e.g. Brandstetter and Hierholzer 2018; Fründt 2019; Hamm and Schönberger 2021a).

In their volume of essays, Berner, Hoffmann, and Lange refer their use of the term sensitive collections back to the 1986 version of the International Council of Museums' (ICOM) *Code for Professional Ethics*.[15] In a revised version 2004, under the heading "Culturally Sensitive Material," ICOM considers "collections of human remains and material of sacred significance" as sensitive. Although Lange (2011a: 15–20) begins the volume's first essay by drawing on international claims for, and already realised, repatriations of human remains stored at German and Austrian institutions, one of the main arguments of the book is to complicate the understanding of what counts as culturally sensitive material. Wishing to rethink the contested category of objects, the authors aim at expanding the definition by including anthropometric accumulations of measuring data, descriptions of bodily features, photographic and moving images, plaster casts, and, last but not least, sound recordings of living people. They consider not only physical artifacts as sensitive but also the applied strategies and procedures constituting this material. In this way, they wish to account for the oftentimes violent situations and problematic circumstances under which the records and collections were compiled. In other words, the advocated widening of the ICOM's code of ethics is more concerned with the associated orders of power and knowledge than with the objects themselves. It is for this reason that Lange pleads for a sensitive treatment of the artifacts' backgrounds and histories of appropriation.[16]

Apart from the debates on the restitution of human remains, the discussion about objects and artifacts which are, on ethical and legal grounds, wrongfully stored in Western museums, universities, and archives, has gained a lot of attention in recent years (e.g. Förster et al. 2018). Attention has grown not only among academics and activists, but also in wider political and public spheres, both in national and international terms.[17] In 2018, Anna-Maria Brandstetter and Vera Hierholzer covered many of the debate's aspects in an edited volume, in which they brought together a whole range of positions and texts by scholars, curators, and museum professionals. The contributions ranged from studies on Nazi-looted art and Nazi propaganda material to illegally traded or destroyed antiques from West Asia, and from colonial and ethnographic collections to human remains and sensitive nature objects.[18] While all essays focused on specific collections or even single objects, historian Christian Vogel suggested some general reflections in the volume's introductory part.

In his approach to sensitive objects, Vogel (2018) lays his focus on the process of *how* objects *become* sensitive. Similar to Berner, Hoffmann, and Lange, he states that objects are not sensitive of their own accord, but that certain contexts turn them into sensitive material. Vogel makes a case for concentrating on the objects' historicity and the diverging meanings ascribed to them, depending on time and context (31). From his point of view, and with respect to accounts in cultural history, one has to ask for whom, when, under which conditions, and due to which practices an object becomes sensitive (32). Accordingly, Vogel emphasises the transformative and mobile character of objects. Particularly with regard to museum and scientific collections, gathered items were turned into objects of knowledge (*Wissensdinge*). They were integrated into existing scientific paradigms, which reinforced certain systems of ordering and classification. This observation leads Vogel to speak of modes of de-sensitising when, for instance, collectors, scholars, or the museum staff removed sacred or ritual objects from their original contexts of use and converted them into research objects or objects of exposition. This perspective is easily translatable to sound objects and the de-contextualisation of ethnographic knowledges. Below, I will return to the notion of sensitive knowledges when drawing on the content of Hussein's sound recording.

In recent years, as Vogel points out, more and more scholars and museum experts seek to re-contextualise objects and piece together the fragmentary information attached to them. Often, the holding institution does not know much about single objects or, at times, entire collections. Given these attempts at re-contextualising, Vogel sees potential for re-sensitisation. With reference to anthropologist Larissa Förster (2013), however, he also contends that intentions to re-contextualise objects have not usually arisen from within institutions. Förster makes clear that this trend has rather originated among circles of post- and decolonial scholars, activists, or descendants.

In the remainder of this chapter, my aim is to draw on the aspects that render Hussein's voice recording a sensitive object and part of a larger sensitive collection and archive. Ensuing from the approaches of Berner, Hoffmann, and Lange as well as Vogel, I show that Hussein's sound file not only bears witness to disparate orders of power and knowledge, but also to the sound object's transformative condition depending on when—and by whom—meaning was or is attached to it (see also Chapter 7). In this respect, the notion of the sensitive is twofold: conceptually, it refers to the representation of collections in terms of their problematic provenance and their asymmetrical mode of production. Further, it refers to the object's embeddedness in a (colonial) knowledge system. But the notion also relates to sensitivities in the literal sense, to the violation of feelings, intimacy, and piety. This is the case when culturally sensitive issues and details are treated in an insensitive, disrespectful, or hurtful manner, as the participants of the collective listening workshop expressed.

Bayume Mohamed Hussein and the Institute for Sound Research

bassi wacheni jawabu
la kujibu makatibu,
nandike nini, sahibu?
na yote mmesikia.

Stop to give an answer,
to reply to the officials.
What should I write, my friend?
You've heard everything.

The personal information form (*Personal-Bogen*) archived together with Hussein's audio recording includes some basic information, which nevertheless contained important facts for compiling his biographical trajectories (see figure 6-1).[19] One learns that Hussein was born on February 2, 1904, in Dar es Salaam where he lived until he was nine years old. He received basic schooling in Swahili and Arabic, both in Dar es Salaam and in the coastal towns of Lindi and Mikindani, where his family resided after 1913. His father was from Khartoum in Sudan. His mother came from the Kilimanjaro region in Tanzania. From the form, one also learns that his father was a Nubian soldier, whereas Hussein's occupation is listed as "Askari, now waiter."[20] Conducting extensive research on Hussein's biography, Marianne Bechhaus-Gerst (2007: 37) revealed that his father, Adam Mohamed, was recruited to the so-called East African Campaign. In 1914, Hussein joined his father's company, being ten years old at the time. Bechhaus-Gerst assumes that Hussein's father was one of the victims of the Battle of Mahiwa fought between German and British Imperial forces in October 1917. Hussein's father might thus not have survived the hostile actions of the First World War.[21]

Little is known about the period of more than ten years from the end of the First World War until Hussein's arrival in Germany in 1929. Bechhaus-Gerst points out that there is generally a lack of sources about what happened to Askari soldiers after the war. What is known is that Hussein spent time in Zanzibar, where he signed up to become a waiter on one of the German steamers plying between the East African coast, Cape Town, and Hamburg. Eventually, one of these ships brought Hussein to Europe. A few months after settling down in Berlin, Hussein found employment as a waiter at the leisure facility *Haus Vaterland* (House of the Fatherland). The multi-storeyed building, located at *Potsdamer Platz* in the centre of the capital and then owned by the Kempinski Hotel Group, comprised a number of restaurants and bars with a rich entertainment program.[22] Established in 1928, the place of amusement was well-known for its commercial exoticism, hiring many Black artists and employees of Colour. Since the late 1920s, the employment circumstances for Black performers and People of Colour deteriorated as a response to a tight job market and general economic and political crisis, changing for the worse when the National Socialists seized power.

Weaved into the storyline of an experimental film by Hito Steyerl (1998), both Hussein and *Haus Vaterland* take on a prominent role in the film's complex formal structure.[23] Examining transnational migration movements, the video essay correlates a variety of historical layers relevant for the histories of public space(s) in Berlin over the past two hundred years, ranging from colonial and fascist to post/socialist entanglements. Excavating these different, seemingly forgotten layers, the filmmaker herself defines her visual practice as an archaeology of amnesia (Steyerl 2003: 47). Diachronically shedding light on the use of 'foreign' labour, the film contrasts the precarious situation of performers of Colour employed in the entertainment sector of Weimar Germany with racist sentiments of German construction workers fearing the competition with migrant

Abschrift

Lautabteilung (staatl. Lautinstitut) Berlin NW 7

PERSONAL-BOGEN

Nr.: ....   Ort: Berlin ....

Datum: .... 25.7.34 ....

Laut-Aufnahme Nr. LA 1373 ....   Zeitangabe: .... 11 h. ....

Dauer der Aufnahme: 4 Min. ....   Durchmesser der Platte: ..... 30 cm .....

Raum der Aufnahme: ..... Institut für Lautforschung ....

Art der Aufnahme und Titel (Sprechaufnahme, Gesangsaufnahme,

Choraufnahme, Instrumentenaufnahme, Orchesteraufnahme): ... Sprechaufnahme ....

.... Hochzeit der Suaheli I.

(Ndoa ya harusi ya Wasuaheli)

Name (in der Muttersprache geschrieben): Bayuma Muhamed Husein ....

Name (lateinisch geschrieben): ....

Vorname: Bayuma ....   Anschrift: Bln-Heinersdorf, Idunastr. 42

Wann geboren (oder ungefähres Alter)? 22.2. 1904 ....

Wo geboren (Heimatprovinz)? .... Daressalaam ....

Welche größere Stadt liegt in der Nähe des Geburtsortes: Daressalaam ....

Wo gelebt in den ersten 6 Jahren? .... Daressalaam ....

Wo gelebt vom 7. bis 20. Lebensjahr? seit 1913 in Lindi, Mikindani

Was für Schulbildung? *Suaheli u. Arabisch (Elementarschule)*

Wo die Schule besucht? ...... Daressalaam, Lindi ....

Wo gelebt vom 20. Lebensjahr? Daressalaam, seit 1930 Berlin ....

Aus welchem Ort (bezw. Sprachbezirk) stammt der Vater? Khartum ....

Aus welchem Ort (bezw. Sprachbezirk) stammt die Mutter? Kilimanjaro ....

Beruf des Vaters? .... Soldat ....

Welchem Volksstamm angehörig? (Vater Nubier) ....

Welche Sprache als Muttersprache? .... Suaheli ....

Welche Sprachen spricht er außerdem? deutsch, etwas arabisch, etwas englisch, etwas
indisch.

Kann er lesen? ...... ja ....   Welche Sprachen? Suaheli, deutsch, arabisch ....

Kann er schreiben? ..... ja ....   Welche Sprachen? Suaheli (lat. und arab. Schrift)

Spielt er ein Instrument (evtl. aus der Heimat)? ... Trommel ....

Singt oder spielt er moderne europäische Musikweisen? ...... nein ....

Religion: Mohammed. ....   Beruf: Askari, jetzt Kellner ....

Vorgeschlagen von: 1. Prof. Westermann ....

2. A. Schröder ....

Beschaffenheit der Stimme: 1. Urteil des Fachmannes
(des Assistenten):

2. Urteil des Direktors der Lautabteilung
(seines Stellvertreters):

Die Lauturkunde wird beglaubigt:

gez. Westermann

Figure 6-1: Personal information form (*Personal-Bogen*), LA 1373.
July 25, 1934. LAHUB.

labourers during the years after the Berlin Wall came down. Tackling questions of the state and citizenship, the film also shows how Hussein's passport was revoked and substituted by a so-called alien passport in 1933. Two years later, Hussein lost his job at *Haus Vaterland*, presumably after a colleague accused him of embezzlement (Bechhaus-Gerst 2007: 78–81). After this, Hussein had to make a living out of casual employment, small parts in colonial exhibitions and film productions, and temporary contracts as an assistant at the university.

Returning to the university and the archived sound recording of Hussein, it must be noted that the written files housed at the *Lautarchiv* do not entail a transcription or translation of the recording's content. By studying the personal information form, one solely gets to know the sound recording's type and title: "Wedding of the Swahili" (*Hochzeit der Suaheli*). An edited version of the recording's content can be found in a textbook, officially published in 1935. As part of the so-called Sound Library (*Lautbibliothek*), consisting of short textbooks featuring transcriptions, transliterations, and translations of a wide range of languages and dialects, Hussein's text formed the basis for phonetic and language learning.[24] When looking at other Swahili grammars and dictionaries edited during the nineteenth and early twentieth century (some of which are also referenced in the textbook's introduction), it does not seem unusual to collect stories and poetry or (as in this case) ethnographic texts for the aim of language instruction (e.g. Meinhof 1928; Steere 1870; Velten 1910). However, after first consulting Swahili speakers in Berlin, they immediately said that they find it, in fact, unusual for a person—and a male person in particular—to speak so bluntly about marriage traditions and all their concomitant practices.[25] Usually, this would only happen among family members or close friends, possibly even only among people of the same age or gender. Such traditions would not be recounted that openly—not to mention put in writing, or even recorded and archived. Once I heard this, it was clear to me that the asymmetrical circumstances allowing for the making of the voice recording are not the only ones fraught with problems. All the more, the recording's content must be considered sensitive. On a further note, the recording also got me thinking about applied scientific practices in general, and about ethnographic practices in particular.

As a standard practice 'in the field,' missionaries and later ethnographers would ask (usually male) informants to elaborate on cultural traditions and everyday life practices. This information was then included in the writings of the particular anthropologist or missionary, travel writer or 'explorer.' The knowledge, commonly received from a single—considered to be representative—informant, was oftentimes not collated with others, but rather abstracted

Figure 6-2: Mohammed Bayume Hussein and Arnulf Schroeder in front of the recording device. 039-7022-15. Bildarchiv der Deutschen Kolonialgesellschaft, Universitätsbibliothek Frankfurt am Main.

and generalised to being valid for an entire community, language group, geographical region, and even, all too often in an essentialist sense, all Black people. As a result, a distance was created both between the informant and the gathered information, and between the ethnographer and the informant, who most often remained anonymous. Torn out of context in terms of source, time, and place, knowledges and histories were positioned in opposition to the naturalised figure of the researcher. Considered to be an authoritative and 'objective' observer, information and fact gatherer, the *white* and male researcher usually remained—in a refined manner—invisible and unquestioned.

In Hussein's case, however, and even though the text was scripted and then recited during the recording session, one listens directly to the informant or "narrator" (1935: 3), as Schroeder writes in his preface. Ostensibly, one perceives the ethnographic content in an unmediated way and not in a written or otherwise transmitted form. The first, yet soon revised, assumption Jasmin and

Figure 6-3: Mohammed Bayume Hussein and Arnulf Schroeder in front of a map. 039-7022-41. Bildarchiv der Deutschen Kolonialgesellschaft, Universitätsbibliothek Frankfurt am Main.

I made was that Hussein might have delivered the text in an informal setting before recording it. We thought that Hussein perhaps dictated it in a one-to-one situation, an impression supported by the staged photograph displaying Hussein next to the recordist Schroeder.

Probably taken at the Institute for Sound Research, the photograph shows the two men sitting in front of a bookshelf storing metal cans that might contain wax cylinders (see figure 6-2). In the foreground, on the right side of the photograph, one can see a wooden pedestal to which the gramophone's turntable is attached. Hussein, wearing a suit, is holding a sheet of paper with both of his hands. He faces the document; his mouth stands slightly open as if he is reading to Schroeder, who is sitting to his left, looking at Hussein. Schroeder is also wearing a suit. On his lapel one can see a Nazi pin—a black swastika on white background. I remember that, when I first encountered the photograph, printed in poor quality on a book page, I could not immediately decipher, nor believe, that the pin really carried the emblem of a *Hakenkreuz*. In front of Schroeder lies a stack of papers. Wearing headphones and holding a pen in his right hand, he acts as if he is writing down what he is hearing. Was he listening to Hussein's voice directly or via the headphones? Having the staged character of the photograph in mind, one wonders why Schroeder is wearing headphones in the first place, since Hussein does not speak into a microphone or the gramophone's horn.[26]

In a second photograph, we see Hussein and Schroeder standing in front of a wall-mounted map of the African continent, as one can read in the map's bottom left corner (see figure 6-3). Turning his back to the camera, Hussein is pointing with both of his hands and two fingers to Dar es Salaam, his place of birth. Schroeder, to Hussein's right, does not face the map but inclines his body down to Hussein, as if he is trying to make eye contact with him. I am describing these visual sources in all their details, as I assume that they were orchestrated in a meticulous manner. I imagine that the photographs were staged in order to draw a specific picture of the two displayed protagonists, to give a specific sense of their performance of academic knowledge production.

Whether or not the actual recording situation was anything like the first photograph leads one to believe remains, however, uncertain. Assuredly, a script was drawn up forming the template for the sound recording and ultimately the textbook. Presuming that the audio recording came about with the intention of producing Swahili language-learning material, the selection of the text prompts many questions that were also tackled by the workshop discussants. From correspondences stored at the university archive, it is possible to verify that Schroeder was not the only one involved in the editing process of the publication—though, unsurprisingly, it is solely his name that is mentioned on the cover. Hussein had also been consulted during the editing, and then admonished by the secretary to hand in his corrections in time, though Schroeder also had to be reminded several times to adhere to the deadlines.[27] It is in a similar vein that historian Sara Pugach argues that:

> although Europeans considered themselves the primary 'authors' of African language grammars, dictionaries, and Bibles, it is more apt to say that the texts were *co-authored* by Africans, since they supplied most of the raw data in their role as informants. (2018: 19, emphasis in the original)

Apart from the phonetic text, transcription, and German translation of Hussein's recording, the Sound Library's publication contains two additional short texts allegedly also authored by Hussein. The two texts bear the titles "The Role of the Woman" (*Die Rolle der Frau*) and "The Work in the Fields" (*Die Feldarbeit*). Contrary to Jasmin's and my first assumption, the other workshop participants soon agreed that all three texts seemed so uncommonly detailed (and thus 'typical' German), suggesting that a German scholar composed all of them. Below, I come back to more of the listeners' conclusions.

In addition to the ethnographic texts, Schroeder included lists of words and numbers in Swahili, though they were recorded in a different Swahili dialect. The lists stemmed from the colonial soldier Asmani Ahmat (approx. 1892–?) from the Comoros, a French colonial soldier who had recited them in the German POW camp in Wünsdorf, close to Berlin, in November 1918.[28] The recording belongs to a series of sound files recorded by the Africanist Martin Heepe (1887–1961), who was a member of the Royal Prussian Phonographic Commission during the First World War. Later, Heepe would become a staff member of the Prussian State Library's Sound Department and Hussein's superior at the Seminar for Oriental Languages. In his preface, Schroeder explains that he added the list of words because the audio recordings and accompanying text edition should serve as a teaching aid for language instruction. He writes that he had found Ahmat's record containing Swahili vocabularies in the archive's holdings. Schroeder also mentions a, presumably dictated, handwritten text does not perfectly correspond with what is heard on the record. Combing through the *Lautarchiv*'s files, it can be assumed that Schroeder was referring to a recording of the same speaker (Asmani Ahmat) recorded by the Africanist Carl Meinhof (1857–1944)[29] one year earlier, in November 1917.[30]

At this point, it seems especially important to ask why publishing Swahili content by speakers of completely different backgrounds and places of origins did not seem as a contradiction.[31] It almost leads one to believe that neither the content nor the linguistic and phonetic nuances really seemed to matter with respect to the purpose of language learning. Other textbooks, also based on sound recordings of prisoners of war recorded during the First World War, had been published as part of the series of the *Lautbibliothek* since 1926. Yet, in most cases, there is no mention of the date and—from a present point of view— the problematic circumstances under which the recordings came into being. Apparently, the editors did not consider the inclusion of these details meaningful or necessary. For me, the crucial question is how a public institution, such as the university, should handle these kinds of publications and their accessibility, being well aware of the recordings' difficult origins and content (see also Fründt 2019: 136–137).[32] Without wishing to neglect the fact that this, of course, also applies to many other publications entailing contents ranging from outdated scientific findings to racist, discriminatory, and/or propagandistic accounts, I still believe that the university bears a particular (ethical) responsibility with regard to this specific body of publications produced at its very own research facilities.[33]

Diedrich Westermann: 'Facts are wanted, not opinions.'

asili twali wqjinga,   Formerly we were fools.
werevu wetu maninga,   Our wisdom was superficial.
kana watu si wqjinga   But if people were not fools,
hatukuwa watu pia.   we wouldn't have been dehumanized.

In order to shed light on the practices and presuppositions connected to the recording of Hussein, taking a closer look at university professor Diedrich Westermann and his writing seems particularly worthwhile. For both the history of the *Lautarchiv* as well as the then emergent field of African studies, Westermann is a prominent figure. In the following, the focus will primarily lay on one short but very revealing text by him.

In the article titled "The Missionary as an Anthropological Field-Worker," first published in English in 1931, Westermann elaborates on his version of and vision for missionary work. For him, missionary work implies both the willingness to study indigenous life and to serve scientific interests.[34] In his opening passage, Westermann emphasises that his "remarks are not addressed to specialists, but to those Europeans and Africans working in Africa who have for professional reasons an interest in getting to know the native better and, if possible, in making this knowledge available to a wider circle" (164). In his further elaboration, one gets the impression that Westermann, despite the fact that he published the text in an academic journal, merely wrote it as a recommendation for missionaries. The article describes how to gather knowledge from and about colonial subjects in order to serve both the political purpose of "creating a new religious, moral, and often social order" and the "science of ethnology" (164).[35] In the past, Westermann explains, opportunities to produce anthropological knowledge in places where missions were set up were too often missed.

Before proceeding to an academic career, and becoming one of the first full professors and hence a key figure in the establishment of *Afrikanistik* (African language and cultural studies) in Germany, Westermann had been trained as a Lutheran missionary.[36] His occupation at the North German Bremen Mission brought him to the German colony of Togo in 1901, 1903, and again in 1907 (Meier 1995: 1). The linguistic research he conducted during his time in Togo is said to have triggered his main interest in Sudanese languages. Throughout Westermann's academic life, Peter Kallaway (2017: 873) argues, these trips were of particular importance for his scholarly work. When trying to grasp Westermann's ambiguous academic habitus, it is striking to observe how he distinguishes between the intentions of missionary work aiming at transforming "the inner life" (Westermann 1931: 164) of the people, and scholarly interests trying "to save what can be saved" (165). While Westermann does not generally speak against missionary movements, he nevertheless holds the opinion that conventional missionary work 'destroys' vernacular practices in ways that hinder the implementation of a new social order (see also Chapter 7). In other words, he favours the gathering of knowledge in, and detailed study of, colonised regions in order to best implement missionary ethics and colonial ideals.

Westermann conveys the impression of being an expert in both anthropological fieldwork and missionary work. His article thus pursues two goals: the improvement of missionary work, by emphasising the importance of studying vernacular life, and the opportunity for anthropologists to benefit from lay people working in the field. At the same time, I understand Westermann and his writing as emblematic for the fact that, particularly in the emergent field of African studies, professional distinctions were still rather fluid. Many considered it beneficial that Westermann combined both professions, and was therefore able to connect research on linguistics and phonetics to anthropological and theological, political and historical questions.[37]

Outlining anthropology's legacy of the institutionalisation of fieldwork in the late nineteenth and early twentieth century, James Clifford draws on the notion of the 'armchair anthropologist.' Clifford explains how the anthropologist used to depend on ethnographic information gathered by other people or, if at all, only undertook shorter (museum) expeditions. It was only gradually that the anthropologist started turning to more in-depth and interactive methods. Clifford suggests that metropolitan scholars of the time, such as Franz Boas (1858–1942) or Bronisław Malinowski (1884–1942), felt the need to dissociate their practice and knowledge production from the one of the missionary, colonial officer, or travel writer, described as the "disciplinary Other" (1997: 195). "The fieldworker's professional difference from the missionary, based on real discrepancies of agenda and attitude," Clifford states, "has had to be asserted against equally real areas of overlap and dependency" (196). I argue that Westermann, as opposed to many others, did not seem to feel the need to defend and legitimate his professional authority in the same way, since he saw himself aligned with both spheres. Yet his sense of being an academic, and therefore superior to the missionary, still seems salient in his writing. On the one hand, Westermann emphasises that the missionary should learn from the anthropology scholar. On the other hand, he is nonetheless making a case for the missionary endeavour, valuing the extended period of time the missionary would spend in one particular place, studying and speaking local languages. Throughout his academic career, Westermann endorsed the detailed and comparative study of vernacular languages and indigenous life as the key for mission work as well as colonial government. This ties in with other positions of the time, promoting the British doctrine of indirect rule, which implied a "culturalist/adaptationist view of colonial policy" (Kallaway 2017: 878). According to Kallaway, Westermann took up an entangled position at the crossroads of religious, scientific, and ideological views. Kallaway is Emeritus Professor at the University of Cape Town and has published widely on the history of education, science, and politics in late (British) colonial Africa. With his special interest in the inter-war years and the interaction between missionary educators, philanthropists, and colonial governments, it does not seem surprising that the German missionary and linguist Diedrich Westermann, a then internationally well-known figure, became the focus of Kallaway's attention. Likewise, it does not come as a surprise that it was an international scholar, and not someone from within the German academic landscape, who sharply pointed out Westermann's ambiguous position towards colonial and Nazi policy.

In his article, "Diedrich Westermann and the Ambiguities of Colonial Science in the Inter-War Era" (2017), Kallaway elaborates on Westermann's belief that successful missionary work primarily builds on understanding the people's way of life and studying their language. Considering the increasing impact of modernisation, Westermann was of the opinion that it had to be the task of the discipline of anthropology to document indigenous cultures before further transformation could not be rolled back. This also corresponds with the ideas of the 'salvage paradigm,' which I will draw on in more detail in the next chapter. Kallaway shows that Westermann believed that colonial rule should be guided by scientific facts and findings (and not by opinions, as stated in this section's heading, which cites Westermann). For Westermann, this understanding embodied the core of any kind of social development. Kallaway's observations underscore the entanglements of colonial science and policy as personified by Westermann and other figures of the time.[38] While Kallaway suggests that Westermann rarely commented on issues of concrete political measures, I argue that Westermann's attitude towards, and actual influence on, colonial policy-making nevertheless manifests in his lectures and writing. In a short article, published during wartime in 1941, Westermann clearly states his view on anthropology as a colonial science and its role for National Socialist's colonial policy:

> For us, anthropology has to be, in a deeper sense than before, a colonial science. This is a requirement of the colonial responsibility, which will be taken on by Germany after the end of the war. Anthropology's task is to study indigenous peoples [*Naturvölker*], as the colonial task is also concerned with them. Colonial policy, particularly in Africa, is native policy. (1941b: 1)[39]

Coming back to Westermann's article from ten years earlier, and to the question of the acquisition of both immaterial and material knowledge, it is striking that Westermann draws a distinction between the practices of acquiring language skills and collecting ethnographic artifacts. Accordingly, he explains, "ethnographical objects can be collected without linguistic knowledge" (1931: 168). First-hand information, by contrast, should ideally be compiled in the informant's first language, if necessary, with the help of an interpreter or translator. Here, Westermann's emphasis on linguistic work, as opposed to the study and acquisition of material culture, stands out. However, with regard to the sound recording at hand, I argue that the composition of Hussein's texts (elaborating on cultural practices of the Swahili without specifying local peculiarities or the origin of this knowledge) can be compared to the practice of collecting ethnographic objects, rather than to that of intense fieldwork and language studies. Oftentimes the purchase of ethnographic objects (be they works of art, ritual or religious artifacts, or everyday items) was contingent upon practical conditions and coincidence, or determined by emerging commercial interests and local (art) markets that served and depended on Western collectors, merchants, and scholars. Eventually, this also relates to the understanding of the complex histories of colonialism in more general terms, taking into account heterogeneous fields of interaction. "African resistance, collaboration, and accommodation in all their forms," Gaurav Desai states, "are as much part of the history of colonialism, both on the social as well as epistemological plane, as are the various actions and intents of the European colonizers" (2001: 4).

Another striking aspect of Westermann's article is his distinct attitude towards collecting sensitive information in missionary and ethnographic contexts. Westermann subscribes to the view that "no one must ever be urged to say more than he really wishes or feels he is at liberty to say; he must on no account be put in an awkward position" (1931: 170). Further, he elaborates that "it is inadvisable to try to elicit information regarding matters about which by native law the native is forbidden to speak, or about which, for other reasons, he would prefer to remain silent" (171–172). On yet another note, he warns that, with regard to information of a ritual nature, "the investigator [...] should be very discreet in the use he makes of the knowledge" (172). Nevertheless, one cannot help but notice that Westermann is not completely against gaining and using such knowledge. At a later point, he writes that people might share certain information only with informants belonging to the same community. In such a case, Westermann recommends consulting someone "who could go back again to the same people, should it be necessary to fill up gaps in the story or to ask about matters the native does not like to speak about before a European" (173).

These statements, which seem paradoxical from a present point of view, did not, however, appear incompatible back then. They appeal to Westermann's understanding of a certain set of ethics and humanistic ideals. Yet, for me, these assertions highlight his stance of cultural racism. In a similar vein, cultural anthropologist Sabine Jell-Bahlsen describes Westermann's contradictory positioning as oscillating between paternalism and sheer racism. "In spite of his positive, if paternalistic, attitude towards Black Africans," she states, "his political views never veered from official doctrine" (1985: 324). This perception becomes particularly apparent when considering the radically shifting political climate in Germany during Westermann's professional career. Once a colonial empire, striving after colonial powers like France, Britain, and other imperial states, Germany was showing great efforts to regain power in colonial territories after the First World War.[40] With the coming into power of the National Socialists, these efforts did not abate (at least until 1943) but were rather on the upswing, receiving additional funding and the support of academic expertise. Concerning the growth of the general and scientific racisms during the Nazi period, Jell-Bahlsen notes: "Like the Nazis, Westermann constantly identified race with culture and language, and although his examples were drawn from Africa, his theories were easily adapted to Europe" (324). Although Westermann's racist sentiments may have been defined culturally and linguistically, and were, for that matter, distinct from biological racism, they rested on people's alleged inferior linguistic and cultural development (see also Pugach 2012).

In spite of the fact that Westermann never became a member of the NSDAP, the advancement of his academic career during the Nazi period cannot be denied.[41] As many other university members, Westermann represents someone whose academic career benefited from, and whose professional agenda was highly influenced by, the changing political environment (Lange 2017c; Mischek 2000; Stoecker 2008a). Comparing Westermann to Eugen Fischer (1874–1967), a prominent proponent of racial superiority and Nazi eugenics, anthropologist Udo Mischek (2000: 71) depicts both men as scholars who utilised their research strategically to gain political impact and to advance their academic authority. Yet in the course of de-Nazification, Westermann's political enmeshment barely seemed to matter.[42] Westermann did not face major personal or material disadvantages after the Second World War, and could soon continue with his scholarly activities. It became, however, difficult for him to receive funding for new research projects, given the different priorities of the Russian authorities. For the most part, the existing secondary literature on Westermann shows the difficulty of unravelling his ambivalent position before, during, and after the Second World War (e.g. Eckert 2010; Heyden 2003; Meier 1995; Stoecker 2008a). While Kallaway convincingly emphasises Westermann's ambiguous actions and his fateful role under the Nazi regime, his text nonetheless gives the impression that Westermann's story of academic success is not to be completely dispelled. According to Stoecker (2008a: 19), one reason for this is that large parts of scholarship still recount histories of science as heroic *his*tories of progress. These are heroic stories in which complicity and racism hardly fit.[43]

Black Teaching Assistants between Objectification, Complicity, and Agency

wakangia na Wazungu
wakatuawinia na mafungu
wakatonesha matungu
na miji kuikimbia.

Then the Europeans came.
They scattered us into groups.
They added more pain to us,
and we fled the towns.

Even after the First World War and the end of Germany's formal colonial rule, the academy remained an incisive space where the continuing effects of colonialism, exploitation, and racism stood out. This is one of the conclusions in Stoecker's (2008a: 85) comprehensive account of the history of African studies in Berlin between 1919 and 1945. Stoecker's observations can be linked to the racialised figures of language and teaching assistants (*Sprach- und Lehrgehilfe*[44]), who held an ambiguous status in and for post/imperial Germany. Considered as the best educated among colonial subjects, willing to contribute to and collaborate with the colonial project, their appointments within the university were, at the same time, located at the bottom of the academic scale. Facing discrimination and harassment, they had to survive on non-permanent and usually precarious part-time contracts. Reduced to linguistic, phonetic, and anthropological research objects, but simultaneously indispensable as informants and teachers, they need to be understood as a constitutive part of academic research and teaching. As laid out by Pugach, the teaching assistants must be considered integral to the project of colonial knowledge production in imperial Germany. Pugach carried out extensive research on the history of colonial linguistics and the role of Black teaching assistants in the heartlands of colonial science in Germany—namely, Hamburg and Berlin.[45] For the period between 1814 and 1945, she comprehends that the teaching assistants "may have been despised or looked down upon because of their 'race', but it was difficult to deny their pedagogical importance" (270: 120).

At the time, members of the university did not usually problematise or reflect on modes of objectification and racialisation. The opposite was the case. Westermann, for instance, described the language assistants as *his* 'objects.' Against the backdrop of the financially precarious situation of German academia after the end of the First World War, he writes in a letter to a representative of the North German Missionary Association (*Norddeutsche Misssionsgesellschaft*):

> Poverty does not allow us to keep native lecturers. However, I found a way to replace them, at least with respect to the linguistic tutorials. The ministry granted credit for the purpose of consulting natives, who are staying in Berlin permanently or temporarily, as *objects* for *my* tutorials for a longer or shorter period of time. In this way, I get natives from all parts in Africa, and not only them, I have also had Japanese, Chinese, Hungarians, Russians, Lithuanians as *objects*. (Westermann to Schlunk, April 9, 1923, my emphasis)[46]

Are such statements the expression of Westermann's general authoritarian and paternalistic attitude? Or, does the paragraph reveal the mindset of the time, of the *white* scholar being able to consult and 'use' colonised or allegedly inferior subjects for any possible purpose? Certainly, the unequal distribution of symbolic and economic capital, as well as the ambivalent dependency on the part of the academics on their assistants' knowledge, has always shaped—and continues to shape—the relationship between *white* scholars and Black language assistants.

While official archives provide a number of sources, such as the above-cited correspondence, in which Westermann and others talk *about* the teaching assistants, documents containing voices by the assistants themselves commenting on their status and occupation in Germany can rarely be found.[47] As other scholars have emphasised, the status of the language assistants is very difficult to shed light on, due to the paucity of primary sources (Knopf 2018: 87–88; Pugach 2007: 120; Pugach 2012: 142–143; Stoecker 2008a: 49). How then, I ask, might it be possible to illuminate their role in relation to processes of colonial knowledge production be it in terms of the production of anthropological and linguistic treatises, or the actual language instructions at the Seminar for Oriental Languages? From archival documents, one can deduce which, and how many, lessons non-Western teaching assistants were giving. However, what the lessons and interactions between the instructors and students might have actually looked like can hardly be reconstructed. Comparing the roles of Black and *white* lecturers, Pugach makes the following observation:

> One of the most significant features in both classroom and laboratory was the division of workload between Germans and Africans. The Germans were the lecturers who 'translated' African grammar and vocabulary into terms students could understand. The African's main job was to demonstrate correct pronunciation and elocution. Meinhof believed that their roles could not be reversed. (2018: 24)

Pugach continues her comparison, elaborating on the setting 'in the field,' in contrast to the situation at Carl Meinhof's Phonetics Laboratory in Hamburg:

> The African at the laboratory shared some similarities with the informants who had worked with missionaries and administrators in the field, but this comparison can go only so far. In the field, Africans explained the particulars of their language to the Europeans. In the laboratory, Africans did not comment on the grammatical or morphological characteristics of the languages, merely speaking words from them so that they could be repeated back. (24)

What is conveyed in these juxtapositions is the clear allocation of tasks and particular roles to be filled: the *white*, male lecturer as the knowledge carrier, who uses the assistant as a 'living phonograph' and nothing else.[48] How, then, can one picture the relationship between a Black lecturer teaching *white* students who were meant to live, work, conduct research in, or secure[49] colonial territories, once Germany reclaimed its colonies—as was the ambition of the growing group of colonial revisionists during the 1920s and 1930s? Did the colonised teacher, in this way, become an accomplice of the (future) coloniser? Hussein, for his part, had been an active agent in the colonial revisionist movement in Berlin since his arrival in Germany in 1929. Many archival and visual sources document Hussein's participation in various events of the German Colonial Union or comparable institutions (Bechhaus-Gerst 2007: 82–93).[50] However, there is also evidence of other lecturers being members of the anti-colonial movement in Germany.[51] In both scenarios—collaborating with but also challenging the colonial project—anti-/colonial subjects trusted that eventually they would be given equal civil rights (e.g. Kuck 2014).[52] Pugach comprehends the assistants' complicated status, ranging from racialised research subjects and objects, collaborators and accomplices, to agents of their own life plans, in the following way:

> African assistants both rebelled against and complied with the images of their languages and people that the Germans presented. The *Lektoren* therefore both subverted and confirmed European notions of race; they questioned their placement in racial hierarchies but also, in some instances, reasserted those same positions for personal political or economic gain. (2012: 20, emphasis in the original)

Collaborations between the Colonial and the Male Gaze

kwa kizungu andikeni	*Write in European style,*
wasia na khati za deni,	*wills and credit documents.*
lugha lolote tieni,	*Use any language.*
pia tutazipokea.	*We will accept them.*

In addition to the previously applied modes of listening in Chapter 3 and 5, and as introduced at the outset of this chapter, the following comprises yet another methodological mediation, namely *collective listening*. The initial reason for approaching the recording through collective listening was quite simply my lack of expertise in Swahili. As in the previous case studies, my access to Hussein's historical audio recording was limited to appraising the quality of his voice, describing the noise of the recording device, and noticing pauses, hesitations, or other irregularities on the record. I thus detected limitations in my attempts to make sense of the things I heard, or study the (fragmentary) written material attached to the archived sound. Can I trust the historical translation? What does a person's voice, their stumbling, hesitating, or pausing convey? How does one assess the relationship between the content and the way the content was vocally transmitted? In order to approach these practical and intersubjective questions, I sensed that it would be worthwhile and, in fact, necessary to consult other people. Thus, with the help of Jasmin Mahazi, we invited Swahili speakers to engage with the sound recording and share their views on the (sonic) material and its (social) content. A collaborative approach and analysis allowed our engagement with the source material to be broadened and intensified.

I perceive collective listening as a way to renounce traditional academic knowledge production, by recognising different bodies of knowledge and experience as relevant for the meaning and interpretation of sound. Kate Lacey (2013: 1–4), for example, historicises different modes of listening, proving that listening is an active rather than a passive practice. Focusing on the politics of listening, the media historian argues that listening collectives ought to be understood as discursively constituted groups of people interacting with and in social spheres. Following her emphasis on listening publics, I understand collective listening as a mode in which the qualities of plurality and intersubjectivity matter. In other words, listening is seen, here, neither as a merely receptive mode of consumption nor as an isolated, individual experience. By contrast, collective listening is understood as a situated and actively engaging, yet open-ended practice.

In total, eight participants (including Jasmin and myself) took part in the workshop, which was organised at Humboldt University in January 2019.[53] At the time of the workshop, all participants were involved either in the academic field of African studies and/or active members of the East-African diaspora in Germany.[54] After listening to Hussein's sound recording collectively, our conversation began as follows:

Asmau Nitardy: *He was definitely reading something out loud. From a book.*
Lutz Diegner: *Yes, it wasn't his text.*
Vitale Kazimoto: *It wasn't written by him, he had to read it.*
Stephanie Lämmert: *Exactly.*

Lutz Diegner: *So one would say, an absolutely unnatural speech situation. And then this sing-song is very special.*
Asmau Nitardy: *Yes, exactly.*

These comments show that the listeners' first responses focused on the way in which the speaker vocalised the things heard on the record: Hussein read out, he did not speak freely. The words and sentences sounded "unnatural;" other remarks described them as "impersonal," as spoken "without feeling"—"without a feeling for the language." Hussein's intonation was referred to as a peculiar "sing-song," meaning the emphasis of the so-called stress accent of the Swahili language.[55]

For me—the only person in the room without an understanding of Swahili, but nonetheless familiar with the sound recording and the sing-song tone referred to—, it was striking that all listeners were in agreement after their first listening experience, thus reinforcing each other's observations. I had provided the participants with some basic information about the speaker's biography and the poorly documented recording situation in 1934. Some of them were familiar with Hussein and his story; some had knowledge of the sound recording before Jasmin and I invited them to take part in the workshop, and I had sent them the digital version of the sound file in preparation for the event. The recorded text is divided into two files, corresponding with the front and back side of the record. Both soundtracks contain little more than four minutes of sound (which was comparatively long, given the technical capabilities of the time). The text itself consists of fifty-one sentences, each describing one step or act of a Swahili wedding, beginning with the groom's parents searching for an adequate future wife, and concluding with remarks on how husband and wife should treat each other when sharing a home.[56]

While the listeners focused mostly on the speaker's voice and the pace and flow of his delivery, their initial remarks also relate to the recording's content. Why did Vitale Kazimoto and Lutz Diegner feel so certain that the text was not Hussein's, that it was not written by him? Why did Asmau Nitardy declare that "he was simply 'used' to reproducing it as sound"? These impressions derive not only from the "unnatural," "hesitant," "distanced," and "impersonal" voice, as described by the participants. The listeners shared the opinion that a man of African descent, born and raised in regions of Eastern Africa at the beginning of the twentieth century, would not deliberately choose to talk about intimate details of Swahili wedding customs in public. "Did he have to do this," one of the participants asked, "or was it his decision to talk about this topic?"

Like the workshop discussants, I also directed my interest towards the recording's content. Asmau Nitardy, who wondered whether Hussein had chosen the topic of the recording himself, described the content as "culturally insensitive." To her, it was "unusual" and "not so natural" that a *man* would share intimate details about Swahili marriage—an event she considered to be a "woman's affair." Before attending the workshop, she had listened to the sound file together with her husband and her mother, who had had similar reactions. She told us that her husband had a sense of embarrassment, and that her mother felt a little uncomfortable while listening to the record. Her mother speculated that the recorded voice may have been a European who learned a Swahili tinged with a Tanzanian accent. Recognising the practices indicated in the text, her Swahili mother considered it odd that a man would formulate and record the information in such vivid detail—an extent of detail people would go into, but usually not publicly.

I have deliberately chosen not to reproduce the actual text. To me, it is problematic enough that this particular text and many others of its kind, elaborating on cultural traditions in a disrespectful manner and with an insensitive choice of words, are accessible in public university libraries without contextualisation. While it is my aim to contextualise and historicise the recording, I still ask my readers to exercise a sympathetic understanding towards my decision to leave out the exact wording. Certainly, there are ways to talk about Swahili matrimonial practices without infringing on the rights to privacy and intimacy, in a manner less invasive and compromising.[57] My decision not to reproduce the content stems from the conviction that the text is offensive, hurtful to people, and should not be displayed. For most of the participants, it was especially the choice of words and details that drew a negative picture of something that, in other contexts, would be associated with pride and honour. For them, the language was emblematic of the European perspective and the colonial gaze seeking spectacle and alterity. Consequently, I think the more important question is what the historicity of the sound recording can tell us about regimes of representation and colonial knowledge production. In addition, the listeners' observations led to a questioning of the access policies of the archive. What does the expressed unease portend for the current archival practices of the *Lautarchiv*? What does it mean for the future of the Humboldt Forum? Should the recording still be accessible to anyone who requests it from the archive? Would it be enough to include some sort of disclaimer or warning as part of the online catalogue to avoid the possibility of painful listening experiences?[58] Who would, or should, make these decisions and on what grounds?

For me, what followed from the collective listening were two strik-ing insights. First, the listeners shared the opinion that the information and details included in the recording must have hailed from a woman—a female informant. Second, the participants assumed that a German scholar was clearly involved in the compilation of the text. To most of them, the chosen language and wording were so 'typically' German—rich in detail and pedantic in form. Lutz Diegner suspected a German scholar composed, or at least edited, the text based on somebody else's knowledge. He also suspected the scholar might have written down the text in German before retranslating it into Swahili.[59] "It was written down just like that," Asmau Nitardy commented, "without a feeling for or thinking about who was going to read it."

In light of the discussion, my pondering over Hussein's sound recording and its content, over anthropological research practices and the male gaze, had reached a completely new level. From the outset of my research, and as shown in more detail in Chapter 5, I was struck by the fact that the presence (or the *absent presences*) of women in historical archives and records in general, and in the *Lautarchiv*'s holdings in particular, is often imparted by material *about* women rather than *by* women. Women never, or at most rarely, appeared as speakers or knowledge carriers and producers themselves. Yet, not only did the recording speak *about* women, but the very content stemmed *from* and should have been articulated, if at all, *by* women. With regard to the history of early anthropology, it was usually privileged, male, and *white* scholars who estab-lished their ethnographic research on (participant) observations, in addition to knowledge they received from 'native middlemen'—informants, interpreters, and translators (Pugach 2012: 6).[60] Often, the people they worked with were well-respected men among their community because of their gender, age, and membership in local or cosmopolitan elites. Subsequently, not only the colonial eye but also the gaze of local men mattered. It also follows that the gendered (male) gaze can occasionally occur in a collaborative, doubly effective mode. In other words, female presences were excluded from the order of knowledge dominated by both colonising and colonised male subjects.

In the context of the colonial and gendered making of knowledge, the pub-lication *The Customs of the Swahili People* (*Sitten und Gebräuche der Suaheli*), edited by Carl Velten (1862–1935) and published in 1903, represents only one of many examples. The book's subject matter ranges from birth and children's games, to the main occupations of men and women, to slavery and legal con-ventions. The book, Velten writes in the preface, consists of a body of texts, noted down by 'native informants' on his request during a stay in East Africa.[61]

However, Velten, who served as an official translator to the imperial government, does not specify when and where this stay took place, and with whom he interacted. Was he in contact with one or several local researchers—with men or women? What was their social background? Contrary to many others in his field, Velten at least mentions that he edited the texts together with Mtoro bin Mwenyi Bakari (1869–1927), who had been a Swahili lecturer at the Seminar for Oriental Languages in Berlin since 1900.[62] Yet, for historian Katharina Oguntoye, it is a clear case: "He [Bakari] authored a book about *The Customs of the Swahili People*, which was the most important source for the social and cultural history of the Swahili before colonisation. The book was published under the name of his superior, Dr C. Velten" (1997b: 20).[63] On the one hand, it seems crucial to disclose the fact that it was often not the editor inscribed on the book cover but the informant or translator who narrated, authored, or edited the collected texts, stories, and poems. Sometimes, the editors credited the informant or assistant's name in the preface; yet most of the time, they did not. In this way, they concealed and silenced authorship and collective modes of knowledge production. On the other hand, most of these collections of texts appear as products of epistemic violence and practices of *othering*, as Hussein's case exemplifies compellingly.

In this light, the four-liners acting as epigraphs for each section of this chapter, which belong to a longer poem by an anonymous author, constitute a remarkable exception. Bearing the title *Chairi kwa Wazungu* (*Poem for the Europeans*), each verse is highly critical of the colonial government and practices of collecting material and intellectual property of colonised subjects in East Africa. Velten included the poem in a volume on *Prose and Poetry of the Swahili* (*Prosa und Poesie der Suaheli*). In a footnote, he comments:

> In the year 1895, in a circular note at the insistence of the editor, the Swahili people of the coast were asked to write down riddles, sayings, fables, etc. and to send them to the government. Thereon, a poet from Bagamajo [sic] sent this poem as his response without, however, mentioning his name. The poet belongs to those dissatisfied elements who refuse to make friends with the reign of the Europeans. (1907: 367)[64]

Swahili expert and translator Katrin Bromber (2003: 48) supposes that Velten included the piece of poetry despite the author's critical attitude because of the poem's artistic quality. Ironically, he inserted it in a collection of panegyric poems praising German colonial rule and rulers.[65] Velten probably saw no problems with the ways in which he was collecting information and knowledge, which was criticised in the poem. Nor did he take seriously the author's demand articulated in the last line of the first verse: "*Don't ask for more.*" It seems paradoxical that this vocal criticism (even if anonymous) would not have caught recent scholarly attention if it had not been published in the 'colonial library' (Desai 2001; Mudimbe 1988). Does it develop its resistant quality and subversive potential only today? How did readers receive it back then?

Returning to the gendered dimensions of appropriating knowledge, I revisited a paragraph in Westermann's account of the missionary as anthropological field-worker that I had not considered before in my attempt to analyse his approach to the gathering of (sensitive) ethnographic information.

> While it may be valuable to obtain authentic records of the life of the people from others, it is still more important to observe and study the actual thing at first hand. A division of the work between men and women is worth considering, as a woman will be able to get into touch with the life of the women much more easily than a man, and this opens up a large field that can only be dealt with by women. Among the missionaries there are today many women, who, by their education and knowledge of African languages, are specially qualified to take up this neglected part of the work and to say what the African woman is, what she does, what she thinks, and what the present changes in woman's life mean. (1931: 170)

Significantly, women have always been part of colonial encounters between Western missionaries, travellers, or researchers and members of *othered* groups—most prominently in the role of accompanying wives, on both sides.[66] Yet these female presences have been silenced. They have been invisibilised by incorporating the women's share in their husbands' work or banishing it to the footnotes (e.g. Karttunen 1994; Loosen 2014; Tedlock 1995). Today, it seems impossible to determine whether the information included in the sound recording's text originated from a female narration. "We simply won't know," is the prosaic answer by anthropologist Barbara Tedlock (1995: 271) who has famously written about the "silent wife-ethnographers" and their (often unpaid and unacknowledged) contribution to their husbands' ethnographic work and writing. Consequently, I am inclined to ask: what about the silent wife-informants? Their role seems to be an even more unacknowledged chapter in anthropology's collective history. In the above-quoted paragraph, Westermann does not address the way in which male scholars had previously been collecting information—without the help of trained and 'qualified' women. He similarly does not indicate that it was this 'neglected part' of a woman's life in particular that might entail sensitive knowledge. Two pages later, however, he does declare that "it must not be forgotten that there are certain things that must not be mentioned and that the native is naturally loth to tell a stranger anything about the life or customs of *his* people" (1931: 172, my emphasis).

I am returning to Westermann and his depiction of gender divisions at this point, because it ties in with the assertion of one of the workshop participants. Stephanie Lämmert stated that Hussein's sound recording "is a source that likely shows more about the colonial gaze [...] and also about the cooperation between the colonial gaze and the male gaze." In my final remarks on the listening workshop, it is my aim to tie this statement back to two conceptual strands: the notion of *academic silencing* and the concept of *sensitive collections*.

In view of my line of reasoning throughout this chapter, I see the practice of academic silencing playing out on three different, yet correlating, levels. First, there is the failure to acknowledge the contributions of informants, interpreters, and assistants to colonial knowledge production and education. Not crediting them with authorship, co-authorship, and co-teaching might be the most obvious lapse in light of the practices of academic knowledge production in the colonial metropolis. Second, academic silence and exclusion become apparent with regard to recent discourses within German academia. I began this chapter pointing out that scholarship has not yet fully grappled with Hussein's sound recording—and thus literally his voice. I later touched upon the notion of silence, when drawing on Westermann's career path in Nazi Germany. Evidently, there are historical accounts portraying the history of professionalising African studies and Westermann's role within these processes. However, there seems to be a lack of more critical approaches to the protagonists involved. In my view, the literature, even *if* naming the fact that Westermann and German African studies benefited from and thrived under the Nazi regime, still seems to venerate the scientific achievements of Westermann and his colleagues. I, therefore, call for the contextualisation of a knowledge production that rests on assumptions of superiority and the maintenance of (cultural) racisms. Finally, the third and last level, which only came to light against the backdrop of the workshop, is the silencing of female knowledge(s).

From a present-day perspective, and alluding to the concept of sensitive collections, Britta Lange asks, in the closing remarks of an article on anthropological collecting during colonialism: "How *systematically* do our [Western] sciences and the knowledge derived from them build upon situations of duress, and how *inherent* are such practices of transgression in our [Western] theories?" (2013b: 66, emphasis in the original)[67] To rephrase these questions as statements, I say: Western sciences and the knowledge derived from them build *systematically* upon situations of duress, and such practices of transgression are *inherent* in Western theories. In my view, only after admitting this fact does the next step, the attempt to decolonise the epistemic frameworks our theories and disciplines rest upon, become possible (see also Chapter 3). Only then can we identify situations of duress and epistemic violence. Only then can we avoid further acts of transgression, in terms of the violation of cultural, religious, social, or gender-specific boundaries.

Against the backdrop of Hussein's sound recording—a source of colonial knowledge production—I laid out the sensitive nature of the archival document. Understanding the sound object as evidence of colonial power and colonial knowledge regimes, it remains Hussein's individual voice that one listens to and projects certain associations onto. "He was in a colonial jam," is the way in which workshop participant Frank Daffa tried to make sense of Hussein's position and decision to do the recording. Did Hussein indeed feel at a loss, or did he simply perform a job without taking it too personally? Did he feel caught up in his own values and Western curiosity—this genuine 'craving' for knowledge? Might this be one reason for his hesitant and impersonal tone of voice, which all listeners described as their first hearing impression? Stephanie Lämmert shared the perception that she "thought that this hesitance—which one senses—rather has something to do with the fact that he was maybe somehow distancing himself from the content instead of reading the text for the first time." If we are to understand this distancing from the content literally, one may wonder if this was a move Hussein claimed for himself more generally. He understood his lifestyle as modern (rather than traditional); he advocated Western science (rather than non-Western knowledges); and he felt equal to his collaborators in the colonial metropolis (rather than to people in his former homes).

Reflecting on the decision to organise a collective listening workshop, the participants' impressions of and thoughts on this acoustic source were crucial in the attempt to approach the sound recording through an intersectional lens and in a collective mode. All workshop participants tried to make sense of the event in the past. We tried to get a feel for the past moment by paying special attention not only to the recording's content but also to the mode in which the content was transmitted: to the speaker's intonation and timbre, the pace and flow, and other nuances of vocal expression, which could never have been expressed in the same way in a written source. It was through the presence of Hussein's voice that some participants sensed a connection to the historical subject. For some, the link was Berlin, the city they live in; for others, it was the university, the institution they also work for or study at. Rukia Bakari, for her part, felt a linkage on yet a different level, sharing her intuition that "the informant must have been a woman to have given those details. So maybe that was my connection at that point that maybe there is a woman involved 'cause the man wouldn't give those details."

Heepe and Hussein

yote tukayafuata,	*We'll followed* [sic] *all of this.*
hatuna kutatata,	*We don't argue.*
kulla neno mwalipata,	*You got every word.*
sina kuwatilia.	*I don't have anything to add.*

Following the listening workshop, I felt that a more effective heuristic approach to Hussein and his acoustic legacy than the one offered in the workshop seemed hardly possible. Sharing impressions and exchanging hypotheses with others was crucial for the multidirectional exploration of the acoustic trace of a colonial subject that materialised under metropolitan conditions. Yet my search for and engagement with archival sources of and about Hussein did not end with the workshop session. On the limited number of occasions in which Hussein's name appears in the holdings of the university archive, one finds his name connected to a person Hussein seemed to harbour the strongest resentment towards, namely Martin Heepe. Holger Stoecker (2008a: 19) depicts Heepe as being the 'second Berlin Africanist' for many years (the first being Westermann). Moreover, Stoecker points out that a critical account of Heepe's biography is yet to be written. For me, however, it seems quite fitting that a critical investigation of one of the most recalcitrant characters in the institutional history of German African studies has yet to be conducted.

Earlier in this chapter, I mentioned Heepe as a person intimately involved with the history of the *Lautarchiv*. Having studied theology, philosophy, and (in the broadest sense) African languages in Leipzig, Halle, Erlangen, and Berlin,

Heepe started his academic career as a research assistant at the then emerging Colonial Institute in Hamburg in 1910. When the First World War began, he was away on a study trip to East Africa. Held in custody as prisoner of war in September 1916, and following a time of imprisonment in Belgian Congo, England, and France, Heepe was able to return to Germany by the end of 1917 (owing to an exchange of prisoners). At that point, he became a member of the Royal Prussian Phonographic Commission (1915–1918), supervising sound recordings made in German POW camps. This collaboration came about most likely through Carl Meinhof, who Heepe had previously studied and worked with in Berlin and Hamburg. Along with Otto Dempwollf (1871–1938) and Paul Hambruch (1882–1933), both trained in linguistics and anthropology, Meinhof was in charge of the 'African recordings' conducted by the Phonographic Commission. After the First World War, Heepe was appointed a library position at the newly founded Sound Department of the Prussian State Library in 1921, before he became a member of the Philosophical Faculty at the Friedrich Wilhelm University and a lecturer at the Seminar for Oriental Languages. The Seminar was most likely the place where Heepe and Hussein first met in 1931.

Regarded as an expert of Bantu languages, Heepe taught courses in Sandawe and Swahili both at the Philosophical Faculty of Berlin University and at the Seminar for Oriental Languages from 1922. He worked and taught jointly with native speakers in Hamburg and later Berlin before and again after the First World War. Presumably, Heepe instructed Swahili tutorials together with Hussein over a period of ten years, from 1931 until 1941. Among his circle of colleagues and students, Heepe was known for being a difficult character, as someone always asking for trouble, regularly harassing his students, denouncing colleagues and assistants.[68] In 1940, after a number of incidents, the university instigated proceedings against Heepe, aiming to block his promotion to a tenured professor at the Faculty of Foreign Studies. Apart from the personal disagreements, the adduced arguments against Heepe were that he had stopped publishing his work in 1929 and neglected his teaching, causing offence to his colleagues and students. When Gerhard Knothe (1877–1945) put himself forward to take over some of his Swahili classes, Heepe intervened claiming that he was the only person permitted to instruct Swahili, and that Knothe must not engage with Hussein in any teaching activities.[69] Knothe was born and raised in a German missionary family in South Africa. After he had to leave South Africa because of the First World War, he and his family tried to start a new life in Berlin. In 1926, he became a visiting lecturer for South African languages at the Seminar for Oriental Languages.

From archived documents and the university's personnel files, one learns that the university dealt with the 'Heepe case' on the level of the Ministry of Science, Education and National Culture and the Faculty's deanery. In a letter to the minister, the associate dean expounded the concerns and complaints regarding Heepe, attesting his report by adding the statements of several members of the university. Among the letter's five attachments, one finds a written complaint by Hussein.[70] Dating from April 2, 1941, Hussein wrote to the associate dean of the Faculty of Foreign Studies, wishing to resign from his post at the university.

> As I have already explained to you in person, I am unable to continue my work in the upcoming semester. The reason for this lies in the fact that Prof. Heepe interferes in my personal life in the strongest terms. [...] I am dependent on additional income. Prof. Heepe does not want to grant this additional income; as soon as he notices that I have an additional income, he contacts the firms via phone or personal visits until such a time where I am dismissed. There is no legal basis for Prof. Heepe's actions, since I do not have a contract with either the former *Hochschule für Politik* nor with the university that prohibits me from having additional income. For these reasons, I am unable to continue working with Prof. Heepe, and I therefore ask you to consider this letter as my resignation. However, I always remain willing to continue working with Prof. Knothe. Hail Hitler! (Hussein to the associate dean of the Faculty of Foreign Studies, April 2, 1941, transcript of the original letter, my emphasis)[71]

If this formal complaint was yet another attempt to stand up for his rights, Hussein did not succeed, however. In an additional letter to the ministry, the rector undermined Hussein's efforts. Explaining that he invited both Heepe and Knothe to a hearing in order to close the 'Heepe case,' the rector stated that he decided against summoning Hussein to the hearing of the university's legal committee, although Hussein was mentioned as a witness in this affair. To me, the rector's depiction of "the language assistant Hussein as a coloured foreigner" sounds condescending.[72] It is a gesture of dismissal of Hussein as a relevant and reliable witness, even though Heepe's behaviour affected Hussein in the most existential terms. It seems striking that Hussein would rather have quit his employment at the university, facing financial distress and precarity as a result, than to continue working under Heepe and be subjected to his harassment and discriminatory actions.

It remains unknown whether it might have been Heepe who accused Hussein of having an affair with a *white* woman and thus denounced him for 'racial defilement' to the Berlin authorities a few months after this episode. While Heepe did not become a tenured professor, he remained employed at the university until the end of the Second World War. Hussein's life, in turn, would change drastically in the course of the year 1941. Shortly after arresting Hussein and detaining him at the police prison of the *Gestapo* at Berlin-*Alexanderplatz*, the police imprisoned him without a trial at the concentration camp *Sachsenhausen* in Oranienburg, close to Berlin in September 1941. It is a tragic fact that Hussein would not leave the camp's premises alive (Bechhaus-Gerst 2007: 140–150; Stoecker 2008a: 100–101).

The university did not feel accountable for Hussein but responded with his formal dismissal in November 1941. By the end of the year, his wife, Maria Hussein (née Schwadner), whom Hussein had been married to since 1933, filed for a divorce, which became final the next year, in August 1942. It remains unclear whether the *Gestapo* pressured her into this decision, as was the case for many other (Jewish) families. Hussein and his wife had two legitimate children, who both died in early childhood. Hussein's first and oldest child, Heinz Bodo, was born to a different mother in 1933, but raised by Hussein and his wife, Maria. While Maria Hussein disappears from the archives after 1943, it is known that Heinz Bodo outlived his father by a few months, but lost his life during the last months of the bombing of Berlin, on March 3, 1945.[73] Hussein had died four months earlier, on November 24, 1944, after three years of imprisonment. Presumably, he died from one of the many infectious diseases circulating in *Sachsenhausen* among both inmates and guards. Today, one can find a gravestone at a military cemetery in Berlin-*Reinickendorf* where Hussein was buried in January 1945.

In 2007, a tripping stone (*Stolperstein*) was installed in front of Hussein and his family's last place of residence in the Berlin city centre at *Brunnenstraße* 193. It was the first commemorative stone dedicated to a Black victim of Nazi terror and persecution since the inception of the decentralised memorial project in 1992.

Conclusion

tama yangu, nikomele	*I end my poem.*
haya yangu matungole,	*This is my composition.*
uamke walilele,	*Wake up, those who have slept,*
huna tena kusinzia.	*and don't sleep anymore!*

I end my chapter. This is my composition. This chapter represents my way of engaging with the sonic trace of the historical figure of Bayume Mohamed Hussein. By means of new reading strategies and the practice of collective listening, this chapter manoeuvred between notions of (1) adding to the colonial archive, (2) giving thought to a possible 'second life,' and (3) creating a whole new archive consisting of contemporary and intersubjective projections and speculations.

I began this chapter by drawing attention to the fact that the legacies of colonial migrations and the Black diaspora in Germany still do not appear as crucial and substantial parts of German historiography and collective memory. In this respect, Sebastian Conrad's (2002: 148) understanding of a twofold marginalisation is still valid. On the one hand, the historian points out that concepts of the West and modernity are usually not understood by tracing their entangled and multipolar conditions. On the other hand, colonial Germany is still considered as an exception on the global scale, often presented as no more than an appendix to German or global history. However, one has to admit that discourses have slowly started to shift over the past decades. The growing attention to Germany's colonial past in public and political spheres is the result of the longstanding work and effort of various postcolonial academics and activists.[74]

In line with the above, I showed how exploring particular moments in the biography of a single character makes it possible to elicit entangled and minoritised histories of colonial Germany. Shedding light on different forms of academic silencing—then and now—allowed me to take a closer look at Hussein and parts of his life in order to point to the discursive contexts he, as a colonial subject, was embedded in. I took the sonic document as a starting point for thinking about the making and transmission of colonial knowledges in the past, leading to a collaborative engagement in the present. In this way, I was able to deal with the problematic practices associated with the production of Hussein's sound file and the accompanying written material. Creating a new, experimental, and situational field site by setting up a collective space for listening to the acoustic trace together, Jasmin and I opened a path back into the past, enabling the formation of a new archive in the present.

Positioning themselves in relation to the things heard, the workshop participants established connections between the voice and its producer, between Hussein's perceptible, or rather audible, discomfort and the formalised setting. We discussed the relation between the described cultural practice and the way it was translated into the colonial knowledge system—both in a discursive, but also in a literal sense, as the recording was used for purposes of colonial education. Together we developed relationships between the past and the present, between one's own subjective listening experience and that of the other listeners. This exchange illuminated not only possible ways of reading, or rather listening to, the source material. It also allowed us to problematise the difficult circumstances under which the material came into being, how it was archived, and how it is accessed today. In this way, it was possible to discuss different notions of the sensitive, as presented in my theoretical account of the concept of sensitive collections. It is my belief that the notion of sensitive collections, as well as the practice of collective listening, was helpful in order to find a mode and language in which to approach and speak about the sonic material.

Drawing attention to yet another individual, I pointed to the figure of Diedrich Westermann, who is closely linked to the history of the *Lautarchiv* during the Nazi period, and even more so to the institutionalisation of African studies. The positions of power Westermann climbed to during his career, as well as his particular views on colonial Africa and its people, allowed him to influence and shape research methodologies and agendas. His way of thinking rested, on the one hand, on taking up a paternalistic position and, on the other, on propagating cultural and linguistic racisms. Accordingly, both Westermann and Hussein appear as decisive figures for the discourses relevant to this book, namely those of the practices of colonial knowledge production and their materialisations; as well as the question of how to deal with these metropolitan figurations in the present and future. Conceptually, drawing on Hussein and Westermann allowed me to develop my argument under one of the premises of historical ethnography. As introduced in Chapter 2, historical ethnography asks for moments of relationality, ambiguity, and difference both in the past and present. It remained my priority to foreground hitherto forgotten or hidden traces and to rethink and reinterpret what can be known about Bayume Mohamed Hussein and his life in connection to both colonial and postcolonial Germany. The two characters—though on completely different levels—occupy controversial places within the colonial discourse. Do we understand Hussein

as a pawn in the hands of the powerful? Or, do we consider his actions as resil-
ient manoeuvres between different, yet entangled, worlds and borders, attempting to contest and cross racial boundaries?

Hussein fought German bureaucracy to be paid as a fully recognised member of the German colonial army; he aspired to make a career as an actor and
performer in the German colonial film and entertainment industry; and lastly,
he strove to receive credit for his knowledge and language expertise, which was
utilised in academic and colonial enterprises. Hussein went far, but he never
fully succeeded. He did not receive adequate payment, he did not become a successful actor, and he decided to leave the institution of the university because of
its discriminatory environment. Though this might overstep the mark, I cannot
help but wonder whether Hussein's and Westermann's ambition is one of the
connections one can draw between the two. Did they not both grasp the opportunities laid out in front of them? When it comes to Westermann, I showed
that the accumulation of his political and academic authority seemed mutually
dependent; he used one to push the other. Yet with Hussein, one has to note
that all his life decisions seem to have been of an existential nature: decisions on
how to live and make a living in a state under colonial rule, in a colonialist and
soon fascist metropolis, within the racial (dis)order of things. Hussein was ultimately not able to survive the prevailing racial inequalities of the illegitimate,
oppressive state and social order. Remembering Bayume Mohamed Hussein
today means remembering a colonial past that does not end with Germany's
formal colonialism, but persists in personal biographies, institutional settings,
and knowledge systems.

7

... THE ACOUSTIC

Listening and Preserving, Sound and Vision

There are two narrative threads pervading this book, which I have yet to discuss in detail. The first and most obvious strand concerns the acoustic, the object of sound, and conceptions of listening. The second, more subtle, strand regards practices of preserving and the historical paradigm of 'salvage anthropology' (e.g. Clifford 1986, 1987). As my points of departure in this chapter, I choose crucial accounts by eminent sound and media scholars. Jonathan Sterne (2003) and Brian Hochman (2014), for instance, carried out major research on the interrelationship between early sound technologies and anthropology. Placing emphasis on cultural practices, their interests lie with the social and cultural implications of media history. In their works, both scholars show that media history is inseparable from ideologies of race and difference. This chapter therefore seeks to position the history of the *Lautarchiv* in the nexus between technology and race. How can one best assess the epistemic field of the employed technologies and media practices? Are they the consequence and/or constitutive elements of discourses of race and difference? While Hochman is primarily concerned with change and development in the histories of media technology and anthropology, Sterne is more interested in the histories of sound reproduction and preservation, both of which he introduces as cultural techniques. Though the two scholars mainly concentrate their research on North American histories, I believe it is a worthwhile endeavour to consult and redirect their accounts to examine European and German contexts. Hence, this chapter intends to connect their thought to the history of the *Lautarchiv* and the recording practices I have been dealing with in the previous chapters.

At the heart of this book are three case studies enacting three different listening practices. Employing these modes of listening allowed me to reflect on three approaches to different sonic events. Conceptually, I discussed notions of the ethnographic and archival by drawing on the project of historical anthropology and looking into genealogies of archival theories (see Chapter 2 and 4). In doing so, I constructed the theoretical framework of my approach to my object of study—the *Lautarchiv*. This chapter expands my conceptual structure by utilising analytical premises stemming from the fields of sound studies and media history.

Crucial to the analysis of sound, the auditory, and the acoustic is the conviction that historical sound objects change over time. They change over time depending on the perspective and context within which one perceives objects of sound as historical sources. Another notion that is crucial to the investigation of sound is that of changing listening practices, as media historian Kate Lacey has convincingly demonstrated. With regard to the complex processes of modernisation, Lacey discusses Western practices of listening in mediated public life, paying special attention to what she terms the "modern media age" (2013: 11), beginning in the 1870s and encompassing a multitude of different media histories. In her insightful study on the politics and experience of listening, Lacey understands "listening to be a cultural practice that changes under changing historical and material conditions" (18). She goes on to note: "Like any other cultural practice, listening is embedded in the complex realities of unequal power relations, cultural specificities and the dynamics of continuity and change" (22). In line with Sterne, one of Lacey's central concerns is to argue that narratives of modernity have long been overlooked transfigurations of the auditory and practices of listening in favour of focusing on conditions of vision, space, or time. This chapter therefore tackles the question to what extent a shift of attention towards the acoustic, as well as towards epistemologies of listening, can modify an approach to formations of the modern world and perceptions of modern thinking. This is of particular significance when understanding the enterprise of the *Lautarchiv* as a manifestation of constituent principles of modernity.

The distinction between vision and sound was and continues to be highly controversial, not only with regard to notions of modernity. For a considerable period of time, turns proclaimed as *iconic, pictorial*, or *visual*, as well as the fields of visual culture and visual history, have been well-established in the humanities. Likewise, notions of the *material turn* and material culture studies in addition to the discursive field of a new materialism, gained importance as new analytical lenses and sites of inquiry. Over the last decades, the idea of an *acoustic, auditory*, or *sonic turn* has frequently been invoked but does not (yet) seem to have the same impact across disciplines (e.g. Braun 2017; Meyer 2008).[1] Although this book concentrates mainly on sound as a pertinent object of knowledge, and listening as an instructive concept of knowing, it also aims to explore analytical synergies emerging from a multidirectional approach, combining different senses, materialities, and schools of thought. This chapter thus also considers conceptual ideas drawn from broader realms in media studies and visual anthropology. For certain branches in visual anthropology, for instance, the question of how to deal with photographic records from the colonial past has been an important issue; an issue, as I show, that seems to be directly applicable to sonic records generated under colonial conditions.

In this book, it is not historical imagery but single sound documents from the past that have formed the points of access around which I clustered my analysis. In each case study, my attempt was to carve out the sonic conditions of the source material. In part, however, this also meant including other material, such as texts or images. More often than not, it was precisely the interplay among, or the opposition to, different media formats that informed my interpretation in the first place. Using a methodology of juxtaposition, my wish was to negotiate the specificity of particular sound events against the background of their emergence in the past, their assessment over time, and their adoption in the present. Exploring different listening practices—both in synchronic and diachronic terms—was crucial for the interpretation of the sound events. Here, it became particularly evident why focusing on changing practices of listening and diverging listening positions can be so decisive.

This chapter focuses on the relationship between race and technology in general, and race and sound in particular. By drawing on different approaches from sound, media, and cultural history, I show that historical and discursive layers correlate not only with each other but also with stipulations of the archive. This brings me back to my examination of the archive in Chapter 4 and leads me to think of genealogies of media and archives together. I then turn to the paradigm of salvage anthropology, by recalling sections of my three case studies and salvage anthropology's effects on the history of the *Lautarchiv*. As the chapter progresses, I ask in what ways phenomena of sound were constitutive of formations of modernity. In this regard, attention to the imperative of objectivity (or more precisely, the notion of *mechanical objectivity*) is as important as a focus on changing scientific techniques and figurations of the scientific self and its objects. I continue to discuss rationales of vision and an essentialising impetus related to visuality. While the engagement with sound also faces the risk of naturalisation, I point to possibilities of denaturalising sound through, for instance, *sonic imagination* (Sterne 2012b) or the *practice of vibration* (Eidsheim 2015). Finally, the last part of this chapter draws on both contrasting and shared characteristics of visual anthropology and what might be called *sonic anthropology*, before concluding by highlighting the analytical strengths I see in the field of sound studies for my work.

Recording Sound, Constructing Race

"Our imaginaries of race have been technologized and our imaginings of technology have been racialized" (2009: 2). This is how media scholar Lynne Joyrich puts it in the preface to a special issue of the journal *Camera Obscura*, edited together with Wendy H. K. Chun. With reference to the special issue's title "Race and/as Technology," Chun (2009: 7) begins her introduction by claiming that race should be regarded *as* a technology or a media form in order to better understand it as a construct of race. With this evocative, and for some, provocative, call, the editors Joyrich and Chun push discourses on race and technology further, opening up discussions, as they argue, beyond essentialised notions of race and difference. In her essay, Chun contends that mobile media technologies serve(d) both cultural and biological constructs of race. Consequently, understanding race as a form of technology allows us to reveal its mobile quality.

For my investigation of the *Lautarchiv*, the notion of race as technology and how this notion can be used to illuminate the ramifications of racial discourses seem equally relevant. In the context of the *Lautarchiv*, racial discourses have been and continue to be mobilised and negotiated. Following Joyrich and Chun, and applying their arguments to sound, it is possible to trace how race has been constituted via sound technologies and how, in turn, sound recordings have been constituted by formations of race. Would the *Lautarchiv*'s initial collection of sound recordings of (colonial) prisoners of war have been imaginable without the race question? Would the emerging entertainment industry in Western metropoleis have been as commercially successful without exoticisation and racialisation? And would the institutionalisation of a range of academic disciplines, such as anthropology or linguistics, have succeeded without the political and social patronage of a *white* and Christian mainstream society? Answering these rhetorical questions in the negative, it follows that the *Lautarchiv*'s very basis served, and even rested on, constructs of race and difference and their multiple mobilisations.

The contributions to the aforementioned special issue mainly concentrate on modes of visualisation and visual technologies. Therefore, Brian Hochman's historical study of modern media technologies offers valuable supplements, as he looks at the intersections between sonic and racial discourses. Hochman productively correlates his thoughts on early sound technologies with practices of colour photography and documentary film. His focus on racial formations is key to exploring the relations between race and sound. According to Hochman, for contemporaries, "the promise of media and the problem of race were inextricably linked" (2014: xii). This points towards the fact that the emergence of the phonograph is closely interconnected with both discursive formations of race and the paradigm of salvage anthropology—or *Savage Preservation*, as the title of Hochman's book suggests.

While I strongly doubt that one must invoke the figure of the 'savage,' which in my view is always derogatory, even when it comes with deconstructive intentions, I follow Hochman in his preoccupation with the motif of salvage as a central analytical lens. Under the premise of media archaeology (see also Chapter 4), Hochman's study pursues two main objectives. Besides shedding light on—both well- and lesser-known—historical figures, Hochman shows "that ideologies of race and difference are absolutely necessary to the story of media history in the United States" (xx). To him, this story often remains to be told in neutral terms of progress and social use. One of the strengths of media archaeology is that it does not attempt to trace a linear and teleological path of technological development, but points to the ruptures, detours, and (dis)continuities of modern media technology. The concept of salvage prompts Hochman to argue that his "book performs a salvage operation of a different sort" (xxiv). By building his case studies on 'residual' media objects, implying new or alternative stories, Hochman claims to be saving these objects from oblivion.

Deriving his definition of salvage anthropology from James Clifford, Hochman suggests that the logic of the salvage paradigm "reduces culture to little more than a 'disappearing object' to be collected, classified, and preserved" (xiii, referencing Clifford 1986: 112–113). Following from this, Hochman outlines two important assumptions reaching back to nineteenth-century traditions of the Western academy that form the basis of salvage mentality. First, he mentions the dominant and essentialising conviction that the world is structured by difference and racially divided by culture, religion, and bodies. This concept was not limited to human spheres but included the encyclopaedic interest in other species, organisms, and artifacts. Particularly during the nineteenth century, natural and human sciences, such as zoology and botany as well as philosophy and the gradually institutionalised discipline of anthropology, strengthened this conviction. Second, Hochman emphasises the prevailing sentiment of a linear understanding of the historical development of humankind, leading from 'savagery' over 'barbarism' to 'civilization.'[2] The desire to understand and order the world, then, was dependent on the accumulation of natural, anthropological, and ethnographic artifacts and data, which was gathered in Western knowledge institutions and then newly-established national museums. The collecting strategies involved the development of systemised recording techniques and media for cataloguing, classifying, and comparing the compiled knowledge. In many cases, this meant applying methods derived from the natural sciences to the humanities, a point I will come back to below (see also Kaschuba 1999 [2006]: 52–54).

While the subtitle to Hochman's book lays emphasis on the *Ethnographic Origins of Modern Media Technology*, Sterne, for his part, promises no less than to examine the *Cultural Origins of Sound Reproduction*. Sterne's account goes far beyond the consideration of ethnographic practices. For instance, he links the history of sound preservation to the larger context of socio-cultural histories of practices of embalming dead bodies and canning food. Sterne associates these cultural techniques with a general Western struggle against decay and a nineteenth-century "culture of death" (2003: 305). In this way, he pinpoints particular historical situations that brought forth advancements, such as canning or recording sound. Despite the impressive scope of Sterne's study, I wish to limit my attention to his remarks on what he calls "audio or phonographic ethnography" (311).

Sterne describes the emergence of the possibility of sound reproduction and its application to ethnographic purposes as a logical "extension of the preservative ethos at the turn of the twentieth century" (324). He juxtaposes the initial assertion of the phonograph's inventor, Thomas Alva Edison, with anthropology's agendas. While Edison promised to save the voices of dying individuals, prevailing doctrines in anthropology intended to capture entire cultures that were presumably threatened with extinction. Linking questions of sound to different senses of time, Sterne connects anthropology's desire to preserve the melodies of 'dying cultures' back to Johannes Fabian's deconstruction of ethnographic time. With reference to Fabian's 'denial of coeval existence' as performed by US American anthropologists, Sterne explains that the scholars located Native Americans "in a different temporal zone" (312, referencing Fabian 1983). As opposed to European anthropologists who mostly went on field expeditions outside of Europe, North American anthropologists acted in the same geographic space as the ethnographic *Other*.[3] This spatial simultaneity explains why nineteenth-century anthropologists were in need of another marker of difference in order to disconnect themselves from their research objects: the marker being time.

Sterne suggests that contrasting academic positions influenced US American anthropologists. While evolutionist cultural theories continued to play a major role, more pluralistic, empirical, and relativistic tendencies were also gaining ground. The latter stood in the scholarly tradition of German-born Franz Boas and his students. Despite this more nuanced differentiation, it was, nonetheless, a dominant sense of cultural difference and a belief in constant change that were crucial to the ethnographic practice of recording *tradition* by means of the *modern* technology of the phonograph. The aim was to capture fragmented pieces of a present which would soon become the past. The idea was to preserve this past for the upcoming generations of an anticipated future (see also Chapter 2). In *The Audible Past*, Sterne frequently returns to notions of time and temporality. With regard to phonographic ethnography, he discovers that:

> The very idea of making recordings for listeners in a distant and unknown future [...] carries within it a distinctively threefold sense of time: this time is at once (1) a linear, progressive historical time, (2) the internally consistent time on a record, a present cut into fragments, and (3) the almost geologic time of the physical recordings itself. (310)

To give a brief example of these three notions of time, I return to the historical figure of Heinrich Lüders and the recording activities that took place during the First World War, before recalling this context in more detail below. Here, I point to the recordist's aspirations, indicating at least three objectives that can be associated with the triple temporality, as described by Sterne. First, Lüders felt it was a unique opportunity and his scholarly duty to document what he presumed to be a 'natural' historical process of one dominant language (modern Nepalese) slowly replacing a multitude of other languages.[4] Second, he wished to capture this process of a changing use of vocabulary among the imprisoned soldiers of so-called Gurkha regiments, by recording traditional folk tales and songs. Hence, Lüders wished to cut into the present moment as he encountered it in the camps; a moment that would soon be part of the past. Lastly, Lüders' contemporaries had faith in the enduring quality of the material of shellac. However, perhaps because Lüders approached the new medium with a certain scepticism, or because no one could confidently predict how permanent the material actually was, Lüders and his colleagues invested a lot of additional effort into taking notes and making transliterations of the tales and songs they recorded. Back then, the institution of what is today known as the *Lautarchiv* did not yet exist. The necessary collaboration with locally-based record companies was, however, already well underway. Despite Wilhelm Doegen's vision to found a sound archive and voice museum, it was not until 1920 that the Sound Department at the Prussian State Library was officially established.

During the early years of the phonograph and its successor, the gramophone, institutional frameworks were not yet in place. From the very beginning, sound pioneers had, nevertheless, a future for the reproduction and preservation of sound in mind. They presumed that this future would offer the necessary institutional and technological features. The phonographic ethnographers Doegen emulated had similar visions. "The speaking dead needed a cemetery for their resonant tombs" (327), Sterne metaphorically states, stressing the necessity for the establishment of a new archival infrastructure.

> The sound archives that could and actually did preserve recordings for future generations were themselves part of the anthropological impulse towards preservation. They derived their justification from the ethics of the disciplines of anthropology, musicology, and linguistics. Beyond sharing the temporal sensibility of their contemporaries in the phonograph industry and elsewhere, academic and government researchers had the added justification of systematic study and research. (328)

This implicit contingency between media and archive history will be the point of departure for the following pages. I argue that when recounting the history of recording and reproducing sound, one must also pay attention to the history of preserving and archiving sound. At the same time, these parallel histories need to be approached as consistently interrelated with academic, economic, material, political, racist, and social forces.

Historical Subjects and (Disappearing) Objects

This section, then, suggests that it is hardly possible to tell a media history of recording sound without also considering the history of archival notions of preserving sound. These parallel histories, I argue, need to be approached against the backdrop of broader historical and discursive media formations. When attempting to do media history, one can pose a number of different research questions. One can ask how modern ideas of communication developed, how modes of perception changed, or what political choices and social structures promoted and/or interfered with certain transformations. Hence, doing media and sound history implies a multiplicity of intellectual projects. Like Hochman, media historian Lisa Gitelman (2008: 1) makes the case that media history should not be confined to an apolitical history of technological progress of changing methods and devices. Rather, her starting point in *Always Already New* is to understand media as historical subjects. For Gitelman, addressing media in the plural—as complicated and at times contradictory historical subjects with social and cultural histories—is a way to prevent the tendency to naturalise or essentialise them. Gitelman holds the opinion that media is all too often depicted as one unified technology, thereby neglecting the plurality of media and its discursive impact. There are media histories, she argues, trying to prove that one type of history, for instance, one that focuses on technological progress, would be more revelatory than one that concentrates on, say, media epistemologies or social practices (2). Eidsheim voices similar unease when it comes to the common notion of a singular "figure of sound" (2015: 2; see also Novak and Sakakeeny 2015: 7). Explaining that sound would too often be viewed as a stable, static, and naturalised referent, Eidsheim promotes an understanding of sonic events as highly dynamic, multi-faceted, and multi-sensorial phenomena. Below, I shall return to Eidsheim's suggestion to reconceptualise the understanding of sounds as fixed by means of the practice of vibration. I will draw further on her politics of listening and her call for "listening to listening" (2019: 57).

In my account of *the archival* in Chapter 4, I stressed that the archive can be understood as a medium of history, encoding certain knowledges and narratives. This chapter adds to this understanding with the depiction of the *Lautarchiv* as an object, or rather subject, of a nuanced media history. According to Gitelman, "history of emergent media [...] is partly the history of history, of what (and who) gets preserved—written down, printed up, recorded, filmed, taped, or scanned—and why" (2008: 26). Earlier in her book, she argues: "If history is a term that means both what happened in the past and the varied practices of representing that past, then media are historical at several different levels" (5). As I hope to have shown in this book, the *Lautarchiv* serves as a remarkable example of the exploration of events in the past, and of considering different practices of representing this past in the present (see Chapter 2). In Chapter 4, I emphasised that the archive in its discursive form bears little relation to formal archival institutions or—and this is important for the point I wish to make here—to media. The archive as dispositive deems only certain statements and knowledges imaginable. In this sense, the medial status of the archive and its meaning remain diffuse. Hence, in media archaeology, the Foucauldian archive as 'the law of what can be said' becomes a medial law—regulating the production and transmission "of what could be deployed [...] in the order of things" (Foucault: 1972 [1969]: 145). In other words, when bringing the archive together with notions of history and media, the archive becomes a medium of knowledge and a device of its transmission.

Another intention of my conceptual account of the archive was to show to what extent and on what grounds theorising the politics of the archive may be productive for engaging with the physical archive and actual archival histories. I pointed out that this means being capable of handling the idea of the archive as two analytical objects; walking a tightrope between the two bodies of the archive—the literal and the metaphoric (Ebeling and Günzel 2009: 10). At this stage, I continue my reflections on the practices and politics of archiving, arguing that one might benefit from taking into account broader concepts of preserving and doctrines of salvaging. I refer to literal practices of preserving, but also to more conceptual ideas and past ideologies, such as Sterne's above-mentioned assertion of a Western 'preservative ethos' in the nineteenth and early twentieth century. In what follows, I contemplate the question of how this ethos played out both in the history of anthropology, and with regard to the *Lautarchiv*'s enterprise—which, as this book argues, is strongly linked to the anthropological project.

As indicated before, practices of preservation have found an expression in the discipline of anthropology in rather drastic ways. It was especially during its founding phase in the nineteenth century that scholarly strands in anthropology resorted to unilinear and evolutionist cultural theories, which were closely connected to the idea of modernity's inevitable progression (Kaschuba 1999 [2006]: 25; Stangl 2000: 75–77). For a crucial period of time, the salvage paradigm was an important principle in European and North American anthropology, causing lasting repercussions, even after the discipline's reorientation.[5] According to Wolfgang Kaschuba (1999 [2006]: 54), the paradigm was also part of the discipline's compensatory strategy of *looking back* in order to tackle the contingent challenges of the present and future, the acceleration of industrialisation and urbanisation processes.

It was James Clifford who notably problematised the legacy of the salvage mentality, which affected ongoing developments and schools of thought in the field. In his contribution to *Writing Culture* (1986), co-edited with George E. Marcus, Clifford connects the problem of representational strategies and practices specific to the production of ethnographic texts to the formerly dominant motif of salvage. At the time, he claimed that the 'allegory of salvage' remains ingrained in the theory and practice of ethnography (112–113; see also Clifford 1987: 121). However, a lot has changed since Clifford made these assertions. For example, a lot has changed since a number of anthropologists pushed the debate on writing culture forward, since the crisis of representation was proclaimed, since post- and decolonial critique became an integral part of certain branches in anthropological scholarship and other academic, political, and social spheres. If doing media and sound history is more complex than following up on media change and technological development, as Gitelman states, the same can be said about tracing the genealogies of anthropological and ethnographic knowledge production. Shedding light on epistemological legacies in all their complexity must go beyond the examination of changing scholarly mentalities and practices of documenting, interpreting, and writing. In order to retrace the connection to the knowledge regimes relevant to this book, the following presents a retrospective view on my case studies and the ways in which they are linked to the salvage paradigm. I bring to bear my unpacking of the 'allegory of salvage' and its echo in each recording act—in each colonial situation and sonic event—this book examines. In a next step, I relate the intentions expressed in the recording practices to broader understandings of configurations of modernity and the imperative of objectivity.

The *Lautarchiv* and the Salvage Paradigm

> The discourse of salvage anthropology was perhaps the most powerful force shaping nineteenth-century ethnology and the development of both German and non-German ethnographic museums. It combined feelings of urgency, loss, and possibility with scientific competence to create a sense of purpose that demanded extraordinary sacrifices to possess cultural artifacts. (Penny 2002: 52)

> The aim was not to protect the cultures 'threatened with extinction' by improving the political circumstances, but rather to compile as

comprehensive anthropological-ethnological collections and multi-
media documentations as possible. (Lange 2013a: 107–108)[6]

These two quotes by H. Glenn Penny and Britta Lange illustrate not only the
impact the salvage paradigm had on the institutionalisation of anthropology but
also the institutionalisation of ethnographic collections in German-speaking
contexts. In his work on the discipline of anthropology and ethnographic
museums in imperial Germany, Penny examines the political means and affec-
tive strategies shaping dominant discourses of the time. For Lange (2013a:
107), the quintessential assertion of salvage anthropology is that the salvage
paradigm was not a *social* but a *media(l)* project. As Lange shows, this holds
particularly true for the studies undertaken in German and Austro-Hungarian
POW camps during the First World War, to which she dedicated a large part
of her academic work (see also Chapter 3). In line with Penny, Lange notes that
scholars mobilised the salvage paradigm and 'feelings of urgency' to legitimate
their research agenda. In this way, anthropologists and collectors alike sought to
obtain funding for their field expeditions abroad or, alternatively, the research
site of an internment camp 'at home.' Salvage anthropology claimed to know
which ethnicised and racialised groups should be documented and studied,
archived and preserved, even exhibited and displayed publicly (Clifford 1987:
122). Recontextualising the *Lautarchiv*'s material against the backdrop of the
history of anthropology and media history, and their respective relationship to
the salvage paradigm, thus seems to be of key importance. How, I therefore ask,
did salvage anthropology find expression in the three case studies of this book?
        As part of my first case study, in Chapter 3, I took a close look at the
Orientalist Heinrich Lüders. Lüders considered it a rare opportunity to gather
linguistic data among soldiers of the Gurkha regiments in the British Indian
Army. Between 1916 and 1918, Lüders and his colleague Wilhelm Schulze
compiled a considerable amount of sound recordings and transcriptions of
so-called Gurkha soldiers, first imprisoned in a POW camp in Germany and
later Romania. Due to the longstanding and cross-generational service in the
British Indian Regiments, during most of which the soldiers were stationed in
regions of pre-partition northern India, their knowledge of Tibeto-Burman
languages was in the process of being replaced due to the dominant use of the
Indo-Aryan languages, such as Nepali, Hindi, and Hindustani. Against this
backdrop, it was Lüders' intention to study the linguistic proficiencies among
Nepalese members of the British Indian troops, wishing to capture their 'remaining' language knowledge and vocabulary. As the Indologist himself highlighted,

many of the young soldiers were neither recruited nor born in Nepal. In most of the cases, they were born and raised on Indian military bases as so-called "line-boys" (Lüders 1925: 126). Consequently, the majority of them had little or no knowledge of other native languages. Lüders stated that there were only a few soldiers left with a first language other than Nepalese. His scholarly interest was directed towards documenting which parts of the vocabulary the speakers adapted in their narratives and songs. He asked which words and phrases they integrated into Nepalese and which they no longer used and thus, in a way, 'lost' over time. I analysed Lüders' accounts with reference to Fabian, who famously deconstructed anthropology's Eurocentric methodologies and belief in cultural and racial stratification. Following Fabian, I argued that, in his writing, Lüders positioned the knowledge and use of Tibeto-Burman languages on a preceding temporal and lower cultural stage. While Lüders did not expect Tibeto-Burman languages to disappear, he nevertheless held the opinion that the languages were losing speakers because of the effects of labour movements and the homogenising force of modernisation under colonial rule in South Asia. In view of processes of modernisation—in this case expressed primarily in the form of military labour regimes—it was Lüders' Eurocentric wish to salvage processes of changing linguistic genealogies among the *Other*.

In my second case study, I dealt with sound recorded at a metropolitan colonial spectacle, a so-called *India Show*. Here, I went back to the very beginnings of the *Lautarchiv*'s predecessor and sibling institution, the Berlin Phonogram Archive (see Chapter 5). Transpiring simultaneously with the archive's formation, I discussed the emergence of comparative musicology at the turn of the twentieth century, which became known as the Berlin School. I showed that the field of study was highly influenced by, if not constitutive of, the conviction that Western scholarship had to study *and* preserve non-Western music traditions before the allegedly relentless impact of modernity became too strong. I pointed out that leading figures in comparative musicology of the time, such as Carl Stumpf, Erich Moritz von Hornbostel, and Otto Abraham, welcomed the opportunities to explore music as part of and during colonial spectacles in the Western metropolis. In their attempt to gather as much empirical data as possible, Stumpf, Hornbostel, and Abraham used every opportunity to collect melodies and songs that were foreign to them. They made their own recordings during performances in the imperial capital, commissioned traveling researchers whom they equipped with a phonograph, or exchanged recordings with other archives and phonographic companies (Ames 2003: 300, referencing Stumpf 2000 [1908]). Musicologists and anthropologists alike had to deal with the fact that non-Western performers were often well aware of common Western expectations and imaginations of allegedly 'authentic' and 'exotic' musical representations, and met them in order to earn a living. "Performers resisted anthropologists' designs," Andrew Zimmerman writes, "for they were cosmopolitan cultural hybrids, often with political agendas of their own, rather than the pure natural peoples anthropologists wished to study" (2001: 7). The promise of early sound technology to 'fix' and salvage music traditions by turning ephemeral sound into tangible objects seemed simply too tempting for many musicologists and anthropologists. Yet it must be noted that the technical setup only allowed for recording those who were willing to go on record. Hence, the contextual and technological possibilities of the time prescribed what could be salvaged. In other words, the musicologist and his apparatus—as documentarians—prescribed the availability and interpretability of the empirical data. "They [were] active participants in the culture that he claim[ed] they study from the outside" (2003: 320), Sterne explains with regard to the US American anthropologist and early sound ethnographer Jesse Walter Fewkes (1850–1930).

In the previous chapter, and the last of my three case studies, I drew on accounts of former missionary and influential Africanist, Diedrich Westermann. I discussed an essay in which Westermann (1931) wrote about both of his professions, elaborating on possibilities of their mutual improvement. Here, I also observed resemblances to the principles of salvage anthropology. Since Westermann was well-aware and in support of social and political transformations set in motion by missionary work and colonial rule, he promoted the urgency to gather as much knowledge about vernacular languages and indigenous life as possible. He was convinced that this racialised knowledge was useful and necessary for the implementation of social development in the colonies. At the same time, Westermann cautioned that modernisation would cause an undesirable level of so-called detribalisation.[7] In the longer term, according to Westermann, this would endanger colonial governing and the deployment of non-*white* labour. In his patronising rhetoric, he claimed that people from the African continent

> 'were losing the basis of their existence (the tribe) ... (and) had lost Lebenslust, Lebensinhalt, Lebenszweck [love of life, content of life and purpose of life]. When a race no longer knew what it was living for, it might well be in danger of decay.' (Tilley 2011: 238, quoting remarks made by Westermann in 1929)

As evinced in this quote, Westermann's assumptions must also be seen as being in line with the principles of indirect rule, for which ethnicised knowledge of vernacular languages and customs was regarded as indispensable. Following Hochman, and considering Westermann's general attitude, I argue that, for Westermann, the salvage endeavour was not merely a *media project*, but a "moral imperative" (Hochman 2014: xv): 'disappearing cultures and people' had to be salvaged from 'losing the basis of their existence.' Westermann made this argument out of his paternalistic, and ostensibly humanistic, concern that African people could lose their 'purpose of life.' What pervades Westermann's statements is his cultural racism, which saw language and culture as markers of alterity and inferiority. Forging a bridge back to Lange's assertion that the salvage paradigm pursued a media and not a social project, my point here demonstrates the paradigm's patronising and morally charged character. For Westermann, salvaging knowledge was a moral project—despite the double standard of those morals.

From this selective overview of my three case studies, it is clear that the salvage operation and constructs of race play out in nuanced ways and on different levels in the *Lautarchiv*. The notion of salvage becomes a common condition that subsists through the *Lautarchiv*'s activities under colonial conditions. The elements of 'urgency, loss, and possibility,' alluded to in Penny's quote at the outset to this section, matter for all three cases. It strikes one as remarkable that it is a particular attitude towards modernisation processes on the part of the recordists that is fundamental to the divergent sound projects. In all three cases, the narrative of technological progress, as manifested through the modern device of the gramophone, epitomises ambivalent, if not antithetical, notions. Sound reproduction promised the possibility of archiving—and thus objectifying—the speech and music of the ethnographic *Other*. Yet by studying the ethnographic *Other*, the anthropological project also sought to define its own society and legitimise its cultural superiority through the mirror of the *Other* (Kaschuba 1999 [2006]: 32). At the same time, modernisation processes, not least in the form of technological innovation, were one of the catalysts for the destruction of what the academy wished to rescue and secure—that is, the categories of difference it needed to define itself against. This points to only some of the contradictions scholars of the nineteenth and early twentieth century had to face. The following pages deal with yet another discrepancy between prevailing epistemic ideals and the figuration of the scientific self.

Making Difference Audible and the Imperative of Objectivity

The idea of 'scientific objectivity' finds its expression not only in the afore-mentioned examples from the case studies in this book, but also in the general characteristics of the salvage paradigm and the recording procedures described. The scholars involved in the *Lautarchiv*'s recording activities were confident in their disciplinary authority and scientific performance—be it in the fields of linguistics, comparative musicology, or anthropology. In their eminent book *Objectivity* (2007), Lorraine Daston and Peter Galison follow the history of sci-entific objectivity as a guiding concept, carving out the interrelations between epistemic concepts and scientific practices. By examining images in anthropo-logical atlases, mainly from the nineteenth but also from the first half of the twentieth century, the two scholars demonstrate how image-making and visual-ising techniques shaped both subjects and objects of science at the time. Ideals like *truth-to-nature* and *mechanical objectivity* were attempts to restrain the scholar's subjectivity, which, however, seemed to function as a necessary defini-tional counterpart to objectivity. In this way, a scientific self was cultivated that converged knowing and knower (36–37). In reference to Daston and Galison, Lange (2013a: 15) poses the question of whether and how the postulate of sci-entific objectivity can be used for the examination of the production of other media, such as film or sound recordings. I understand objectivity as a historical concept—a concept constituting a scientific paradigm, shaping hypotheses, methods, and results.

In German-speaking contexts, physical anthropology is an anthropology that was and is conceived as a natural science. Here, knowledge production was based on the practice of compiling physical collections—in many cases, consisting of human remains. This compilation of physical objects—or rather subjects—coincided with the practice of generating new objects of knowledge, which depended, for instance, on detailed body descriptions. In her work, Lange has been concerned with the disciplinary history of physical anthropology in German-speaking academia. Her interests lie with research practices of collect-ing and/or producing data, rather than with the physical objects themselves (see also Chapter 6, on the concept of sensitive collections). For Lange, it is crucial to study the practices of generating data since it is precisely these techniques that create the discipline's objects of study—epistemic objects that would not exist without, and do not exist prior to, the scientific urge for knowledge. She places special focus on visualising techniques that constitute anthropological and ethnographic data in the form of metric, numerical, visual, but also acoustic information. According to her, (physical) anthropologists sought to make human characteristics visible by compiling anthropometric information, such as measuring data, body descriptions, photographs, films, plaster casts, and sound recordings. The applied visualising techniques constituted new objects of knowledge. Tables, schemes, and graphics promised to make humans 'measurable' and 'objectively' comparable. At the same time, as anthropologist Andre Gingrich writes, "machines and tools of measurement and documentation shaped the reified relation between superior 'white' researchers and their inferiorized and dehumanized alien objects of research" (2010: 372). It was about making difference visible—by making it legible and measurable. In the case of sound, instead, it was about making difference audible.

In her engagement with historical sound recordings, Lange (2011a: 31–37) introduces the term audibilisation (*Hörbarmachung*), as analogous to visualisation (*Sichtbarmachung*). Audibilisation describes the practice of creating objects of sound, understood as sonic objects of knowledge. Historically, recording sound with a technological device has been an active and effective process of producing linguistic, phonetic, musicological, or anthropological knowledge by constructing and maintaining difference. But Lange further states that compiling sound recordings for linguistic, phonetic, musicological, or anthropological purposes has also always made other things audible. For instance, historical sound recordings make the human voice audible as a characteristic and unique sign of an individual.[8] Sound files reveal early sound technology with its distinctive noise; and they might also contain messages addressed to future audiences.

Anthropological techniques and media technologies brought about new epistemic objects, not least by means of *mechanical objectivity*. In this way, the object of sound became a crucial element not only for anthropological, but also linguistic and musicological knowledge production. What is so striking about Lange's argument is that it allows me to make sense of the particular conditions of the sonic events dealt with in this book. "The sound recordings [...]," Lange claims, "are not authentic traces of people, but artificial documents producing a scientific sound object" (2013: 49).[9] Hence, the sound recordings can only be understood in their artificial and constructed nature—that of serving modernity's imperatives of objectivity and technological progress. However, as Lange suggests, mediated sound can also contain other, unintended, even subversive traces: traces undermining such imperatives—implicitly or explicitly, in technological or epistemological terms. As I have shown in this book, one way to make these traces visible, or audible, is through different modes of listening. This book, then, performs another form of audibilisation—an audibilisation that seeks to account for certain limitations and boundaries (see Chapter 3 on failed listening), ruptures and distinct technological conditions (see Chapter 5 on close listening), and the power over who is speaking and who is listening (see Chapter 6 on collective listening).

Sonic Imaginations and Sensory Economies

Returning to approaches in sound studies, the undermining quality of figurations of sound and voice, as well as practices of listening and hearing, can also be explored in other ways. Possibly, and as suggested by Sterne (2012b: 9), drawing on the notion of *sonic imaginations* can be a pertinent tool to examine sound phenomena. For Sterne, tensions between different knowledges of sound are characterised by the desire to rely, on the one hand, on familiar ways and vocabularies of approaching, knowing, and analysing sound as practiced in one's own field, and on the other hand, the attempt to detach oneself from this familiar knowledge, and turn to other ways of knowing sound. "Sound studies," Sterne believes, "should be a central meeting place where sonic imaginations go to be challenged, nurtured, refreshed and transformed" (10). It is in this sense, then, that a sound studies approach to historical sounds from the *Lautarchiv* makes it possible to challenge presumably stable notions of sound and its meaning, and instead accounts for a multiplicity of the audible and its intelligibility.

In their collection of *Keywords in Sound*, Novak and Sakakeeny (2015: 7) emphasise, too, that sound is not a stable object, technologically determined, or perceptible in general or universal terms. But Sterne (2003: 14) points out that many theorists and historians of sound do in fact understand hearing as having static, transhistorical, and 'natural' qualities. In his litany of difference, Sterne brings together a supposedly naturalised and timeless set of attributes of hearing as opposed to seeing. In this, by now famous, audiovisual litany, hearing is considered to be spherical and immersive, tending towards subjectivity and affect. With these attributes, hearing is falsely equated with listening and is only intelligible in opposition to seeing and vision. Seeing, in turn, is considered directional and perspectival, leaning towards objectivity and intellect. Sterne points out the risk that, in this antithetical depiction, one sense appears intelligible only in opposition and in an excluding stance to another sense. In his work, he aims at dismantling and rethinking such ostensibly transhistorical and universal constructs of sound and hearing. He therefore reminds his readers time and again that listening and seeing are learned bodily practices and historically-shaped cultural techniques that create(d) centuries of Western (and Christian) knowledge, thought, and cultural theory.[10]

In the ideologically charged list of differences, it is not only a mutual conditionality of the two senses that becomes *visible*. Indeed, a privileging of the sense of vision over hearing is exposed. The opposition shows that seeing is idealised in its association with modernity's rationality and reason, while hearing signifies the opposite, "manifesting a kind of pure interiority" (15). What follows is that examining sound and hearing succeeds all too often solely by distinguishing it from vision and seeing. This is another reason for Sterne to call for refiguring sound. He wishes to "reopen the question of the sources of rationality and modern ways of knowing" (18). Ultimately, this leads me back to efforts to deconstruct the sound/vision binary and tackle the 'hegemony of vision' within conceptions of modernity. While the sense of seeing and the status of vision are crucial fields of inquiry in cultural theory and history, the sense of hearing and the object of sound have long been ignored as a theoretical subject matter. This is particularly astonishing considering the multitude of sound phenomena that ought to be understood as a direct consequence of the invention of modernity. At the heart of Sterne's work lies thus the call for taking "seriously the role of sound and hearing in modern life [...] to trouble the visualist definition of *modernity*" (3, emphasis in the original).

The editors of the volume *Sensible Objects* (2006) have a slightly different understanding when it comes to prioritising one sense over another in terms of figurations of modernity. To Elizabeth Edwards, Chris Gosden, and Ruth B. Phillips, it is a variety of sensory experiences and mechanisms of control that are integral to modernity. For instance, they refer to transformations of smell and noise through sanitation and industrialisation. While admitting that vision plays a dominant role in and for the analysis of colonial and modernist experiences, Edwards, Gosden, and Phillips *see* hearing as one of the two "primary senses for the production of rational knowledge" (7). They therefore attempt to tackle the fact that the Western sensory schema elides feeling, smelling, and tasting by classifying these senses as negligible. Instead, they advocate for a multi-sensory approach when exploring objects and other trajectories of sensory economies of colonialism and modernity. "Thinking through the senses" (2), they posit, means to understand vision as only one possible way to grasp colonial encounters and the material traces accumulated in Western institutions. I will come back to the notion of a multi-sensory approach in the conclusion to this chapter.

Anthropology's Visual and Acoustic Legacies

The preoccupation with questions of visuality and the colonial gaze in general, and anthropology's visual legacy in particular, is a rich and varied field of study. The urgency to deal with anthropology's visual archives emerged not least as a response to, and in the aftermath of growing concerns regarding the discipline's knowledge making processes.[11] By contrast, work on acoustic legacies and the relationship between anthropology and phonography does not have such long-standing trajectories of critical debate to look back to. This is why the following section explores which analytical angles, developed in the realms of visual anthropology and visual history, may be transferable to acoustic legacies. However, it is not my aim to consider the entire range of extensive scholarship on the entangled relations between anthropology and photography (e.g. Edwards 2001; Pinney 2011; Sekula 1989), not to mention the massive body of literature on linkages between photography and history (by scholars such as Walter Benjamin, Siegfried Kracauer, or Roland Barthes). Rather, I concentrate on introducing perspectives from visual anthropology to what might be considered an approach of *sonic anthropology*.

When looking at anthropology's visualising practices of the past, there seem to be certain traits shared with the sonic practices I outlined previously. But there are also striking differences between visual and sonic traces. In often contrasting ways, the two legacies have left both epistemic and literal marks in a variety of disciplines and institutions. In material terms alone, visual holdings of historical imagery surpass acoustic repositories—not only in Berlin. In this study, the holdings of the *Lautarchiv* are the starting point for an investigation of the practices and histories associated with the different archival collections housed at the sound archive. As outlined in my introduction, the archive's core consists of 4,500 shellac records and almost the same number of duplicates.[12] From this massive accumulation, however, only a relatively small number of files suggest an immediate connection to colonial presences and colonial knowledge production. Appraising these files, I decided to examine the modest amount of five recordings as part of my case studies.

A quantitative distinction hence becomes obvious when considering the sheer number of archival records, as well as the extent of research carried out on the history of anthropology's relationship with visuality. Quantity becomes further apparent with regard to the efforts undertaken over the past decades on the part of ethnographic museums and other knowledge institutions to deal with their audiovisual collections from colonial times. This effort includes large digitisation and cataloguing projects, providing online access to digital collections, and reaching out to descendants and other possible stakeholders. In this context, attempts by postcolonial subjects to re-appropriate visual objects from the archives are tremendously important (e.g. Edwards and Morton 2009). But the predominance of visuality cannot be explained in quantitative terms alone. Visuality and the question of representation play out on different levels, both past and present. Photographs from the past, categorised as 'anthropological' or 'ethnographic,' indicate different visualising practices. Understood as indexical traces, they served and partly continue to serve as sources of evidence and truth—and often as markers of difference. As collection items, they fill hundreds and thousands of pages and registers; they are hidden in drawers, forgotten in museum depots, public and private archives. As exhibition objects, ethnographic museums often show them either as illustrative large-scale projections or in dimmed showcases in an effort to protect what is displayed from natural light and the irreverent gaze.

During the nineteenth and early twentieth century, Edwards argues, the predominance of visuality related to "an ordering of knowledge that was itself premised on a privileging of vision on which photography was both constitutive and constituted" (2001: 11). In anthropology, the 'ordering of knowledge' through photographic technologies found its most instrumentalising expression in anthropometric imagery. It did not take long until anthropologists employed anthropometric methods during their field trips, compiling large amounts of visual and measuring data. Today, these racialising images belong to the most contentious collections in the visual colonial archive. In the catalogues of ethnographic collections, there exist many photographs not taken 'in the field' but in professional photo studios or at research institutions in the (Western) metropolis. Here, the same distinction between different collection types applies as for acoustic collections. Colonial photography did not solely originate in colonised territories, but in the imperial metropolis as well. The fact that all of the sound recordings housed at the *Lautarchiv* were compiled in Germany and Europe[13] prompted me to consider the *Lautarchiv* a colonial archive 'at home,' generated in the heart of the European metropolis.[14]

As the subtitle of her book, *Photographs, Anthropology, and Museums*, suggests, Elizabeth Edwards aims to uncover the interdependent relationship between medium, discipline, and institution. In her introduction, Edwards mentions that she deliberately chose to concentrate on specific photographic events, arguing that her conceptual and methodological ideas "might be extended to other bodies of material and to contribute to a broader understanding" (4) of the relationship between media and institutions. I wish to take Edwards up on this, although she may be alluding to other bodies of imagery and broader questions of photography, ethnography, and history than other media, such as sound. Yet in Chapter 4, I already showed how Edwards' thoughts on the colonial archive 'at home,' which in her case refers to visual archives in British institutions, also offer valuable incentives for the metropolitan archive I am dealing with. One of the crucial questions Edwards, like many other visual anthropologists, poses is how to work with, through, and against colonial photography. Likewise, and as a common thread throughout this book, students of colonialism ask how to move within—along and against the grain of—the colonial archive. As for my part, I wonder how to tell histories with, through, and against colonial sounds.

Important for Edwards' research on historical imagery is the assumption that focusing on surface and content alone will reveal only the obvious. "Instead," she claims, "one should concentrate on detail" (2). Paying attention to the photographs' historicity, meaning the intersecting histories of photographic practices, is key when wishing to address details and "little narratives" (3; see also my introduction). Together with Christopher Morton, Edwards advocates for "a more nuanced approach in which the production, dissemination, consumption, possession and display of photographs are all considered as generating photography's situational and historical meanings" (2009: 6). Ultimately, this may also offer insight into the question of how and when canonical, yet fluid, (historical) categories deem photos as 'ethnographic' or 'anthropological.' Understanding photographs from the past as highly ambiguous and time-contingent media fits in with my depiction of sound recordings from the past. In both cases, the temporal ambiguity arises from the notion of a captured piece of the past retrieved and seized in the present. As conceived in nineteenth-century anthropology, a fragment of space and time becomes a placeholder for some sort of imagined and arbitrary whole.

While photographic technologies promised to fix observed realities, cultures, and not least, race, they in fact fabricated and reified those realities, cultures, and race. Yet anthropologist Deborah Poole shows that:

the understanding of race that emerges from a history of anthropological photography is clearly as much about the instability of the
photograph as ethnological evidence and the unshakeable suspicion
that perhaps things are not what they appear to be as it is about fixing the native subject as a particular racial type. (2005: 165)

It is this search for moments of fracture that might manifest a possibility to
counter initial promises of stability by means of technology. What seems to
sustain the work of visual anthropologists and postcolonial subjects alike is this
ambivalent condition of historical photographs. On the one hand, photographs
are symbols of the asymmetries of power caused by the epistemic framing of
their production. On the other hand, photographs also carry the potential of
contesting established colonial histories and epistemologies. In her case studies,
Edwards looks for destabilising points of fracture in order to find alternative
histories and new narrative spaces—"even in the most dense colonial documents" (2001: 12). A similar stance applies to the institution of the archive and
the (ethnographic) museum. As highly contested places because of their histories of colonial complicity, they have simultaneously become places of debate
and renewal. After all, it is the colonial archive, which keeps and reifies colonial
documents, where both visual and acoustic legacies emerge. It is the archive,
with its practices and politics, in which both legacies become decodable and
possibly recodable.

Moreover, Edwards sees the relevance in investigating the social and material biographies of photographs. In this, she follows important thinkers, such
as Arjun Appadurai (1986) and Igor Kopytoff (1986) in their accounts of the
social life and an anthropology of things. The photograph, Edwards says, "must
be examined through the process of its production, exchange, and consumption" (2001: 13). "Integral to social biography," she goes on:

is the way in which the meaning of photographs, generated by viewers, depends on the context of their viewing, and their dependence
on written or spoken 'text' to control semiotic energy and anchor
meaning in relation to embodied subjectivities of the viewer. These
are acts upon photographs, and result in shifts in its meaning and
performance, over time and space [...]. (14)

What strikes me here is the emphasis Edwards lays on the viewer and their
viewing. This perspective seems easily translatable into the listener and their

listening. Depending on their contexts, viewers and listeners alike generate situational, and hence shifting, meaning. In one moment, a sound recording stands for a language sample of a specific language type. In the next moment, it is the recording's medium, the material of shellac, which bears witness to early sound technology and a colonial commodity. And in yet another moment, the same sound recording can act as the acoustic testament of a historical subject, which may have left no other trace.

Edwards believes that the concept of the objects' social biographies can be linked to questions of materiality. "What things are made of and how they are materially presented," she argues, "relates directly to their social, economic and political discourses and their function as documents" (15). For her, this also alludes to the *model of visual economy* as developed by Poole. Poole introduces this concept in order to refer to the "organization of people, ideas, and objects" (1997: 8). For her, the principles of visual economy involve at least three levels of organisation: the production of images, their circulation, and the value attached to them within specific cultural and discursive systems. Again, I suggest translating this concept to the notion of a *model of sonic economy*. In doing so, questions arise as to who produced the *Lautarchiv*'s sound recordings, how and in which form they circulated, and what kind of meaning they stood and stand for.[15]

There are plenty of conceptual and methodological strands in visual anthropology and visual history that tie in with the sonic contexts of the *Lautarchiv*. Nevertheless, inquiries into historical sound cannot assemble their analytical toolkit exclusively from approaches to visual legacies. Sound studies share questions and concerns with other domains, but also address very distinct analytical problems. In the following, I return to positions from the field of sound studies once more, to show that sound scholars draw from a variety of influences and approaches.

Historicising Sound

Reflexivity, historicity, and *positionality*—for Sterne, these are crucial cornerstones of the field of sound studies. While these key parameters resonate throughout the book, they have not always appeared merely in relation to sound and its analysis. The previous section, for instance, showed that visuality and anthropological photography are fluid categories, embedded in broader and mobile contexts of knowledge, and therefore require a nuanced and reflexive approach. The following, then, aims to pinpoint how the object of sound and its inquiry relate to concepts of reflexivity, historicity, and positionality.

> Sound students produce and transform knowledge about sound and in the process reflexively attend to the (cultural, political, environmental, aesthetic...) stakes of that knowledge production. By *reflexivity*, I [Sterne] refer to arguments developed by Pierre Bourdieu and Donna Haraway. Both argue that knowers must place themselves in relation to what it is they want to know: they must account for their own positions and prejudices, lest scholars misattribute them as qualities of the object of study. This means that if we use concepts drawn from the study of human auditory perception, we must account for the *historicity* of that knowledge [...]. Depending on the positioning of hearers, a space may sound totally different. [...] Hearing requires *positionality*. (Sterne 2012b: 3–4, my emphasis)

Naturally, expecting a high degree of reflexivity from knowers and knowledge producers is not unique to the field of sound studies, as the reference to Pierre Bourdieu and Donna Haraway illustrates. Phenomena of sound can evoke many research interests and questions, emerging discursively and from a pool of possible concerns (see also Chapter 4 and my discussion of Arlette Farge). Accordingly, the research questions I developed are not inherent to my object of study, but bound to my position and the trajectories I wish to follow. In a similar vein, Paul Ricœur (2004: 177) reminds us that what constitutes historical knowledge is exactly the reciprocity between trace, document, and question. It is important to acknowledge that Sterne regards reflexivity as a constitutive pillar of any approach to sound. His argument stands in stark contrast to the previous assertions in this chapter, where I drew on the paradigm of objectivity and the desire to disconnect knowledge production from a scientific self. Likewise, a demand for reflexivity and historicity seems to contradict the premises of early sound reproduction. At the turn of the twentieth century, the phonograph was seen as a surgical instrument that could dissect speech and music in their formal structures (Ames 2003: 314). It was assumed that sound could be fixed on a recording medium like a corpse on a dissecting table. For the imperative of (mechanical) objectivity, the historicity of knowledge associated with sound, sound technology, and auditory practices was not a driving factor. However, just as practices of listening change, so do other modes of perception and conception of sound. It is in this vein that Novak and Sakakeeny (2015: 6) warn against the risk of generalising sound and ignoring historical and cultural particularities of sonic categories. Instead, they plead for destabilising and denaturalising sound as a static and distinct object. Finally, I hope Sterne's reminder that 'hearing requires positionality' resonates through all of my chapters, both through the different modes of listening and the conceptual framing. Eidsheim even goes so far as to advocate a radical shift towards a focus on processes of hearing, away from the essentialised figure of sound. According to her, this shift allows for allocating certain qualities not to the object of sound but to the one who studies the object. As stressed in my introduction, I follow Eidsheim's credo that listening is always already political for ways of listening reflect "the listener's historical, cultural, social, political, moral, ethical, academic, or any other positionality" (2019: 58).

In *The Race of Sound* (2019), Eidsheim takes the project of denaturalising sound to a new level. One of her central arguments is to pay more attention to hearing and the politics of listening. Although Eidsheim looks at contemporary practices of racialised constructs of sound, she also points to the long history of scientific racism and to genealogies of practices of measuring race by sonic means. Arguing "that the body has been objectified and used as a measure of race and as evidence of innate racial difference," she suggests that "voice is equally objectified, entrained, and used as a 'measure' of race (i.e., a feature that is believed to represent something specific but has the power to do so only through social consensus)" (17). Eidsheim's recent work can be seen as a continuation of her earlier research interests in the relation between voice, performativity, and race. Conceptually, her work ties in with what Sterne (2003: 13) had already called for in *The Audible Past*: showing that sound is a variable and not a constant; understanding that sound is not a distinct object of research, but requires attention to its historical particularity and discursive embeddedness. Yet, as Kara Keeling made clear at a lecture in Berlin in 2018, Eidsheim's assertions must be understood in more radical terms. For Keeling, Eidsheim's earlier monograph, *Sensing Sound* (2015) was a radical intervention, not only for the discipline of musicology, but also for the broader field of sound studies.[16] With the aim to re-envision how to think about sound and music, Eidsheim revisits practices of listening by means of a multi-sensory perspective—*the practice of vibration*. By approaching music (and sound) in terms of a vibrational practice, Eidsheim wants to consider all aural, tactile, spatial, physical, and material sensations. The practice of vibration takes into account the nonfixity of music, "and recognizes that it always comes into being through an unfolding and dynamic material set of relations" (2015: 10). As the previous chapters suggest, I follow Eidsheim in her understanding of sound as a multi-layered phenomenon and as defined by the one who listens.

The interventionist work of Eidsheim illustrates that sound studies are neither a unified field of study, nor based on unified methodologies, concepts, and research questions. Nevertheless, over the past decades, there have been attempts to map genealogies of sound research, of common concepts, and terminologies. Today, one can consult an impressive body of literature that deals with the question of what sound studies *are* and what they *do*. There exists a wide range of basic research, anthologies, and emerging journals that bring together a whole array of theories and disciplines (e.g. Novak and Sakakeeny 2015; Papenburg and Schulze 2016; Pinch and Bjisterveld 2011; Radano and Olaniyan 2016; Smith 2004; Sterne 2012a).[17] Sound scholarship found its niche in a variety of disciplines, ranging from history and musicology, anthropology and architecture, to media, literary and cultural studies. Despite intra-disciplinary discourses on sound, there is also the conviction that sound is "a problem that cuts across academic disciplines, methods and objects" (Sterne 2012b: 5). It is this traversing character of sound that makes sound studies a multi-faceted and a transdisciplinary project, where nurturing and contradictory forces exist side by side. However, one also has to acknowledge, as most of the anthologies and research networks admit, that "the field as a whole has remained deeply committed to Western intellectual lineages and histories" (Novak and Sakakeeny 2015: 7).[18]

A common thread in the scholarly field of sound studies is to understand sound as an analytical problem, which means to assess sound in all its multi-valence—ranging from music and vibration to voice, noise, and silence. With this understanding also comes the idea that "sound studies is an academic field in the humanities and social sciences defined by combination of object and approach" (Sterne 2012b: 4). In this book, especially with regard to the three case studies, the combination of object and approach becomes evident. My three case studies evolved around specific sound *objects*; in each case study, the *approach* was concerned with a different mode of and reflection upon listening and knowing sound. As Karin Bijsterveld (2019: 5) suggests, sonic skills and their analyses are not limited to practices of listening, but include practices of making, recording, storing, and retrieving sound. Thinking sonically allows us to address the big questions of cultural crises (Sterne 2012b: 3), characterised not least by the coloniality of power and knowledge. Subsequently, this book aimed to pose the big question of how to work through colonial and postcolonial discourses by means of thinking with and through sound. In the course of this study, I have taken principles of sound studies as key vectors, arguing that approaches to the *Lautarchiv* must be transdisciplinary, multitemporal *and* multisensorial.

Conclusion

By bringing together strands from the field of sound studies, and in particular from sound and media history, this chapter aimed to complement and complete the conceptual framing of this book. Concentrating on lineages of the salvage paradigm, moreover, it sought to recall and discuss aspects of the history of anthropology. For both contexts—the genealogy of the medium of the gramophone and the discipline of anthropology—, a reflection on ideologies of race and difference was of crucial significance. I demonstrated that constructs of race have to be understood as constitutive, and at the same time as the outcome, of early sound reproduction, preservation, and exploration. In reference to perspectives in cultural history and theory, I structured my analytical approach by focusing on the role of media practices and listening techniques. Within the investigation of sound phenomena, the attention on practices, those of hearing and listening in particular, allows us to shift our awareness first and foremost to the one who listens—but also to the one who makes, records, stores, and retrieves sound.

In reference to Poole's *model of visual economy*, developed as part of her account of vision, race, and modernity of the Andean world, this chapter suggests that it may be worth thinking in terms of a *model of sonic economy*. A model of sonic economy attends to the production, circulation, and transformation of concepts and practices related to mediated sound and the auditory. It also allows for describing moments of transition of the material entity of sound in temporal, material, and spatial terms. Inscribed on wax plates, the recorded sound was transferred to copper masters and pressed to shellac discs. From archival backup copies on tapes and CDs, it was transferred into digital MP3 and WAV files. As Poole (1997: 9–13) argues, the material forms of photographs follow their respective social, economic, and political function. On the one hand, the initial collection of shellac records was supposed to form the core of an archive yet to be institutionally established. At the same time, the records also served as a product that could be exchanged between archival institutions, circulated among researchers, and purchased by interested listeners. The backup copies, on the other hand, remain in the archive, while the digital files are constantly downloaded and shared, thereby crossing disciplinary and discursive boundaries, imaginary and actual borders (Hennig 2016: 362–363).

"They were made for a reason," Edwards writes. Photographs are "objects created with a clear biographical intention: they are inextricably linked to the past, but they are also about the future – a moment, fixed and active in the present, specifically to communicate the past in the future" (2001: 14). For Edwards, the 'desire' to transfer a past present into the future is "fundamental to the act of photography" (14). In this chapter, I showed that the same can be said about the act of recording sound. However, even if objects are created with a 'clear biographical intention,' their social and discursive career does not necessarily continue to follow the path set out by their initial purpose of production. Rather, *the social life of things* is mobile and versatile (Appadurai 1986). Thinking in terms of social and cultural biographies of things, historical photographs as well as sound recordings appear as active and mobile objects that change depending on multiple and shifting modes of producing meaning.

It is not only objects that are mobile; concepts, technologies, and practices are too. At the very beginning of this chapter, and with reference to Chun and Joyrich, I showed how understanding race as a mobilising technology allows us to grasp the complexities of racial assemblages. Following the argument that sound technologies mobilise race formations and that, in turn, race constitutes sound recordings, I showed that objects of sound and practices of listening should be regarded as pertinent lenses for understanding figurations of modernity. This also ties in with the work of those who point out that constructions of race and conceptions of European modernity are inextricably linked (e.g. Bruns, Hampf, and Kämpf 2018; Conrad and Randeria 2013 [2002]). Furthermore, with a focus on the sonic, it is possible to oppose the powerful trope of the hegemony of vision. It becomes possible to counter the common critique that conceptions of modernity privilege the visual over the acoustic—a prominent concern of scholars subscribing to the field of sound studies (Morat and Ziemer 2018: IX).

Looking back on my depictions of the archival in Chapter 4, I wished to recall the peculiarities of the notions of both the discursive archive and the sound archive. Thinking critically in archival terms may include possible prospects for the sound archive's future, and may even serve the attempt at decolonising the *Lautarchiv*. In an interview dealing with the big question-mark hovering over the future of *the archive*, Petra Löffler advocates the concept of thinking in terms of an archive of relations (Kuster, Lange, and Löffler 2019: 106). Together with Brigitta Kuster and Britta Lange, Löffler discusses topics ranging from the politics of collecting and the colonial archive to possibilities of decolonising knowledge. Löffler understands the archive of relations as not defined by the institution, by materiality, or by ownership. Rather, the media scholar argues, one should shift the attention to practices of the archive. How does one archive and de-archive, Löffler asks. For me, this assertion is another move away from a rather normative figure—the figure of the archive—and towards an understanding of dynamic practices of exchange, circulation, and assemblage. In her thoughts on the practices and politics of the archive, Lange holds the opinion that one must reflect on epistemology and on questions of knowledge production in terms of both the past and the present. In other words, decolonising the archive becomes possible only through decolonising knowledge and knowledge making (see also Chapter 6).

With respect to archival practices, Löffler also wonders whether the search for what was not archived, what did not fit the colonial logic of the archive, can be understood as a subversive practice of the non-archived. In relation to the colonial sound archive, the non-archived has two facets. First, it refers to the archival order, which abided by specific ideas regarding who, and for what purpose, should or should not go on record. Secondly, it relates to the ones who refused to give their voice, to the ones who did not conform to the archival order. The manifest absence of female voices among the sound recordings, for instance, was not opposed to the archival logic, as discussed in detail in Chapter 5. When engaging with the acoustic traces that have been archived, when reflecting on different modes of listening of the past and the present, one also needs to consider silences and non-sounds, which account for the untold testimonies that have neither been inscribed on wax nor archived, but can only be imagined. However, as discussed previously, listening to silence and considering archival gaps comes with two risks: one risk is the desire to fill those gaps in the sense of repair and closure. A second is the peril of (re)constituting gaps and silences by the act of re-codifying and updating them. Considering Eidsheim's account that the "definition of sound is dependent on who is listening" (2015: 151), the question, then, is how does one define silence. Following the perception of sound not as a fixed figure but a "composite of visual, textural, discursive, and other kinds of information" (Eidsheim 2012: 9), I argue, allows for the possibility and, in fact, the necessity to speak about silence and absence as determined by a multiplicity of information.

8
Coda

The Future/s of the *Lautarchiv*

This book explored different avenues for rethinking the acoustic legacies of the colonial archive, discussing different conceptual lenses and modes of listening. It is my hope that the deep drills I conducted in this study, both in terms of case studies as well as theoretical and disciplinary positions, will inspire further engagement with and research on the *Lautarchiv*. As mentioned in my introduction and at various points in this book, it is difficult to foresee the future of the *Lautarchiv* at its new location: the Humboldt Forum. Sceptical voices may argue that the mere shell and architecture of the Forum alone—the copy of a Prussian king's castle, an emblem of European hegemony—precludes any possibility of critical engagement. For me, the decision to partly reconstruct the City Palace is a sign of the persistence of hegemonic regimes of representation that tend to follow Royal Prussian narratives, rather than a reflection of the contemporary post-migrant German society and its trajectories.[1] Nevertheless, I hope that my analyses of traces that attest to these trajectories will spur further reflection on post/colonial conditions of the present and future: in particular, the difficulty of dealing with Germany's colonial legacies. The hope remains that institutions such as the Humboldt Forum can become places of open debate and continuous negotiation—of challenging established national narratives and collective memories. Regardless of the prospects of the Humboldt Forum in the years to come, I am convinced that going back to an archival project from the past can contribute to imagining future archival projects and to raising awareness of colonial continuities.

On the final pages of this book, I intend to touch upon two different scenarios I see in relation to the *Lautarchiv* and this study. The first part deals with exemplary contemporary archival projects that seek to document heterogeneous histories. These projects aim to replace narratives that fail to account for global entanglements and migratory movements, inequalities and (epistemic) violence. I examine how these projects can be linked to prospects for the *Lautarchiv* as part of the Humboldt Forum. The second part ventures into the political now. Here, I discuss a specific development in current European asylum politics: with Germany and its Federal Office for Migration and Refugees at the forefront, speech analysis technology is used to compile voice samples of asylum seekers to determine their countries of origin and hence their asylum status. In this process of building a voice archive, albeit one with different political intentions, I draw an analogy between the *Lautarchiv* and the present-day practice of producing speech samples for the purpose of providing evidence; evidence that proves racial and cultural difference or a presumed stable resemblance between spoken language and geopolitical borders (Pfeifer forthcoming). As discussed in the previous chapter, both of these objectives echo the nexus of race and technology, pointing to the construction of race and difference as simultaneously constitutive of and constituted by technology.

* * *

The oral history project *Archive of Refuge* is one of the current archival projects I would like to discuss. Launched in late 2021, *Archive of Refuge* was curated by Manuela Bojadžijev and Carolin Emcke, in collaboration with a number of other intellectuals, scholars, and activists. While one of the aims of this study was to show that sources from the *Lautarchiv* bear witness to global entanglements before the second half of the twentieth century, *Archive of Refuge* sought to assemble memories of migration as part of Germany's post-war history. The outcome of the project is a digital commemorative site featuring forty-one multilingual video interviews, lasting several hours, with people who immigrated to East and West Germany between 1945 and 2016. The project's goal was to provide an innovative tool—that is, an online archive—to narrate German history: a history that is intrinsically connected to (im)migration.[2]

Linking the two archival projects—the *Lautarchiv* and *Archive of Refuge*—is a balancing act. While the first project was intended to attest to the narrative of Germany as a nation of technological and scientific progress, the latter seeks to show that migratory movements are an integral part of German society and history. While one project was conceived to form a science-based repository proving cultural and racial difference, the other wished to create a pool of (re)sources to be used in political education and critical migration research. In these concluding remarks, I suggest that the *Lautarchiv* can be seen both as a counter-archive and a reference point for projects such as *Archive of Refuge*. In my approach to the *Lautarchiv*, it became manifest how the politics of the archive determine narratives and memories of past, present, and future. My study thus joins the ranks of many, but still too few, readings of the archive against the grain, which attempt to unravel the power of the constitution of archives, the production of history, and the formation of cultural memory. Here, I seek to demonstrate how different intentionalities and ways of using technologies affect the politics of the archive.

In its design as an institutionally embedded archive, *Archive of Refuge* forms a repository that is 'filled' once and can then be visited and used online. This, however, does not mean that the archive, once it has been constituted, is complete and finished. Rather, its primary purpose lies in its continuous use and in the ever-new inquiries and interpretations that arise from diverse groups of users. At the beginning of the twenty-first century, none other than Stuart Hall (2001) and Arjun Appadurai (2003) advocated for the vision of a *living archive*. For Hall, describing the archive as living "means present, on-going, continuing, unfinished, open-ended" (2001: 89). At first glance, this seems to contradict common ideas of the archive as referring exclusively to the past; of the archive as a closed set of sources. Yet, against the backdrop of this book, it should be clear that in dealing with the archive—both as an institution and a concept—, there is the need for reflection in a threefold manner: one needs to reflect on the moment of the archive's genesis, on its fragmentary and fragile status, and on the moment(s) of its retrieval (see Chapter 2 and 4). It was one of the challenges of this book to account for these different moments, to grasp the *Lautarchiv* as a discursive formation, marked by gaps and ruptures, and defined by transformations rather than fixed presences and meanings.

Visions of the living archive emerged long before the idea for *Archive of Refuge* was born and long before "the long summer of migration" (Hess et al. 2017), in 2015, prompted many people to feel differently about flight and displacement (in both solidary and anti-humanitarian ways). *Archive of Refuge* is one possible answer to the public discourse on migration, which has been and is being fuelled by volatile and heated debates in the realm of media and politics. While Hall reflected on the "living archive of the diaspora" (2001: 89) by examining each term in detail: living, archive, and diaspora, Appadurai wrote about what he would call the *migrant archive*. In line with Hall, who depicted the living archive as a "continuous production" (91), Appadurai understands the migrant archive as "a continuous and conscious work of the imagination, seeking in collective memory an ethical basis for the sustainable reproduction of cultural identities in the new society" (2003: 23). I agree with Appadurai's view that the migrant archive, as well as the work of imagination, is of vital importance for the creation and re-creation of cultural identities. Furthermore, as suggested by Michael Rothberg and previously discussed in this book, it seems worthwhile to approach collective memory as multidirectional. *Archive of Refuge*, a collection of distinct and individual stories, has become a site where these stories—which ultimately do not focus exclusively on migration and flight at all—productively overlap, connect, or contradict each other, allowing for ongoing and possibly conflicting negotiations. "When the productive, inter-cultural dynamic of multidirectional memory is explicitly claimed," Rothberg writes, there is "the potential to create new forms of solidarity and new visions of justice" (2009: 5).[3] As far as the Humboldt Forum is concerned, even after its opening, I wonder whether there is a chance that the museum project will ever live up to this explicit claim: to be open to dynamic rather than static museum and memory practices.

According to Appadurai, the migrant archive operates "outside the official spheres of both the home society and the new society" (2003: 23). It consists of archival documents and traces that are part of everyday life: textual, visual, and oral archives, all serving as deliberate repositories for memories outside the remit of the state. A striking example of the constitution of a migrant archive is DOMiD—the Documentation Centre and Museum of Migration in Germany.[4] As a non-governmental organisation, DOMiD was founded by a small group of migrants from Turkey, who made it their task to collect and preserve testimonials bearing witness to the diverse histories of migration in Germany.[5] In 2020, DOMiD celebrated its thirtieth anniversary, now com-prising an archive of more than one hundred thousand documents and arti-facts reflecting the post-migrant German society. One year earlier, in 2019, the organisation announced that a central and publicly funded museum—the *'Haus der Einwanderungsgesellschaft'*—is set to open in Cologne in 2023.[6] The founding of a central museum had been the subject of controversial discussion for decades, and represents a future archive and exhibition project that will operate and mediate within both official and non-governmental structures.

As has been stressed before, the *Lautarchiv* differs from other archives because its sources were exclusively produced for the purpose of the archive (see Chapter 4). In this sense, the *Lautarchiv* is similar to a project like *Archive of Refuge*. In contrast to DOMiD, neither the *Lautarchiv* nor *Archive of Refuge* form repositories to be filled with already existing documents or traces that have survived purposely or accidentally. Nevertheless, I deemed it important to show that the records produced and preserved at the *Lautarchiv* are inflected by the contingency of history. It was the state of a global war that offered German scholars a site of research almost literally on their doorsteps. It was the rise of the global labour market that not only brought non-*white* military troops and labour corps to the European theatres of war, but also recruited non-*white* people to perform at commercial sites of exoticisation and colonial sensationalism. It was the prolonged and constant mobility of people and goods, of ideas and ideologies. As Europeans set out to mission sites, colonial trading bases, and settler colonies in search of a better or different future, non-Europeans entered the colonial centres in Europe. In most cases, it was, however, impossible for them to fully arrive and settle in Europe. Both then and now, the notion of the *Other* who keeps arriving hovers over the reality of migration to Europe and Germany. In this sense, Regina Römhild (2018: 78) argues, the concept of post-migration can help us to negotiate the political category of migration as a category of difference without invalidating the significance of migration as a political practice.

By rethinking archival categories and established historiographies, a primary goal of my research was to draw attention to the discontinuities of the archive and the contingency of the *Lautarchiv*'s history. Likewise, DOMiD and *Archive of Refuge* attempt to challenge the grand national narrative by assembling divergent memories of migration and post-migration. Both archival projects seek to document a variety of stories, dating from different times and relating to a range of experiences of flight, exile, and belonging. In doing so, they strive to trace specific genealogies of migratory and diasporic histories, yet without wanting to homogenise the different conditions under which migration has taken place and continues to take place. The projects demonstrate that migratory histories have a lasting impact on and continue to shape German society: a wealthy and heterogeneous society, in which, however, wealth, recognition, and representation are unequally distributed along various axes of power and (structural) discrimination. Both DOMiD and *Archive of Refuge* testify to causes of postcolonial (amongst many others) migratory movements. A crucial point of reference might be the slogan 'we are here because you were there,' as famously coined by novelist Ambalavaner Sivanandan (1923–2018). This slogan has been adopted by post/migrants, refugees, and activists since the 1980s, but has received renewed attention in protests against the current European border regime. In recent years, Appadurai has made the provocative proposal to redefine museum objects of the Berlin ethnographic collections that have been moved to the Humboldt Forum as 'accidental refugees.' Unlike most human migrants, Appadurai states, the objects "did not come to Germany willingly or by their own volition" (2017: 407)—the objects are *here* because adventurers, collectors, and scholars were *there*. Museum objects usually stand for fixed meanings, for the meaning and function they supposedly had in the context of their original location or in the past. Those meanings are not usually about the processes of their circulation and relocation, about the conditions that brought the objects to the Berlin depots. In the case of human migrants and refugees, it is the other way around: their stories are usually determined by translocation and displacement. Appadurai argues that both refugee humans and refugee objects are in need of new stories. For him, a "better balance could be achieved if refugee objects and refugee humans could be seen as complex and interactive mixtures of stability and dislocation" (407).

Returning to Appadurai's earlier essay "Archive and Aspiration" (2003), it is not materiality, but the stories of museum collections and the uses of archives that determine their design, agency, and intentionalities. What Appadurai observes is a Cartesian split between the archive's materiality—"its paper, its textures, its dust, its files, its buildings"—and the archive's spirit of "pastness." For him, it is not the materiality but this spirit—a "deep sacrality of the past" (15)—that invigorates the archive. With regard to this orientation towards the past, Appadurai diagnoses a certain fuzziness and a lack of understanding of what defines the archive and the past as sacralised. As discussed in Chapter 2, Appadurai belongs to the group of anthropologists who wonder why the field's foci are occupied with relations between past and present, and less with questions of futurity and the future (e.g. Appadurai 2013; Bryant and Knight 2019). What resonates in Appadurai's critique is that, in many cases, the focus on the past and the archive is charged with notions of the 'sacred' nation state, of national heritage, and national imaginations. Appadurai wishes to move away from the analytical category of the nation state, from thinking in delimited containers, in terms of space, time, and identity. Similarly, this study sought to overcome the notion of national heritage. I have shown that perceiving the acoustic legacies of the *Lautarchiv* as static and linear national heritage only tells half the story. As emphasised at various points throughout this book, in disciplines such as linguistics and anthropology, established narratives of practices of collecting and archiving, of the history of the city of Berlin and the Humboldt University silence colonial entanglements as the unequal conditions on which many of such institutions and practices rest. In my opinion, the Humboldt Forum must become a site where these conditions come to the fore, where the very existence of the ethnographic collections of the Ethnological Museum of Berlin, as well as the *Lautarchiv*'s sound collections, testifies to their colonial trajectories.

While this study has largely focused on refiguring the archive and narratives of the past, a project like *Archive of Refuge* can intervene in the divisions that exist between past, present, and future. Revolving around post-war history, *Archive of Refuge* is intended to serve as an educational tool capable of shaping new solidarities and alternative futures: futures in which official German narratives attest to the post-migrant society, one consisting of and building on contrapuntal memories. Can the Humboldt Forum also be a place that mediates between past, present, and future? Is this what the combination of reconstructed and new architectural facades could enable after all?

The diasporic and migrant archive is understood to be highly active and interactive. One way for the *Lautarchiv*, as well as projects like *Archive of Refuge* and DOMiD, to remain alive, is to place emphasis on political education and research inquiries that (re)negotiate and relate to the stories preserved in the archives in different ways. In this sense, the *Lautarchiv* can also be understood as a living archive. It is my hope that this book keeps the *Lautarchiv* alive by listening to and becoming part of the archived stories. In the words of Britta Lange, this means that "the stories of the others are connected to our stories through listening, they become part of our story and we become part of theirs. We are drawn into it. We listen to the story, but we are also part of the story if we listen now" (2019: 204–205).[7] Given this book's focus on listening, I ask whether the Humboldt Forum can also become a site of listening. Only time will tell if the Forum can be a place where visitors and the stories told in the exhibition spaces—through objects and archives—meet, cross, and possibly merge.

The *Lautarchiv*, DOMiD, and the *Archive of Refuge* offer the possibility to negotiate individual memories and personal stories alongside shared narratives and collective memories, all in one place—the site of the digital archive. I trust that both the practice of revisiting historical archives and that of building new, open-ended archives helps to form rich and sustainable collective memories in the present and for the future. Inspired by Appadurai, I want to believe in archives where "new solidarities might produce memories, rather than just waiting for them" (2003: 25).

* * *

As indicated at the beginning of these final pages, I want to conclude by touching upon a completely different and alarming instance of another current archival project. One might say that it is the opposite of the migrant archive seeking new solidarities and collective memories. This archive is the other side of the coin of the living archive; it is related to what has become known as 'migration management.' I am referring to the collection of (biometric) data by the German Federal Office for Migration and Refugees. In 2016, the governmental institution introduced the nationwide use of biometric tools in asylum procedures. Referred to as 'integrated identity management,' the IT tools include the standardised transliteration of names into Latin characters, the analysis and interpretation of mobile phone data, as well as biometric facial and voice recognition software (Biselli 2018).[8] In these concluding remarks, I wish to compare the use and supposed usefulness of these ongoing racialising techniques with procedures that have been implemented within the scope of the *Lautarchiv*. In doing so, I will concentrate on the use of biometric voice analysis software. Voice analysis for the identification of the 'ethnic origin' of asylum seekers, which, according to German law, determines the right to asylum, is not a new phenomenon in 'migration management.' Language experts and speech analysts have been consulted for analyses of regional dialects since 1998. Specialists have been asked to examine interview recordings to determine the credibility of information provided by the applicants (Biselli 2017). What is new is that the practice is no longer carried out by humans, but outsourced to a software program for so-called voice biometrics.

In a presentation at the 15th biennial conference of the European Association of Social Anthropologists (EASA) in Stockholm in 2018, media scholar Michelle Pfeifer argued that the software is seen as an allegedly efficient, secure, and legitimate system for determining asylum.[9] Pfeifer pointed out that the focus on voice analysis shifts attention from the 'content' of asylum narratives to a supposedly stable relationship between phonetics and territory. In her talk, Pfeifer not only discussed these contemporary racialising techniques, she also suggested that certain genealogies of identification technologies lead us back to the German colonies, to the colonial monitoring of mobility and belonging.[10] I wish to add to the discussion initiated by Pfeifer, by arguing that it is certainly important and revealing to revisit the German colony, but that it is not necessarily required in order to trace colonial genealogies. Instead, there are genealogies to be found in the colonial metropolis of a certain way of understanding the voice as stable and measurable data, to be analysed by technocratic means. I suggest that this rationale reaches back to the beginning of the twentieth century, and to the project of the *Lautarchiv*.

One of the most obvious similarities between practices of compiling speech samples then and now is, in fact, the disregard for the 'content;' it is the presumptuous conviction that content, context, and form can be ignored when a specific agenda is pursued. In the case of the *Lautarchiv*, the linguists usually showed no interest in the content of the sound recordings. They showed no interest in the life stories and individual situations of the people recorded, apart from biographical information regarding the geographical origins of their families, their level of education, as well as their language and writing skills. Nor did it appear necessary to refer to the circumstances in which the recordings were made, when subsequently used and published. For the recordists, the most important aspect was the moment of recording, whether the people recorded adhered to the agreed texts, whether the technical setup worked, whether the sound quality was good. Information about biographical language backgrounds was systematically noted, but neither comprehensively evaluated nor verified. As I was able to show with regard to the edition of a Swahili textbook from the series of the so-called Sound Library, the various dialectal influences did not contradict the purpose of basic language training of future colonial personnel (see Chapter 6).

In the asylum procedure, all that matters is the credibility of the narrative. It is the logic of suspicion that calls for additional instruments by which to verify the narrative. What hovers over the implementation of biometric technologies is the assumption that technology cannot be wrong, cannot fail, whereas human practice can. Just as the sound project of the past rested on 'objective' and measurable data, generated by the technical device of the gramophone, today's systems rely on computer-based technologies. But as can be shown, not only is the error rate (still) quite high, but also the context in which the recordings are produced is disregarded (Biselli 2017, 2018, 2020). In recordings lasting two minutes each, asylum applicants are asked to describe an image. The computer then generates percentages of the extent to which the speech sample corresponds with a particular regional dialect. The fact that speakers in such a situation might adapt to the language of the respective case worker/translator, or may choose a standardised language and vocabulary, is not taken into account in the interpretation of the sample. In this way, language is constructed as stable and fixed, neglecting that humans—as language carriers—are mobile, that dialects are fluid and language is living.

Although this scenario seems far removed from the *Lautarchiv*, there are, as shown, certain genealogical moments of similarity. I see tragic continuities of the project of the *Lautarchiv*, in which, under the auspices of science and technology, power is exercised and ostensibly absolute knowledge is produced. However, it must be stressed that the recording procedures of the *Lautarchiv* did not compromise the (future/post-internment) mobility of the people recorded, whereas the voice analysis software is capable of doing just that. Against this backdrop, I wish to conclude on two counts. On the one hand, I plead for more research to be invested in carving out the genealogies of colonial technologies and biopolitics (e.g. Madörin forthcoming; Pfeifer forthcoming). On the other hand, the development of new technologies, as well as the contexts of use of seemingly new techniques, demand critical investigation and evaluation. Otherwise, I cannot help but wonder what researchers—anthropologists and critical migration scholars—will be doing in a hundred years' time, when they look back at the archives of the German Federal Office for Migration and Refugees, and at the tens of thousands of speech samples compiled by a state institution. How will they tackle the difficult task of dealing with the acoustic legacies of the European border regime?

Appendix
List of German Institutions

Berlin Anthropological Society (*Berliner Anthropologische Gesellschaft*)

Berlin Museum of Decorative Arts (*Kunstgewerbemuseum Berlin*)

Berlin Phonogram Archive (*Berliner Phonogramm-Archiv*)

Berlin Society for Anthropology, Ethnology and Prehistory (*Berliner Gesellschaft für Anthropologie, Ethnologie und Urgeschichte*)

Berlin Society for Folklore Studies (*Berliner Gesellschaft für Volkskunde*)

Berlin University (*Berliner Universität*)

Berlin Zoological Garden (*Berliner Zoologischer Garten*)

City Palace (*Stadtschloss*)

Ethnological Museum of Berlin (*Ethnologisches Museum Berlin*)

Faculty of Foreign Affairs (*Auslandswissenschaftliche Fakultät*)

Friedrich Wilhelm University in Berlin (*Friedrich-Wilhelms-Universität zu Berlin*)

German-African Business Association (*Afrika-Verein der deutschen Wirtschaft*)

German-Foreign Association of Academics (*Deutsch-ausländischer Akademiker-Club*)

Half Moon Camp (*Halbmondlager*)

Hamburg Colonial Institute (*Hamburgisches Kolonialinstitut*)

Humboldt University of Berlin (*Humboldt-Universität zu Berlin*)

Imperial Colonial Office (*Reichskolonialamt*)

Institute for Sound Research (*Institut für Lautforschung*)

Intelligence Bureau for the East (*Nachrichtenstelle für den Orient*)

Museum of European Cultures (*Museum Europäischer Kulturen*)

Museum for German Traditional Costumes and Domestic Products (*Museum für Deutsche Volkstrachten und Erzeugnisse des Hausgewerbes*)

North German Missionary Association (*Norddeutsche Missionsgesellschaft*)

Reich Colonial League (*Reichskolonialbund*)

Royal Prussian Phonographic Commission (*Königlich Preußische Phonographische Kommission*)

Palace of the Republic (*Palast der Republik*)
Prussian State Library (*Preußische Staatsbibliothek*)
Seminar for Colonial Languages (*Seminar für Kolonialsprachen*)
Seminar for Oriental Languages (*Seminar für Orientalische Sprachen*)
Sound Commission (*Lautkommission*)
Sound Department (*Lautabteilung*)
Sound Library (*Lautbibliothek*)
Stadtmuseum Berlin Foundation (*Stiftung Stadtmuseum Berlin*)

Notes

1 Introduction

1   The exhibition lasted from October 14, 2016 to May 14, 2017, see https://www.dhm. de/en/ausstellungen/ archive/2016/german-colonialism.html [last accessed March 30, 2020].

2   Further below, I will elaborate on the genesis of the archive's collections relevant to this book. In an account of the *Lautarchiv*'s history, Britta Lange (2017a) discusses why the term sound *archive* (*Lautarchiv*) became the official name for the collection of historical sound recordings, which, she argues, was partly due to the founding of similar institutions, such as the phonogram archives in Vienna (1899) and Berlin (1900, officially 1904). Other comparable institutions were established in Saint Petersburg (1903), Zurich (1909), Paris (1911), Copenhagen (1913), and Budapest (1914).

3   Here, I am inspired not least by Elizabeth Edwards and Christopher Morton, who had similar intentions regarding anthropology's visual legacies in their edited volume *Photography, Anthropology and History: Expanding the Frame* (2009).

4   "[D]ie Abwesenheit [...], die, obwohl diese Abwesenheit im physischen Sinne endgültig ist, doch in eine 'meta-physische' oder medial gestützte Anwesenheit verwandelt werden kann." All translations are my own, unless otherwise noted.

5   The Humboldt Forum will appear at various points in this book and will also be the subject of my concluding remarks in the coda.

6   See e.g. the website of the NoHumboldt21! campaign starting in 2013, http://www. no-humboldt21.de/ [last accessed March 11, 2020], NoHumboldt21! 2017, and the digital project BARAZANI.berlin: Forum Colonialism and Resistance, https:// barazani.berlin/ [last accessed February 17, 2021].

7   The palace of the Hohenzollern dynasty was first built in 1442 and was extended several times in the course of its history. From 1701, it served as a royal Prussian, and from 1871 as an imperial German, residence. From 1921, it housed the Berlin Museum of Decorative Arts (*Kunstgewerbemuseum Berlin*), among other institutions. Partially damaged and burnt down during the Second World War, the GDR government decided to demolish the palace in 1950. In the 1970s, the modernist Palace of the Republic

(*Palast der Republik*) was built on the very same spot. The building was closed in 1990 and gradually demolished from 2006 to 2009.

8   For more information on the planning process of the Humboldt Forum and the controversial discussions accompanying it, see e.g. Bose 2013, 2016; Förster and Bose 2015; Oswald 2022; Thiemeyer 2019.

9   I myself was one of those student assistants, taking over the work from my predecessor and passing it on to my replacement. Working at the *Lautarchiv* has decisively influenced the direction of my research and my perspective on the administrative organisation of the archive's holdings.

10   A comprehensive history of the *Lautarchiv* before and during the Second World War, in the post-war years, the GDR and post-unification periods, up to its relocation to the Humboldt Forum has yet to be written. For particular historical accounts of the *Lautarchiv*, see e.g. Hennig 2016; Kaplan 2013; Lange 2017a; Mahrenholz 2003; Mehnert 1996; Meyer-Kalkus 2015.

11   The archive's core consists of more than 4,500 shellac discs (excluding duplicates), containing music and speech recorded in various contexts between 1909 and 1944. Other archival objects of the *Lautarchiv* include wax cylinders, commercial records, records made from gelatin or acetate, photographs, phonetic instruments, and specialised literature.

12   As it is common practice in German anti-racist contexts, I write *white* in italics to emphasise that *white* refers to a political position of power.

13   From 1909, Wilhelm Doegen (1877–1967), the technical and logistical director of the Phonographic Commission, pursued the objective of producing sound recordings for the purpose of Anglophone and French-language research and teaching.

14   From 1917, the chemist Ludwig Darmstaedter (1846–1927) funded the production of the so-called Darmstaedter Autograph Collection of male politicians and scientists of the time (see LAHUB, AUT 1–74).

15   On analogies between material objects and sound objects, see e.g. Lange 2017a.

16   Bose was a musicologist interested in German folk songs and the 'musicological study of race.' In 1939, he submitted his habilitation on *Sound Styles as Racial Characteristics* (*Klangstile als Rassenmerkmale*). He was involved in the pseudo-scientific activities of the *SS-Ahnenerbe*, a think tank in Nazi Germany operating between 1935 and 1945. For more on Bose and his position at the Institute for Sound Research, see Lange 2017c: 340–342.

2 THE ETHNOGRAPHIC …

1   In her account, Stoler concentrated on records of the colonial period of the Dutch West Indies from the nineteenth century, stored in the National Archives of the Netherlands located in The Hague.

2   See my engagement with the Orientalists Heinrich Lüders (1869–1943) and Helmuth von Glasenapp (1891–1863) in Chapter 3, the discussion on the hybrid figure of the merchant John George Hagenbeck (1900–1959) in Chapter 5, or the positions of the Africanists Diedrich Westermann (1875–1956) and Martin Heepe (1887–1961) in Chapter 6.

3   Whereas Römhild and Knecht base their argument on the premise of two anthropologies, Andre Gingrich speaks of a triangular institutional construct. Drawing particularly on later institutional constellations, after the First World War, Gingrich (2010: 373–375) also includes physical anthropology as integral to German-speaking anthropology (see also Penny and Bunzl 2003).

4   Wolfgang Kaschuba (2006 [1999]: 139–141) points out that both *Volkskunde* and *Völkerkunde* contributed to the production of naturalised ideas of an *ethnos*—an ethnicised identity—defined by lineage and territory. This is also connected with German citizenship law, which until twenty years ago still emanated exclusively from *ius sanguinis* ('right to blood') and not from *ius soli* ('right to land').

5   In contrast to the institutional formation of the discipline of sociology and the development of more progressive social theories by eminent scholars, such as Max Weber (1864–1920) or Georg Simmel (1858–1918), folklore studies used to be dedicated to the study, collection, and preservation of peasant traditions and folkloristic artifacts. As discussed in more detail in Chapter 7, notions of preservation or salvage, and the role of collections, archives, and museums seemed equally important to developments in all anthropologies (Kaschuba 2006 [1999]: 47–54). Under the Nazi regime, fascist and racist doctrines appropriated the rhetoric of folklore studies, which partly mutated "into a handmaiden of national socialist ideology" (Bendix 2012: 365).

6   In 1869, Rudolf Virchow (1821–1902), Adolf Bastian (1826–1905), and Robert Hartmann (1831–1896) founded the Berlin Anthropological Society (*Berliner Anthropologische Gesellschaft*), from which the Berlin Society for Anthropology, Ethnology and Prehistory (*Berliner Gesellschaft für Anthropologie, Ethnologie und Urgeschichte*) emerged. In 1873, the founding of an ethnographic museum followed, which was mainly based on historical collections of the Royal *Kunstkammer*. Adolf Bastian became head of the collection and first director in 1886. Three years later, in 1889, the Museum for German Traditional Costumes and Domestic Products (*Museum für Deutsche Volkstrachten und Erzeugnisse des Hausgewerbes*) was founded, which is today the Museum of European Cultures (*Museum Europäischer Kulturen*). In the same year, Karl Weinhold (1832–1901) founded the Berlin Society for Folklore Studies (*Berliner Gesellschaft für Volkskunde*). Another year later, the journal *Zeitschrift für Volkskunde* emerged, which was previously (from 1859) called *Zeitschrift für*

Völkerpsychologie und Sprachwissenschaft. Already before that, Wilhelm Heinrich Riehl (1823–1897) had attempted to institutionalise folklore studies. Later, some would refer to him as one of the founding figures of *Volkskunde* (e.g. Kaschuba 2006 [1999]: 42–46).

7   On a related note, Randeria (1999b: 375) has convincingly shown how the initial disciplinary division between sociology on the one hand, and anthropology and area studies on the other, manifested and kept on reproducing a division between the idea of a European modernity and its allegedly 'un- or premodern' counterparts (see also Fabian 1983; Randeria and Römhild 2013).

8   Macdonald previously addressed these ideas in her essay "Trafficking in History: Multitemporal Practices," published ten years earlier in 2003; see also Macdonald 2012.

9   The use of the ethnographic present, of course, alludes to Johannes Fabian's *Time and the Other* (1983). In this context, however, the practice of freezing the ethnographic subject in time does not necessarily relate to a colonised ethnographic *Other*.

10   Another highlight was the commemoration of the centenary of the beginning of the First World War in 2014 and in the following years. In numerous academic publications and news articles, history and art exhibitions, documentaries and radio broadcasts, conferences and public discussions, the sound recordings of prisoners of war received more and more attention both in public and academic spheres.

11   By a post-migrant society, I mean a society in which migration and mobility are understood as constitutive parts of society and not as something that concerns only a few members (e.g. Foroutan, Karakayali, and Spielhaus 2018). The term resembles the notion of a postcolonial world for which colonial processes in the past and present are constitutive (e.g. Bojadzijev and Römhild 2014).

12   Michael Rothberg (2009) coined the concept of a *multidirectional memory*, by which he does not mean a fixed understanding of remembrance, but rather ongoing negotiations and the possibility of cross-references and borrowing between different memories. For him, the concept draws attention to dynamic processes of transfer between diverse spatial, temporal, and cultural sites. For more on the persistence of essentialised and ethnicised notions of identity in German memory culture, see Rothberg and Yildiz 2011: 35–37.

13   For more on notions of future and futurity as missing temporal elements in conceptualisations of historical anthropology and in the discipline of European ethnology, see Chakkalakal 2018: 172–173.

14   While the Sound Department's focus was to record German-speaking dialects and idioms, this did not contradict self-assertive practices, but rather reinforced a sense of national identity, which was simultaneously produced and reproduced (Lange 2017c: 354).

15   On contingency and the archive, see also Appadurai 2003: 15–16.

16   "Die historische Anthropologie ist nicht zuletzt deshalb theoretisch und thematisch innovativ, weil sie Fragen zu stellen gelernt hat, die es ermöglichen, von einem erweiterten Verständnis menschlicher Spuren auszugehen, und weil sie umgekehrt diese Sensibilität für das *tracing* der Vergangenheit mit neuen erkenntnistheoretischen und methodischen Überlegungen zur Frage, wie 'historische Fakten' konstruiert werden, verbunden hat."

3   Failed Listening

1   The term *lascar* originally came into common usage to refer to Indian sailors. By the mid-eighteenth century, the term also included sailors from other places in the non-Western world (e.g. Myers 1994). According to Ravi Ahuja (2005), it was not a self-designation and had the connotation of inferiority and coercion.

2   "Sepoys and labourers were largely recruited from the 'races'—non-literate or semi-literate peasant-warrior classes of northern India who joined the army largely out of financial need, though a number of them also prided themselves on their martial traditions and links with the army" (Das 2011a: 6). Below, I will return to the martial race ideology.

3   Here, I was also influenced by Jack Halberstam's *The Art of Queer Failure* (2011), in which Halberstam depicts the notion of failure as a form of critique of not meeting normative standards. Halberstam references José Esteban Muñoz (1999) and Scott Sandage (2005) as two important scholars who first produced elaborate accounts on queer failure. For me, it is important to note that the accounts of all three queer theorists attach great importance to an intersectional perspective that problematises not only gender, but addresses also other factors, such as race and class.

4   Wishing to understand the "discourse of failure in our times" (2020: 1) in relation to debt and crisis in the worlds of Wall Street and Silicon Valley, Arjun Appadurai and Neta Alexander go so far as to speak of "failure studies" (3; see also Alexander 2017: 15–18). In their book, they draw from schools of thought in science, business, queer studies, and infrastructure studies.

5   For more on the politics of listening and the call for a listening to listening, see Eidsheim 2019: 57–60 and Chapter 7.

6   See LAHUB, personal information form PK 642 (recorded on January 2, 1917): "Urteil des Kommissars: sehr helle Fistelstimme."

7   See LAHUB, personal information form PK 1155-1159 (recorded on February 7, 1918): "Urteil des Kommissars: helle Mittelstimme mit hinreichend deutlicher Konsonanz und nasalierten Lauten."

8   As Lange made this point prior to the centenary of the beginning of the First World War, one has to admit that subaltern or entangled historiographies have been made more visible since then (see e.g. Bromber et al. 2018; Das 2011b; Liebau et al. 2010).

9   In 2014, a survey by the British Council revealed a general lack of knowledge among the population about the global impact of the First World War. While respondents from countries such as the UK, Egypt, France, Germany, Russia, and Turkey showed little awareness, knowledge was lowest among Indians (Sharma 2014). The journalist Manimugdha Sharma, who has been reporting on the history of the First World War and the commemoration events in India for the *Times of India* since 2014, also reported on the survey. He was one of my interview partners during my research stay in New Delhi and informed me about the media coverage of the commemoration of the First World War in India.

10   At a later point in her essay, Visweswaran draws on her ambivalent feelings about how she ended up "working on India" (2003 [1994]: 108) in the US academy, positioning herself as a second-generation person of Indian descent.

11   For a long time, information on the *Lautarchiv*'s collection and its access politics were only provided in German. In 2017, the *Lautarchiv*'s website was translated into English. However, the online catalogue is still only available in German. Hence, international users are still often dependent on the support of the archival staff.

12   Randeria preferred the term *entangled* in her attempt to rethink Eurocentric theories of modernisation. She chose the term over *multiple* (Eisenstadt 2000), *alternative* (Gaonkar 2001), or *vernacular* (Knauft 2002) modernities, because, to her, the notion of the *entangled* is able to replace a hierarchical view with an emphasis on reciprocal, though unequal, conditionalities (Randeria 2009: 42).

13   My great-grandfather (1901–1956) on my mother's side acted as a missionary for European colonists in Brazil from 1925 until 1938. As newlyweds, he and my great-grandmother (1904–1999) were initially supposed to be sent to the German colony of New Guinea, which had been seized by Australian forces during the First World War. In 1927, my grandmother (1927–2019) was born, the oldest of three daughters and one son, in the state of Espírito Santo in Brazil. In 1938, the family returned to Germany. On my father's side, my grandfather (1916–2007) was a pharmacy student when he was conscripted, serving on the Eastern Front during the Second World War.

14   Mall Singh was recorded on December 11, 1916 (see LAHUB, PK 619).

15   For theoretical analyses of the film, see Balke 2009 and Gordon 2011. Balke (2009: 74) discusses the stylistic idea of arranging the documentary as the product of the failure of another, the film as it was originally conceptualised, thus reflecting on cinematic practice as yet another recording medium.

16   For more on the film and the exhibition project, *The Making of...Ghosts*, see https://halfmoonfiles.de/en/4/making-of/home [last accessed April 12, 2020].

17   *Poste restante* is also known as general delivery. It describes a system in which the post office holds someone's mail until the recipient collects it.

18   Jasbahadur Rai was recorded on June 6, 1916 (see LAHUB, PK 307 and 308).

19   Sundar Singh was recorded on January 5, 1917, the same day as Baldeo Singh (see LAHUB, PK 676).

20   Gangaram Gurung was recorded on May 31, 1916 (see LAHUB, PK 271). The drawings are part of the Otto Stiehl Collection housed at the Museum of European Cultures in Berlin (see VIII Eu 27625, 27626, 27627).

21   Liebau's wish to contribute to and intervene in global and military history also corresponds with the aim of the transnational research project *Cultural Exchange in a time of Global Conflict: Colonials, Neutrals and Belligerents during the First World War* (2013–2016), of which she and a group of distinguished international scholars were part.

22   For instance, George Abraham Grierson (1851–1941) also used the text in *The Linguistic Survey of India*, conducted between 1894 and 1928.

23   Motilal's recordings were produced on June 3, 1916 (see LAHUB, PK 279). Him Bahadur was recorded on the same day (see LAHUB, PK 283).

24 In total, 1.4 million South Asian combatants (90,000) and non-combatants (50,000) were involved in the First World War. Approximately a thousand military prisoners of war and about the same number of civilian internees were interned in German camps (e.g. Liebau 2018).

25 See LAHUB, Mohammed Hanif (PK 1149, story and song in Hindi), Mohammed Hossin (PK 1150–1152, story in Bengali); Wahed Box Ustagar (PK 1153, 1154, story and song in Bengali); Keramat Ali (PK 1155–1159, poems, stories, and songs in Bengali); Albert Newton (PK 1160, 1161, stories in Hindi). Other *lascars* were interned in camps in Güstrow, Havelberg, and Parchim (Lange 2011c: 181).

26 See LAHUB, PK 1150, 1151, 1152.

27 The mentioned ship is not to be mistaken for the *SS Clan Mactavish* (built in 1920), which was torpedoed and sunk by the German submarine U-159 in the Indian Ocean, with the loss of 61 lives, during the Second World War, on October 8, 1942.

28 For the entire translation into English by Santanu Das, see Lange 2011c: 181–182.

29 In total, seven recordings on five records exist of Keramat Ali, LAHUB, PK 1155_1 (school poetry), PK 1155_2 (tale), PK 1156 (tale), 1157 (tale), PK 1158_1 (folk song), PK 1158_2 (folk song), PK 1159_1 (Bengali Alphabet).

30 "More than four million non-white men were involved in the war, including two million African and over a million Indian. Indeed, if one had been at Ypres during the war years, one would have seen Indian sepoys, *tirailleurs Senegalais*, North African *saphis*, Chinese and Indi-Chinese workers, Maori Pioneer battalion and First Nations Canadians, in addition to white troops and workers" (Das 2011a: 6, emphasis in the original). For more on German-Indian entanglements and *lascar* seamen, see e.g. Jan 2018, (forthcoming); Roy 2011.

31 Since Narendra Modi of the Bharatiya Janata Party (BJP) was elected and re-elected Indian Prime Minister in 2014 and 2019, one can observe changes in the state's memory politics. Between 2014 and 2018, Modi participated in numerous local and international public events commemorating the First World War. While I do not want to deny that the government wishes to pay tribute to the fallen soldiers, the symbolic politics behind these public performances seem unmistakable. In my reading, they reflect the effort of the Indian head of state to be on par with international leaders, portraying India as a powerful nation fighting for the cause of peace. In February 2019, Modi inaugurated a National War Memorial honoring the Indian Armed Forces. The Memorial was built in the city centre of New Delhi near India Gate, which was established by the British in 1921 and inaugurated in 1931. India Gate commemorates soldiers of the British Indian Army who died in the First World War (1914–1918) and the Second Anglo-Afghan War (1878–1880).

32 The Zehrensdorf Indian Cemetery, located not far from the former Wünsdorf campsite, is the final resting place for 206 Indian soldiers who died in captivity.

33 See LAHUB, PK 642_1 (song), PK 647_1 (song, sung by three singers), PK 647_2 (spoken song), PK 652_1 (tale), PK 652_2 (song), PK 673_2 (tale).

34 See LAHUB, personal information form PK 673 (January 5, 1917) "Baldeo Singh schreit zum Schluss ohne Aufforderung *Guten Abend*."

35   It should be stressed, however, that Said's analysis refers to the British and French academy and cannot fully be translated to the German context. For an account on German Orientalists, see e.g. Marchand 2009.

36   In 1917, Felix von Luschan published a commissioned book featuring one hundred lithographs drawn by the artist Hermann Struck (1876–1944) in the Wünsdorf camp. Luschan (1917) contributed a scientific preface about "The Basics of Anthropology."

37   For more on Stumpf and Hornbostel and the beginnings of the Berlin Phonogram Archive, see Chapter 5.

38   In total, they recorded 1,030 wax cylinders that ended up at the Phonogram Archive of the Ethnological Museum of Berlin (e.g. Ziegler 2006). Additionally, the Commission recorded 1,650 shellac records in seventy (of 175) POW camps, compiling samples of over two hundred languages and dialects (Meyer-Kalkus 2015: 53).

39   Along with a number of African internees from the French troops, the German military command had arranged to relocate soldiers from the British Indian Army to occupied territories in Romania, starting in spring 1917.

40   In the letter, it says: "The Sikhs especially will strongly resist on religious grounds any attempt made by Europeans to touch any part of the body and more particularly the head. Further, such measurements are associated by Indians with criminals. We beg to warn the Government that the laudable scientific curiosity of German Professors will be attended with very unpleasant consequences" (Lange 2011c: 160, referencing the letter from IIC to Baron von Wesendonk/Ministry of Foreign Affairs, dated May 31, 1916; PAAA, R21256: 271). Despite the protest letter, measurements among Sikh soldiers did take place, forming the basis for Eickstedt's doctoral thesis (*Rassenelemente der Sikh*, 1921). It is not known whether some of the internees opposed the practice.

41   For a biographical account of Eickstedt's life, see Preuß 2009; see also Lange 2013a: 132–136.

42   After the Indian Rebellion of 1857, army officials of British India created the theory of 'martial' and 'non-martial races.' The stereotype-based construct particularly served military propaganda and recruitment. 'The Gurkhas' (soldiers formerly recruited in Nepal) were considered to be a 'martial race' because they remained loyal to the British during the rebellion. The designation of Gurkha soldiers is still widely used today (e.g. Omissi 1994; Streets 2004).

43   "Als Professor Wilhelm Schulze und ich uns in den Gefangenenlagern dem Studium des Khas [Nepali] zuwandten, da konnten wir freilich unsern braven Gurkhas den eigentlichen Zweck unserer Wißbegierde nicht begreiflich machen, aber das hat sie nicht abgehalten, uns willig zu helfen. Sie schienen einen gewissen Stolz zu empfinden, daß wir gerade ihrer Sprache so besondere Aufmerksamkeit zuwandten. Viele, vielleicht die meisten, waren des Lesens und Schreibens kundig; sie hatten die für ihre Sprache gebräuchliche Schrift allerdings nicht als Kinder, sondern erst während ihrer Dienstzeit erlernt. Manche waren auch imstande, selbstständig aus dem Gedächtnis längere Erzählungen niederzuschreiben. [...] Die meisten freilich trauten es sich nicht zu, eine zusammenhängende Geschichte zu erzählen. Sie zogen es vor, ein Lied vorzutragen, sei

es allein, sei es in Gemeinschaft mit anderen. Unter den Liedern sind gewiß einzelne, die schon seit alter Zeit bei festlichen Zusammenkünften [...] erklungen sind. "

44   See Oppenheim's *Denkschrift betreffend die Revolutionierung der islamischen Gebiete unserer Feinde* (*Memorandum on Revolutionizing the Islamic Territories of Our Enemies*), written in October 1914 and republished in 2018.

45   "Die Aufgabe bestand im wesentlichen darin, daß die Inder zunächst veranlaßt wurden, den Text einer Erzählung oder eines Liedes aufzuschreiben, dieser wurde dann mit ihnen durchgesprochen und schließlich von Professor Doegen aufgenommen. Die Erfüllung dieser Aufgabe war oft schwierig, weil die Gefangenen natürlich alle kein Englisch konnten, ich mich mit ihnen daher nur in Hindi verständigen konnte; zudem gab es auch solche, die Analphabeten waren, deren Texte man also lediglich abhören und nachschreiben konnte. Wenn die Ergebnisse dieser Studien der Natur der Sache nach auch manche Fehlerquellen aufweisen mußten, so kam doch auf diese Weise eine große Sammlung zusammen, die leider nicht wie geplant als Buch veröffentlicht worden ist."

46   "Diese Aufnahmen hatten kein wissenschaftliches 'Nachleben' – bis zu ihrer Wiederentdeckung als historische Bestände des Archivs *durch das Archiv selbst*. So scheint es auch berechtigt, bei den Tonaufnahmen von Kriegsgefangenen von einem 'archivalischen' Projekt, einem Sammelprojekt (Scheer 2010) zu sprechen, das sich hauptsächlich den Interessen des Archivs selbst verdankte und dementsprechend nicht vollständig mit einer der beteiligten wissenschaftlichen Disziplinen – Anthropologie, Ethnografie, Orientalistik, Linguistik, vergleichende Musikwissenschaft – kompatibel war."

47   While disciplinary boundaries may have not been that clearly defined at the time, it was mostly linguists who contributed essays to the volume. Felix von Luschan, who had been in charge of the Phonographic Commission's group on (physical) anthropology in the camps, was not included (see also Lange 2013a: 126–127).

48   "Die Schöpfung lebendiger Kultururkunden, die die Jahrtausende überdauern."

49   For more on post-imperial colonial revisionism and colonial fantasies in German popular culture and the academy, see e.g. Bechhaus-Gerst 2018a; Laak 2003, 2018; see also Chapter 7.

50   For more on Bengali *jatra* and *tappa*, see e.g. Banerjee 1989.

4   ... THE ARCHIVAL ...

1   In retrospect, Stoler (2009: 44) argues that the *archival turn* had already set in before Derrida's publication *Archive Fever* (1996 [1995]). For her, the turn was characterised first and foremost by the shift from seeing the 'archive-as-source' to an understanding of the 'archive-as-subject,' in particular as implemented by scholars committed to critical history. For more on the *archival turn*, see also Eichhorn 2013: 4–9.

2   Alluding to the archival sensations famously described by Farge (2013 [1989]) and Carolyn Steedman (2001a), and by trying to find the 'pulse' of the archive, Stoler points out that, for her, "the colonial archives are the bitter aftertaste of empire, the morsels left for us, their voracious contemporary reader" (2009: 19).

3   The essay was originally given as a lecture at the opening of the Freud Museum in London in 1994.

4   In this context, see also *Hegel, Haiti, and Universal History* (2009) by philosopher Susan Buck-Morss.

5   It may not come as a surprise that the literary reference texts, as well as the works of natural scientists, on which Richards mounts his argument were all written by *white* men of the elite. The only historically situated female agent is Rosa Luxemburg (1871–1919). Richards (1993: 91) references her as a representative socialist and coeval with H. G. Wells (1866–1946). In characterisations of imperial or colonial archives, female subjects do not usually appear in the picture; their absence seems seldom to be of relevance. Without wanting to make Richards part of the imperial project, it is nevertheless striking that he does not consider the lack of female references as a missing or incomplete part of his own assertions. I ask myself, however, whether female authors and poets, or the few female scientists of the Victorian time, did not react to or deal with imperial imaginations, utopian spaces, and perceptions of a colonial world. Did *white* women not take part in imagining a unitary natural world comprehensible through practices of collecting and classifying information?

6   Here, Roque and Wagner (2012: 9) refer to Sherry Ortner's eminent article "Resistance and the Problem of Ethnographic Refusal" (1995), in which the anthropologist criticises (postcolonial) studies on the subject of resistance for keeping up with the dichotomy of (Western) domination and (subaltern) resistance (see also Stoler and Cooper 1997: 6).

7   Nevertheless, Gayatri C. Spivak, herself member of the Subaltern Studies Group, has to be considered an early critic of the idea of a re-examination of the past by focusing on the question of subalternity. By raising issues of gender and race, Spivak (e.g. 1985, 1988) argued for complicating and expanding readings of the archives.

8   For more on the parallel histories of the possibility of sound reproduction and archiving, see Sterne 2003 and Chapter 7.

5   Close Listening

1   In the following, I opt to mainly use the term *Völkerschau* so as not to conceal the degrading practice of ethnicising peoples (*Völker-*) and the practice of exhibiting (*-schau*). Other terms used in the literature are human zoo, ethnic show, commercial ethnography, ethnographic exhibition, or colonial/exotic spectacle.

2   A remarkable example of an engagement with the history and repercussions of a specific colonial spectacle is the permanent exhibition "zurückgeschaut" at one of the district museums in Berlin. The exhibition deals with the first German colonial exhibition at *Treptower Park* in 1896. As a joint project of the museum and two NGOs (*Initiative Schwarze Menschen in Deutschland* and *Berlin Postkolonial*), the exhibition opened in October 2017. What is so unique about the project is that it was collaboratively planned and realised. The exhibition will be permanently on display while constantly being updated (last in October 2021). Although Germany's colonial past has been the subject of special and temporary exhibitions in recent years, it is still usually not part of the canonical historical narrative told in public museums. For more information on the project, see http://zurueckgeschaut.de/ [last accessed April 11, 2020].

3   Founded in 2006, the Pirate Party Germany achieved an election result of 8.9 percent and became part of the opposition in Berlin in 2011. In the 2016 and 2021 elections, the party did not win any seats in the Berlin House of Representatives.

4   See Magalski 2014: written request by representative Philipp Magalski (Pirates), printed matter 17 / 14 643, September 25, 2014.

5   During the course of my research, the Zoological Garden set up an exhibition and published a book, both dealing with the history of the zoo. The small permanent exhibition opened in December 2016. Two years later, the social historian Clemens Maier-Wolthausen (2019) published a comprehensive historical account of the last 175 years of the institution's history. One might argue that, against the background of the German paradigm of *Vergangenheitsaufarbeitung* (dealing with or working through the past), a permanent exhibition and a publication appear to suffice for the process of coming to terms with difficult institutional pasts. However, I see many more layers to the (colonial) histories of the zoo and would therefore wish for constant and multiple ways of dealing with them. For example, both the exhibition and the illustrated book reproduce exoticising representations of colonial subjects by drawing on historical imagery and wording. In this way, stereotypical representations are updated rather than contested or overcome.

6   In her compelling work, Susann Lewerenz (2017) lays special focus on migrant show troupes, which, as she points out, have so far gone almost unnoticed in academic research. The historian is particularly interested in looking at processes of interaction and exchange within the entertainment sector during the inter-war period.

7   According to Thode-Arora (1996: 116 and 126), the organizers became more liberal towards the performers after the First World War. Before that, they preferred performers

with poor skills in European languages in order to limit the interaction and exchange between artists and audience.

8   One current and ongoing example of these kinds of struggles is of course the debate around the Humboldt Forum. As explained in my introduction, the Humboldt Forum hosts (ethnographic) collections of the Ethnological Museum of Berlin and the Museum of Asian Art. Significant parts of the collections of both museums have given rise to demands for clarifying their provenance.

9   In 2006, Susanne Ziegler published a comprehensive catalogue of the wax cylinder recordings housed at the Berlin Phonogram Archive. Although Ziegler mentions the fact that she transcribes all spellings and terms appearing in the original documents, she does not make clear that, in doing so, problematic and racialising terms are being reproduced. Instead, she argues that, for the purposes of the book and due to missing expertise, (less offensive) contemporary terms could not be included. Moreover, the author neither makes clear whether sound recordings were produced in colonial entertainment environments, nor points out the lack of this information.

10   In 1933, Hornbostel first emigrated to Switzerland and later to the US, before settling in Cambridge, UK, where he died in 1935. Only through an intersectional and nuanced lens, capable of grasping ambiguities, does it seem possible to approach a biography as complicated as Hornbostel's. Pursued in the wake of the Nazi dictatorship, Hornbostel must also be seen against the background of the complicity between comparative musicology and *white* theories of supremacy. For more on the precarious histories of Jewish biographies related to the disciplines of anthropology and their associated institutions, see Kremmler (forthcoming).

11   Vanessa Agnew (2005: 42) argues that the discipline of comparative musicology, unlike anthropology, has not been described as having been established in conjunction with (German) colonialism. According to Agnew, this is because comparative musicology was primarily seen as a domestic phenomenon and more of an 'armchair' discipline.

12   For more on Prince Dido and his family's stay in Germany in 1886, see e.g. Gouaffo 2013.

13   "Carl Hagenbeck verlangt keinerlei Arbeit von der Truppe, nur den Leuten ihre Sitten und Gebräuche zu zeigen."

14   Compelling exceptions are the works of Susann Lewerenz for the German and Priya Srinivasan for the Indian and US contexts. For more on the nexus between the increasing commercialisation of *Völkerschauen* and the mobility of non-*white* people in and to Germany during the imperial era, see Lewerenz 2017: 40–48. For an account of the female and non-*white* labouring body acting simultaneously as artist and labourer in the US at the end of the nineteenth and the beginning of the twentieth century, see Srinivasan 2009, 2012.

15   In 1925 and 1927, Wilhelm Doegen set out to record the sounds of animals at the circus in Berlin and at the Zoological Garden in Dresden. See LAHUB, LA 511–517 and LA 841–847. For more on recordings of non-human voices, see e.g. Reimann 2014. Other performers, also involved in the urban entertainment scene, were recorded directly at the

Sound Department, and later at the Institute for Sound Research or at the premises of the record label of the *Berlin Lindström AG*.

16   See LAHUB, recordings LA 734–739, LA 823–826.

17   See AZGB, OØ/1/114.

18   The document's enumeration ends with a list of animals included in the show: nine elephants, ten zebus, twenty sheep and goats, three ponies, and an indefinite number of snakes and monkeys.

19   See HUB-Archive, IfL no. 7, 8, and 9, correspondence between Doegen and Schrader.

20   John George Hagenbeck's father was John Hagenbeck (1866–1940), whose own father was the half-brother of the merchant and zoo director Carl Hagenbeck (1844–1913). The business of colonial spectacles and *Völkerschauen* is closely connected with the name Carl Hagenbeck who had been organising ethnographic exhibitions in Germany since 1875. Today, he is thought of as an influential figure who "brought the animal trade from the margins to the mainstream of colonial commerce, [...] [and] moved the practice of human display from the fairground to the zoological garden. [...] He made it 'respectable' and therefore easily consumable by the widest possible audience including (but not restricted to) the broad middle classes" (Ames 2008: 207). John George Hagenbeck's mother (whom we do not know more about) was Sinhalese.

21   Hans Virchow is one of the sons of the physician and anthropologist Rudolf Virchow (1821–1902).

22   Carl Hagenbeck was a member of the Berlin Society for Anthropology, Ethnology and Prehistory (*Berliner Gesellschaft für Anthropologie, Ethnologie und Urgeschichte*), founded by aforementioned Rudolf Virchow and Adolf Bastian in 1869.

23   Other female voices appear solely in the sound recordings of German idioms and other dialects. Women are otherwise in evidence only when male individuals refer to them in speech or song as, for example, their wives, lovers, mothers, or sisters.

24   See LAHUB, personal information form LA 824.

25   Kovvali Viracaryalu was recorded on September 28, 1926 (see LAHUB, LA 734 and 735).

26   The personal information form was based on a template designed and used for sound recordings of male soldiers and civil internees compiled at POW camps during the First World War (see Chapter 3).

27   In addition to the sound recordings compiled in POW camps during the First World War, photographic portraits of a number of internees were taken. However, a lot of them got lost and were not archived. The few documented photographs stored at the *Lautarchiv* contain neither the name of the internee depicted nor that of the photographer.

28   Interestingly, in Judith Butler's theory of gender performativity, vocality is an almost completely omitted aspect. According to Anette Schlichter (2011: 32), Butler touches upon the material qualities of the voice, its mediation and technologies, only on the surface, thereby fostering thinking of the body without a voice.

29   See LAHUB, personal information form LA 824. By contrast, Priya Srinivasan refers to Indian women dancers exactly the other way around, describing them as "married to members of the party of jugglers who accompany them" (2009: 3).

30   *Patira*: sandalwood paste.

31   "*Bal*: a metrical continuation to emphasise the previous note in continuation to the further line" (note by the translator).

32   "1. O Geliebter! Wenn du mich verlässtest [sic], wie soll ich es ertragen? 2. Der Böse Amor in seiner Grausamkeit hat mich rasend gemacht! 3. Ist es recht, mich zu quälen, indem du so sehr hinhörst auf (Gott weiss) was (für) Einflüsterungen des Bösen (Amors) (betreffs mir einer vorzuziehenden Schönen)? 4. (zur Freundin gewandt:) Wie oft sagte er 'Steh auf und komm!' und strich mir Sandelpaste an den Hals. Nach einem Monat (noch) duftet(e) sie. 5. = 1. 6. O Mädchen, die Worte die er sprach. Mein Denken schwand dahin. 7. In dieser Welt gäbe es nicht meinesgleichen: (so) dachte ich. 8. = 1."

33   G. Manoja is Professor at the Department of English at the Palmuru University in India. I thank Madhumeeta Sinha for introducing me to Professor Manoja.

34   Priya Srinivasan refers to *devadāsīs* performing in Europe or the US as "dancing girls" (2009: 7) or "temple dancers" (2012: 52) from South India, although this simplifies the practices of *devadāsīs* in India, and especially their role under colonial rule. Since the nineteenth century, Indian female dancers, whether they came from the north or south of India, were also associated with the iconic image of the bayadere—an 'oriental' dancing girl. For more on the *devadāsī* practice, see e.g. Soneji 2012. For more on the tradition of *javalis*, see particularly pages 95–111.

35   "Was wir hören, ist nicht unbedingt eine Ergänzung oder Vervollständigung dessen, was wir sehen. Was wir sehen, wollen wir nicht unbedingt um Hörbares erweitern. Aber was wir hören, möchten wir – MitteleuropäerInnen – gerne mit etwas Sichtbarem in Verbindung bringen, einer Quelle des Tons, dem Wissen um seinen Ursprung."

36   I found the photograph at the archive of the Berlin City Museum, which houses a special collection on 'variety, circus, and cabaret' mostly consisting of visual material donated by private collectors. See *Stiftung Stadtmuseum Berlin, Lehmann Sammlung.*

37   As part of the digitisation process, the record's content was divided into four pieces of sound. The first part (LA 824_1) contains the song performed in Telugu, the second part (LA 824_2) an interrupted version. The third part comprises a second version of the song and the last part (LA 824_4) counting in cardinal numbers from one to twenty in Telugu.

38   See LAHUB, personal information form LA 824.

39   "Töne – verstanden nicht als 'authentische' Äußerung des Menschen, sondern als Hörbarmachungen – scheinen den Verhörten mehr als Messdaten, Fotografien und Gipsabgüsse die Möglichkeit zu geben, kurzzeitig und in bestimmten Grenzen als Subjekt zu agieren und aus dem wissenschaftlich verordneten Objektstatus herauszutreten. Während sie ein Sprachbeispiel liefern, das die Forscher zufrieden stellt, haben sie zugleich auf der technischen Ebene die Möglichkeit zu irritieren, indem sie Pausen machen, lachen, den verabredeten Text abändern oder Teile davon auslassen."

40 See LAHUB, PK 649. The recording belongs to the Indian colonial soldier Chote Singh (approx. 1888–?), who was recorded on January 2, 3, and 5, 1917.

41 The concept leads back to Yann Moulier Boutang (1998), who first postulated the hypothesis of an autonomy of migration in his account of post-operaism.

42 In 1939, after the beginning of the Second World War, the British arrested John Hagenbeck senior and detached him from his property. He died in Colombo in 1940.

43 "Kein anderer Impresario zeigt in seinem Werk trotz eines europäischen Überlegenheitsgefühls und der damit verknüpften paternalistischen Haltung des Völkerschauleiters so viel Respekt vor der künstlerischen Leistung einzelner, so viel Sympathie und Anteilnahme gegenüber den Teilnehmern. Um die Lebensmittel für die Menschen mit verschiedenen Religionen und Speisegewohnheiten kümmerte er sich meist an jedem Gastspielort persönlich, den Kindern erfüllten er und seine Frau ihre Wünsche nach Spielzeug, besonderer Kleidung, Vergnügungsausflügen oder zärtlichem Kuscheln."

44 "Ich möchte hierzu bemerken, daß ich als Europäer niemals die Überfahrt für eine weiße Frau, die sich hier mit einem Inder verheiratet hat, bezahlen würde; denn was die Frau drüben erwartet, ahnt sie nicht. Die Europäer werden mit ihr nicht verkehren, und der Mann hat von seinen Landsleuten nur Kränkungen zu erwarten, weil sie eine Heirat mit einer weißen Frau nicht anerkennen. Ein gebildeter Inder wird einer europäischen Frau nie zumuten, mit ihm in seine Heimat zu gehen und nach den dortigen Sitten und Gebräuchen zu leben."

45 "Noch sind die Schranken, die Asien und Europa trennen, zu hoch, und es werden wohl erst Tausende von Jahren vergehen müssen, um eine Verbrüderung herbeizuführen, wie sie sich so mancher Mensch vorstellt. Um die Asiaten zu verstehen, muß man selbst Asiate sein, um uns Europäer zu verstehen, muß man immer Europäer sein."

46 "Es ist nun nicht immer leicht, aus dem vorliegenden Material das Richtige herauszufinden, und oft muß man persönlich an Ort und Stelle fahren, um die Eignung des Bewerbers zu prüfen. In den meisten Fällen wird man sehr enttäuscht, wenn man die so hoch angepriesene Attraktion zu sehen bekommt, und der Bewerber ist fassungslos, wenn man ihm einen ablehnenden Bescheid gibt, denn er kann nicht verstehen, daß mir seine Leistungen nicht genügen, da er doch bei seinen Landsleuten einen so überreichen Beifall erntet. Hierbei fällt die offensichtlich entgegengesetzte Geschmacksrichtung zwischen Europa und Indien auf."

47 See LAHUB, personal information form LA 823, her age and place of birth were noted on the personal information form LA 733 (see below).

48 See LAHUB, personal information form LA 736.

49 Sometimes, the recordists would also whisper or prompt the practiced texts selected for the recording. While, in most cases, the technical device would not, or rather could not, capture these whispering sounds, in a few recordings the scholar's whispering is vaguely audible. Sometimes, it is even mentioned on the personal information form that the text or words were prompted (*vorgeflüstert*).

50 "Lautaufnahme Nr. 823, Stueck 1, Umschrift des Blattes in Tamil-Schrift = des für die Aufnahme bestimmten, aber bei dieser nicht benutzten Diktates der Sprecherin. Das

Diktat, welches ohne Stockungen und Aenderungen gegeben wurde, zeigt, in wie hohem Grade Sprecherin bei der Aufnahme befangen war."

51   See LAHUB, written documentation LA 823.

52   The same story was also recorded by Sanmuga Soragar on September 28, 1926, at four in the afternoon. The translation of his recording is not identical with Rajamanikkam's version (see LAHUB, personal information form LA 736).

53   "Jemand hatte zwei Frauen geheiratet: Die beiden Frauen hatten je ein Kind. Er starb. Später starb (auch) ein Kind. Dem einen (andern) Kinde gaben alle beide Milch und zogen (es so) auf. Nachdem sie in Streit miteinander gekommen, sagten sie (jede von ihnen): es ist meins, es ist meins! Sie gingen zum Richter und sagten (dasselbe). Da Ihm (plur. maj.) nicht klar war, wer recht hatte, sprach Er: 'Hau dieses Kind in zwei Stücke und gib jeder Person ein Stück!' Die eine sagte 'Gut!' Die anderen sagte: 'Das Kind darf nicht zerhauen werden! Übergebt es jener!' Auf diesen ihren Ausspruch hin erkannte Er, dass das Kind ihres war, übergab es ihr und bestrafte die andere (Da sagte der Richter 'Das Kind ist ihres!' Und übergab es ihr; die andere (aber) bestrafte Er)."

54   At the time of my research, Viswajith was a Master student from India at the University of Potsdam. He was introduced to me by a mutual friend. I thank him for providing this translation from Tamil to English.

55   See LAHUB, personal information form LA 733.

56   See LAHUB, press archive, "Lautaufnahmen indischer Sprachdenkmäler" (Brauchschweiger Landeszeitung, October 11, 1926).

57   See LAHUB, written documentation LA 733.

58   See LAHUB, press archive, "Kunst und Wissenschaft. Ein indischer Abend" (Börsenzeitung, May 15, 1926).

59   Additional sound recordings belonging to the *Lautarchiv*'s collections can, for instance, be found at the University of Halle, at the Phonogram Archive in Vienna, or in Doegen's personal inheritance located at the German Historical Museum in Berlin.

60   However, in 1921, in the minutes of a meeting of the future Sound Commission, it was mentioned that women should be included in the recordings of German dialects and idioms, as they would be better at 'preserving' the language, although often they would also be the ones to 'transplant' the dialect of their home. See HUB-Archive, IfL no. 9, minutes, October 10, 1921.

61   However, this could also be the Eurocentric and hetero-normative perception of those who registered Venkatamma's professional occupation as her husband's companion. It remains questionable whether the artistic team did perhaps only feel complete as a couple, in which one does not accompany the other, but both are regarded as equal performers.

6   Collective Listening

1   These four lines form the beginning of the poem *Chairi kwa Wazungu* (*Poem for the Europeans*), composed by an unknown author from Bagamoyo in today's Tanzania. Carl Velten (1862–1935) initially published the poem in a volume on *Prose and Poetry of the Swahili* in 1907. For the poem's translation in its full length (by Katrin Bromber), see Miehe et al. 2002: 372–374. I made a selection of the poem's four-liners to open each section of this chapter. For me, the lines of poetry symbolise moments of subversion and critique, recorded by and surviving in the colonial archive. As the author wrote the poem "for the Europeans," I feel that it is in some sense directed to me. It remains up to my readers to decide whether the lines appeal to them, and, if so, in what way.

2   For further literature on Hussein, see e.g. Bechhaus-Gerst 1997, 2007, 2013; Breiter 2002; Knopf 2013, 2018; KZ-Gedenkstätte Neuengamme 2018; Oguntoye 1997a; Reed-Anderson 2000 [1995]; Stoecker 2008a.

3   From the time of his arrival in Germany, he was known as Bayume Mohamed Hussein, which became Mohamed Husen, presumably a self-chosen, Germanised adaptation (Bechhaus-Gerst 2007: 11–12). In the following, I will nevertheless use the name Bayume Mohamed Hussein, although in German postcolonial academic and public discourse he is still often called Mohamed Husen.

4   The *Seminar* was founded in 1887 and was renamed *Auslandshochschule* in 1936. Later, it merged into the University's Faculty of Foreign Studies, which opened in 1939.

5   Using the term ethnographic (text) can be ambivalent given its colonial ballast. Here, the genre of ethnographic texts refers to the writings of early anthropologists, missionaries, travel writers, and colonial civil servants. For more on the genre in colonial contexts, see Bromber 2003: 39.

6   With good reason, historian Anja Laukötter (2013: 27) problematises the use of the term 'anthropological material.' According to Laukötter, the term expresses a distancing from, or even a form of concealment of, what the material actually consists of: images of people, human remains, measuring and observational data of bodily features such as skin, hair, or eye colour. For Laukötter, anthropological material therefore denotes forms of a problematic appropriation of the human body.

7   Although the sound document's existence is mentioned, for example, in Hussein's biography (Bechhaus-Gerst 2007: 121–123), Holger Stoecker's account of the history of African studies in Berlin between 1919 and 1945 (2008a: 135–136), and the documentary film *Majub's Journey* (2013) by Eva Knopf, none of them seem to consider the audio file and its content to be an essential object worth analysing.

8   The former Sound Department of the Prussian State Library was officially converted into the Institute for Sound Research on February 14, 1934 (Stoecker 2008a: 134). Since then, the *Lautarchiv*'s holdings have been in the possession of the university.

9   In November 1921, the Ministry of Cultural Affairs set up a Sound Commission (*Lautkommission*) to advise the Prussian State Library's Sound Department on selecting language experts and recording contexts. Members of the Commission were the General

Director of the Prussian State Library, members of the Academy of Sciences, as well as professors of Berlin University—namely, Alois Brandl, Heinrich Lüders, and Wilhelm Schulze—who had already been members of the Phonographic Commission (1915–1918). See HUB-Archive, IfL no. 9, minutes of the meeting regarding the future Sound Commission, October 10, 1921.

10   Schroeder submitted his doctoral thesis on *Sounds of the Wendish (Sorbian) dialect of Schleife in Upper Lusatia (Die Laute des wendischen (sorbischen) Dialekts von Schleife in der Oberlausitz)* in 1938. As one can read in the preface to his thesis, written by the linguist Reinhold Olesch (1910–1990) in 1958, Schroeder died during the last days of the Second World War.

11   In total, Hussein was part of twenty-three film productions realised between 1934 and 1941 (Bechhaus-Gerst 2007: 114). For more on film productions of the Weimar period and the question of race and representation, see e.g. Nagl 2009.

12   "Diese Bilder zu zeigen, bedeutet, auch die rassistischen Stereotype, die Husseins Rollen prägten, zu aktualisieren und in die Zukunft zu tragen. Sie nicht zu zeigen, würde bedeuten, Mohamed Hussein in den Archiven zu vergessen, oder zumindest den Versuch zu unterlassen, ihn noch einmal in die (Film-)Geschichte einzuschreiben. Wie aber kann seine Geschichte erzählt werden?"

13   "Die Tonaufnahmen von Kriegsgefangenen sind fraglos eine sensible Sammlung – eine Sammlung, die unter sensiblen Umständen entstand, unter Ausnutzung einer militärischen und kolonialen Machtposition, unter Überschreitung von kulturellen, religiösen, sozialen, möglicherweise auch körperlichen Grenzen der Sprecher."

14   Bechhaus-Gerst (2007: 114 and 166) mentions an artists' almanac (*Künstler-Almanach*) from 1941, in which Hussein advertises his language skills and other competencies. She also refers to Hussein's contracts with different production companies, as well as the letterhead used by him.

15   As a response to prominent claims of restitution, ICOM first published *Ethics of Acquisition* in 1970, followed by the *Code of Professional Ethics* in 1986. Since then, ICOM has revised the guidelines several times, and translated them into different languages. A German version was published in 2010.

16   One reason why ICOM does not include media relates to the matter of property. The recording media belonged to the researchers; the results of the (anthropometric) procedures were considered scientific knowledge and thus the intellectual property of the researcher and not of the person examined (Lange 2013b: 55).

17   See e.g. the restitution report by Felwine Sarr and Bénédicte Savoy (2018), commissioned by the French Ministry of Culture.

18   See also my contribution to the volume, which focuses on a single sound object from the *Lautarchiv* and its sensitive nature (Hilden 2018a).

19   See LAHUB, personal information form LA 1373 / 1374.

20   Notably, it was not listed that Hussein had been working as a language and teaching assistant at the Seminar for Oriental Languages since 1931.

21   On the German side, General Paul von Lettow-Vorbeck (1870–1964) led the combat operations during the war. He was the commander of the German so-called *Schutztruppe*

(colonial protection force) in the colony of German East Africa. Today, Lettow-Vorbeck is considered a war criminal (Knopf 2018: 90).

22   In 1937, the Nazis dispossessed the firm M. Kempinski & Co of the *Haus Vaterland*. Together with his family, Berthold Kempinski's (1843–1910) son-in-law Richard Unger (1866–1947) emigrated to the US during the Second World War (Bechhaus-Gerst 2007: 81).

23   For a detailed discussion of Steyerl's film, see e.g. Gerhardt 2007.

24   See *Lautbibliothek der Lautabteilung der Preußischen Staatsbibliothek,* Berlin. Under the title *Sound Library*, the publication series was irregularly published between 1926 and 1952. Little is known about the use of these publications and accompanying discs. We do not know whether and how they were used in classroom settings or for private teaching and study purposes. In the university archive, one finds inquiries concerning specific published sound recordings that one could purchase via the archive. In the catalogue, published by the Prussian State Library in 1932, one finds the available titles and prices (*Lautabteilung* 1932). When the *Lautabteilung* merged into the newly founded Institute for Sound Research, Diedrich Westermann took over the editorship.

25   This stems from a personal conversation and e-mail correspondence with Jasmin Mahazi, who listened to the sound recording together with her relatives (July 11, 2018).

26   In 1925, the development of electroacoustic recording technologies superseded earlier mechanic methods (Morat and Blanck 2015: 707). The Institute for Sound Research also implemented this new technology.

27   See HUB-Archive, IfL no. 21, letter to "Muhamed Husein Bajuma [sic]," November 25, 1935.

28   See LAHUB, PK 1508 (November 11, 1918).

29   For more on Meinhof, see e.g. Pugach 2012. In her introduction, Pugach comprehends: "Many of Meinhof's theories on language and ethnicity were uncompromisingly racist, including his contention that the lightest-skinned African 'tribes' were usually the ones whose members spoke the most sophisticated languages, or his assertion that the more vowels a language had, the more primitive it was" (2).

30   See LAHUB, PK 1108 (November 24, 1917). From the personal information form referring to this recording, one learns that this particular audio file, containing a narrative about the speaker's personal life, was not recorded on the site of the POW camp but at the corporate headquarters of the Odeon Company located in the centre of Berlin, approximately fifty kilometres from the internment camp.

31   According to the archival script, both speakers, Hussein and Ahmat, spoke several different languages. According to his personal information form, Hussein spoke Swahili and German, a bit of Arabic, English, and "Indian [sic]." Ahmat's first language is listed as Mwali dialect, but he also knew Swahili, French, and Arabic.

32   The *Guidelines for German Museums: Care of Collections from Colonial Contexts* by the German Museum Association (first published in May 2018, followed by a revised version in July 2019) distinguishes between three object categories: (1) objects from formal colonial rule contexts, (2) objects from regions which were not subject to formal colonial rule, and (3) objects that reflect colonialism. The third case refers to objects reflecting

colonial thinking and/or conveying stereotypes based on colonial racism. As examples, the guidelines name: colonial propaganda, advertising products, and works of the visual and performing arts. For me, it is astonishing that this category is somehow limited to visual material and that the guidelines do not include scientific literature and textbooks.

33   For more on the discourse of Nazi propaganda material in public/university libraries, see e.g. Rösch 2018.

34   The article was published in the academic journal *Africa*, which was founded by the *International Institute of African Languages and Cultures* (IIALC) in London in 1926, and which still exists today. For more on the IIALC and the emergent scientific community within African studies, see e.g. Stoecker 2008a; Tilley 2011.

35   In a footnote, Westermann (1931) acknowledges that colonial officers also contributed to anthropological research, but this fact would not be the focus of his text.

36   The first to become professor for African linguistics in Germany at the Hamburg Colonial Institute (*Hamburgisches Kolonialinstitut*) in 1909 was Carl Meinhof, a former pastor. One year before, Westermann took over Meinhof's previous position as a lecturer at the Seminar for Oriental Languages in Berlin. Westermann became a full professor for African languages and cultures at Berlin University in 1925, despite lacking a traditional academic career and qualification.

37   Stoecker (2008a: 218 and 238) describes Westermann's academic habitus as representing his disciplinary field in its entirety and not only a subfield. Stoecker also emphasises that the nexus between colonial science and colonial politics gained in importance under Westermann.

38   In the context of enhancing colonial policies and control, Helen Tilley speaks of "the application of scientific knowledge and its complement, scientific colonialism" (2011: 4).

39   "Die Völkerkunde muß für uns heute in tieferem Sinne als früher eine koloniale Wissenschaft sein. Das ist eine Forderung der kolonialen Verantwortung, die Deutschland nach Beendigung des Krieges übernehmen wird. Aufgabe der Völkerkunde ist das Studium der Naturvölker, und mit eben diesen hat es auch die koloniale Tätigkeit zu tun. Kolonialpolitik ist zumal in Afrika Eingeborenenpolitik." For more of Westermann's writing during the Nazi period, see e.g. Westermann 1941a.

40   While the concept of *Lebensraum* under Nazi rule is predominantly associated with the ideology of a territorial expansion into and colonisation of Central and Eastern Europe (*Generalplan Ost*), it can also be related to the colonial ambitions in Africa as pursued by the Colonial Policy Office of the NSDAP (Jell-Bahlsen 1985: 324).

41   From 1938 to 1941, Westermann was chair of the Berlin Society for Anthropology, Ethnology, and Prehistory (*Berliner Gesellschaft für Anthropologie, Ethnologie und Urgeschichte*). From 1940 to 1945, he was editor of the *Koloniale Rundschau*. In 1942, he became chair of the African Department of the Faculty of Foreign Studies. In 1947, the Institute for Asian and African Studies which still exists today, arose from this department (Stoecker 2008a: 112).

42   Despite several attempts, Westermann's colleague and early member of the SA, Martin Heepe, had difficulties finding employment at the university after the war. In December 1945, Heepe was dismissed; in February 1946, the Russian authorities

prohibited him from entering university premises (HUB-Archive, personnel file Martin Heepe, vol. 1, 64–65). However, in May 1949, he was rehabilitated (HUB-Archive, personnel file Martin Heepe, vol. 3, 22).

43   In her, so far unpublished, master's thesis, Julia Weitzel (2018) also addresses Westermann's ambiguous role in her examination of the *Lautarchiv*'s sound recordings of Bonifatius Folli (1877–1947) from Togo, who was a long-standing assistant of Westermann and co-taught Ewe at Berlin University. For the sound recordings of Folli, see LAHUB LA 1183-1185 and 1412, 1411.

44   According to Stoecker (2013: 73), the term *Sprach- und Lehrgehilfe* was primarily used for people of African descent. The term stands for the wilfully marked distinction between the *white* teacher and the ostensibly less educated and dependent Black assistant.

45   For an account of Carl Meinhof's Phonetics Laboratory at the Seminar for Colonial Languages (*Seminar für Kolonialsprachen*) in Hamburg, see Pugach 2018: 24–28.

46   "Eingeborene Lektoren zu halten erlaubt uns die Armut nicht. Ich habe aber einen Weg gefunden, sie zu ersetzen, wenigstens für die eigentlich sprachwissenschaftlichen Übungen. Vom Ministerium habe ich mir einen Kredit bewilligen lassen zu dem Zweck, dafür Eingeborene, die sich dauernd oder vorübergehend in Berlin aufhalten, für längere oder kürzere Zeit zu meinen Übungen als Objekte heranzuziehen. Ich erhalte so Eingeborene aus allen Teilen Afrikas, und nicht nur sie, ich habe ferner Japaner, Chinesen, Ungarn, Russen, Litauer als Objekte gehabt" (cited in Stoecker 2008a: 83).

47   In the university's archive, the name of the language assistant Bonifatius Folli, for instance, most frequently appears when Westermann makes claims for (extra) payments for Folli, whose employment was always only temporarily approved. Once again, this illustrates Westermann's position of power, and his patronising attitude of looking after his employees. See HUB-Archive, IfL no. 6, correspondence between Westermann and the *Reichskolonialbund* (Reich Colonial League) concerning the financial support for Folli and Abdullah bin Juma (1893–1952, Hussein's replacement after 1941) to cover the expenses of a dentist visit, September 26 and October 20, 1944. For a biographical account of Folli's life, see Stoecker 2008a and 2008b.

48   This quote hails from the British missionary William Henry Temple Gairdner (1873–1928). In a memorandum, entitled *Missionary training methods on the Continent*, from 1912, he referred to non-Western teaching assistants as "living phonographs" to be "cranked up" whenever needed (cited in Pugach 2007: 128).

49   Between 1937 and 1939, the *Auslandshochschule* offered advanced education (applied language courses, lessons in applied geography and colonial science) for members of the police (Stoecker 2008a: 108–109).

50   Hussein (alongside many other Black people and People of Colour living and working in Germany during the Nazi regime) took part in the German Africa Show (*Deutsche Afrika-Schau*), an officially sponsored colonial exhibition touring throughout Germany from 1936 until its ban in 1940 (Lewerenz 2006).

51   See e.g. Mdachi bin Sharifu, a Swahili lecturer who signed an anti-colonial petition in 1919, which became known as the *Dibobe Petition* (Stoecker 2008a: 58). In talks held in Berlin during the same period, he spoke about the discrimination he was facing and the

insufficient payment he received at the Seminar for Oriental Languages (Wimmelbücker 2009: 91). Important anti-colonial networks of the time included: *Bund Neues Vaterland*, founded in 1914, *Liga gegen die Kolonialgreuel und Unterdrückung*, founded in 1926, *Liga zur Verteidigung der N[sic]rasse* (see also *Ligue de la Defence dela Race N[sic]*), founded in 1928 (Stoecker 2013: 76 and 81).

52   A well-known example of this tension is the so-called *Dibobe Petition*. In 1919, Martin Dibobe (1876–1922), a Berlin underground train driver, submitted a petition to the German National Assembly in Weimar together with a group of seventeen other people, all born in Cameroon. While the thirty-two claims covered demands such as equality before the law and full access to public posts, the petition also included loyalty towards colonial Germany. For Nathanael Kuck (2014: 149), the petition was an expression of a growing political consciousness among colonial subjects living in Berlin.

53   I thank the *Humboldt-Universitäts-Gesellschaft* and the *Humboldt Labor* for funding the workshop and my collaboration with Jasmin Mahazi.

54   At the time, Rukia Bakari was a doctoral fellow at the Institute of African Studies, University of Leipzig, and visited Berlin to participate in the workshop. Frank Daffa was pursuing a second degree in African studies at Humboldt University, where he occasionally taught Swahili. He had first heard of the story of Hussein when attending a screening of Eva Knopf's documentary film at the Goethe Institute in Dar es Salam in 2014. Vitale Kazimoto was a long-standing member of the Tanzanian diaspora movement in Berlin. For more than twenty years, he had taught Swahili language and literature at Humboldt University, where he saw a number of (*white*) Swahili lecturers come and go. Kazimoto was familiar with the historical figure of Hussein and his story but did not know much about the sound recording before the workshop. Lutz Diegner and Stephanie Lämmert both studied and then worked in the field of African studies. Diegner was a lecturer in Swahili at Humboldt University, while Lämmert was a post-doctoral researcher at the Max Planck Institute for Human Development in Berlin. Diegner felt it was his responsibility to engage with Hussein's story. After all, he saw his and Kazimoto's appointments at the university as a continuing legacy of the institution's history. As a manager responsible for East Africa, Asmau Nitardy worked for the German–African Business Association (*Afrika-Verein der deutschen Wirtschaft*). She took part in the workshop out of personal interest.

55   The quotes are taken from my transcription and translation of the workshop, which took place at Humboldt University on January 16, 2019. We conducted the workshop mostly in German and partly in English.

56   Apparently, the record ended before Hussein could read out the text in full. For this reason, the last five sentences are only available in the accompanying textbook (Schroeder 1935).

57   During the workshop, Frank Daffa and Jasmin Mahazi, for instance, referred to poetic and metaphorical texts and wedding songs performed by women. Asmau Nitardy mentioned an exhibition she was impressed with, on Swahili cultural practices of the past and present at the National Museum of Kenya in Lamu. Contrasting, contesting, and

even invalidating this difficult archival source by means of (female) art practices of poetry or music would be the task of another chapter, if not another research project entirely.

58   While not consistently, more and more institutions are employing the practice of including a trigger warning in their digital archives, making users aware that historical content can contain wording that may be outdated or offensive.

59   During my research, and after bringing together a number of people with a variety of expertise and opinions, I was not able to prove whether the text stemmed from an already published book or another source available to Schroeder.

60   The method of participant observation is usually credited to Bronisław Malinowski and his students in the UK, as well as Franz Boas and his students in the US. Margaret Mead (1901–1978) was also important in advocating and practicing participant observation. Moreover, Mead must be referenced in relation to the issue of the (non-)involvement of female informants (e.g. Mead 1929).

61   In another book, *Narrations of the Swahili* (*Schilderungen der Suaheli*), edited and translated by Carl Velten in 1901, he claims that, for the first time, a volume was published consisting of travelogues for the most part written down by Africans and not by Europeans.

62   Bakari was born in Tanzania in 1869. He came to Berlin in 1900, where he started working at the Seminar for Oriental Languages. For more on his life in Germany and his position as a Swahili lecturer, see e.g. Oguntoye 1997b; Wimmelbücker 2009.

63   "Er verfasste ein Buch über die ‚Sitten und Gebräuche der Suaheli‚ das die wichtigste Quelle für die Sozial- und Kulturgeschichte der Suaheli vor der Kolonisation war. Das Buch erschien unter dem Namen seines Vorgesetzten Dr. C. Velten."

64   "Im Jahre 1895 wurde die Suaheli-Bevölkerung an der Küste durch ein Suaheli-Rundschreiben auf Veranlassung des Herausgebers aufgefordert, Rätsel, Sprichwörter, Märchen usw. aufzuschreiben und an das Gouvernement einzusenden. Ein Dichter aus Bagamajo [sic] sandte darauf dieses Gedicht als Antwort ein, ohne aber seinen Namen zu nennen. Der Dichter gehört jedenfalls zu den unzufriedenen Elementen, die sich mit der Herrschaft der Europäer wenig befreunden können."

65   The collection of poems refers to Hermann von Wissmann (1853–1905), Lothar von Trotha (1848–1920), and the Kaiser Wilhelm II (1859–1941), among others.

66   In colonial territories and missionary sites, *white* women were also present as, for instance, missionary sisters, teachers, or nurses.

67   "Wie *systematisch* bauen unsere Wissenschaften und das daraus abgeleitete Wissen auf Zwangssituationen auf, und wie *inhärent* sind unseren Theorien solche Praktiken der Grenzüberschreitung?"

68   Since 1932, Heepe had been an active member of the SA, the paramilitary branch of the NSDAP.

69   See HUB-Archive, personnel file Martin Heepe, vol. 2, 21 and 23.

70   The five attachments consisted of: (1) a letter by Westerman finding fault with Heepe's lack of publications, (2) a note for the files explaining the dispute between Knothe and Heepe, (3) a letter by Knothe to the associate dean elaborating on the same dispute, (4) a letter by Hussein to the associate dean complaining about Heepe, and (5) statements by

the janitor reporting on lectures cancelled by Heepe. See HUB-Archive, personnel file Martin Heepe, vol. 2, 15–25.

71   "Wie ich Ihnen schon mündlich erklärte, bin ich ausserstande, im kommenden Semester meine Tätigkeit fortzusetzen. Der Grund hierfür liegt darin, dass Herr Prof. Heepe in mein Privatleben auf das stärkste eingreift. [...] Ich bin auf Nebenverdienste angewiesen. Diesen Nebenverdienst will Prof. Heepe mir nicht zugestehen, sowie er bemerkt, dass ich einen Nebenverdienst habe, wendet er sich telefonisch oder durch persönliche Besuche an die Firmen und belästigt diese so lange, bis ich entlassen werde. Eine rechtliche Grundlage für dieses Vorgehen hat Prof. Heepe nicht, denn ich besitze keinen Vertrag, weder mit der früheren Hochschule für Politik noch mit der Universität, der mir verbietet, noch andere Einkünfte zu haben. Aus diesen Gründen bin ich völlig ausserstande, noch weiter mit Herrn Prof. Heepe zu arbeiten und bitte, dieses Schreiben in diesem Sinne als Kündigung aufzufassen. Dagegen bin ich jederzeit bereit, mit Herrn Dr. Knothe weiter zu arbeiten. Heil Hitler!"

72   Rector to the Minister of Science, Education and National Culture, July 31, 1941, see HUB-Archive, personnel file Martin Heepe, vol. 2, 35. "Ich habe daraufhin Prof. Heepe und den in die Angelegenheit verwickelten Dr. Gerhard Knothe durch den Rechtsrat vernehmen lassen, weil ich hoffte, von mir aus die Dinge ins Reine bringen zu können, dagegen von der Vernehmung des ebenfalls als Zeugen gegen Prof. Heepe benannten Sprachgehilfen Bajuma [sic] Hussein als eines farbigen Ausländers abgesehen."

73   Bodo Hussein's burial site is located at the protestant cemetery *Neuer Dorotheenstädtischer Friedhof* in Berlin-Wedding (Bechhaus-Gerst 2007: 155).

74   For an account of these developments in academic and museum contexts, see e.g. Conrad 2019; Habermas 2019.

7   ... THE ACOUSTIC

1   In the preface to the volume *acoustic turn*, Petra Maria Meyer (2008: 13) emphasises that, in her opinion, all turns, from the linguistic to the performative, contain notions of the acoustic.

2   This threefold periodisation derives from the Scottish philosopher Adam Ferguson (1723–1816) and the US American anthropologist Lewis Henry Morgan (1818–1881).

3   The notion of a shared geographic space ties in directly with the history of violent settler colonialism in the Americas, the militant struggles over land, and the genocidal policies towards Native Americans. It is a tragic paradox that anthropologists aimed at preserving traditions and cultures by turning them into artifacts, while the US government sought to systematically destroy them (Sterne 2003: 331).

4   In his writing, Lüders (1925: 134–135) refers to Khas (Nepalese) as the lingua franca of Nepal and of Nepalese people living outside of the kingdom. The kingdom lasted from 1786 until the monarchy's abolishment in 2008.

5   The paradigms of 'salvage' and 'survival' were, however, not restricted to non-European anthropology, as, for instance, Elizabeth Edwards shows in her work on British folklore studies and photographic surveys, undertaken in the UK in the late nineteenth century. According to Edwards, anxieties of cultural disappearance also applied to a "broader cultural matrix concerned with the ethnographic and archaeological delineation of the racial and cultural origins of British people" (2009: 71). For the German context, see also Kaschuba 1999 [2006]: 26 and 38.

6   "Es ging nicht darum, die 'vom Aussterben bedrohten' Kulturen durch Verbesserung der politischen Umstände zu schützen, sondern das Ziel war, möglichst umfassende anthropologisch-ethnologische Sammlungen und eine multimediale Dokumentation anzulegen."

7   Detribalisation, as seen from a colonialist point of view, seems to be a paradox. On the one hand, colonisers saw themselves as being on a 'civilizing mission' that implemented the Christian faith, permanent settlements, and Western infrastructure. Colonial officials detached colonised subjects from their traditional territories and cultural practices in order to exploit their labour force. On the other hand, colonised subjects were not supposed to become 'too' urban and/or nationalist, as in the phase of decolonisation (Eckert 2004: 478).

8   In the same vein as Lange's argument, Anette Schlichter writes that "historical sound detaches itself from its source but keeps a corporeal connection to it through the singularity of voice" (2011: 33). In opposition to this, Eidsheim argues that voice is not innate but cultural, not unique but collective. In her opinion, the "voice's source is not the singer; it's the listener" (2019: 40).

9   "Die Tonaufnahmen [...] sind keine authentische Spur der Menschen, sondern artifizielle Dokumente, die einen wissenschaftlichen Hörgegenstand herstellen."

10 The audiovisual litany includes eleven phrases. For the list in its entirety, see Sterne 2003: 15.

11   The works of aforementioned Johannes Fabian (1983), James Clifford and George E. Marcus (1986), among others, played a major role in promoting this shift.

12   In comparison to the *Lautarchiv*, the historical collections of the Berlin Phonogram Archive (dating from 1893 to 1954) comprise more than 16,000 wax cylinders alone.

13   By contrast, a majority of sound media amassed at the Berlin Phonogram Archive stem from travels and field trips to the non-European world.

14   In North America, anthropologists compiled recordings both 'in the field' and in the metropolis. See e.g. Sterne's (2003: 321–325) account of the 'studio ethos,' as embodied by anthropologists Alice Cunningham Fletcher (1838–1923) and Frances Densmore (1867–1957).

15   From its inception, recorded sound was constituted discursively and intended as a mobile object. A person's voice externalised on a sound carrier was supposed to outlive the person and reach other generations to come. Yet sound objects were also commercial products. The formation of the *Lautarchiv* was never free from economic and commercial determinants. The mobility of recorded sound required a vast infrastructure of technical expertise, equipment, and material. Hence, record companies that were Berlin-based but operated globally had to be, and always were, involved in the institution's enterprise (Lange 2019: 65–66).

16   For this argument, I am thankful to Kara Keeling's lecture "'I Feel Love:' Race, Gender, Technē, and the (Im)Proper Sonic Habitus" at the conference *Un/Sounding Gender*, which took place at *Humboldt-Universität zu Berlin* in June 2018 (for my conference report, see Hilden 2018b).

17   For sound studies in German-speaking contexts, see e.g. Morat and Ziemer 2018; Network 'Hör-Wissen im Wandel' 2017.

18   See e.g. Steingo and Sykes 2019 as an attempt to address and overcome this critique.

8 Coda

1 As explained in Chapter 2, I borrow the notion of post-migration from critical migration research, which regards migration and mobility as constitutive components of German society (e.g. Bojadžijev and Römhild 2014; Foroutan, Karakayali, and Spielhaus 2018).

2 For more information, see https://archivderflucht.hkw.de/en/ [last accessed March 16, 2022].

3 For more on dynamics between migrant archives and Holocaust memory in Germany, see Rothberg and Yildiz 2011: 37–38.

4 See https://domid.org/en/ [last accessed March 19, 2020].

5 Initially, it was founded as a non-profit organisation called DOMiT: the Documentation Centre and Museum of Migration from Turkey.

6 In 2017, DOMiD launched a virtual migration museum. The idea of the digital museum is not to offer a complete history of migration, but to concentrate on a selection of new and thus far overlooked topics. It aims to constantly expand the virtual exhibition of objects and themes. For more information, see https://virtuelles-migrationsmuseum.org/en/ [last accessed March 31, 2020].

7 "Die Geschichten der Anderen sind mit unseren Geschichten durch das Zuhören verbunden, sie werden Teil unserer Geschichte und wir ihrer. Wir werden hineingezogen. Wir hören der Geschichte zu, aber wir sind auch Teil der Geschichte, wenn wir jetzt hören [...]."

8 Over the past few years, Anna Biselli, computer scientist, journalist, and Internet activist, has reported on the use of biometric technologies in the administration of asylum procedures, as well as on other matters of state surveillance in Germany. Biselli evaluates official documents of the German Federal Office for Migration and Refugees as well as minor interpellations to the Federal Government and the Federal Ministry of the Interior.

9 I thank Michelle Pfeifer for generously providing me with the manuscript of her presentation, "Racializing Migrancy: Genealogies of Managing Mobility in Germany and Its Colonies," which she gave at a panel on *Migrantizing Europe*, convened by Arjun Appadurai and Regina Römhild. Her contribution is based on her doctoral research project at New York University's Department of Media, Culture, and Communication.

10 Here, Pfeifer refers to a 1907 decree, in the German colony German South-West Africa, according to which every colonial subject had to register and wear a pass-badge as a means of identification (see also Zimmerer 2008; Madörin [forthcoming]).

Bibliography

Adam, Jens, Regina Römhild, Manuela Bojadžijev, Michi Knecht, Paweł Lewicki, Nurhak Polat, and Rika Spiekermann, eds. 2019a. *Europa dezentrieren: Globale Verflechtungen neu denken*. Frankfurt am Main: Campus.

———, Manuela Bojadžijev, Michi Knecht, Paweł Lewicki, Nurhak Polat, Regina Römhild, and Rika Spiekermann. 2019b. "Europa dezentrieren: Programm und Perspektiven einer Anthropologie reflexiver Europäisierung." In *Europa dezentrieren: Globale Verflechtungen neu denken*, ed. by Jens Adam, Regina Römhild, Manuela Bojadžijev, Michi Knecht, Paweł Lewicki, Nurhak Polat, and Rika Spiekermann, 7–33. Frankfurt am Main: Campus.

Agnew, Vanessa. 2005. "The Colonialist Beginnings of Comparative Musicology." In *Germany's Colonial Pasts*, ed. by Eric Ames, Marcia Klotz, and Lora Wildenthal, 41–60. Lincoln: University of Nebraska Press.

Ahmed, Sara. 2010. "Feminist Killjoys (And Other Willful Subjects)." *The Scholar and Feminist Online* 8 (3).

Ahuja, Ravi. 2005. "Die 'Lenksamkeit' des 'Lascars.' Regulierungsszenarien eines transterritorialen Arbeitsmarktes in der ersten Hälfte des 20. Jahrhunderts." *Geschichte und Gesellschaft* 31 (3): 323–353.

Aitken, Robbie, and Eve Rosenhaft. 2013a. *Black Germany: The Making and Unmaking of a Diaspora Community, 1884–1960*. Cambridge: Cambridge University Press.

———, eds. 2013b. *Africa in Europe: Studies in Transnational Practice in the Long Twentieth Century*. Liverpool: Liverpool University Press.

Alexander, Neta. 2017. "Rage against the Machine: Buffering, Noise, and Perpetual Anxiety in the Age of Connected Viewing." *Cinema Journal* 56 (2): 1–24.

Ames, Eric. 2003. "The Sound of Evolution." *Modernism/Modernity* 10 (3): 297–325.

———. 2008. "Seeing the Imaginary: On the Popular Reception of Wild West Shows in Germany, 1885–1910." In *Human Zoos: Science and Spectacle in the Age of Colonial Empires*, ed. by Pascal Blanchard, Nicolas Bancel, Gilles Boëtsch, Éric Deroo, Sandrine Lemaire, and Charles Fürsdick, 205–219. Liverpool: Liverpool University Press.

Amin, Shahid. 1995. *Event, Metaphor, Memory: Chauri Chaura 1922–1992*. Berkeley, Los Angeles, and London: University of California Press.

———. 2002. *Alternative Histories: A View from India*. Calcutta: Centre for Studies in Social Sciences.

Anonymous. 1907. "Chairi kwa Wazungu." Composed by an unknown author from Bagamoyo, Tanzania, in 1895. In *Prosa und Poesie der Suaheli*, ed. by Carl Velten, 367–370. Berlin: author's edition. Translation by Katrin Bromber. 2002. In *Kala Shairi: German East Africa in Swahili Poems*, ed. by Gudrun Miehe, Katrin Bromber, Said Khamis, Ralf Großerhode, and Hilke Meyer-Bahlburg, 372–374. Köln: Rüdiger Köppe Verlag.

Appadurai, Arjun, ed. 1986. *The Social Life of Things: Commodities in Cultural Perspective*. Cambridge: Cambridge University Press.

———. 2003. "Archive and Aspiration." In *Information is Alive: Art and Theory on Archiving and Retrieving Data*, ed. by Susan Charlton, Arjen Mulder, and Joke Brouwer, 14–25. Rotterdam: NAI Publishers.

———. 2013. *The Future as Cultural Fact: Essays on the Global Condition*. London and New York: Verso.

———. 2017. "Museum Objects as Accidental Refugees." *Historische Anthropologie* 25 (3): 401–408.

———, and Neta Alexander. 2020. *Failure*. Cambridge: Polity Press.

Ardener, Edwin. 1989. "The Construction of History: 'Vestiges of Creation.'" In *History and Ethnicity*, ed. by Elizabeth Tonkin, Mayron McDonald, and Malcolm Chapman, 22–33. London: Routledge.

Arondekar, Anjali. 2009. *For the Record: On Sexuality and the Colonial Archive in India*. Durham and London: Duke University Press.

———, Ann Cvetkovich, Christina B. Hanhardt, Regina Kunzel, Tavia Nyong'o, Juana María Rodríguez, and Susan Stryker. 2015. "Queering Archives: A Roundtable Discussion." *Radical History Review* 122: 211–231.

Asad, Talal, ed. 1995 [1973]. *Anthropology and the Colonial Encounter*. Atlantic Highlands: Humanities Press.

Assmann, Aleida. 2008. "Canon and Archive." In *Cultural Memory Studies: An International and Interdisciplinary Handbook*, ed. by Astrid Erll and Ansgar Nünning, 97–107. Berlin and New York: De Gruyter.

Axel, Brian K. 2002. "Introduction: Historical Anthropology and Its Vicissitudes." In *From the Margins: Historical Anthropology and Its Futures*, ed. by Axel K. Brian, 1–44. Durham and London: Duke University Press.

Ayim, May, Katharina Oguntoye, and Dagmar Schultz, eds. 1986. *Farbe bekennen: Afro-deutsche Frauen auf den Spuren ihrer Geschichte*. Berlin: Orlanda.

Bach, Jonathan. 2017. *What Remains: Everyday Encounters with the Socialist Past in Germany*. New York: Columbia University Press.

Balke, Friedrich. 2009. "Rete mirabile: Die Zirkulation der Stimmen in Philip Scheffners Halfmoon Files." *Sprache und Literatur* 40 (2): 58–78.

Banerjee, Sumanta. 1989. *The Parlour and the Streets: Elite and Popular Culture in Nineteenth Century Calcutta*. Calcutta: Seagull Books.

Basu, Paul, and Ferdinand De Jong. 2016. "Utopian Archives, Decolonial Affordances: Introduction to special issue." *Social Anthropology* 24 (1): 5–19.

Bayer, Kirsten, and Jürgen-K. Mahrenholz. 2000. "'Stimmen der Völker.' Das Berliner Lautarchiv." In *Theater der Natur und Kunst*, ed. by Horst Bredekamp, Jochen Brüning, and Cornelia Weber, 117–128. Berlin: Humboldt-Universität zu Berlin.

Bechhaus-Gerst, Marianne. 1997. "Afrikaner in Deutschland 1933–1945." *1999. Zeitschrift für Sozialgeschichte des 20. und 21. Jahrhunderts* 4: 10–31.

———. 2007. *Treu bis in den Tod: Von Deutsch-Ostafrika nach Sachsenhausen. Eine Lebensgeschichte*, Berlin: Ch. Links.

———. 2013. "Menschen Afrikanischer Herkunft in Berlin 1918–1945." In *Black Berlin: Die deutsche Metropole und ihre afrikanische Diaspora in Geschichte und Gegenwart*, ed. by Oumar Diallo and Joachim Zeller, 89–111. Berlin: Metropol Verlag.

———. 2018a. "'Nie liebt eine Mutter ihr Kind mehr, als wenn es krank ist.' Der Kolonialrevisionismus (1919–1943)." In *Deutschland Postkolonial? Die Gegenwart der imperialen Vergangenheit*, ed. by Marianne Bechhaus-Gerst and Joachim Zeller, 101–122. Berlin: Metropol Verlag.

———. 2018b. "Welche Farbe hat die Nation? Afrodeutsche (Gegen-)Stimmen." In *Deutschland Postkolonial? Die Gegenwart der imperialen Vergangenheit*, ed. by Marianne Bechhaus-Gerst and Joachim Zeller, 243–263. Berlin: Metropol Verlag.

Bendix, Regina. 2012. "Folklore Studies in German-speaking Europe since 1945." In *A Companion to Folklore*, ed. by Regina Bendix and Galit Hasan-Rokem, 364–390. Oxford: Wiley-Blackwell.

Berner, Margit, Anette Hoffmann, and Britta Lange, eds. 2011. *Sensible Sammlungen: Aus dem anthropologischen Depot*. Hamburg: Philo Fine Arts.

Bhambra, Gurminder K., and Boaventura de Sousa Santos. 2017. "Introduction: Global Challenges for Sociology." *Sociology*: 1–8.

Bijsterveld, Karin. 2018. *Sonic Skills: Listening for Knowledge in Science, Medicine and Engineering (1920s–Present)*. London: Palgrave Macmillan.

Binder, Beate. 2009. *Streitfall Stadtmitte: Der Berliner Schlossplatz*. Köln: Böhlau Verlag.

———, and Sabine Hess. 2011. "Intersektionalität aus der Perspektive der Europäischen Ethnologie." In *Intersektionalität Revisited*, ed. by Sabine Hess, Nikola Langreiter, and Elisabeth Timm, 15–52. Bielefeld: transcript.

Biselli, Anna. 2017. "Digitalisierte Migrationskontrolle: Wenn Technik über Asyl entscheidet." *Netzpolitik*, November 24, 2017. https://netzpolitik.org/2017/digitalisierte-migrationskontrolle-wenn-technik-ueber-asyl-entscheidet/ [last accessed April 1, 2020].

———. 2018. "Die IT-Tools des BAMF: Fehler vorprogrammiert." *Netzpolitik*, December 28, 2018. https://netzpolitik.org/2018/die-it-tools-des-bamf-fehler-vorprogrammiert/ [last accessed April 1, 2020].

———. 2020. "Dialektanalyse bei Geflüchteten: Automatisiertes Misstrauen." *Netzpolitik*, January 9, 2020. https://netzpolitik.org/2020/automatisiertes-misstrauen/ [last accessed April 1, 2020].

Blanchard, Pascal, Nicolas Bancel, Gilles Boëtsch, Éric Deroo, Sandrine Lemaire, and Charles Fürsdick, eds. 2008 [2002]. *Human Zoos: Science and Spectacle in the Age of Colonial Empires*. Liverpool: Liverpool University Press.

Bojadžijev, Manuela. 2011. "Das Spiel der Autonomie der Migration." *Zeitschrift für Kulturwissenschaften* 5 (2): 139–145.

———, and Regina Römhild. 2014. "Was kommt nach dem 'transnational turn'? Perspektiven für eine kritische Migrationsforschung." In *Vom Rand ins Zentrum: Perspektiven einer kritischen Migrationsforschung*, ed. by Labor Migration, 10–24. Berlin: Panama Verlag.

Bose, Friedrich von. 2013. "The Making of Berlin's Humboldt-Forum: Negotiating History and the Cultural Politics of Place." *darkmatter*. http://www.darkmatter101.org/site/2013/11/18/the-making-of-berlin%e2%80%99s-humboldt-forum-negotiating-history-and-the-cultural-politics-of-place/ [last accessed April 2, 2020].

———, and Larissa Förster. 2015. "Jenseits der Institution: Für eine erweiterte Diskussion ethnologischer Museumspraxis." *Zeitschrift für Kulturwissenschaften* 5: 95–122.

———. 2016. *Das Humboldt-Forum: Eine Ethnografie seiner Planung*. Berlin: Kadmos.

Braidotti, Rosi. 1994. *Nomadic Subjects: Embodiment and Sexual Difference in Contemporary Feminist Theory*. New York: Columbia University Press.

Brandstetter, Anna-Maria, and Vera Hierholzer, eds. 2018. *Nicht nur Raubkunst! Sensible Dinge in Museen und universitären Sammlungen*. Göttingen: V&R unipress.

Braun, Hans-Joachim. 2017. "An Acoustic Turn? Recent Developments and Future Perspectives of Sound Studies." *AVANT* 8 (1): 75-91.

Breiter, Bastian. 2002. "Der Weg des 'treuen Askari' ins Konzentrationslager: Die Lebensgeschichte des Mohamed Hussein." In *Kolonialmetropole Berlin*, ed. by Ulrich van der Heyden and Joachim Zeller, 215–220. Berlin: Berlin Edition.

Bromber, Katrin. 2003. "Verdienste von Lehrern und Lektoren des Seminars für Orientalische Sprachen zu Berlin im Schaffen und Bewahren von Swahili-Wortkunst." In *Nicht nur Mythen und Märchen: Afrika-Literaturwissenschaft als Herausforderung*, ed. by Flora Veit-Wildt, 34–57. Trier: Wissenschaftlicher Verlag.

———, Katharina Lange, Heike Liebau, and Anorthe Wetzel, eds. 2018. *The Long End of the First World War: Ruptures, Continuities and Memories*. Frankfurt am Main: Campus.

Bruckner, Sierra A. 2003. "Spectacles of (Human) Nature: Commercial Ethnography between Leisure, Learning, and Schaulust." In *Worldly Provincialism: German Anthropology in the Age of Empire*, ed. by H. Glenn Penny and Matti Bunzl, 127–155. Ann Arbor: The University of Michigan Press.

Bruns, Claudia, M. Michaela Hampf. 2018. *Wissen – Transfer – Differenz: Transnationale und interdiskursive Verflechtungen von Rassismen ab 1700*. Göttingen: Wallstein.

Bryant, Rebecca, and Daniel M. Knight. 2019. *The Anthropology of the Future*. Cambridge: Cambridge University Press.

Buck-Morss, Susan. 2009. *Hegel, Haiti, and Universal History*. Pittsburgh: University of Pittsburgh Press.

Burton, Antoinette. 2005. "Introduction: Archive Fever, Archive Stories." In *Archive Stories: Facts, Fictions, and the Writing of History*, ed. by Antoinette Burton, 1–24. Durham and London: Duke University Press.

———. 2011. "Imperial Optics: Empire Histories, Interpretative Methods." In *Empire in Question: Reading, Writing, and Teaching British Imperialism*, ed. by Antoinette Burton, 1–23. Durham and London: Duke University Press.

Carter, Rodney G.S. 2006. "Of Things Said and Unsaid: Power, Archival Silences, and Power in Silences." *Archivaria* 61: 215–233.

Certeau, Michel de. 1988 [1975]. *The Writing of History*, trans. by Tom Conley. New York: Columbia University Press.

Chakkalakal, Silvy. 2018. "Migration in der frühen Kulturanthropologie: Grenzüberschreitende Wissenspraktiken zwischen lokaler Geschichte und globaler Zukunft." *Historische Anthropologie* 26 (2): 149–175.

Chakrabarty, Dipesh. 2000. *Provincializing Europe: Postcolonial Thought and Historical Difference*. Princeton: University of Princeton Press.

Chun, Wendy H. K. 2009. "Introduction: Race and/as Technology; or, How to Do Things to Race." *Camera Obscura* 24 (1): 7–35.

Clifford, James, and George E. Marcus, eds. 1986. *Writing Culture: The Poetics and Politics of Ethnography*. Berkeley, Los Angeles, and London: University of California Press.

———. 1986. "On the Ethnographic Allegory." In *Writing Culture: The Poetics and Politics of Ethnography*, ed. by James Clifford and George E. Marcus, 98–121. Berkeley, Los Angeles, and London: University of California Press.

———. 1987. "Of Other Peoples: Beyond the 'Salvage Paradigm.'" In *Discussions in Contemporary Culture*, ed. by Hal Foster, 121–130. Seattle: Bay Press.

———. 1997. "Spatial Practices: Fieldwork, Travel, and the Discipline of Anthropology." In *Anthropological Locations: Boundaries and Grounds of a Field Science*, ed. by Akhil Gupta and James Ferguson, 185–222. Berkeley, Los Angeles, and London: University of California Press.

Comaroff, Jean, and John Comaroff. 1992. *Ethnography and Historical Imagination*. Boulder: Westview Press.

Conrad, Sebastian. 2002. "Doppelte Marginalisierung: Plädoyer für eine transnationale Perspektive auf die deutsche Geschichte." *Geschichte und Gesellschaft* 28 (1): 145–169.

———, and Shalini Randeria. 2013 [2002]. "Einleitung: Geteilte Geschichten – Europa in einer postkolonialen Welt." In *Jenseits des Eurozentrismus: Postkoloniale Perspektiven in den Geschichts- und Kulturwissenschaften*, ed. by Sebastian Conrad, Shalini Randeria, and Regina Römhild, 32–70. 2nd Edition. Frankfurt am Main: Campus.

———. 2019. "Rückkehr des Verdrängten? Die Erinnerung und den Kolonialismus in Deutschland 1919–2019." *Aus Politik und Zeitgeschichte* 69 (40/42): 28–33.

Crenshaw, Kimberlé. 1989. "Demarginalizing the Intersection of Race and Sex: A Black Feminist Critique of Antidiscrimination Doctrine, Feminist Theory, and Antiracist Politics." *University of Chicago Legal Forum*: 139–168.

———. 1991. "Mapping the Margins: Intersectionality, Identity Politics, and Violence against Women of Color." *Stanford Law Review* 43 (6): 1241–1299.

Das, Santanu. 2005. *Touch and Intimacy in First World War Literature*. Cambridge: Cambridge University Press.

———. 2011a. "The Singing Subaltern." *Parallax* 17 (3): 4–18.

———, ed. 2011b. *Race, Empire and First World War Writing*. Cambridge: Cambridge University Press.

———. 2014. "Indian Sepoy Experience in Europe, 1914–18: Archive, Language, and Feeling." *Twentieth Century British History* 25 (3): 391–417.

———. 2018. *India, Empire and First World War Culture: Writings, Images and Songs.* Cambridge: Cambridge University Press.

Daston, Lorraine, and Peter Galison. 2007. *Objectivity.* New York: Zone Books.

De Genova, Nicholas. 2017. "Introduction: The Borders of Europe and the European Question." In *The Borders of 'Europe': Autonomy of Migration, Tactics of Bordering,* ed. by Nicholas De Genova, 1–35. Durham and London: Duke University Press.

Debray, Régis. 1996 [1994]. *Media Manifestos: On the Technological Transmission of Cultural Forms,* trans. by Eric Rauth. London and New York: Verso.

Derrida, Jaques. 1996 [1995]. *Archive Fever: A Freudian Impression,* trans. by Eric Prenowitz. Chicago and London: University of Chicago Press.

Desai, Gaurav. 2001. *Subject to Colonialism: African Self-Fashioning and the Colonial Library.* Durham and London: Duke University Press.

Diallo, Oumar, and Joachim Zeller, eds. 2013. *Black Berlin: Die deutsche Metropole und ihre afrikanische Diaspora in Geschichte und Gegenwart.* Berlin: Metropol Verlag.

Didi-Huberman, Georges. 2007. "Das Archiv brennt." In *Das Archiv brennt,* ed. by Knut Ebeling and Georges Didi-Huberman, 7–32. Berlin: Kadmos.

Diengdoh, Wanphrang K. 2017. *Because We Did Not Choose.* Documentary Film. India. 92 Minutes.

Doegen, Wilhelm, ed. 1925. *Unter fremden Völkern: Eine neue Völkerkunde.* Berlin: Stollberg.

Ebeling, Knut, and Stephan Günzel. 2009. "Einleitung." In *Archivologie: Theorien des Archivs in Philosophie, Medien und Künsten,* ed. by Knut Ebeling and Stephan Günzel, 7–26. Berlin: Kadmos.

Eckert, Andreas. 2004. "Regulating the Social: Social Security, Social Welfare and the State in Late Colonial Tanzania." *The Journal of African History* 45 (3): 467–489.

———. 2010. "Afrikanische Sprachen und Afrikanistik." In *Geschichte der Universität Unter den Linden 1810–2010,* ed. by Heinz-Elmar Tenorth, 535–546. Berlin: Akademie Verlag.

Edwards, Elizabeth. 2001. *Raw Histories: Photographs, Anthropology and Museums.* Oxford and New York: Berg.

———, Chris Gosden, and Ruth B. Phillips, eds. 2006. *Sensible Objects: Colonialism, Museums and Material Culture.* Oxford and New York: Berg.

———, and Christopher Morton. 2009. "Introduction." In *Photography, Anthropology and History: Expanding the Frame,* ed. by Christopher Morton and Elizabeth Edwards, 1–24. Farnham and Burlington: Ashgate.

———. 2009. "Salvaging Our Past: Photography and Survival." In *Photography, Anthropology and History: Expanding the Frame,* ed. by Elizabeth Edwards and Christopher Morton, 67–88. Farnham and Burlington: Ashgate.

———. 2016. "The Colonial Archival Imaginaire at Home." *Social Anthropology* 24 (1): 52–66.

Eichhorn, Kate. 2013. *The Archival Turn in Feminism: Outrage in Order.* Philadelphia: Temple University Press.

Eickstedt, Egon von. 1921. *Rassenelemente der Sikh.* Berlin.

Eidsheim, Nina S. 2012. "Voice as Action: Towards a Model for Analyzing the Dynamic Construction of Racialized Voice." *Current Musicology* 93: 9–32.

———. 2015. *Sensing Sound: Singing and Listening as Vibrational Practice*. Durham and London: Duke University Press.

———. 2019. *The Race of Sound: Listening, Timbre, and Vocality in African American Music*. Durham and London: Duke University Press.

Eisenstadt, Shmuel N. 2000. *Multiple Modernities*. Cambridge: American Academy of Arts and Sciences.

Ernst, Wolfgang. 2002. *Das Rumoren der Archive: Ordnung aus Unordnung*. Berlin: Merve.

Evans, Andrew D. 2002. "Capturing Race: Anthropology and Photography in German and Austrian Prisoner-of-War Camps during World War I." In *Colonialist Photography: Imag(in)ing Race and Place*, ed. by Eleanor M. Hight and Gary D. Sampson, 226–256. London and New York: Routledge.

———. 2003. "Anthropology at War: Racial Studies of POWs during World War I." In *Worldly Provincialism: German Anthropology in the Age of Empire*, ed. by H. Glenn Penny and Matti Bunzl, 198–228. Michigan: University of Michigan Press.

———. 2010. *Anthropology at War: World War I and Science of Race in Germany*. Chicago and London: University of Chicago Press.

Fabian, Johannes. 1983. *Time and the Other: How Anthropology Makes Its Objects*. New York: Columbia University Press.

Falola, Toyin. 2017. "Ritual Archives." In *The Palgrave Handbook of African Philosophy*, ed. by Adeshina Afolayan and Toyon Falola, 703–728. New York: Palgrave Macmillan.

Farge, Arlette. 2013 [1989]. *The Allure of the Archives*, trans. by Thomas Scott-Railton. New Haven and London: Yale University Press.

———, and Michel Foucault. 2016 [1982]. *Disorderly Families: Infamous Letters from the Bastille Archives*, trans. by Thomas Scott-Railton. Minneapolis: University of Minnesota Press.

Förster, Larissa. 2013. "Öffentliche Kulturinstitution, internationale Forschungsstätte und postkoloniale Kontaktzone: Was ist ethno am ethnologischen Museum?" In *Ethnologie im 21. Jahrhundert*, ed. by Thomas Bierschenk, Matthias Krings, and Carola Lentz, 189–210. Berlin: Reimer.

———, Iris Edenheiser, Sarah Fründt, and Heike Hartmann, eds. 2018. *Provenienzforschung zu ethnografischen Sammlungen der Kolonialzeit: Positionen in der aktuellen Debatte*. Berlin: Humboldt-Universität zu Berlin.

Foroutan, Naika, Juliane Karakayali, and Riem Spielhaus, eds. 2018. *Postmigrantische Perspektiven: Ordnungssysteme, Repräsentationen, Kritik*. Frankfurt am Main: Campus.

Foucault, Michel. 1972 [1969]. *The Archaeology of Knowledge*, trans. by A. M. Sheridan Smith. London and New York: Routledge.

———. 1978. *Dispositive der Macht: Über Sexualität, Wissen und Wahrheit*, trans. by Jutta Kranz, Hans-Joachim Metzger, Ulrich Raulff, Walter Seitter and E. Wehr. Berlin: Merve.

Fründt, Sarah. 2019. "Sensitive Collection." In *Museumsethnologie: Eine Einführung. Theorien, Debatten, Praktiken*, ed. by Iris Edenheiser and Larissa Förster, 137–147. Berlin: Reimer.

Gaonkar, Dilip P., ed. 2001. *Alternative Modernities*. Durham and London: Duke University Press.

Gerhardt, Christina. 2007. "Transnational Germany: Hito Steyerl's Film Die leere Mitte and Two Hundred Years of Border Crossings." *Women in German Yearbook* 23: 205–223.

German Museums Association. 2019. *Guidelines for German Museums: Care of Collections from Colonial Contexts*. 2nd Edition. Berlin.

Gingrich, Andre. 2010. "After the Great War: National Reconfigurations of Anthropology in Late Colonial Times." In *Doing Anthropology in Wartime and War Zones: World War I and the Cultural Sciences in Europe*, ed. by Reinhard Johler, Christian Marchetti, and Monique Scheer, 355–379. Bielefeld: transcript.

Gitelman, Lisa. 2008. *Always Already New: Media, History and the Data of Culture*. Cambridge: Cambridge University Press.

Gouaffo, Albert. 2013. "Prince Dido of Didotown and 'Human Zoos' in Wilhelmine Germany: Strategies for Self-Representation under the Othering Gaze." In *Africa in Europe: Studies in Transnational Practice in the Long Twentieth Century*, ed. by Robbie Aitken and Eve Rosenhaft, 19–33. Liverpool: Liverpool University Press.

Glasenapp, Helmuth von. 1925a. "Der Hinduismus." In *Unter Fremden Völkern: Eine neue Völkerkunde*, ed. by Wilhelm Doegen, 116–125. Berlin: Stollberg.

———. 1925b. "Die Radschputen." In *Unter Fremden Völkern: Eine neue Völkerkunde*, ed. by Wilhelm Doegen, 140–150. Berlin: Stollberg.

———. 1925c. "Die Sikhs." In *Unter Fremden Völkern: Eine neue Völkerkunde*, ed. by Wilhelm Doegen, 151–160. Berlin: Stollberg.

———. 1964. *Meine Lebensreise: Menschen, Länder und Dinge, die ich sah*. Wiesbaden: F. A. Brockhaus.

Gordon, Avery. 2011. "'I'm already in a sort of tomb.' A Reply to Philip Scheffner's The Halfmoon Files." *The South Atlantic Quarterly* 110 (1): 121–154.

Grosse, Pascal. 2003. "Zwischen Privatheit und Öffentlichkeit: Kolonialmigration in Deutschland, 1900–1940." In *Phantasiereiche: Zur Kulturgeschichte des deutschen Kolonialismus*, ed. by Birthe Kundrus, 91–109. Frankfurt am Main: Campus.

Guha, Ranajit. 1997. *Dominance without Hegemony: History and Power in Colonial India*. Cambridge: Harvard University Press.

Gunkel, Hermann. 1987 [1917]. *The Folktale in the Old Testament*. Sheffield: Almond Press.

Ha, Noa. 2014. "Perspektiven urbaner Dekolonisierung: Die europäische Stadt als 'Contact Zone.'" *s u b u r b a n. zeitschrift für kritische stadtforschung* 2 (1): 27–48.

Habermas, Rebekka, and Susanna Burghartz. 2017. "Globale Dinge: Und was wir von ihnen lernen können." *Historische Anthropologie* 25 (3): 301–307.

———. 2017. "Benin Bronzen im Kaiserreich: Oder warum koloniale Objekte so viel Ärger machen." *Historische Anthropologie* 25 (3): 327–352.

———. 2019. "Restitutionsdebatten, koloniale Aphasie und die Frage, was Europa ausmacht." *Aus Politik und Zeitgeschichte* 69 (40/42): 17–22.

Hagenbeck, John George. 1932. *Mit Indiens fahrendem Volk*. Berlin: August Scherl GmbH.

Halberstam, Jack. 2011. *The Queer Art of Failure*. London and Durham: Duke University Press.

Hall, Stuart. 1992. "The West and the Rest: Discourse and Power." In *Formations of Modernity*, ed. by Stuart Hall and Bram Gieben, 275–331. Cambridge: Polity Press.

———, ed. 1997. *Representation: Cultural Representations and Signifying Practices*. London: Thousand Oaks.

———. 2001. "Constituting an Archive." *Third Text* 15 (54): 89–92.

Hamilton, Carolyn, Verne Harris, and Graeme Reid. 2002. "Introduction." In *Refiguring the Archive*, ed. by Carolyn Hamilton, Verne Harris, Michèle Pickover, Graeme Reid, Razia Saleh, and Jane Taylor, 7–17. Cape Town: David Philip.

Hamm, Marion, and Klaus Schönberger, eds. 2021a. *Contentious Cultural Heritages and Arts: A Critical Companion*. Klagenfurt: Wieser Verlag.

———. 2021b. "A Critical Companion: On Contentious Heritages and the Arts, Democracy and a New European Imagination." In *Contentious Cultural Heritages and Arts: A Critical Companion*, ed. by Marion Hamm and Klaus Schönberger, 27–43. Klagenfurt: Wieser Verlag.

Hanke, Christine. 2007. *Zwischen Auflösung und Fixierun: Zur Konstitution von 'Rasse' und 'Geschlecht' in der physischen Anthropologie um 1900*. Bielefeld: transcript.

Haraway, Donna. 1988. "Situated Knowledges: The Science Question in Feminism and the Privilege of Partial Perspective." *Feminist Studies* 14 (3): 575–599.

Hartman, Saidiya. 2008. "Venus in Two Acts." *Small Axe: A Caribbean Journal of Criticism* 26: 1–14.

Hartmann, Heike. 2018. "Andererseits: Zum Umgang mit Objekten in der Ausstellung 'Deutscher Kolonialismus. Fragmente seiner Geschichte und Gegenwart.'" In *Provenienzforschung zu ethnografischen Sammlungen der Kolonialzeit: Positionen in der aktuellen Debatte*, ed. by Larissa Förster, Iris Edenheiser, Sarah Fründt, and Heike Hartmann, 294–264. Berlin: Humboldt-Universität zu Berlin.

Hartmann, Thomas, Jochen Hennig, and Britta Lange. 2015. *Du hast Mein Wort: Juristische und kulturethische Kriterien für die Nutzung der Aufnahmen aus dem Lautarchiv der Humboldt-Universität zu Berlin*. Berlin: Humboldt-Universität zu Berlin.

Haschemi, Elahe Yekani, and Beatrcie Michaelis. 2014. "Queering Archives of Race and Slavery: Or, on Being Wilfully Untimely and Unhappy." In *Postcoloniality – Decoloniality – Black Critique*, ed. by Sabine Broeck and Carsten Junker, 269–283. Frankfurt am Main: Campus.

Hennig, Jochen. 2016. "Wechselnde Formate: Zur rezenten Geschichte der Sprachaufnahmen des Berliner Lautarchivs – ein Bericht." *Berichte zur Wissenschaftsgeschichte* 39: 350–366.

Herzfeld, Michael. 2002. "The Absent Presence: Discourses of Crypto-Colonialism." *The South Atlantic Quarterly* 101 (4): 899–926.

Hess, Sabine, Bernd Kasparek, Stefanie Kron, Mathias Rodatz, Maria Schwertl, and Simon Sontowski, eds. 2017. *Der lange Sommer der Migration*. 2nd Edition. Berlin: Assoziation A.

Heyden, Ulrich van der. 2003. "Vom Seminar für Orientalische Sprachen zum Seminar für Afrikawissenschaften." In *Nicht nur Mythen und Märchen: Afrika-Literaturwissenschaft als Herausforderung*, ed. by Flora Veit-Wildt, 19–33. Trier: Wissenschaftlicher Verlag.

Hilden, Irene. 2015. *Die (Un)Möglichkeit subalterner Artikulation: Zu den Tonaufnahmen aus deutscher Kriegsgefangenenlagern des Ersten Weltkriegs*. 2015. MA thesis, Humboldt-Universität zu Berlin.

———. 2018a. "Who sang this song? Ein akustisches Zeugnis, gefangen zwischen Selbstermächtigung und Objektstatus." In *Nicht nur Raubkunst! Sensible Dinge in Museen und wissenschaftlichen Sammlungen*, ed. by Anna-Marie Brandstetter and Vera Hierholzer, 177–191. Göttingen: V&R unipress.

———. 2018b. Conference Report: "Un/Sounding Gender." June 8, 2018. *H-Soz-Kult*, July 20, 2018. https://www.hsozkult.de/conferencereport/id/tagungsberichte-7798 [last accessed April 29, 2020].

Hochman, Brian. 2014. *Savage Preservation: The Ethnographic Origins of Modern Media Technology*. Minneapolis: University of Minnesota Press.

Hoffmann, Anette. 2014. "Echoes of the Great War: The Recordings of African Prisoners in the First World War." *Open Arts Journal* 3: 7–23.

———. 2015. "Introduction: Listening to Sound Archives." *Social Dynamics: A journal of African Studies* 41 (1): 73–83.

———, and Phindezwa Mnyaka. 2015. "Hearing Voices in the Archive." *Social Dynamics: A Journal of African Studies*. 41 (1): 140–165.

———. 2020. *Kolonialgeschichte hören: Das Echo gewaltsamer Wissensproduktion in historischen Tondokumenten aus dem südlichen Afrika*. Wien/Berlin: mandelbaum verlag.

Hoffmann, Arnd. 2005. *Zufall und Kontingenz in der Geschichtstheorie: Mit zwei Studien zu Theorie und Praxis der Sozialgeschichte*. Frankfurt am Main: Klostermann.

Hoffmann, Christoph. 2004. "Vor dem Apparat: Das Wiener Phonogramm-Archiv." In *Bürokratische Leidenschaften: Kultur- und Mediengeschichte im Archiv*, ed. by Sven Spieker, 281–294. Berlin: Kadmos.

ICOM (International Council of Museums). 2004 [1986]. *Code of Ethics for Museums*. https://icom.museum/en/resources/standards-guidelines/code-of-ethics/ [last accessed August 18, 2022].

Jan, Svenja von. 2018. "Das moderne Indien in deutschen Archiven, 1706–1989 (MIDA): Erste Spuren einer Verflechtungsgeschichte zwischen Hamburg und Indien im 19. und 20. Jahrhundert." *Hamburgische Geschichtsblätter* 9: 53–58.

———. (forthcoming). *Indian Migration and Migrational Networks: Preconditions and Functioning of South Asian Settlement in European and American Port Cities*. PhD diss., Georg-August-Universität Göttingen.

Jell-Bahlsen, Sabine. 1985. "Ethnology and Fascism in Germany." *Dialectical Anthropology* 9: 313–335.

Joyrich, Lynne. 2009. "Preface: Bringing Race and Media Technologies into Focus." *Camera Obscura* 24 (1): 1–5.

Kallaway, Peter. 2015. "Volkskirche, Volkekunde and Apartheid: Lutheran Missions, German Anthropology, and Science in African Education." In *Contested Relations: Protestantism between Southern Africa and Germany from the 1930s to the Apartheid Era*, ed. by Hanns Lessing, Tilmann Dedering, Jürgen Kampmann, and Dirkie Smit, 155–176. Wiesbaden: Harrassowitz Verlag.

————. 2017. "Diedrich Westermann and the Ambiguities of Colonial Science in the Inter-War Era." *The Journal of Imperial and Commonwealth History* 45 (6): 871–893.

Kaplan, Judith. 2013. "'Voices of the People.' Linguistic Research among Germany's Prisoners of War during World War I." *Journal of the History of the Behavioral Sciences* 49 (3): 281–305.

Karttunen, Frances E. 1994. *Between Worlds: Interpreters, Guides, and Survivors*. New Brunswick: Rutgers University Press.

Kaschuba, Wolfgang. 2006 [1999]. *Einführung in die Europäische Ethnologie*. München: C.H. Beck.

Kienitz, Sabine. 2012. "Von Akten, Akteuren und Archiven: Eine kleine Polemik." *Historisches Forum* 14: 107–122.

Knauft, Bruce M., ed. 2002. *Critically Modern: Alternatives, Alterities, Anthropologies*. Bloomington: Indiana University Press.

Knopf, Eva. 2013. *Majub's Journey*. Documentary Film. Germany. 48 Minutes.

————. 2018. "Die Suche nach Mohamed Hussein im kolonialen Archiv: Ein unmögliches Projekt." In *Archive dekolonialisieren: Mediale und epistemische Transformationen in Kunst, Design und Film*, ed. by Eva Knopf, Sophie Lembcke, and Mara Recklies, 83–106. Bielefeld: transcript.

Kopytoff, Igor. 1986. "The cultural biography of things: Commoditization." In *The Social Life of Things: Commodities in Cultural Perspective*, ed. by Arjun Appadurai, 64–91. Cambridge: Cambridge University Press.

Kremmler, Katrin. (forthcoming). *Eurasian Magyars: Postcolonial Perspectives on the Construction of a Nationalist Prehistory in Illiberal Hungary*. PhD diss., Humboldt-Universität zu Berlin.

Kuck, Nathanael. 2014. "Anti-colonialism in a Post-Imperial Environment: The Case of Berlin, 1914–33." *Journal of Contemporary History* 49 (1): 134–159.

Kuster, Brigitta, Britta Lange, and Petra Löffler. 2019. "Archive der Zukunft? Ein Gespräch über Sammlungspolitiken, koloniale Archive und die Dekolonisierung des Wissens." *Zeitschrift für Medienwissenschaft* 20 (11): 96–111.

KZ-Gedenkstätte Neuengamme. 2018. *Verflechtungen: Koloniales und rassistisches Denken und Handeln im Nationalsozialismus. Voraussetzungen, Funktionen, Folgen. Materialien für die Bildungsarbeit*, ed. in collaboration with Universität Augsburg and Universität Hamburg. Hamburg.

Laak, Dirk van. 2003. "'Ist je ein Reich, das es nicht gab, so gut verwaltet worden?' Der imaginäre Ausbau der imperialen Infrastruktur in Deutschland nach 1918." In *Phantasiereiche: Zur Kulturgeschichte des deutschen Kolonialismus*, ed. by Birthe Kundrus, 71–90. Frankfurt am Main: Campus.

————. 2018. "Die deutsche Kolonialgeschichte als Fantasiegeschichte." In *Deutschland Postkolonial? Die Gegenwart der imperialen Vergangenheit*, ed. by Marianne Bechhaus-Gerst and Joachim Zeller, 123–142. Berlin: Metropol Verlag.

Lacey, Kate. 2013. *Listening Publics: The Politics and Experience of Listening in the Media Age*. Cambridge: Polity Press.

Lange, Britta. 2011a. "Sensible Sammlungen." In *Sensible Sammlungen: Aus dem anthropologischen Depot*, ed. by Margit Berner, Anette Hoffmann, and Britta Lange, 15–40. Hamburg: Philo Fine Arts.

———. 2011b. "'Denken Sie selber über diese Sache nach.' Tonaufnahmen in deutschen Gefangenenlagern des Ersten Weltkriegs." In *Sensible Sammlungen: Aus dem anthropologischen Depot*, ed. by Margit Berner, Anette Hoffmann, and Britta Lange, 89–128. Hamburg: Philo Fine Arts.

———. 2011c. "South Asian Soldiers and German Academics: Anthropological, Linguistic and Musicological Field Studies in Prison Camps." In *'When the war began, we heard of several kings.' South Asian Prisoners in World War I Germany*, ed. by Franziska Roy, Heike Liebau, and Ravi Ahuja, 149–184. New Dehli: Social Science Press.

———. 2012. "Was Wir Hören: Aus dem Berliner Lautarchiv." In *Was Wir Sehen: Bilder, Stimmen, Rauschen. Zur Kritik anthropometrischen Sammelns*, ed. by Anette Hoffmann, Britta Lange, and Regina Sarreiter, 61–78. Basel: Basler Afrika Bibliographien.

———. 2013a. *Die Wiener Forschungen an Kriegsgefangenen, 1915–1918: Anthropologische und ethnographische Verfahren im Lager*. Wien: Verlag der Österreichischen Akademie der Wissenschaften.

———. 2013b. "Prekäre Situationen: Anthropologisches Sammeln im Kolonialismus." In *Sammeln, Erforschen, Zurückgeben? Menschliche Gebeine aus der Kolonialzeit in akademischen und musealen Sammlungen*, ed. by Holger Stoecker, Thomas Schnalke, and Andreas Winkelmann, 45–68. Berlin: Ch. Links.

———. 2014. "History and Emotion: The Potential of Laments for Historiography." In *The World during the First World War*, ed. by Herbert Bley and Anorthe Kremers, 371–376. Essen: Klartext-Verlag.

———. 2015a. "Poste Restante, and Messages in Bottles: Sound Recordings of Indian Prisoners in the First World War." *Social Dynamics: A journal for African Studies* 41: 1–17.

———. 2015b. "Geschichten von der Möwe, 1916-1918: Praktiken von *talking* und *speaking* vor dem Grammophon." In *Laute, Bilder, Texte: Register des Archivs*, ed. by Alf Lüdtke and Tobia Nanz, 25–46. Göttingen: V&R unipress.

———. 2017a. "Archive, Collection, Museum: On the History of the Archiving of Voices at the Sound Archive of the Humboldt University." *Journal of Sonic Studies* 13. https://www.researchcatalogue.net/view/326465/326466 [last accessed March 4, 2019].

———. 2017b. "Archival Silences as Historical Silences: Reconsidering Sound Recordings of Prisoners of War (1915–1918) from the Berlin Lautarchiv." *Sound Effects: An Interdisciplinary Journal of Sound and Sound Experience* 7 (3): 47–60.

———. 2017c. "Die Konstruktion des Volks über Hör-Wissen: Tonaufnahmen des Instituts für Lautforschung von 'volksdeutschen Umsiedlern' aus den Jahren 1940/1941." In *Wissensgeschichte des Hörens in der Moderne*, ed. by Netzwerk 'Hör-Wissen im Wandel,' 329–356. Berlin and Boston: De Gruyter.

———. 2019. *Gefangene Stimmen: Tonaufnahmen von Kriegsgefangenen aus dem Lautarchiv 1915–1918*. Berlin: Kadmos.

Laukötter, Anja. 2013. "Gefühl im Feld. Die 'Sammelwut' der Anthropologen in Bezug auf Körperteile und das Konzept der 'Rasse' um die Jahrhundertwende." In *Sammeln,*

Erforschen, Zurückgeben? Menschliche Gebeine aus der Kolonialzeit in akademischen und musealen Sammlungen, ed. by Holger Stoecker, Thomas Schnalke, and Andreas Winkelmann, 24–44. Berlin: Ch. Links.

Lautabteilung. 1932. *Katalog der Lautbibliothek: Phonetische Platten und Umschriften*. Berlin.

Lawy, Jenny R. 2017. "Theorizing Voice: Performativity, Politics and Listening." *Anthropological Theory* 17 (2): 192–215.

Lennartsson, Rebecka. 2012. "Archival Ethnography: Reflections on a Lost Note." *Historisches Forum* 14: 77–92.

Lewerenz, Susann. 2006. *Die Deutsche Afrika-Schau (1935–1940): Rassismus, Kolonialrevisionismus und postkoloniale Auseinandersetzungen im nationalsozialistischen Deutschland*. Frankfurt am Main: Peter Lang Verlag.

———. 2017. *Geteilte Welten: Exotisierte Unterhaltung und Artist*innen of Color in Deutschland 1920–1960*. Köln: Böhlau Verlag.

Liebau, Heike, Katrin Bromber, Katharina Lange, Dyala Hamzah, and Ravi Ahuja, eds. 2010. *The World in World Wars: Experiences, Perceptions and Perspectives from Africa and Asia*. Leiden: Brill.

———. 2018. "A Voice Recording, a Portrait Photo and Three Drawings: Tracing the Life of a Colonial Soldier." *ZMO Working Papers* 20: 1–14.

Loosen, Livia. 2014. *Deutsche Frauen in den Südsee-Kolonien des Kaiserreichs: Alltag und Beziehungen zur indigenen Bevölkerung 1884–1919*. Bielefeld: transcript.

Lorde, Audre. 1984. *Sister Outsider: Essays and Speeches*. Freedom: The Crossing Press.

Lüders, Heinrich. 1925. "Die Gurkhas." In *Unter Fremden Völkern: Eine neue Völkerkunde*, ed. by Wilhelm Doegen, 126–139. Berlin: Stollberg.

Luschan, Felix von. 1917. *Kriegsgefangene: Ein Beitrag Zur Völkerkunde im Weltkriege*. Berlin: Reimer.

Maase, Kasper. 2001. "Das Archiv als Feld? Überlegungen zu einer historischen Ethnographie." In *Die Poesie des Feldes*, ed. by Katharina Eisch and Marion Hamm, 255–271. Tübingen: Tübinger Vereinigung für Volkskunde.

Macdonald, Sharon. 2003. "Trafficking in History: Multitemporal Practices." In *Shifting Grounds: Experiments in Doing Ethnography*, ed. by Ina-Maria Greuvers, Sharon Macdonald, Regina Römhild, Gisela Welz, and Helena Wulff, 93–116. Münster: Lit Verlag.

———. 2009. *Difficult Heritage: Negotiating the Nazi past in Nuremberg and beyond*, London and New York: Routledge.

———. 2012. "Presencing Europe's pasts." In *A Companion to the Anthropology of Europe*, ed. By Ulrich Kockel, Mairead Nic Craith, and Jonas Frykman, 233–252. Chitchester, Wiley-Blackwell.

———. 2013. *Memorylands: Heritage and Identity in Europe Today*. London and New York: Routledge.

———. 2021. "Contentious Collections, Contentious Heritage: Risks and Potentials of Opening Europe's Memory Bank." In *Contentious Cultural Heritages and Arts: A Critical Companion*, ed. by Marion Hamm and Klaus Schönberger, 95–127. Klagenfurt: Wieser Verlag.

Madörin, Anouk. (forthcoming). *Shadow Archives of the European Border Regime: Border and Surveillance Technologies between Colony and Crisis.* PhD diss., Universität Potsdam.

Mahrenholz, Jürgen-K. 2003. "Zum Lautarchiv und seiner wissenschaftlichen Erschließung durch die Datenbank IMAGO." In *Berichte aus dem ICTM-Nationalkomitee Deutschland,* ed. by Marianne Brücker, 131–152. Bamberg: Universitätsbibliothek Bamberg.

Maier-Wolthausen, Clemens. 2019. *Hauptstadt der Tiere: Die Geschichte des ältesten deutschen Zoos.* Berlin: Ch. Links.

Magalski, Phillip. 2014. "Kolonialgeschichte des Zoologischen Gartens: fühlt sich der Senat für die geschichtliche Aufarbeitung einer Berliner Institution verantwortlich?" Printed matter 17 / 14 643. https://kleineanfragen.de/berlin/17/14643-kolonialgeschichte-des-zoologischen-gartens-fuehlt-sich-der-senat-fuer-die-geschichtliche-aufarbeitung-einer.txt [last accessed August 11, 2017].

Marchand, Suzanne L. 2009. *German Orientalism in the Age of Empire: Religion, Race, and Scholarship.* Cambridge: Cambridge University Press.

Martin, Peter, and Christine Alonzo, eds. 2004. *Zwischen Charleston und Stechschritt: Schwarze im Nationalsozialismus.* Hamburg and München: Dölling und Galitz Verlag.

Martínez, Francisco. 2018. "The Serendipity of Anthropological Practice." *Anthropological Journal of European Cultures* 27 (1): 1–6.

Mbembe, Achille. 2002. "The Power of the Archive and Its Limits." In *Refiguring the Archive,* ed. by Carolyn Hamilton, Verne Harris, Michèle Pickover, Graeme Reid, Razia Saleh, and Jane Taylor, 19–26. Cape Town: Philip.

McClintock, Anne. 1995. *Imperial Leather: Race, Gender and Sexuality in the Colonial Contest.* London and New York: Routledge.

Mead, Margaret. 1929. *Coming of Age in Samoa: A Psychological Study of Primitive Youth of Western Civilisation.* London: Cape.

Mehnert, Dieter. 1996. "Historische Schallaufnahmen: Das Lautarchiv an der Humboldt-Universität zu Berlin." In *Studientexte zur Sprachkommunikation: Tagungsband der siebenten Konferenz Elektronische Sprachsignalverarbeitung,* ed. by Dieter Mehnert, 28–45. Dresden: TUD press.

Meier, Wilma. 1995. *Diedrich Westermann: Erforscher afrikanischer Sprachen und Kulturen.* Bremen.

Meinhof, Carl. 1928. *Die Sprache der Suaheli: in Deutsch-Ostafrika,* Berlin: Reimer.

Meyer-Kalkus, Reinhart. 2015. "'Bizarres Philologentum' und Repräsentation akustischer Weltkulturen: Phonographische Sprachaufnahmen aus deutschen Kriegsgefangenenlagern im Ersten Weltkrieg im Berliner Lautarchiv." In *Wege zur Weltliteratur: Komparatistische Perspektiven der Editionswissenschaft,* ed. by Gesa Dane, 43–70. Berlin: Weidler Buchverlag.

Meyer, Petra Maria, ed. 2008. *Acoustic Turn.* München: Wilhelm Fink Verlag.

Mezzadra, Sandro. 2011. "The Gaze of Autonomy: Capitalism, Migration, and Social Struggles." In *The Contested Politics of Mobility: Borderzones and Irregularity,* ed. by Vicki Squire, 121–142. London and New York: Routledge.

Miehe, Gudrun, Katrin Bromber, Said Khamis, Ralf Großerhode, and Hilke Meyer-Bahlburg, eds. 2002. *Kala Shairi: German East Africa in Swahili Poems*. Köln: Rüdiger Köppe Verlag.

Mischek, Udo. 2000. "Autorität außerhalb des Fachs: Diedrich Westermann und Eugen Fischer." In *Ethnologie und Nationalsozialismus*, ed. by Bernhard Streck, 69–82. Gehren: Escher Verlag.

Morat, Daniel. 2011. "Zur Geschichte des Hörens: Ein Forschungsbericht." *Archiv für Sozialgeschichte* 51: 695–716.

———, and Thomas Blanck. 2015. "Geschichte hören: Zum quellenkritischen Umgang mit historischen Tondokumenten." *Geschichte in Wissenschaft und Unterricht* 11/12: 703–726.

———, Hansjakob Ziemer. 2018. "Einleitung." In *Handbuch Sound: Geschichte – Begriffe – Ansätze*, ed. by Daniel Morat and Hansjakob Ziemer, VII–XI. Stuttgart: J.B. Metzler.

Morris, Rosalind C., ed. 2010. *Can the Subaltern Speak? Reflections on the History of an Idea*. New York: Columbia University Press.

Moulier Boutang, Yann. 1998. *De l'esclavage au salariat: Economie historique du salariat bride*. Paris: Presses Universitaires de France.

Mudimbe, Valentin-Yves. 1988. *The Invention of Africa: Gnosis, Philosophy, and the Order of Knowledge*. Bloomington: Indiana University Press.

Muñoz, José Esteban. 1999. *Disidentifications: Queers of Color and the Performance of Politics*. Minneapolis: University of Minnesota Press.

Myers, Norma. 1994. "The Black Poor of London: Initiatives of Eastern Seamen in the Eighteenth and Nineteenth Centuries." *Immigrants and Minorities: Historical Studies in Ethnicity, Migration and Diaspora* 13 (2/3): 7–21.

Nagl, Tobias. 2009. *Die unheimliche Maschine: Rasse und Repräsentation im Weimarer Kino*. München: edition text+kritik.

Network 'Hör-Wissen im Wandel.' 2017. *Wissensgeschichte des Hörens in der Moderne*. Berlin and Boston: De Gruyter.

NoHumboldt21! 2017. *Dekoloniale Einwände gegen das Humboldt-Forum*. Berlin: AfricAvenir International e.V..

Novak, David, and Matt Sakakeeny. 2015. "Introduction." In *Keywords in Sound*, ed. by David Novak and Matt Sakakeeny, 1–11. Durham and London: Duke University Press.

Oguntoye, Katharina. 1997a. *Eine afro-deutsche Geschichte: Zur Lebenssituation von Afrikanern und Afro-Deutschen in Deutschland von 1884 bis 1950*. Berlin: Hoho Verlag.

———. 1997b. "Die Lebensumstände von Afrikanern in Deutschland." In *Metropole Menschen Nahaufnahme: Afrikaner in Berlin*, ed. by Paulette Reed-Anderson, 20–23. Berlin: Ausländerbeauftragte des Senats.

Omissi, David. 1994. *The Sepoy and the Raj: The Indian Army, 1860–1940*. London: Macmillan Press.

Oppenheim, Max von. 2018 [1914]. *Denkschrift betreffend die Revolutionierung der islamischen Gebiete unserer Feinde*. Berlin: Verlag Das Kulturelle Gedächtnis.

Ortner, Sherry B. 1995. "Resistance and the Problem of Ethnographic Refusal." *Society for Comparative Study of Society and History* 10: 173–193.

Oswald, Margareta von. 2022. *Working Through Colonial Collections: An Ethnography of the Ethnological Museum in Berlin*. Leuven: Leuven University Press.

Papadopoulos, Dimitris, and Vassilis Tsianos. 2013. "After Citizenship: Autonomy of Migration, Organisational Ontology and Mobile Commons." *Citizenship Studies* 17 (2): 178–196.

Papenburg, Jens G., and Holger Schulze. 2016. *Sound as Popular Culture: A Research Companion*. Cambridge: MIT Press.

Parzinger, Hermann. 2011. *Das Humboldt-Forum: 'Soviel Welt mit sich verbinden als möglich.' Aufgabe und Bedeutung des wichtigsten Kulturprojekts in Deutschland zu Beginn des 21. Jahrhunderts*, ed. by Stiftung Berliner Schloss. Berlin.

Penny, Glenn H. 2002. *Objects of Culture: Ethnology and Ethnographic Museums in Imperial Germany*. Chapel Hill and London: The University of North Carolina Press.

———, and Matti Bunzl. 2003. "Introduction: Rethinking German Anthropology, Colonialism, and Race." In *Worldly Provincialism: German Anthropology in the Age of Empire*, ed. by Glenn H. Penny and Matti Bunzl, 1–30. Ann Arbor: The University of Michigan Press.

Pfeifer, Michelle. (forthcoming). *Your Voice is (not) Your Passport: The Mediated Voice and Sonic Borders*. Phd diss., New York University.

Pinch, Trevor, and Karin Bijsterveld, eds. 2011. *The Oxford Handbook of Sound Studies*. Oxford and New York: Oxford University Press.

Pinney, Christopher. 2011. *Photography and Anthropology*. London: Reaktion Books.

Pöch, Rudolf. 1916. "Anthropologische Studien an Kriegsgefangenen." In *Die Umschau: Wochenschrift über die Fortschritte in Wissenschaft und Technik*, ed. by J. H. Bechhold, 988–991. Frankfurt am Main.

Poignant, Roslyn. 2004. *Professional Savages: Captive Lives and Western Spectacle*. New Haven and London: Yale University Press.

Poole, Deborah. 1997. *Vision, Race, and Modernity: A Visual Economy of the Andean World*. Princeton and Oxford: Princeton University Press.

———. 2005. "An Excess of Description: Ethnography, Race, and Visual Technologies." *Annual Review of Anthropology* 34: 159–179.

Preuß, Dirk. 2009. *'Anthropologe und Forschungsreisender.' Biographie und Anthropologie Egon Freiherr von Eickstedts (1892–1965)*. München: Herbert Utz Verlag.

Pugach, Sara. 2007. "Of Conjunctions, Comportment, and Clothing: The Place of African Teaching Assistants in Berlin and Hamburg, 1889–1919." In *Ordering Africa: Anthropology, European Imperialism, and the Politics of Knowledge*, ed. by Helen Tilley and Robert J. Gordon, 119–144. Manchester and New York: Manchester University Press.

———. 2012. *Africa in Translation: A History of Colonial Linguistics in Germany and Beyond, 1814–1945*. Michigan: The University of Michigan Press.

———. 2018. "A Short History of African Language Studies in the Nineteenth and Early Twentieth Centuries, with an Emphasis on German Contributions." In *The Routledge Handbook of African Linguistics*, ed. by Augustine Agwquele and Adams Bodomo, 15–32. London and New York: Routledge.

Radano, Ronald, and Tejumola Olaniyan, eds. 2016. *Audible Empire: Music, Global Politics, Critique.* Durham and London: Duke University Press.

Rancière, Jaques. 1994 [1992]. *The Names of History: On the Poetics of Knowledge*, trans. by Hassan Melehy. Minneapolis: University of Minnesota Press.

Randeria, Shalini. 1999a. "Geteilte Geschichte und verwobene Moderne." In *Zukunftsentwürfe: Ideen für eine Kultur der Veränderung*, ed. by Jörn Rüsen, Hanna Leitgeb, and Norbert Jegelka, 87–96. Frankfurt am Main: Campus.

———. 1999b. "Jenseits von Soziologie und soziokultureller Anthropologie: Zur Ortsbestimmung der nichtwestlichen Welt in einer zukünftigen Sozialtheorie." *Soziale Welt* 50: 373–382.

———, and Regina Römhild. 2013. "Das postkoloniale Europa: Verflochtene Genealogien der Gegenwart – Einleitung zur erweiterten Neuauflage." In *Jenseits des Eurozentrismus: Postkoloniale Perspektiven in den Geschichts- und Kulturwissenschaften*, ed. by Sebastian Conrad, Shalini Randeria, and Regina Römhild, 9–31. 2nd Edition. Frankfurt am Main: Campus.

———. 2019. "Das Verborgene entdecken: Zur Geschichte und Methodologie des Verflechtungsansatzes." Shalini Randeria in conversation with Jens Adam and Regina Römhild. In *Europa dezentrieren: Globale Verflechtungen neu denken*, ed. by Jens Adam, Regina Römhild, Manuela Bojadžijev, Michi Knecht, Paweł Lewicki, Nurhak Polat, and Rika Spiekermann, 35–65. Frankfurt am Main: Campus.

Reed-Anderson, Paulette. 1997. *Metropole Menschen Nahaufnahme: Afrikaner in Berlin*. Berlin: Ausländerbeauftragte des Senats.

———. 2000 [1995]. *Rewriting the Footnotes: Berlin und die afrikanische Diaspora*. Berlin: Ausländerbeauftragte des Senats.

Reid, Kirsty and Fiona Paisley. 2017. "Introduction." In *Sources and Methods in Histories of Colonialism: Approaching the Imperial Archive*, ed. by Kirsty Reid and Fiona Paisley, 1–10. London and New York: Routledge.

Reimann, Denise. 2014. "'Art der Aufnahme: T.' Zu den Tierstimmenaufnahmen im Berliner Lautarchiv." *Trajekte* 29: 55–62.

Restrepo, Eduardo, and Arturo Escobar. 2005. "'Other Anthropologies and Anthropology Otherwise.' Steps to a World Anthropologies Framework." *Critique of Anthropology* 25 (2): 99–129.

Rice, Tom. 2015. "Listening." In *Keywords in Sound*, ed. by David Novak and Matt Sakakeeny, 99–111. Durham and London: Duke University Press.

Rich, Adrienne. 1987. "Notes Toward a Politics of Location (1984)." In *Blood, Bread and Poetry: Selected Prose 1979–1985*, ed. by Adrienne Rich, 210–223. London: Virago Press.

Richards, Thomas, 1993. *The Imperial Archive: Knowledge and the Fantasy of Empire*, London: Verso.

Ricœur, Paul. 2004. *Memory, History, Forgetting*, trans. by Kathleen Blamey and David Pellauer. Chicago and London: University of Chicago Press.

Rivoal, Isabelle and Noel B. Salazar. 2013. "Contemporary Ethnographic Practice and the Value of Serendipity." *Social Anthropology* 21 (2): 178–185.

Römhild, Regina. 2009. "Reflexive Europäisierung: Tourismus, Migration und die Mediterranisierung Europas." In *Projekte der Europäisierung: Kulturanthropologische Forschungsperspektiven*, ed. by Annina Lottermann and Gisela Welz, 261–278. Frankfurt am Main: Kulturanthropologische Notizen.

———. 2018. "Europa postmigrantisch: Entdeckungen jenseits ethnischer, nationaler und kolonialer Grenzen." In *Postmigrantische Perspektiven: Ordnungssysteme, Repräsentationen, Kritik*, ed. by Naika Foroutan, Juliane Karakayali, and Riem Spielhaus, 69–82. Frankfurt am Main: Campus.

———, and Michi Knecht. 2019. "Die doppelte Lücke: Postkoloniale ethnologische Perspektiven auf Europa." In *Europa dezentrieren: Globale Verflechtungen neu denken*, ed. by Jens Adam, Regina Römhild, Manuela Bojadžijev, Michi Knecht, Paweł Lewicki, Nurhak Polat, and Rika Spiekermann, 67–79. Frankfurt am Main: Campus.

———. 2021. "Reflexive Europeanisation: Europe in the Making of Global Entanglements." In *Contentious Cultural Heritages and Arts: A Critical Companion*, ed. by Marion Hamm and Klaus Schönberger, 685–701. Klagenfurt: Wieser Verlag.

Roque, Ricardo and Kim A. Wagner. 2012. "Introduction: Engaging Colonial Knowledge." In *Engaging Colonial Knowledge: European Archives in World History*, ed. by Ricardo Roque and Kim A. Wagner, 1–32. London: Palgrave Macmillan.

Rösch, Hermann. 2018. "Eine ethische Herausforderung: Der Zugang zu nationalsozialistischer Propagandaliteratur in Hochschulbibliotheken." In *Nicht nur Raubkunst! Sensible Dinge in Museen und universitären Sammlungen*, ed. by Anna-Maria Brandstetter and Vera Hierholzer, 257–270. Göttingen: V&R unipress.

Rothberg, Michael. 2009. *Multidirectional Memory: Remembering the Holocaust in the Age of Decolonization*. Stanford: Stanford University Press.

———, and Yasemin Yildiz. 2011. "Memory Citizenship: Migrant Archives of Holocaust Remembrance in Contemporary Germany." *Parallax* 17 (4): 32–48.

Roy, Franziska, Heike Liebau, and Ravi Ahuja, eds. 2011. *'When the War Began, We Heard of Several Kings.' South Asian Prisoners in World War I Germany*. New Delhi: Social Science Press.

———, and Heike Liebau. 2011. "Introduction." In *'When the war began, we heard of several kings.' South Asian Prisoners in World War I Germany*, ed. by Franziska Roy, Heike Liebau, and Ravi Ahuja, 1–14. New Dehli: Social Science Press.

———. 2011. "South Asian Civilian Prisoners of War in First World War Germany." In *'When the war began, we heard of several kings.' South Asian Prisoners in World War I Germany*, ed. by Franziska Roy, Heike Liebau, and Ravi Ahuja, 53–95. New Dehli: Social Science Press.

Sarr, Felwine, and Bénédicte Savoy. 2018. *Restituer le patrimoine africain*. Paris: Philippe Rey / Seuil.

Said, Edward W. 1978. *Orientalism*. New York: Pantheon Books.

Sandage, Scott. 2005. *Born Losers: A History of Failure in America*. Cambridge: Harvard University Press.

Scheer, Monique. 2010. "Captive Voices: Phonographic Recordings in the German and Austrian Prisoner-of-War Camps of World War I." In *Doing Anthropology in Wartime and War Zones: World War I and the Cultural Sciences in Europe*, ed. by Reinhard Johler, Christian Marchetti, and Monique Scheer, 279–309. Bielefeld: transcript.

Scheffner, Philip. 2007. *The Halfmoon Files*. Documentary Film. Germany. 87 Minutes.

Schlichter, Annette. 2011. "Do Voices Matter? Vocality, Materiality, Gender Performativity." *Body & Society* 17 (1): 31–52.

Schroeder, Arnulf. 1935. "Suaheli." In *Lautbibliothek: Texte zu den Sprachplatten des Instituts für Lautforschung an der Universität Berlin*, ed. by Diedrich Westermann. Berlin.

———. 1958. *Die Laute des Wendischen (Sorbischen) Dialekts von Schleife in der Oberlausitz: Lautbeschreibung*. Tübingen: May Niemeyer Verlag.

Sekula, Allan. 1986. "The Body and the Archive." *October* 39. 3–64.

Sharma, Manimugdha. 2014. "British Better Informed about India's Key Role in World War I: Survey." *Times of India*, March 30, 2014. https://timesofindia.indiatimes. com/india/British-better-informed-about-Indias-key-role-in-World-War-I-Survey/ articleshow/32933750.cms [last accessed December 13, 2019].

Simon, Artur, ed. 2000. *Das Berliner Phonogramm-Archiv 1900–2000: Sammlungen der traditionellen Musik der Welt*. Berlin: Verlag für Wissenschaft und Bildung.

Singha, Radikha. 2010. "Front Lines and Status Lines: Sepoy and 'Menial' in the Great War 1916–1920." In *The World in World Wars: Experiences, Perceptions and Perspectives from Africa and Asia War 1916–1920*. Heike Liebau, Katrin Bromber, Katharina Lange, Dyala Hamzah, and Ravi Ahuja, 55–106. Leiden: Brill.

Smith, Mark M., ed. 2004. *Hearing History: A Reader*. Athens: University of Georgia Press.

Soneji, Davesh. 2012. *Unfinished Gestures: Devadasis, Memory, and Modernity in South India*. Chicago and London: Chicago University Press.

Spivak, Gayatri C. 1985. "The Rani of Sirmur: An Essay in Reading the Archives." *History and Theory* 24 (3): 247–272.

———. 1988. "Can the Subaltern Speak?" In *Marxism and the Interpretation of Culture*, ed. by Cary Nelson and Lawrence Grossberg, 271–313. Basingstoke: Macmillan.

———. 2006 [1987]. *In Other Worlds: Essays in Cultural Politics*. New York and London: Meuthen.

Srinivasan, Priya. 2009. "The Nautch Women Dancers of the 1880s: Corporeality, US Orientalism, and Anti-Asian Immigration Laws." *Women and Performance: A Journal of Feminist Theory* 19 (1): 3–22.

———. 2012. *Sweating Saris: Indian Dance as Transnational Labor*. Philadelphia: Temple University Press.

Stangl, Burkhard. 2000. *Ethnologie im Ohr: Die Wirkungsgeschichte des Phonographen*. Wien: WUV Universitätsverlag.

Steedman, Carolyn. 2001a. *Dust*. Manchester: Manchester University Press.

———. 2001b. "Something She Called a Fever: Michelet, Derrida, and Dust." *The American Historical Review* 106 (4): 1159–1180.

Steere, Edward. 1870. *Swahili Tales: As Told by Natives of Zanzibar*. London: Bell and Daldy.

Steingo, Gavin, and Jim Sykes, eds. 2019. *Remapping Sound Studies*. Durham and London: Duke University Press.

Sterne, Jonathan. 2003. *The Audible Past: Cultural Origins of Sound Reproduction*. Durham and London: Duke University Press.

———, ed. 2012a. *The Sound Studies Reader*. London and New York: Routledge.

———. 2012b. "Sonic Imaginations." In *The Sound Studies Reader*, ed. by Jonathan Sterne, 1–17. London and New York: Routledge.

———. 2012c. "Hearing, Listening, Deafness." In *The Sound Studies Reader*, ed. by Jonathan Sterne, 19–21. London and New York: Routledge.

Steyerl, Hito. 1998. *Die leere Mitte*. Documentary Film. Germany. 62 Minutes.

———. 2003. "The Empty Center." In *Stuff it: The Video Essay in the Digital Age*, ed. by Ursula Biemann, 47–53. Zürich: Edition Voldemeer.

Stoecker, Holger. 2007. "The Advancement of African Studies in Berlin by the 'Deutsche Forschungsgemeinschaft,' 1920–1945." In *Ordering Africa: Anthropology, European Imperialism, and the Politics of Knowledge*, ed. by Helen Tilley and Robert J. Gordon, 67–94. Manchester and New York: Manchester University Press.

———. 2008a. *Afrikawissenschaften in Berlin von 1919 bis 1945: Zur Geschichte und Topographie eines wissenschaftlichen Netzwerkes*. Stuttgart: Franz Steiner Verlag.

———. 2008b. "Sprachlehrer, Informant, Küchenchef: Der 'preußische' Afrikaner Bonifatius Folli aus Anecho (Togo) im Dienste der Berliner Afrikanistik." In *Unbekannte Biographien: Afrikaner im deutschsprachigen Europa vom 18. Jahrhundert bis zum Ende des Zweiten Weltkrieges*, ed. by Ulrich van der Heyden, 217–237. Edition Zeitgeschichte 26. Werder: Kai Homilius Verlag.

———. 2013. "Lehrer, Informanten, Studienobjekte." In *Black Berlin: Die deutsche Metropole und ihre afrikanische Diaspora in Geschichte und Gegenwart*, ed. by Oumar Diallo and Joachim Zeller, 71–85. Berlin: Metropol Verlag.

Stoler, Ann L., and Frederick Cooper. 1997. "Between Metropole and Colony: Rethinking a Research Agenda." In *Tensions of Empire: Colonial Cultures in a Bourgeois World*, ed. by Frederick Cooper and Ann L. Stoler, 1–56. Berkeley, Los Angeles, and London: University of California Press.

———. 2002a. "Developing Historical Negatives: Race and the (Modernist) Visions of a Colonial State." In *From the Margins: Historical Anthropology and Its Futures*, ed. by Brian K. Axel, 156–185. Durham and London: Duke University Press.

———. 2002b. *Carnal Knowledge and Imperial Power: Race and the Intimate in Colonial Rule*. Berkeley, Los Angeles, and London: University of California Press.

———. 2002c. "Colonial Archives and the Arts of Governance: On the Content in the Form." In *Refiguring the Archive*, ed. by Carolyn Hamilton, Verne Harris, Michèle Pickover, Graeme Reid, Razia Saleh, and Jane Taylor, 83–102. Cape Town: David Philip.

———. 2002d. "Colonial Archives and the Arts of Governance." *Archival Science* 2: 87–109.

———. 2009. *Along the Archival Grain: Epistemic Anxieties and Colonial Common Sense*. Princeton and Oxford: Princeton University Press.

Streets, Heather. 2004. *Martial Races: The Military, Race and Masculinity in British Imperial Culture, 1857–1914*. Manchester and New York: Manchester University Press.

Stumpf, Carl. 2000 [1908]. "Das Berliner Phonogrammarchiv." In *Das Berliner Phonogramm-Archiv 1900–2000: Sammlungen der traditionellen Musik der Welt*, ed. by Artur Simon, 65–84. Berlin: Verlag für Wissenschaft und Bildung.

Tanner, Jakob. 2009. "Historische Anthropologie." In *Handbuch Anthropologie: Der Mensch zwischen Natur, Kultur und Technik*, ed. by Eike Bohlken and Christian Thies, 147–156. Stuttgart: Metzler.

Tedlock, Barbara. 1995. "Works and Wives: On the Sexual Division of Textual Labor." In *Women Writing Culture*, ed. by Ruth Behar and Deborah Gordon, 267–286. Berkeley, Los Angeles, and London: University of California Press.

Thode-Arora, Hilke. 1996. "'Charakteristische Gestalten des Volkslebens': Die Hagenbeckschen Südasien-, Orient- und Afrika-Völkerschauen." In *Fremde Erfahrungen: Asiaten und Afrikaner in Deutschland, Österreich und in der Schweiz bis 1945*, ed. by Gerhard Höpp, 109–134. Berlin: Verlag Das Arabische Buch.

———. 2001. "Völkerschauen in Berlin." In *Kolonialmetropole Berlin: Eine Spurensuche*, ed. by Ulrich van der Heyden, 149–153. Berlin: Berlin Edition.

———. 2008. "Von St. Pauli bis Hagenbeck: Völkerschauen in Hamburg." In *Kolonialismus hierzulande: Eine Spurensuche in Deutschland*, ed. by Ulrich van der Heyden, 330–336. Erfurt: Sutton Verlag GmbH.

———. 2014. *From Samoa with love? Samoa-Völkerschauen im deutschen Kaiserreich – eine Spurensuche*. München: Hirmer.

———. 2021. "The Hagenbeck Ethnic Shows: Recruitment, Organization, and Academic and Popular Responses." In *Staged Otherness: Ethnic Shows in Central and Eastern Europe 1850–1939*, ed. by Dagnosław Demski and Dominika Czarnecka, 45–75, Budapest: Central European University Press.

Tilley, Helen. 2011. *Africa as a Living Laboratory: Empire, Development, and the Problem of Scientific Knowledge, 1870–1950*. Chicago and London: University of Chicago Press.

Thiemeyer, Thomas. 2019. "Cosmopolitanizing Colonial Memories in Germany." *Critical Inquiry* 45: 967–990.

Trouillot, Michel-Rolph. 1995. *Silencing the Past: Power and the Production of History*. Boston: Beacon Press.

Velten, Carl, ed. 1901. *Schilderungen der Suaheli*. Göttingen: Vandenhoeck and Ruprecht.

———. 1903. *Sitten und Gebräuche der Suaheli*. Göttingen: Vandenhoeck and Ruprecht.

———, ed. 1907. *Prosa und Poesie der Suaheli*. Berlin: author's edition.

———. 1910. *Suaheli-Wörterbuch*. Berlin.

Visweswaran, Kamala. 2003 [1994]. *Fictions of Feminist Ethnography*. Minnesota: University of Minnesota Press.

Vogel, Christian. 2018. "Theoretische Annäherungen an sensible Objekte und Sammlungen." In *Nicht nur Raubkunst! Sensible Dinge in Museen und universitären Sammlungen*, ed. by Anna-Maria Brandstetter and Vera Hierholzer, 31–44. Göttingen: V&R unipress.

Weitzel, Julia. 2018. *(Re)konstruierte (Auto)biographien: Spuren finden, lesen, interpretieren im Lautarchiv der Humboldt-Universität zu Berlin. Am Beispiel der Tonaufnahmen von Bonifatius Foli*. MA thesis. Humboldt-Universität zu Berlin.

Westermann, Diedrich. 1931. "The Missionary as an Anthropological Field-Worker." *Africa. Journal of the International African Institute* 4 (2): 164–177.

———. 1941a. "Die koloniale Aufgabe der Völkerkunde." *Koloniale Rundschau* 32: 1–5.

———. 1941b: *Afrika als europäische Aufgabe*. Berlin: Deutscher Verlag.

Wietschorke, Jens. 2010. "Historische Ethnografie: Möglichkeiten und Grenzen eines Konzepts." *Zeitschrift für Volkskunde* 106 (2): 97–124.

———. 2012. "Historische Anthropologie und Europäische Ethnologie: Zur epistemologischen Verklammerung von Geschichte und Gegenwart in einem Forschungsprogramm." *Historisches Forum* 14: 23–35.

———. 2013. "Historische Forschung in der Europäischen Ethnologie: Ein Diskussionsbeitrag." In *Kultur_Kultur: Denken, Forschen, Darstellen*, ed. by Reinhard Johler, Christian Marchetti, Bernhard Tschofen, and Carmen Weith, 206–212. Münster and München: Waxmann Verlag.

Wimmelbücker, Ludger. 2009. *Mtoro bin Mwinyi Bakari: Swahili Lecturer and Author in Germany*. Dar es Salaam: Mkuki na Nyota Publisher.

Zeitlyn, David. 2012. "Anthropology in and of the Archives: Possible Futures and Contingent Pasts. Archives as Anthropological Surrogates." *Annual Review of Anthropology* 41: 461–480.

Ziegler, Susanne. 2006. *Die Wachszylinder des Berliner Phonogramm-Archivs*. Berlin: Staatliche Museen zu Berlin – Preußischer Kulturbesitz.

Zimmerer, Jürgen. 2008. *Genocide in German South-West Africa: The Colonial War of 1904–1908 and Its Aftermath*. London: Merlin Press.

Zimmerman, Andrew. 2001. *Anthropology and Antihumanism in Imperial Germany*. Chicago and London: The University of Chicago Press.

Index